ASIAN DEVELOPMENT OUTLOOK

1998

Special Chapter:
Population and Human Resources

Published for the Asian Development Bank
by Oxford University Press

Oxford University Press

OXFORD NEW YORK ATHENS AUCKLAND BANGKOK BOGOTA
BOMBAY BUENOS AIRES CALCUTTA CAPE TOWN DAR ES SALAAM
DELHI FLORENCE HONG KONG ISTANBUL KARACHI KUALA LUMPUR
MADRAS MADRID MELBOURNE MEXICO CITY NAIROBI PARIS
SINGAPORE TAIPEI TOKYO TORONTO

and associated companies in
Berlin Ibadan

Oxford is a trade mark of Oxford University Press

First published 1998
This impression (lowest digit)
1 3 5 7 9 10 8 6 4 2

Published in the United States
by Oxford University Press, New York

Published for the Asian Development Bank by Oxford University Press

ISBN 0-19-590938-0
ISSN 0117-0481

Printed in Hong Kong

Published by Oxford University Press (China) Ltd.
18/F Warwick House, Taikoo Place, 979 King's Road
Quarry Bay, Hong Kong

FOREWORD

This issue of the *Asian Development Outlook* is the tenth in a series of annual economic reports on the developing member countries (DMCs) of the Asian Development Bank. In the context of developments in the world economy that have included some difficult challenges, this *Outlook* analyzes the DMCs' recent economic performance, assesses their economic prospects, and reviews the policy issues that confront them.

The year 1997 was a difficult one for many countries in developing Asia. Last year's *Outlook* noted the marked slowdown in export growth in East and Southeast Asia during 1996. The substantial decrease in export growth rates was the prelude to the worst year the region has seen since its development began accelerating three decades ago. The export slowdown was followed by a currency and financial crisis that affected much of developing Asia during 1997. The consequences are still unfolding, and are being felt worldwide. Many commercial banks and finance companies in the region were closed, the real estate sector collapsed in some countries, interest rates soared, currencies depreciated rapidly, and many regional stock markets fell to unprecedented lows. In an attempt to rescue Indonesia, Republic of Korea, Philippines, and Thailand, multilateral agencies, including the Asian Development ment Bank, and several countries arranged a $117 billion assistance package, which was the largest such program ever put together.

The financial crisis and its consequences are raising the question of whether the Asian miracle is over. Underlying this discussion is the issue of whether deeper reasons lie behind the crisis, in particular, whether a decline in the countries' competitiveness was a partial cause. The success of Asian countries was initially based on the production and export of labor-intensive manufactures. During the last few years, however, a number of other Asian countries capable of producing at lower costs have reached the same stage in the product cycle. Some of the relatively more developed Asian countries are now failing to meet the challenge presented by these economies and to move up the development ladder.

As a result of the events throughout the year, growth rates in East and Southeast Asia in 1997 were below those in previous years, and given recent events, forecasting the region's performance for 1998 and 1999 is more difficult than before. Nevertheless, projections indicate that growth rates will be modest in 1998, and negative in some countries, as the full impact of the crisis has yet to be felt. The year 1998 will be Asia's most difficult since the 1974 oil crisis recession. However, signs of recovery may begin to appear in 1999.

If, in the past, economies had to adjust to changing international conditions to remain competitive, in the present context such adjustment is imperative. First, the region must resolve its financial crisis. Second, it must implement policies to create, once again, an environment for sustained growth. This will require some reforms of institutions and policies, but I am confident that the affected Asian countries will succeed.

The format of this year's *Outlook* is slightly different from that of previous years. Part I is now divided into two chapters. The first chapter briefly surveys recent growth experience and the short-term prospects for the world economy, and then focuses on the Asian and Pacific region. The second chapter, which is an addition to this year's *Outlook*, discusses the financial crisis facing some of the Asian economies. This chapter shows that, while the massive inflows of capital in the form of direct and portfolio investments during the last decade have been an important determinant of growth, they have also proved to be a major source of macroeconomic instability. The structural weaknesses in the region's financial sectors, in conjunction with inappropriate exchange rate management policies and rapid, short-term capital inflows, have been major contributory factors in precipitating the crisis. Part II discusses each of the 35 DMCs in Asia and the Pacific, analyzing their recent economic performance and assessing their prospects for the next two years. Note that this year's country profiles devote greater attention than in the past to discussions of policy and development issues. Part III addresses the important issue of the role of human resources in economic development. It analyzes the links among population, human resources, and competitiveness and stresses their critical importance as determinants of long-run growth. The analysis provides important insights into the issue of the long-run sustainability of the Asian miracle.

Mitsuo Sato
President

ACKNOWLEDGMENTS

The *Asian Development Outlook 1998* has benefited from the support of and valuable contributions from many individuals, both inside and outside the Asian Development Bank. Special thanks are due to the following Bank staff for comments on various parts of the *Outlook:* Paul Dickie, Kazi F. Jalal, S. Ghon Rhee, Yoshihiro Iwasaki, Edward M. Haugh, Jr., Anita Kelles-Viitanen, Kok Heng Phua, Albab Akanda, Stephen Banta, Indu Bhushan, Jeffrey Liang, Urooj Malik, Narhari Rao, and Ramesh Subramaniam. The following individuals provided critical support, guidance, and advice on various matters relating to the preparation of the *Outlook:* Basudev Dahal, Shoji Nishimoto, Eustace Nonis, G. H. P. B. Van der Linden, and Yang Wei Min. The help and support of the following in preparing the country reports in Part II are deeply appreciated: Nihal Amerasinghe, Werner Schelzig, Thomas Crouch, Khaja Moinuddin, Bruce Murray, Rajat Nag, Filologo Pante, Jr., Frank Polman, and Cedric Saldanha. Bindu Lohani, Charles Currin, and S. A. Chowdhury assisted the *Outlook* team by preparing background writeups or providing research advice. Isidoro David and Bishnu Dev Pant offered support with data-related matters. Robert H. Salamon, Karti Sandilya, Ian Gill, Lynette Mallery and Myo Thant provided advice and assistance in publicizing the *Outlook.*

The prepress work was done by the Printing Unit under the supervision of Raveendranath Rajan. Vicente Angeles of the Printing Unit did the art design for the *Outlook.* The assistance of the Bangladesh Resident Mission, India Resident Mission, Office of Administrative Services, and Office of Computer Services in the preparation of the *Outlook* is also gratefully acknowledged.

Many scholars, policymakers, and economists from international organizations participated in the *Tenth Workshop on Asian Economic Outlook* to discuss the background materials for this issue of the *Outlook.* In particular, we would like to acknowledge the contributions of the following individuals, who either prepared papers or acted as designated commentators: Stephen Yan-Leung Cheung, Andrew Freris, Alejandro Herrin, Vikas Kakar, Rajiv Lall, Geoffrey McNicoll, and Gang Yi.

A number of individuals from outside the Bank prepared background papers for Part II of the *Outlook,* namely: Iwan Azis, Stephen Yan-Leung Cheung, Ian Collins, John Fallon, Tan Khee Giap, Mohamed Jaleel, Jun Il Kim, Eshya Mujahid Muktar, Nguyen Van Quy, Ismail Md. Salleh, Pronob Sen, Shankar Sharma, Nimal Siripala, Chung Shu Wu, and Mao Yushi. Anil Deolalikar and Andrew Mason prepared background papers for Part III.

Several international institutions shared their research material and data with the *Outlook* team. In particular, we would like to acknowledge the contributions of Francesco Caramazza from the International Monetary Fund and Amar Bhattacharya and Kwang Woo Jun from the World Bank, who shared their research on global economic prospects and the financial turbulence in developing Asia and participated in the *Tenth Workshop on Asian Economic Outlook*.

The *Outlook* has benefited extensively from advice and guidance provided by Jere Behrman, Marc Nerlove, and T. N. Srinivasan during the conceptual stage of Part III and from reviews and comments on Part I by John Malcolm Dowling, Jr., Takatoshi Ito, and Salim Rashid. Finally, the *Outlook* team is grateful to Abhijit Banerjee, Paul Krugman, and Frederic Mishkin for graciously permitting the use of their research material for preparing boxes for the *Outlook*.

Jungsoo Lee
Chief Economist

THE *1998 OUTLOOK* TEAM

The *Asian Development Outlook 1998* was prepared by a team drawn from the Economics and Development Resource Center of the Asian Development Bank. M. G. Quibria led this core team, assisted by Douglas Brooks, Dilip K. Das, Rana Hasan, Haider Ali Khan, Pradumna B. Rana, and Reza Siregar. The team included Jesus Felipe, Francis Harrigan, Soo-Nam Oh, Juzhong Zhuang, Emma Banaria, Barbara Carreon, Charissa Castillo, Elizabeth Leuterio, Emma Murray, Aludia Pardo, James Villafuerte, and Cherry Lynn Zafaralla. The core team was assisted by the following members of the Programs Departments, who prepared most of the country reports in Part II of the *Outlook*: Shiladitya Chatterjee, Evelyn Go, David Green, Sophia Ho, Yun-Hwan Kim, Rajiv Kumar, Srinivasa Madhur, Sudipto Mundle, Ernesto M. Pernia, Alessandro Pio, Min Tang, Toru Tatara, Richard Vokes, and Hong Wang. John McCombie and Alice Dowsett edited the *Outlook*. The work was carried out under the overall direction of Bong-Suh Lee, Vice-President (Region West) and the supervision of Jungsoo Lee, Chief Economist.

Many others inside and outside the Asian Development Bank wrote background papers, provided helpful comments, and participated in the *Tenth Workshop on Asian Economic Outlook*, held in Manila on 21-22 October 1997 to discuss the background papers. Contributors and participants are listed in the Acknowledgments. The statistical database and country tables were prepared by staff from the Economic Analysis and Research Division in collaboration with the Statistics and Data Systems Division. Overall administrative coordination was handled by Elizabeth E. Leuterio. James Villafuerte was responsible for preparation of the Statistical Appendix. Ma. Teresa Cabellon, along with Zenaida Acacio, Ma. Lourdes Antonio, Patricia Baysa, Anna Maria Juico, Ma. Lourdes J. Maestro, Eva Olanda, and Anna Liza Silverio, provided secretarial and administrative support. Mercedita Cabañeros was responsible for the layout. Charissa Castillo and Cherry Lynn Zafaralla coordinated production. Mildred Belizario and Reynaldo Cancio provided additional research and technical assistance.

CONTENTS

PART
III

POPULATION AND HUMAN RESOURCES

ACRONYMS AND ABBREVIATIONS

ADE	Asian developing economy
ASEAN	Association of Southeast Asian Nations
BOP	Balance of payment
CDF	Commodity Development Framework (Fiji)
CMEA	Council for Mutual Economic Assistance
CRP	Comprehensive Reform Program (Vanuatu)
DMC	Developing member country
EMU	Economic and Monetary Union
EU	European Union
FAO	Food and Agriculture Organization
FDI	Foreign direct investment
FSM	Federated States of Micronesia
FSU	Former Soviet Union
GDI	Gross domestic investment
GDS	Gross domestic savings
GDP	Gross domestic product
GNP	Gross national product
GNS	Gross national savings
IMF	International Monetary Fund
Lao PDR	Lao People's Democratic Republic
MAS	Monetary Authority of Singapore
MFN	Most Favored Nation
M1	Currency in circulation plus demand deposit
M2	M1 plus savings and time deposit
NIE	Newly industrialized economy
OECD	Organisation for Economic Co-operation and Development
PNG	Papua New Guinea
PRC	People's Republic of China
RBI	Reserve Bank of India
R&D	Research and development
RERF	Revenue Equalization Reserve Fund (Kiribati)
SOE	State-owned enterprise
UN	United Nations
UNIDO	United Nations Industrial Development Organization
WTO	World Trade Organization

DEFINITIONS

The classification of economies by major analytic or geographic groupings such as industrial countries, developing countries, Africa, Latin America, Middle East and Europe, and transitional countries follows the classification adopted by the International Monetary Fund. Latin America, however, refers to the Western Hemisphere in that classification and transitional countries include Kazakstan, Kyrgyz Republic, Mongolia, and Uzbekistan, which are for the purposes of this *Outlook* included in Asia.

For the purposes of this *Outlook*, the following apply:

- **Newly industrialized economies (NIEs)** comprise Hong Kong, China; Republic of Korea; Singapore; and Taipei,China.
- **East Asia** comprises the NIEs, People's Republic of China, and Mongolia.
- **South Asia** comprises Bangladesh, Bhutan, India, Maldives, Nepal, Pakistan, and Sri Lanka.
- **Southeast Asia** comprises Cambodia, Indonesia, Lao People's Democratic Republic, Malaysia, Myanmar, Philippines, Thailand, and Viet Nam.
- **Central Asian republics** comprise Kazakstan, Kyrgyz Republic, and Uzbekistan.
- **Pacific islands** comprise Cook Islands, Fiji, Kiribati, Marshall Islands, Federated States of Micronesia, Papua New Guinea, Samoa, Solomon Islands, Tonga, Tuvalu, and Vanuatu.
- **Developing Asia** refers to the 35 developing member countries of the Asian Development Bank discussed in this *Outlook*.

Billion is 1,000 million.
Trillion is 1,000 billion.
Tons are metric tons, equal to 1,000 kilograms or 2,204.6 pounds.
Unless otherwise specified, the symbol $ means United States dollars; dollars are current US dollars.
The symbol ... in tables indicates that data are not available or not applicable.

This *Outlook* is based on data available up to 15 March 1998.

PART I

Developing Asia and the World

ECONOMIC DEVELOPMENTS AND PROSPECTS

The world economy posted another year of robust growth in 1997, yet inflation remained subdued. At the same time, a number of transitional economies of Central and Eastern Europe, along with the Central Asian republics, showed encouraging results in their economic growth. Notwithstanding the slowdown of the Southeast Asian countries, developing Asia continued to post the fastest growth rates in the world. The financial turmoil, which started in Thailand, spilled over to some other Southeast Asian economies and to the Republic of Korea (henceforth referred to as Korea), and the outlook for the global economy in 1998 will depend on a satisfactory response to this crisis. As concerns Asia, the strength of the economy of the People's Republic of China (PRC) and its currency will become the anchor for regional economic stability in 1998. While Southeast Asian and East Asian economies will experience drastic slowdowns in gross domestic product (GDP) growth rates in 1998, moderate slowdowns are also expected in the industrial economies.

The world economy is currently undergoing a massive transformation. The twin forces of globalization and of the information and communications revolution will have ramifications whose extent is unknown. The year 1997 witnessed continued widening and deepening of globalization through trade liberalization in goods and services and in financial markets. Propelled by the increased worldwide competition brought about largely by globalization and the enhanced productivity that resulted from technological advances, the world economy posted yet another year of robust growth, largely unaccompanied by significant inflationary pressures. The presence of robust growth and the absence of inflation have led to widespread debate as to whether the world economy has seen the end of business cycles.

Although globalization brought new prosperity to the world economy as a whole, it was distributed unevenly across regions. While the industrial economies experienced uninterrupted growth with modest inflation, several Southeast Asian economies that had come to take rapid growth for granted went through an unprecedented, cataclysmic financial crisis. Unless these countries manage to resolve the crisis, its adverse effects will spill over not only to other Asian economies, but also to other regions, undermining the industrial economies' current robust performance. However, dealing with such crisis successfully is beyond the capacity of any individual country, and requires a coordinated effort that involves the major industrial economies and the international financial institutions. As external factors become more important in shaping nations' economic destinies, for countries to set and achieve domestic economic targets unilaterally becomes difficult, if not impossible. Globalization has eroded individual governments' scope and autonomy in policymaking, which has resulted in a need for greater international cooperation and coordination even for problems previously perceived as largely domestic. This is perhaps the most important lesson learned from the 1997-1998 financial crisis in Asia.

THE WORLD ECONOMY

Despite the Asian financial crisis that began in July 1997, the growth of the world economy was strong at 3.2 percent in 1997. This was not only a higher rate than in 1996, but also exceeded the average for the preceding five years by 0.9 percentage points. Continued solid growth accompanied by low inflation in the United Kingdom and the United States underpinned this favorable economic performance, which was aided by a strong recovery in Canada and a gradual revival of economic activity in Continental Europe.

Inflation remained low in most countries, reflecting a commitment to price stability that was perhaps greater than at any time since the 1950s. The steep fall in oil prices and a more moderate decline in other commodity prices helped keep the inflation rate in check. Reduced demand for oil during the first half of 1997 and a substantial increase in production caused the drop in oil prices. The mild winter of 1997/98 in Europe and the United States, and a significant drop in demand from the ailing Asian economies will worsen the outlook for oil prices in 1998. Grain prices firmed up in the first quarter of 1997, but subsequently eased back. Some commodities, such as coffee and tea, saw a sharp increase in their prices in 1997. The prices of industrial raw materials rose from a trough reached in the third quarter of 1996, but this was short-lived: the increase faltered a year later. The prevalent low inflation rates and stable exchange rates (except in Southeast Asia) resulted in relatively low world real interest rates, another factor in the favorable growth rates experienced during 1997.

World trade grew exceptionally rapidly in 1994 and 1995, slowed down in 1996, but rebounded in 1997 to 9 percent because of a recovery in trade between the countries of the Organisation for Economic Co-operation and Development (OECD). The United States' imports (and to a lesser extent its exports) grew quickly, and the export performances of France, Germany, and Japan showed marked improvement. A number of factors favor the continued rapid expansion of world trade in the long run, including policy changes resulting from the Uruguay Round of Trade Negotiations, new multilateral initiatives to reduce trade barriers (such as the agreements on information technology, telecommunications, and financial services), further unilateral trade liberalization by a number of developing countries, cost reductions in transportation and communications, and continued growth in multinational production networks.

The structure of world trade has continued to change. Notably, commercial services (travel, transport, communications, and financial and professional services) have continued to increase in importance. During 1986-1995 commercial services grew at a rate of 12.5 percent per year, faster than the growth in merchandise trade of 9.5 percent per year. By 1996 trade in commercial services was worth $1.2 trillion, which represented 20 percent of total world trade. Projections indicate that this rate will continue in the medium term, and possibly accelerate, partly because of the continuing impact of the information technology revolution, but also because of the multilateral liberalization of trade in services under the General Agreement on Trade in Services, negotiated under the auspices of the World Trade Organization (WTO). More than 40 countries signed the Information Technology Agreement in March 1997. The signatories, who account for more than 90 percent of world trade in information technology, are committed to phasing out tariffs on these products between 2000 and 2004.

Projections indicate that a substantial redirection of trade flows is likely to occur in 1998. Thus, the trade deficit with Asia is forecast to narrow from about $42 billion in 1997 to less than $10 billion in 1998.

International private capital flows to emerging market economies more than doubled in real terms between 1991 and 1996, when they reached a total of almost $300 billion. Much of these flows has gone to the Asian emerging market economies as a result of the more open global financial system and the rapid growth rates of many of the recipient countries. However, global cyclical factors also affect the cost and availability of these financial flows, as does the perception that, in certain cases, countries' large current account deficits (the counterpart of the capital inflows) may not be sustainable. A consequence of the Asian crisis will be a much more cautious approach to international lending to the developing countries, including the newly industrialized economies (NIEs), by the financial institutions of the industrial countries. In 1997 private capital flows to the emerging markets fell by one third, with Indonesia, Korea, and Malaysia experiencing the largest falls. These countries experienced a net outflow of more than $10 billion, compared with capital inflows of $93 billion in the previous year. Forecasts suggest that in 1998 the Asian financial crisis will cause a slowdown in world growth by about one percentage point, and in trade by about half a percentage point.

Industrial Countries

The output of the 29 OECD economies grew by 3 percent in 1997, the highest rate since 1989. One of the main reasons for this was the third successive year of rapid growth in the seven largest economies, namely, Canada, France, Germany, Italy, Japan, United Kingdom, and United States. During 1997 the United States' economy grew by 3.8 percent, its highest rate this decade. Switzerland's economy grew by 0.6 percent in 1997, which represented an improvement compared to its decline of 0.2 percent in 1996. Australia and New Zealand also experienced rapid growth rates in 1997 of 3 and 3.3 percent, respectively.

Labor market conditions were good in 1997 in the United Kingdom and the United States, with unemployment rates of less than 5 percent. However, unemployment was higher in Continental Europe. France, Germany, and Italy, for example, all recorded rates of just over 11 percent in 1997. This was partly due to government policies to meet the Maastricht targets for monetary union (see Box 1.1), which led to tight fiscal policy and contractions in public expenditures. Nevertheless, buoyant household spending in France, vigorous business investment, and in some economies strong export demand, helped maintain output in 1997. Output growth stood at 2.5 percent in France and Germany and a little less than 2 percent in Italy.

The inflation rate was a low 2.5 percent in all the industrial economies during 1997, except in the United Kingdom, where it was 3.5 percent. The excess demand for assets and products in the United Kingdom and in the United States should lessen as their growth rates moderate and they feel the

spillover effects of the Asian financial crisis. Hence the risk of inflationary pressures increasing in most of the industrial economies in 1998 is minimal. In particular, Switzerland is projected to have a low inflation rate of about 1 percent.

The Asian financial crisis is already affecting private debt repayments to the industrial economies. Asian companies and plant projects canceled or postponed a number of payments due in early 1998. Airbus Industries, for example, lost revenue from some of the Asian airlines, which either postponed or canceled orders for aircraft. In January 1998, the Daewoo Corp. conglomerate of Korea suspended plans to construct factories in France that would have created about 1,000 jobs. With their large portfolios of Asian loans, European banks are heavily exposed to potentially massive losses brought about by bankruptcies in Asia.

Projections indicate that in 1998 the Asian financial crisis will cause a fall of 0.6 percentage points in output and 0.5 percentage points in export growth in the OECD countries. Among the OECD countries, Japan is projected to be hardest hit, with declines of 1.4 percentage points in output and 0.6 percentage points in export growth. Australia and New Zealand are also likely to be hard hit because of their dependence on trade with and tourism from the Pacific Rim countries. Unemployment in Continental Europe is unlikely to improve, because the commitment of many of these countries to meet the Maastricht conditions will continue to be deflationary. Export growth will fall, partly because of the collapse of purchasing power in the Southeast Asian economies, and partly because of increased competitiveness from Asian exports (especially from Korea) as a result of the large currency depreciations in the region.

Transitional Economies

Output fell in the transitional economies of Central and Eastern Europe in 1996, although by less than in the past. In 1997 growth became positive, but only at a moderate rate of between 1 and 2 percent. The Baltic states, the Czech and Slovak republics, and Hungary have been undergoing stabilization and reform programs, which began to show encouraging results in the form of moderate growth in 1997. Poland's growth rate and level of investment have increased markedly in recent years as a result of its

Box 1.1 European Monetary Union May Help Future Asian Growth

In February 1992 European governments signed the Treaty on European Union, eventually known as the Maastricht Treaty, after the town in the Netherlands where it was signed. This treaty extended and incorporated the 1957 Treaty of Rome, the founding act of the European Community. In accordance with the Maastricht Treaty, the European governments were committed to stabilize the fluctuations in the region's currencies through the Exchange Rate Mechanism, which minimizes exchange rate volatility between the member countries.

In addition to exchange rate stability, the treaty stipulates a convergence criteria for macroeconomic policies and performances that the member countries must meet. The criteria include maintaining a domestic inflation rate of not more than 1.5 percentage points above the average of the three best performing states, an average nominal ten-year bond yield of not more than 2 percentage points above that of the three countries with the lowest inflation, a government deficit of not more than 3 percent of GDP, and government debt of not more than 60 percent of GDP. The Maastricht Treaty does allow some flexibility in the implementation of the convergence criteria. For example, both the government deficit and debt limit might be infringed as long as the numbers have declined substantially and have come close to the targets.

In addition to France and Germany, around eight countries are expected to enter the European Monetary Union (EMU) at the beginning of 1999. From January 1999 until the middle of 2002, the currencies of these countries will coexist alongside a new European currency, the euro, and the exchange rates will be permanently fixed. A major objective of creating a common currency is to harmonize and coordinate the monetary and fiscal policies of the member countries under the direct supervision of a European Central Bank.

Successful implementation of the EMU will result in significant efficiency gains arising from eliminating intra-European foreign exchange risk and transaction costs; doing away with any cross-border price discrepancies; and simplifying the assessment of intra-European investment decisions, thereby leading to a more efficient spatial allocation of resources. The EMU should also make the member countries more competitive through greater intra-European competition.

However, a country faces possible disadvantages in joining the EMU that include the loss of macroeconomic policy instruments. Whether in the long run the economic benefits of the EMU outweigh the costs is still an unresolved issue. Nevertheless, the EMU will almost certainly be formed in January 1999, and many European governments strongly believe that the benefits will outweigh the costs. The United Kingdom is opting not to join the EMU immediately, but is expected to participate eventually when it considers that the economic conditions are right.

The Asian countries are likely to benefit from the formation of the EMU in two ways. The first is through greater trade with Europe, and the second is through greater investment by European countries in Asian financial markets. Although no significant rise in trade between the Asian developing economies and the European Union (EU) is likely in the initial years of the EMU, in the longer run, increased trade flows are likely. At the initial stage, given that the euro is likely to be relatively weak in relation to the US dollar because of uncertainties and the lack of complete market confidence and that many Asian currencies will still be closely linked to the US dollar, the EU might experience a greater increase in exports to Asia than the other way around. This may not, however, be the general case, especially for those Southeast Asian

---

efforts to establish a market-based economy. The fall in economic activity in Russia may have bottomed out and begun to pick up. Armenia, Azerbaijan, Georgia, Kazakstan, and Kyrgyz Republic are benefiting from sustained growth.

Several transitional economies made progress in controlling inflation in 1996 and 1997, especially the economies of the Commonwealth of Independent States other than the Central Asian republics. Croatia and Yugoslavia had suffered hyperinflation in the early 1990s, when inflation ran at more than

1,000 percent per year, but by 1997 they had brought the inflation rate down to 30 percent. Russia and Ukraine brought their inflation further under control, with a rate of 15 percent prevailing in 1997. Bulgaria and Romania were the least successful in controlling inflation.

Many of the transitional economies still need to develop instruments and institutions through which to operate monetary policy in a market economy. The financial systems are still rudimentary and subject to substantial nonperforming loans.

countries that have recently undergone massive devaluations with respect to the US dollar and the European currencies.

In the medium to long term, the increased growth of the EU and a strengthening of the euro are likely to lead to an increase in the growth of imports from the Asian countries. Given the stringent convergence criteria and the large combined level of output of the member countries, which will exceed that of the United States, the EMU has the potential to develop into a large market. Real income should rise and generate greater aggregate demand for imports, including those of the Asian developing economies. Accordingly, export growth from the Asian economies to the EMU will accelerate.

On the investment side, expected higher returns in the Asian fixed income portfolio will provide an excellent alternative destination for investments from the EU economies. The introduction of the euro and the convergence in macroeconomic policies and performances will greatly reduce risks in the fixed income portfolio markets of participating countries. When the convergence process is complete, the emergence of a large and liquid euro-denominated assets market will have the potential to match that of the United States in size. Yet, because of convergence, investors in euro-denominated assets will have only one set of yields to choose from. These will provide significant opportunities for the development of the Asian fixed income portfolio markets (denominated in local currencies). Given the diversity in the overall macroeconomic and business environments among the Asian developing economies, the expanding Asian markets will offer EMU investors with another possible source of risk diversification and higher return assets, subject to a risk premium. The Asian equity markets may similarly benefit from the emergence of the EMU.

The restructuring of state-owned enterprises has been inadequate and tax collection is weak. This has resulted in the inability of the governments to honor their financial obligations. If they are to complete the transition process successfully, they will have to devise appropriate reforms to deal with these issues.

Those transitional economies whose structural adjustment process is sufficiently advanced have started attracting both short-term and long-term capital inflows. In 1997 foreign financing made up about two thirds of the gross investment in Armenia and Azerbaijan and around 20 to 30 percent in Georgia and Turkmenistan. These capital inflows, which are associated with widening external imbalances, bring with them the risk of a sudden reversal, especially if they are short term.

The smaller transitional economies, in particular, should pursue further macroeconomic and stabilization reforms. Some, like Lithuania, have learnt from the Asian financial turmoil and have moved from fixed to flexible exchange rate regimes. At the same time, they have introduced a wider range of financial institutions and instruments into the market.

THE DEVELOPING ECONOMIES

The developing economies have continued to experience some of the world's fastest growth rates, except for the Southeast Asian countries, whose growth collapsed toward the end of 1997. The developing countries are in their sixth year of sustained growth, and on average experienced growth rates of 7.5 percent in 1996 and about 6 percent in 1997. The year 1997 was the first time in this decade that the average growth rate of the Southeast Asian economies fell well below the rate for the South Asian economies. The same is expected to hold true for 1998 and 1999.

Given that most countries experienced low or declining inflation rates and generally had prudent fiscal policies in place, this suggests that they have significantly reduced the threat to growth from policy imbalances. However, a few countries that are lagging behind in implementing policy reforms risk being marginalized in a rapidly integrating world economy. In addition, the ongoing turmoil in Southeast Asia implies that the average inflation rate in these economies will continue to increase in 1998.

Private capital inflows rose by almost a third in 1996 compared to 1995 and reached record levels. Of these flows, foreign direct investment (FDI) amounted to $129 billion, 34 percent more than in 1995. The PRC was the largest recipient, accounting for a third of all FDI flows to developing economies.

Export performance was also buoyant, and the ratio of goods traded internationally to output continued to rise.

The Non-Asian Developing Economies

The non-Asian developing economies generally experienced rapid growth in 1997, although there was some diversity in their individual performances. The main question that arises for 1998 is the extent to which the ongoing Asian financial crisis will adversely affect their growth rates through trade flows or changes in global commodity and financial markets.

Africa. After a period of protracted decline in economic growth, faster growth resumed in 1996 in at least 22 African economies. The agriculture and mining sectors were the largest contributors to this boost in growth. Agricultural output improved—mostly because of better weather conditions—in all countries of northern Africa; some countries recorded cereal yield increases of 50 percent. Nevertheless, even if the current growth rate persists, for African economies to reach the per capita income levels they enjoyed in 1980 will take ten years.

Growth continued in 1997, albeit at a slower pace than in 1996. GDP grew some 3 percent, compared to 4.4 percent in 1996. Drought and civil wars led to slowdowns in several economies, such as Eritrea, Kenya, and Somalia. Weakening non-oil commodity prices also affected growth rates adversely. However, the two main factors responsible for the slowdown in 1997 were the decline in both oil prices and agricultural production. Severe drought in 1997 led to famine in countries such as Burundi, Congo Republic, Democratic Republic of Congo, Kenya, and Uganda.

In many African countries, sustained policy reforms and macroeconomic stability have created an environment conducive to investment and increased production. African economies are also benefiting from increased demand for their exports. In addition, geological surveys financed by aid funds are contributing to increased interest in exploiting mineral deposits. Gold production has increased in several countries in western and southern Africa, except in the Republic of South Africa, and the output of other minerals and metals increased in 1997 in several economies, particularly in Zaire, Zambia, and Zimbabwe. Higher prices and new mining codes with more clearly defined rights and obligations of foreign investors have contributed to rising production in the mining sector.

The franc zone countries, such as Côte d'Ivoire, Mali, and Senegal, experienced continued recovery following their exchange rate adjustments in 1994 and the accompanying economic reform policies. Botswana, Malawi, and Uganda also enjoyed robust growth as a result of market-oriented reforms and greater macroeconomic discipline. Kenya introduced legislation for a new Central Bank, and Mozambique, Tanzania, and Zimbabwe restructured their banking sectors. In contrast, Nigeria's economic performance remained disappointing because of failure in these areas. The Republic of South Africa's growth has not yet responded to its recent economic reforms, and GDP grew slightly more than 1 percent in 1997.

The recent financial crisis in Asia will have repercussions for Africa's growth in 1998, especially as those Asian countries have become some of Africa's fastest growing trading partners.

Latin America. With strong export growth in many Latin American and Caribbean countries, economic growth has been gathering momentum. Since the end of the Mexican crisis of 1995, most countries in the region, especially Argentina, Chile, Mexico, and Venezuela, have continued to recover. Regional output grew at a rate of close to 5 percent in 1997, but this fell short of the region's trend growth rate of 5.5 percent and of the 6 percent required to bring down the growing unemployment rate.

Buoyant exports and external finance played particularly important roles in Argentina's, Chile's, and Mexico's economic turnarounds. However, the Chilean economy, which in 1997 experienced its 13th year of consecutive growth and is the strongest in the region, was in danger of overheating in 1996 and introduced deflationary policies. Brazil has a large external deficit. Its consumption-led boom in 1996 was moderated in 1997 by a tightening of monetary policy. For other economies in the region, improved macroeconomic discipline and intensified structural reform efforts are improving the growth outlook.

Inflation continued its decline toward single digits, and many Latin American governments have placed inflation control high on their priority lists. To accomplish this they have introduced fiscal restraint and stringent monetary policies. The result was that in 1997 inflation was lower than in 1996 in 10 countries and remained stable in 11 others.

Argentina saw one of the lowest rates of inflation in the world. In contrast, inflation increased to a record 100 percent in Venezuela following price liberalization and a major devaluation.

The virtually complete implementation of the Southern Cone Common Market arrangement has led to an expansion of intraregional trade in general, and of grains in particular. Argentina, especially, has capitalized on export opportunities, mainly to Brazil. Mexico, which is still benefiting from postcrisis depreciation, continued to revive its export performance.

The regional savings rate averaged 20 percent during the mid-1990s, which is lower than that of the East Asian economies. Before 1995, the Latin American economies failed to attract substantial foreign capital because of a lack of market confidence. However, in recent years the investment rate has exceeded the savings rate because of the rapid increase in financial flows since 1995.

The East and Southeast Asian currency depreciations are projected to have an impact on the region, which is likely to lose export competitiveness. As a precaution, in early 1998 Brazil widened the bands in which its currency is permitted to fluctuate against the US dollar to maintain its international competitiveness. This change will permit a more rapid depreciation of the real in relation to the US dollar in 1998, as compared with 1997, when the real depreciated by 7.5 percent. Argentina's growth will experience some repercussions from the financial turmoil in Asia because of its loss of competitiveness compared with the Southeast Asian economies. Chile and Colombia will not be affected as much because of measures adopted to discourage short-term capital financing.

The Middle East. In 1996 the region's GDP rose for the first time since 1992, reflecting strong growth in Bahrain, Kuwait, Oman, Qatar, and Saudi Arabia. This was due to a steep rise in oil prices and an accompanying increase in oil production. The increased oil revenues helped reduce fiscal deficits and led to a marked improvement in the current account imbalances of most of these economies.

Economic reforms and economic diversification played a major role in stimulating growth rates by increasing the private sector's performance. As a result, the weakening of oil prices in 1997 did not lead to a decline in the average GDP growth rate.

Several other countries in the region, such as Iraq, Jordan, and Turkey, also recorded noticeably higher growth rates in 1997 than in 1996. In contrast, Israel's growth rate declined sharply in 1997 as a result of the tightening of fiscal policy and a slowdown in inflows of foreign investment as concerns about the peace process mounted.

The Asian and Pacific Developing Economies

The growth rate of 8.2 percent recorded for the Asian developing economies as a whole in 1995 fell to 7.5 percent in 1996. The Asian crisis contributed to a further slowdown in the growth rate to 6.1 percent in 1997 (Table 1.1). The rate is projected to be about 4 percent in 1998, with some recovery in 1999.

These average growth rates in 1997 conceal the fact that there were wide diversities in economic performance across the region. Indeed, except for the Central Asian republics, GDP growth in all subregions of Asia declined, including the Pacific islands which experienced negative growth. However, the most conspicuous slowdown was in Southeast Asia, where the growth remained positive but declined to almost half of the level achieved in 1996. The PRC as well as the NIEs also experienced some slowdown in growth in 1997 but still remained high at 6 percent and above. The South Asian economies experienced a moderate slowdown; however, the performances of the individual countries differed. While Bangladesh and Sri Lanka performed well, the growth rates for India and Pakistan were disappointing.

During 1996 the Asian developing economies managed to control inflation reasonably successfully. Many have seen stable prices for the last four years. The average rate of consumer price inflation fell to 6.7 percent in 1996, from 9.4 percent in 1995, helped considerably by stringent fiscal and monetary policies. And despite the substantial depreciation of the currencies of the Southeast Asian economies, the subregion's inflation rate further declined to 5.6 percent in 1997. However, given the economic problems currently besetting some of these countries, Southeast Asia's average inflation rate is expected to worsen to 12.9 percent in 1998.

In 1996 current account deficits represented 1.2 percent of GDP. The situation however improved in 1997 to less than 1 percent of GDP, at which time

Table 1.1   Selected Economic Indicators: Developing Asia, 1995-1999

Item	1995	1996	1997	1998	1999
Gross domestic product (annual percentage change)					
Developing Asia	8.2	7.5	6.1	4.0	5.1
Newly industrialized economies	7.4	6.4	6.0	2.2	4.3
PRC and Mongolia	10.5	9.6	8.8	7.2	6.8
Central Asian republics	-5.5	3.9	7.8	na	na
Southeast Asia	8.2	7.1	3.9	-0.4	2.4
South Asia	6.6	6.8	4.8	6.4	6.7
Pacific islands	-1.7	3.3	-4.1	na	na
Inflation (percentage change in CPI)					
Developing Asia	9.4	6.7	4.3	6.9	6.5
Newly industrialized economies	4.6	4.3	3.5	6.1	4.9
PRC and Mongolia	17.1	8.3	2.8	4.0	6.0
Central Asian republics	83.6	36.5	24.8	na	na
Southeast Asia	7.3	6.6	5.6	12.9	8.7
South Asia	9.9	9.3	7.1	7.4	7.5
Pacific islands	11.7	8.6	3.9	na	na
Current account balance (percentage of GDP)					
Developing Asia	-1.1	-1.2	0.0	1.1	0.5
Newly industrialized economies	1.2	0.2	1.4	4.5	2.7
PRC and Mongolia	0.2	0.9	2.2	0.9	0.4
Central Asian republics	-10.8	-17.2	-8.5	na	na
Southeast Asia	-5.9	-5.5	-4.1	-1.4	-0.2
South Asia	-2.4	-2.4	-2.0	-2.1	-2.4
Pacific islands	8.3	2.8	-3.9	na	na
Debt-service ratio (percent of goods and services exports)					
Developing Asia	15.2	17.3	18.2	16.6	16.8
Newly industrialized economies	na	na	na	na	na
PRC and Mongolia	9.9	10.1	9.8	11.0	11.0
Central Asian republics	3.1	3.9	na	na	na
Southeast Asia	14.4	18.5	23.9	19.1	19.9
South Asia	32.7	35.7	29.3	27.6	26.7
Pacific islands	17.4	16.5	na	na	na

na Not available.
CPI consumer price index.

the total amounted to $0.8 billion. These deficits were the result of an excess of investment over savings, despite the five percentage point increase in the savings rate that has occurred since the 1980s, mainly because of the region's rising prosperity. Until recently, the high-investing countries had little difficulty in funding these deficits: because of their rapid growth rates, international investors viewed them as attractive propositions. Short- and long-term capital flows—especially to Indonesia, Malaysia, and

Thailand, and more recently to the Philippines— increased rapidly in recent years. However, the situation facing these countries has changed dramatically since the last half of 1997 in the wake of the recent financial crisis. Foreign financing has become an important factor in Southeast Asia's rate of rapid growth, but the failure to introduce necessary institutional and regulatory reforms within the financial sectors was a major contributor to the crisis. The absence of such reforms made using capital inflows productively particularly difficult for these econo-mies, especially in generating industrial develop-ment. Many Asian economies are now burdened with insolvent financial institutions and firms. Currencies that were linked to the appreciating US dollar aggravated these economic problems and contributed to further destabilization. Some of the other factors that together helped destabilize several Asian economies during the latter half of 1997 included skill shortages, infrastructure inadequacies, and the slow pace of structural reforms. In the past, rapid growth rates had concealed these structural weaknesses, which have only recently come to light with the region's economic slowdown.

The Newly Industrialized Economies. The average GDP growth rate of the NIEs—Hong Kong, China; Korea; Singapore; and Taipei,China—declined from 6.4 percent in 1996 to 6 percent in 1997, largely because of a sharp fall in world demand for and prices of electronics, semiconductors, steel, and petro-chemicals that resulted in poor export performance.

The average inflation rate declined from about 4.3 percent in 1996 to 3.5 percent in 1997. Singapore actually saw a slight increase in its consumer price index in 1997. In the case of Hong Kong, China, moderate inflationary pressure arose mostly from domestic markets through wages and rentals in the early part of 1997, but this was offset by low rises in import prices and a drop in property prices during the last quarter of 1997. At 5.7 percent, the 1997 inflation rate remained close to its 1996 level. The rapid depreciation of the Korean won in December 1997 will not be reflected in the rate of inflation for a few months; in fact inflation was actually slightly lower in 1997 than in 1996. Taipei,China saw one of the lowest inflation rates, 0.9 percent in 1997, down from 3.1 percent in 1996.

Weak market sentiment resulted from uncer-tainties about currencies. This, together with the bursting of the asset bubble (especially in the pro-perty market), resulted in a sharp fall in equity mar-kets in 1997. The Hong Kong Hang Seng Index, the Singapore Strait Times Index, and the Taipei Weighted Stock Exchange Index all fell significantly. By contrast, notwithstanding a drop in the last two months of 1997, the Seoul Composite Index still managed to report a modest increase in value.

Korea, in particular, faced a difficult financial situation in 1997. Over the course of the year the

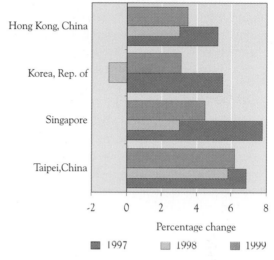

Figure 1.1 Real GDP Growth: Newly Industrialized Economies, 1997-1999

Percentage change

■ 1997   ■ 1998   ■ 1999

Source: Appendix Table A1.

Korean won depreciated by about 44 percent, from W844 to the US dollar to W1,503 to the US dollar. This was the result of concern about credit-worthiness in the wake of corporate bankruptcies, some conglomerates' and banks' financial difficulties, large stocks of unproductive assets financed by overseas capital, and continued depreciation of the Japanese yen in early 1997. The Monetary Authority intervened in both the spot and future markets; however, the end result was an approximately $30 billion loss in foreign reserves. By the end of 1997 Korea had less than the three months' import cover recommended by the IMF.

In early December 1997, Korea agreed with the IMF on a $57 billion bailout package to ease immediate liquidity constraints. The conditions of the package were as follows. The government would (i) close insolvent financial institutions; (ii) raise the ceiling of foreign equity ownership from 50 to 55 percent in 1998; (iii) scale down the GDP growth target for 1998 to 3 percent; (iv) reduce the cur-rent account deficit to 1 percent of GDP; and (v) hold inflation to less than 5 percent, implying even higher real interest rates than those that prevailed in 1997. On 24 December 1997 the Minister of Finance announced a series of financial reforms that will be presented to the National Assembly. The actual implementation of the reforms, which will include liberalizing the capital market, restructuring the financial industry, removing restrictions on foreign stock ownership, and changing the bankruptcy laws, will have a major impact on the economy's future prospects. Similar proposals in November 1997 were defeated in the National Assembly because of labor unrest.

The outlook for the NIEs in 1998 will be influenced by the Asian crisis. GDP is forecast to grow by only 2.2 percent and all the NIEs will experience a slowdown. Hong Kong, China's growth rate is expected to be about 3 percent in 1998. The need to support the currency peg will necessitate high interest rates and the fall in asset prices is projected to continue. The decline in Southeast Asia's purchasing power will adversely affect Hong Kong, China's tourist trade, which accounts for 40 percent of its service exports. Singapore's growth rate is projected to fall to 3 percent in 1998, and the fall in demand from Southeast Asia will also affect its tourist trade and exports. Korea is predicted to see the greatest slowdown, with negative growth in 1998 of 1 percent.

The projected inflation rates for 1998 show wide diversity. Korea's marked depreciation will lead to higher import prices, which is likely to cause a rise in inflation. Singapore and Taipei,China will see some increase in their rates of inflation, but these will be only moderate. Hong Kong, China is actually projected to see a fall in inflation, an effect of the decline in asset prices.

The PRC and Mongolia. The deceleration in the PRC's growth rate that began in 1994 continued through 1996, even though growth remained robust at 9.6 percent that year. The government's GDP growth target for 1997 was 10 percent, but the actual figure was 8.8 percent. The economy achieved a much needed soft landing through a combination of administrative measures and macroeconomic policies that included (i) administrative restrictions on the level of investment, (ii) careful management of Central Bank credit to the financial system, (iii) increased administered interest rates on commercial bank loans, and (iv) price controls on essential commodities. The strength of the currency, the renminbi, helped hold down the costs of imported inputs.

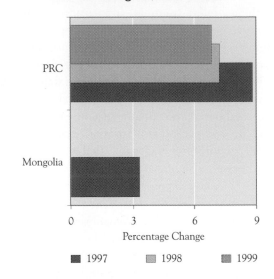

Figure 1.2 Real GDP Growth PRC and Mongolia, 1997-1999

Percentage Change

■ 1997   ▨ 1998   ▨ 1999

Note: 1998 and 1999 forecasts for Mongolia are not available.
Source: Appendix Table A1.

However, a result of the stabilization program was high enterprise arrears and an increase in urban unemployment rates. The adverse impact was particularly severe on township and village enterprises. These are rural, nonagricultural, nonstate enterprises that accounted for nearly half of the PRC's industrial output and one third of its exports in 1997. In recent years they have been growing at about double the rate of the overall economy. However, 15 percent of them are now making losses, and the value of these losses grew by 25 percent in the first ten months of 1997.

Although the 1997 Asian financial crisis has not affected the economy severely to date, it is projected to undermine economic performance slightly in 1998 and 1999. Growth in each of these years is projected to be about 7 percent. This will be partly the result of a weakening in demand from those Asian developing countries that currently account for about one third of the PRC's total exports. Furthermore, most of the export-oriented township and village enterprises are expected to experience some erosion in their competitiveness compared with Southeast Asian exporters.

In addition, high levels of corporate debt and volatility in Asia's equity markets may limit many firms' willingness to invest in the PRC. However, foreign investment has become more important for economic growth because of (i) the slow pace of state-owned enterprise reform, (ii) the weakening of domestic aggregate demand, and (iii) the like-lihood of reduced export growth brought about by the enhanced competitiveness of Southeast Asian exports.

The growth rate of Mongolia's GDP slowed down from 6.3 percent in 1995 to 2.4 percent in 1996, but improved slightly to around 3 percent in 1997. The reduced economic growth rate of the last two years reflected declining international prices of copper and cashmere, and a crisis in the domestic banking sector that resulted in the liquidation of two of Mongolia's largest banks. The 1996 economic downturn adversely affected savings and investment, while in 1997 expenditures faced considerable pressures because of a decline in tax revenues. In addition, the government abolished import duties, which accounted for 10 percent of fiscal revenues. With the establishment of a medium-term stabiliza-tion program, inflation declined from a peak of 268 percent per year in 1993 to about 20 percent in 1997. The significant depreciation of the domestic cur-rency, the tugrik, in 1996 and 1997 did not improve trade performance. This resulted in a current ac-count deficit equal to 5.6 percent of GDP in 1997. As concessional external financial flows could not fully cover this deficit, the government had to draw down its reserves.

The Central Asian Republics. The three developing member countries of the Asian Development Bank among the Central Asian republics—Kazakstan, Kyrgyz Republic, and Uzbekistan—are in the process of converting their centrally planned economies into market-oriented systems. To this end, all three have implemented programs agreed on with the Inter-national Monetary Fund (IMF), with varying degrees of success. Because of the radical economic trans-formation these countries have undertaken, their economies recorded negative GDP growth rates for several years prior to 1996. Declines of more than 10 percent per year were not uncommon. However, 1996 and 1997 saw an expansion in output. In 1997 the Kyrgyz Republic grew most rapidly at 10.4 per-cent, while Kazakstan's growth rate was 2 percent and Uzbekistan's stood at 5.2 percent.

Agricultural output suffered because of adverse weather conditions, particularly in

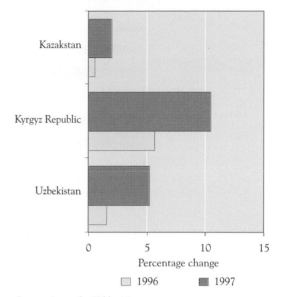

**Figure 1.3 Real GDP Growth:
Central Asian Republics, 1996-1997**

Percentage change

☐ 1996   ■ 1997

Source. Appendix Table A1.

Kazakstan and Uzbekistan, which partly explains their modest growth rates in 1997. Stabilization programs resulted in smaller budget deficits and lower inflation rates in 1997. In 1993 the average rate of inflation was more than 1,000 percent, but by 1996 this had fallen to 36.5 percent. Neverthe-less, commitment to further structural reforms should be a key component of the governments' macroeconomic stabilization programs. These re-forms should include (i) agriculture reform, (ii) en-terprise and industry reform (both in the real and financial sectors), and (iii) tax reform and public expenditure management. The success of these re-forms is critical as most of these countries are heavily dependent on foreign capital.

The Southeast Asian Economies. The financial crisis that affected Southeast Asia dominated the last half of 1997. In 1996 growth stood at 7.1 percent, but in 1997 this fell to less than 4 percent, the lowest fig-ure in two decades. The inflation rate declined from 6.6 percent in 1996 to 5.6 percent in 1997. How-ever, this is projected to rise in 1998 when the sub-stantial depreciations will be fully reflected in the retail price index. In 1997 price controls, the post-ponement of increases in electricity and gas prices, and wage and salary cuts all helped to moderate the

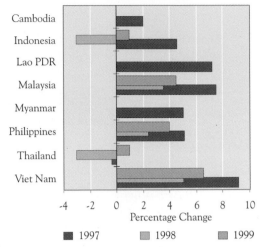

**Figure 1.4 Real GDP Growth
Southeast Asia, 1997-1999**

Percentage Change

■ 1997   ■ 1998   ■ 1999

Note: 1998 and 1999 forecasts for Cambodia, Lao PDR,
and Myanmar are not available.
Source: Appendix Table A1.

This has increased the vulnerability of the banking and capital markets, and has exposed the weaknesses and inconsistencies in macroeconomic policy management. In the absence of adequate institutional, regulatory, and supervisory frameworks, excessive amounts of capital inflows were channeled to the real estate and other speculative sectors.

Several of the economies had to raise interest rates to high levels during the course of the crisis, especially Indonesia, which had raised its short-term rates to 30.5 percent by January 1998, and Thailand, which had raised them to 27 percent. In addition, the currencies in these economies depreciated substantially. Governments announced the postponement and review of large infrastructure projects in the hope that such actions would improve their fiscal position and restore investors' confidence.

During 1990 to 1996 the large and growing current account deficits that all the Southeast Asian countries had experienced were a key concern. In 1995 and 1996 the deficits for Indonesia, Thailand, and Viet Nam rose to their highest levels ever. The international financial markets were concerned about the possibility that short-term, volatile capital flows were financing these deficits and about the increasing share of consumer goods in total imports. In 1997, however, Southeast Asia's current account deficit fell sharply to around $24 billion dollars, compared to $34 billion in 1996. Indonesia and the Philippines, for example, saw a marked increase in their export growth in 1997.

The Southeast Asian countries have been suffering from labor shortages at several skill levels, particularly of managerial and technically trained manpower. To remedy the shortages, both the public and private sectors have taken steps to increase the provision of education and training. As a short-run measure, the economies, especially Malaysia and Thailand, will have to place greater reliance on imported skilled and unskilled labor. Paradoxically, however, the crisis has forced these governments to limit the use of imported labor. For instance, in January 1998 Malaysia announced a plan to deport foreign workers to stem the rise in unemployment. This will have an adverse effect not only on Indonesia, whose nationals make up one of Malaysia's largest expatriate worker groups, but also the Philippines and Thailand.

The problems have been compounded by one of the worst natural catastrophes to hit the South-

increase in prices in the subregion temporarily. Only Lao PDR experienced a large increase in its inflation rate from 13 percent in 1996 to 19.5 percent in 1997.

Thailand's crisis had its manifestations in the first half of 1997, when the Thai baht repeatedly came under strong speculative pressure. During the second half of the year other Southeast Asian currencies, such as the Philippine peso, the Malaysian ringgit, and the Indonesian rupiah, also came under severe speculative pressure. The spillover effect of the crisis also led to a depreciation of Viet Nam's dong by about 19 percent compared with its value against the US dollar at the end of 1996. In some Southeast Asian economies, however, the currency crisis was more than merely a matter of contagion, but reflected fundamental weaknesses.

The crisis unveiled many interrelated problems that pose challenges for macroeconomic, banking, and capital markets management; governance; institutional capabilities; and human resource development. Both governments and the private sector will have to face this challenge, especially in the aftermath of financial liberalization. More important, the recent globalization of financial markets has resulted in a world of highly mobile capital.

east Asian countries: El Niño, a phenomenon caused by the warming of the surface waters of the eastern Pacific Ocean (see Box 1.2). In 1997 El Niño was responsible for severe drought, widespread forest fires, marked increases in health problems, and the resultant economic difficulties throughout the subregion.

The economic outlook for 1998 is extremely uncertain and will depend largely on the extent to which governments can implement the various IMF rescue packages (see the following section on the Financial Crisis in Asia). Projections indicate that Southeast Asia can expect negative growth of 0.4 percent in 1998, with the Philippines performing the least badly. The huge private sector debt burden in Indonesia and Thailand in particular will have a major impact on the economic performance of Southeast Asia in 1998 and 1999.

As a result of depreciation and the rapid increase in import prices, inflation is expected to increase to 12.9 percent in 1998. Indonesia is projected to be particularly hard hit, with an inflation rate of about 20 percent.

Current account imbalances are likely to improve in 1998, partly because of the slower growth, and partly because of the improved competitiveness of exports. Regional deficits are projected to improve to $6.1 billion in 1998 and $0.9 billion in 1999.

The South Asian Economies. Despite a number of infrastructural bottlenecks, the South Asian economies grew at an average rate of 6.8 percent per year between 1994 and 1996, a higher rate than in the immediate past, reflecting the positive impact of recent policy reforms. In 1997, however, the growth rate for South Asian economies declined to less than 5 percent.

The wide disparities in growth between the subregion's countries largely reflected differences in the growth of agriculture and manufacturing, together with the rate of investment. India grew at a slower pace of 5 percent in 1997, in contrast to 7.5 percent in 1996, because of weather-related factors and subdued demand for manufacturing. Pakistan performed poorly as well and its overall growth rate dropped from 4.6 percent in 1996 to 3.1 percent in 1997. Sri Lanka, by contrast, had fast growth in both agriculture and manufacturing, and as a result, its growth rate increased from 3.8 percent in 1996 to 6.3 percent in 1997. Bangladesh grew

rapidly in agriculture, but lagged in manufacturing. The economy grew at 5.7 percent in 1997, a slightly higher rate than the 5.4 percent recorded in 1996.

The inflation rate for the subregion declined from 9.3 percent in 1996, to around 7 percent in 1997. Bangladesh was able to maintain its inflation rate at about 4 percent in 1997, the lowest in the subregion, because of low increases in food prices. A recovery of agricultural output, a slowdown of money supply growth, and improved supply conditions for basic products permitted Sri Lanka's inflation rate to fall from 15.9 percent in 1996 to less than 10 percent in 1997. In Pakistan, a decline in the rate of growth in agriculture and industry largely explained the increase in the inflation rate from 10.8 percent in 1996 to 11.6 percent in 1997. Factors that helped restrain the rise were lower interest rates and the liberalization of trade, with the consequent reduction in import tariffs.

The total trade deficit for the subregion was more than $24 billion in 1997, approximately $1.5 billion more than in 1996. Bangladesh reported a noteworthy improvement, whereas India's current account deficit increased by nearly $2.3 billion. The rise in imports was to some extent necessary to meet the domestic shortfall of basic necessities, such as

Figure 1.5 Real GDP Growth: South Asia, 1997-1999

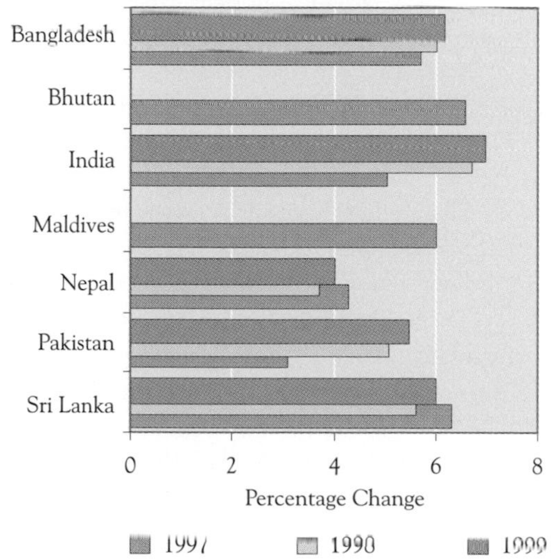

Note: 1998 and 1999 forecasts for Bhutan and Maldives are not available.
Source: Appendix Table A1.

Box 1.2 El Niño: Nature Plays Havoc with the Southeast Asian Economies

El Niño is a natural climatic phenomenon that occurs every 2 to 7 years and lasts up to 18 months. It is caused by a warming of the surface waters of the eastern Pacific Ocean, near the equator, that dramatically alters global wind and rainfall patterns. The present occurrence of El Niño started in early March 1997 and is expected to continue until May 1998.

The present El Niño brought the severest drought in 50 years to Indonesia, Malaysia, Philippines, Singapore, and Thailand. This decreased the acreage devoted to rice, delayed rice planting, and induced farmers to switch to low-yielding but early maturing varieties in 1998. In some remote areas the fall in production of rice and other crops has led to famine. According to an estimate by the Philippine Department of Agriculture, despite measures to mitigate the effects of El Niño, some 230,000 tons of rice may be lost because of the dry spell in the Central Luzon region. In the provinces of Bulacan and Pampanga, some farmers refrained from planting rice in anticipation that El Niño would persist until June 1998. Drought also led to a serious rice shortage in Mindanao, which was assuaged by 100,000 tons of rice imported from Thailand, where rice harvests were not as severely affected. However, even in Thailand, more than 640,000 hectares of farmland in 22 provinces suffered from the prolonged drought, which damaged more than 70 percent of the first corn crop. El Niño has also prompted fish shoals to migrate from the Cook Islands to cooler waters, thereby depriving local fishermen of their livelihood. The situation was so severe in Sumatra that in 1997 the Government of Indonesia allocated nearly Rp1 trillion ($220 million at the early December 1997 exchange rate of $1 to Rp4,500) for the importation of essential food items, including 100,000 tons of rice.

The production of key commercial crops, such as tea, cocoa, and palm oil, has suffered to varying degrees; but the most serious impact has been on coffee bean production, which is expected to be 40 percent below normal.

El Niño has also caused water shortages for both domestic and industrial use. Since its onset, Malaysia and Singapore have received only a third of their normal rainfall. Water reserves in Singapore, which is largely dependent on Malaysia for its supplies, have sunk to record lows. In the Philippines, water levels in reservoirs have reached critically low levels. A shortage of drinking water in the Cook Islands has resulted in the spread of cholera, with many deaths. Papua New Guinea has declared a state of emergency and has had to close its gold mines, the principal source of revenue, due to lack of water.

Because of the drought, El Niño has been associated with the devastating forest fires that occurred in Indonesia during August to October 1997. These fires, which destroyed millions of hectares of forest, enveloped Southeast Asia in a poisonous haze and caused enormous losses in terms of resources, environmental quality, human health, and tourism revenues throughout the subregion. In Central Kalimantan, a province in Indonesia, the concentration of dust particles in the air reached almost 3,000 milligrams per cubic meter, more than ten times the tolerable limit of 260 milligrams per cubic meter. The consequences ranged from the closure of many industrial plants to threats to the survival of endangered wild animals such as tigers, rhinoceroses, and elephants, especially in the jungles of Indonesia.

The poor visibility caused by the haze led to temporary cancellation of most airline flights and dramatically reduced tourism, which normally accounts for $20 billion in revenues. According to one estimate, Malaysian Airlines alone lost $1.95 million in canceled bookings during the period. Hotel revenues also fell as occupancy rates decreased by at least 10 percent.

The prevalence of illness has increased significantly in the affected countries. In Malaysia, for example, asthma cases increased by two thirds. The increase in upper respiratory tract infections was 22 percent for adults and 11 percent for children, while conjunctivitis cases rose by 61 percent and 44 percent respectively. In 1997 Singapore reported a marked increase in acute respiratory tract infections. The number of asthma cases and other respiratory ailments also increased significantly in southern Philippines.

In sum, El Niño's economic impact on Indonesia, Malaysia, Philippines, Singapore, and the Pacific islands was considerable. According to one estimate, the damage wrought by El Niño worldwide will easily exceed $20 billion, an amount significantly larger than the damage caused by El Niño in 1982/83. For countries such as Indonesia, Malaysia, and Philippines, which were the hardest hit by El Niño, the economic impact is projected to cause a fall in output of 1 percent in 1998.

food. The liberalization of trade also encouraged a higher volume of imports. The position was made worse in 1997 by an increase in the trade deficit in services and a fall in net transfers of earnings from expatriate workers. Export performance was weak, and although the subregion's currencies depreciated in the latter half of 1997, they did not do so to the same extent as the Southeast Asian currencies. Without further adjustments in exchange rates, major export sectors, such as garments, textiles, plastics, and synthetic fibers that compete with exports from other Asian economies, will be adversely affected. Pakistan, whose fiscal and current account deficits both increased to around 6 percent of GDP, experienced the most serious macroeconomic imbalances.

A legacy of South Asia's inward-looking policies and the reforms that commenced in the early 1990s, but which remain incomplete, is the persistence of a relatively small external sector. Unlike the economics of the Association of Southeast Asian Nations, regional economic cooperation is somewhat limited; this should, however, increase with the creation of new regional bodies like the South Asia Preferential Trade Agreement. As trade and economic reforms in these countries progress, they will become better integrated both with each other and with the world economy. India, for example, overtook Japan as Sri Lanka's main source of imports in 1996.

However, a few cases of governments failing to honor past commitments and the slow implementation of economic reforms have raised some concerns. A highly publicized case was India's civil aviation sector, which was to be opened up to foreign investment, but where the government subsequently reversed its decision. Furthermore, governments have made inadequate progress in liberalizing trade, modernizing banking, and privatizing state enterprises. The IMF's Enhanced Structural Adjustment Facility loan of $1.6 billion to Pakistan is conditional on successful implementation of a structural adjustment program.

Projections indicate that the South Asian economies will grow at an average rate of 6.4 percent in 1998. Pakistan is expected to grow at 5.1 percent, two percentage points faster than in 1997, and Sri Lanka is projected to grow at a more moderate rate of 5.6 percent, as opposed to 6.3 percent in 1997. However, the other economic indicators for 1998, namely, rates of investment and saving, fiscal and current account balances, and inflation, are projected to confirm the overall improvement in the economies' fundamentals.

With the exception of Nepal and Pakistan, the subregion's inflation rate will deteriorate slightly in 1998, with 7.4 percent projected average rate. This will be the outcome of adverse weather conditions in 1997 and the slow pace of economic reform. The projected inflation rate for the region is somewhat higher for 1999, despite expectations of more disciplined fiscal expenditures.

The Pacific Islands. The Pacific islands are characterized by a narrow production base; a subsistence sector that supports the bulk of the population; and a small, more organized sector that comprises the government, local units of foreign companies, and banks. The largest economy, Papua New Guinea, dominates the islands' economic performance. A severe drought in Papua New Guinea in the second half of 1997 means that some 650,000 people will need food aid for several months in 1998. While rain has now provided some relief, projections indicate that the current coffee and cocoa crop will be down by 20 percent. The overall growth rate of GDP in 1997 was negative.

Fiji's growth contracted to 1 percent in 1997 from the 3 percent achieved in 1996. This was the outcome of a number of factors, including reduced sugar production because of cyclones, industrial disputes, disappointing gold and garment production, a downturn in the construction industry, and a severe drought in the latter part of 1997.

The economic performance of the other Pacific islands was varied. Growth in Kiribati picked up in 1997 and reached 2 percent as a result of a revival in the copra and fishing industries. After declining by more than 5 percent per year in 1995 and 1996, growth in the Cook Islands increased to 0.5 percent in 1997. Fortunately, the cyclone that hit the main pearl producing island in the latter part of 1997, while it did extensive damage to the infrastructure, did not affect the pearl crop. The other countries in the region that did less well include the Marshall Islands. These are facing extreme economic difficulties, with GDP falling by 5 percent in 1997, despite the high level of US grants. The Federated States of Micronesia recorded a negative growth rate of about 5 percent in 1997. In the Solomon Islands output declined by 1 percent in 1997 after impressive growth in the early 1990s of more than 5 percent per year.

RISKS AND UNCERTAINTIES

Globalization is a double-edged sword. It has brought with it many economic benefits in the form of increased competition and more efficient allocation of resources. At the same time, however, the resulting high mobility of short-term capital can quickly cause major financial problems for any country that international financial markets perceive as having major policy shortcomings.

The financial crisis in Southeast Asia and Korea has left these economies in disarray. The most important policy challenge for the world economic community is to devise a satisfactory response. Failure to address the crisis will not only exacerbate Southeast Asia and Korea's economic problems, but will also further undermine the growth momentum in the rest of the world. In 1998 the crisis is already projected to slow the growth of the United States, the European Union, and the OECD countries by less than 1 percentage point and of Japan by 1.5 percentage points. A full commitment to economic and policy reform is a prerequisite for early recovery and sustained future growth of the afflicted Asian economies. The measures these governments, particularly those of Indonesia and Korea, take in 1998 to deal with the private sector's maturing large external debt will inevitably determine these economies' performance.

Risks exist not only with respect to the East and Southeast Asian economies affected by the financial crisis, but also with respect to other Asian countries that are not directly affected by it, but that are now undertaking policy reforms. These economies, such as those in South Asia and the Central Asian republics, are at various stages of the economic reform process. Uncertainties remain about the level of commitment and implementation and about the speed with which these economies will respond to the reform programs.

The stability of the Chinese renminbi and the Hong Kong dollar will remain an important factor in the region's economic stability. Commitments by the Monetary Authority of Hong Kong and the People's Bank of China to defend the Hong Kong dollar successfully countered speculative pressure against the Hong Kong dollar after the Asian currency crisis erupted in July 1997. As of January 1998, the renminbi had also maintained its rate of exchange with the US dollar. With the rapid depreciation of exchange rates in Southeast Asia and the dramatic fall in some Asian stock market indexes in the past few months, the Hong Kong dollar and the Chinese renminbi may be subject to more speculative attacks. The success with which the authorities defend these exchange rates will have important implications for the recovery of the Asian economies.

Uncertainties also exist with respect to further liberalization of the world trading environment, which is an important determinant of the dynamics of the global economy. In the wake of difficulties facing Asian financial and currency markets, the WTO agenda to liberalize trade in financial services will pose a challenge in 1998 and 1999. In December 1997 negotiators from 70 countries reached agreement on a pact to liberalize trade in financial services, which will bring the financial industry in line with WTO rules. This agreement, which is subject to ratification by each signatory state, is expected to come into force no later than March 1999. However, the process faces a number of obstacles. The first obstacle is institutional. For most developing countries, implementing the pact will require changes in domestic law, which may be hard to achieve. Second, the recent crisis in Asia showed that the liberalization of financial sectors is beset with difficulties. Successful liberalization requires strong national institutional and regulatory frameworks, complemented by adequate human resources expertise. In this respect many developing countries suffer from major weaknesses. Given the volatility of the global capital market and the express hostility of many developing countries to the WTO accord, this compact may remain merely as a symbolic commitment for some time to come.

Finally, an important "exogenous" source of uncertainty is climatic, as this year's economic performance of Southeast Asian countries will amply testify. Although structural changes of the past three decades have reduced the importance of agriculture as a source of income, it continues to be an important determinant of growth in many Asian developing economies.

THE FINANCIAL CRISIS IN ASIA

What caused the Asian financial crisis? How will the crisis affect the prospects for the Asian economies and the world economy? What policy options can the affected economies adopt to overcome the adverse effects of the crisis? Can other vulnerable economies learn any lessons from the crisis? The following chapter provides incisive answers to these questions. It concludes that, notwithstanding the crisis, developing countries must continue with the process of liberalization and integration with the global economy, because the benefits of globalization are too large to ignore.

The most significant event in the world economy in 1997—perhaps in the decade—was the financial crisis that besieged much of Asia. The crisis began in Thailand in July 1997 when the value of the Thai currency plummeted following the country's abandonment of its pegged exchange system. This crisis slowly spilled over and engulfed Indonesia, Republic of Korea (henceforth referred to as Korea), Malaysia, and Philippines by the end of 1997. The currencies of these countries (henceforth collectively called the affected countries) depreciated sharply, and at the same time exerted downward pressures on other currencies perceived to be vulnerable, and not just in Asia.

The financial crisis was also reflected in the principal asset markets, namely, stock markets and real estate markets. Together with exchange rate declines, the fall in asset values adversely affected the health of banks and nonbank financial institutions. In the second half of 1997, many other Asian developing economies also experienced difficulties in all these areas to varying extents. For example, with the notable exceptions of the People's Republic of China (PRC) and Hong Kong, China, the currencies of most other Asian economies depreciated. In many of these economies, real estate values and stock markets fell sharply and financial sectors came

under severe pressure (Figure 1.6 shows changes in nominal exchange rates and composite stock market price indexes). The outcome was that many Asian economies experienced drastic slowdowns in their economic growth and a loss of confidence by foreign investors. The speed and severity of the crisis took everybody by surprise. Even those skeptics who argued that the claims of an Asian economic miracle were overstated, and that it was bound to run into "diminishing returns," did not expect such a precipitous collapse.

THE EVOLUTION OF THE CRISIS

The present currency instability in the region began in July 1997 following the year's second speculative attack on the Thai baht (Box 1.3 presents a chronology of the crisis). The Bank of Thailand, after defending the currency as it had done earlier in May 1997 and losing reserves, finally let the baht float on 2 July 1997. The baht immediately depreciated by about 15 percent in the first week alone (Figure 1.7). The Indonesian rupiah, the Malaysian ringgit, and the Philippine peso also depreciated gradually during that week. The depreciation of the peso and the rupiah gathered further momentum after 11 July 1997 and 14 August 1997, respectively,

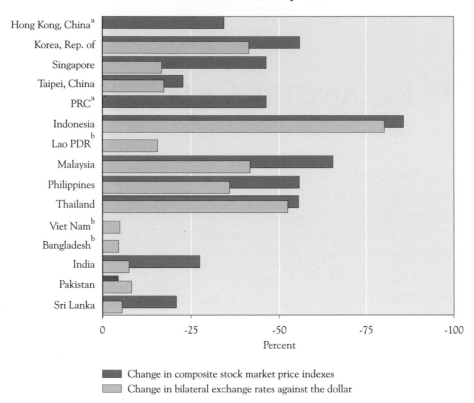

Figure 1.6 Changes in Nominal Bilateral Exchange Rates and Composite Stock Market Price Indexes: Selected DMCs, June 1997 - January 1998

[a] No changes in exchange rates.
[b] Stock market data not available.

Source: Based on data from BLOOMBERG.

when the central banks of these countries adopted more flexible exchange rate policies. Thereafter, Malaysia's Central Bank also gradually reduced its intervention in foreign exchange markets. Since then all four countries have effectively floated their currencies.

Since the end of June 1997 through the end of January 1998, the nominal exchange rate (the dollar price of the local currency) depreciated significantly in all the affected countries. The rupiah depreciated by about 80 percent, the baht by about 53 percent, the won and ringgit by 42 percent, and the peso by about 36 percent. The Korean won was relatively stable until mid-October 1997, when it started to depreciate. The depreciation accelerated further in mid-November 1997. The

authorities widened the exchange rate band for the won to 10 percent in November, and since 16 December have allowed the won to float freely. As the turmoil affected Korea, the world's 11th largest economy, the crisis acquired a new global dimension.

As of mid-January 1998, Indonesia's budget for 1998/99 was invoking skepticism about the government's determination to pursue required reforms, and led to a fresh round of jitters, both regionally and globally. The rupiah hit a record low and affected other currencies as well, thereby sending the turmoil into a new phase. The agreement reached with the International Monetary Fund (IMF) on 15 January 1998 restored some calm to regional stock markets, but has not yet led to significant improvements in currency values.

Box 1.3 Chronology of the Financial Crisis in Asia

2 July 1997	The Bank of Thailand announced a managed float of the baht. This was a trigger for the Asian financial turmoil.
11 July	The Philippine Central Bank allowed the peso to move in a wider band against the dollar.
24 July	The ringgit hit a 38-month low against the dollar.
5 August	Thailand unveiled an austerity plan and a revamping of the financial sector; policies suggested by the International Monetary Fund (IMF) as part of a rescue package.
11 August	The IMF unveiled a rescue package for Thailand that included loans totaling $17.2 billion from the IMF, the Asian Development Bank, the World Bank, and various Asian nations.
14 August	Indonesia abandoned its system of managing the exchange rate through the use of a band and allowed its currency to float.
16 September	Indonesia announced that it would postpone projects worth Rp39 trillion to reduce the budget deficit.
14 October	Thailand established the Financial Restructuring Agency to supervise the overall rehabilitation of the financial sector and help viable companies merge and/or raise capital. It also established the Asset Management Company to liquidate unviable companies.
20-23 October	The Hong Kong, China stock market suffered its heaviest loss ever, shedding nearly a quarter of its value.
31 October	An IMF-led rescue package, with the participation of the Asian Development Bank, the World Bank, and various nations, of $23 billion to Indonesia was announced.
7 November	Asian stocks nose-dived as currency jitters shook Korea and high interest rates and falling property prices rattled Hong Kong, China.
19 November	Deputy finance ministers met in Manila and issued the so-called Manila Framework.
19 November	The Korean government announced plans to increase the funds available to the Korea Asset Management Corporation to purchase nonperforming assets of banks and merchant banks and widened the band for its exchange rate.
24 November	The troubled Tokyo brokerage Yamaichi Securities Co. Ltd., the fourth-largest in Japan, announced that it was closing its doors.
25 November	The yen tumbled to its lowest level against the dollar in more than five years and the Tokyo stock market plunged 5 percent. Standard & Poor's ratings agency lowered Korea's ratings.
3 December	Korean officials and IMF Managing Director Michel Camdessus signed a letter of intent covering an international accord to provide Korea with $57 billion to help the country move out of its financial crisis.
9 December	Rumors that Indonesia's President Suharto was gravely ill swept Southeast Asian currency markets, sending the rupiah into a tailspin.
12 December	Indonesian stocks plunged 7.6 percent and the rupiah sank as concerns about President Suharto's health resurfaced following a report that he would not attend an Asian summit the next week after all.
16 December	Korea moved to a managed float exchange rate regime.
17 December	Japanese Prime Minister Ryutaro Hashimoto announced a special Y2 trillion ($15.7 billion) cut in personal income taxes.
19 December	The Asian Development Bank announced emergency assistance to Indonesia and Korea, amounting to $3.5 billion and $4 billion, respectively.

22 December	Moody's Investors Service downgraded the sovereign debt of four countries, lowering three of them to junk-bond status. Moody's said it had downgraded the foreign currency ceiling for Indonesia's, Korea's, and Malaysia's bonds and bank deposits because of Asia's continuing financial woes. It also downgraded Thailand's foreign currency ceiling for bonds and confirmed the ceiling for bank deposits.
24 December	The IMF and the United States and 12 other nations pledged to provide $10 billion in bailout money to Korea to support its embattled economy. The Indonesian rupiah plunged to a new record low amid reports that the country's short-term debt burden was higher than previously thought.
29 December	The Korean government passed 13 financial sector reform bills that included plans to establish a single supervisory authority by 1 April 1998. The interest rate ceiling of 40 percent was also lifted.
31 December	Indonesia's Ministry of Finance announced a reform package for consolidating and/or merging seven existing banks into three entities by July 1998.
2 January 1998	Major US and European banks announced that they would allow Korean borrowers more time to pay off an estimated $15 billion in short-term debt that had come due on 31 December. The Indonesian rupiah fell sharply against the dollar on a ratings downgrade, and the Malaysian and Philippine currencies also fell as trading resumed in parts of Asia after the New Year holiday.
5 January	Thailand announced that it would ask the IMF to ease the terms of its $17.2 billion bailout package as its currency, the baht, fell to a new low of less than half its mid-1997 value. Prime Minister Chuan Leekpai said Thailand would seek to soften an IMF requirement that it produce a budget surplus in 1998.
7 January	The Indonesian, Malaysian, Philippine, and Thai currencies fell to new lows, dragging stocks down across much of Asia, as Indonesia's budget, announced the previous day, failed to convince investors that these countries were committed to reforming their economies.
15 January	In Indonesia, President Suharto agreed with the IMF on a revised budget and announced additional economic reforms, which included abolishing key monopolies and closing debt-laden banks.
16 January	International lenders completed a plan to roll over Korean short-term debt through 31 March.
27 January	The Government of Indonesia announced a program to rehabilitate the banking sector. The program provides a government guarantee to depositors and creditors of locally incorporated banks for at least two years and creates the Indonesian Bank Restructuring Agency, which will be responsible for rehabilitating unsound banks. In addition, the government proposed an interim freeze on corporate debt-service payments to allow time for lenders and borrowers to work out new arrangements. The temporary freeze would cover financial loans, including bank loans, bonds, and commercial paper, but would exclude trade debt.
29 January	The Government of Korea and a group of 13 leading international banks reached agreement on a plan to extend the maturities of approximately $24 billion of short-term credits to the Korean banking system from one to three years.

As is often the case, investors' confidence deteriorated before the currency crisis hit. Stock markets in Korea and Thailand had been under pressure since the beginning of 1996 (Figure 1.8). In Malaysia and the Philippines, the pressure began in early 1997, and stock prices declined by about 52 and 48 percent, respectively, in local currency terms, between the end of June 1997 and the end of January 1998. In Indonesia, the stock market re-mained buoyant during the early part of the year, but with the onset of the currency crisis it declined sharply, by about 80 percent, between the end of June 1997 and the end of January 1998.

As in many currency crises, the current crisis has not been limited to individual countries, but has spread across the region. Not only neighboring countries, but also financial markets as far away as Latin America, Australia, and New Zealand have felt the

**Figure 1.7 Weekly Nominal Exchange Rates Indexes: Selected Asian Economies,
End of June 1997 - End of January 1998**

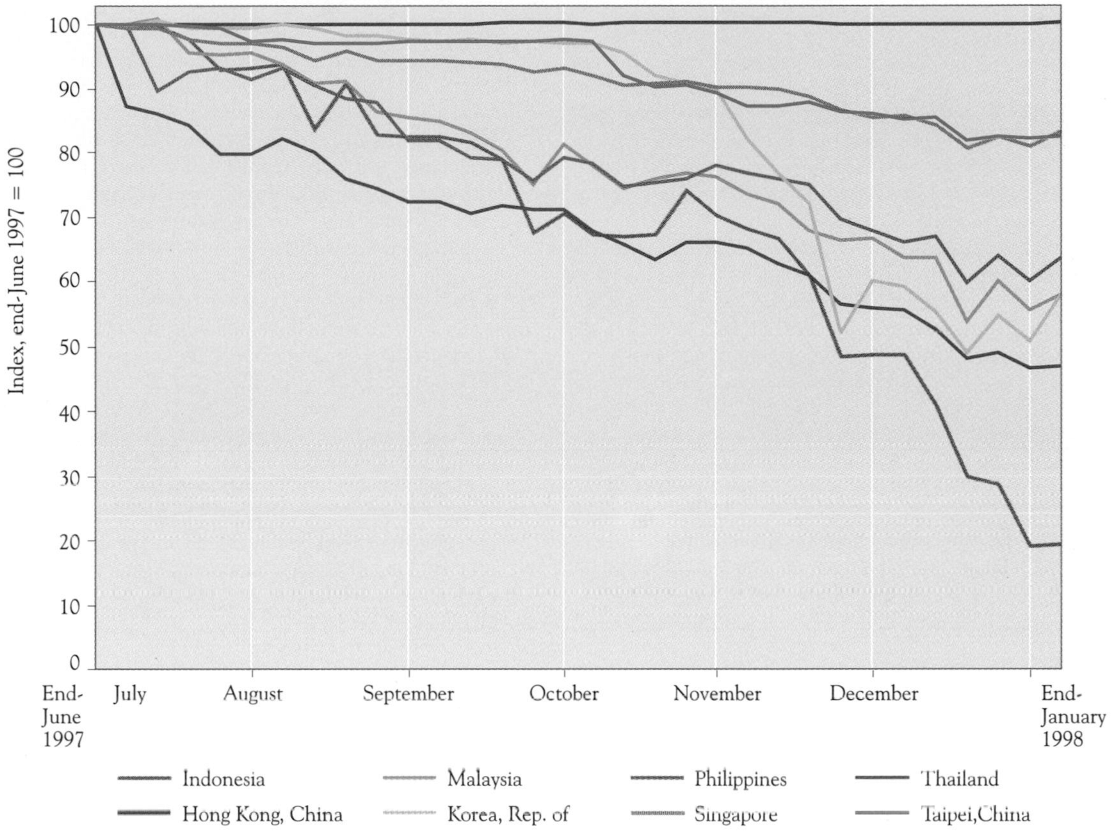

Source: Based on data from BLOOMBERG.

contagion effects of the crisis to varying extents. (See Box 1.4 for an explanation of the contagion effect and how it works.) Between the end of June 1997 through the end of January 1998 the Singapore dollar depreciated by about 17 percent, the Lao kip by about 16 percent, and the Indian and Pakistani rupees by about 18 percent. Despite speculative attacks on a number of occasions and a sharp fall in the Hang Seng Index by about 26 percent from the beginning of July 1997 through the end of January 1998, the Hong Kong dollar has remained firm so far. The principal reason for this firmness is that Hong Kong, China has a sound currency board (a currency board is a fixed exchange rate system where all currency in circulation, and usually all bank reserves, are backed by foreign exchange).

EXPLAINING THE FINANCIAL CRISIS

Currency crises tend to follow a certain pattern. The Latin American crises in the 1980s and the mid-1990s are good examples of this. A country has a fixed or managed exchange rate, and the government engages in profligate spending and runs excessive budget deficits. To sustain these deficits, the government has to follow an expansionary monetary policy, which creates domestic inflation and leads to an appreciation in the real exchange rate and an increase in the trade deficit. (The real exchange rate is the rate at which the goods and services of one country trade for the goods and services of another. An appreciation of the real exchange rate implies that domestic goods and services have become

Box 1.4 How the Contagion Spreads

As illustrated by the recent currency crisis in Asia, currency crises often occur in regional waves rather than in individual countries. This phenomenon has been metaphorically referred to as contagion. While the popular press has talked extensively about contagion, the mechanism of transmission remains largely unexplained. Nevertheless, the economics literature suggests a number of transmission mechanisms.

First, the "contagious" economies are often linked, particularly through trade and financial flows, and often export similar products. Depreciation of the Thai baht, for example, may have an adverse impact on Malaysia's competitiveness, trade, and employment, and hence increase the pressure on the Malaysian government to abandon its own commitment to a pegged exchange rate.

Second, even if the economies are linked only weakly or not at all, they may have some common, but imperfectly observed, characteristics. Once investors have seen one of these countries with common characteristics (say "Latin temperament" or "Asian values") abandon its peg under pressure, they may infer that the others might do the same. For example, in the 1980s, when the Latin American countries suffered a debt crisis, the crisis spread from Mexico to the whole of Latin America. Initially, the Philippines was not affected, even though its policies and debt burden were as bad as those of the affected Latin American countries. However, a year after the onset of the crisis, investors appeared to have decided that the Philippines, a former Spanish colony, was actually more Latin than Asian, and abandoned the country.

Third, the political commitment to defend a fixed exchange rate is subject to "imitative" behavior. If, for example, Thailand has abandoned its peg, for Indonesia and Malaysia to do so becomes politically less costly.

Fourth, some have argued that contagion reflects a certain level of irrationality on the part of investors. This irrationality is often the result of asymmetric incentives. For instance, Korea has had few strong trade links with the financially troubled Southeast Asian economies. If fund managers did not reduce their exposure in Korea and were caught in the devaluation, they would be blamed for lack of diligence. However, if they were proven correct, they would not be rewarded for their insights. Therefore, fund managers feel more compelled to leave Korea once a crisis spreads to neighboring Southeast Asian countries.

Source: Krugman (1998).

---

relatively more expensive compared to foreign goods and services.) If this continues for some time, it becomes apparent to the market that official reserves would be unable to sustain the current exchange rate. Given the pegged exchange rate, this triggers speculative attacks (via the capital account of the balance of payments) on the currency.

This can explain many of the currency crises in emerging markets. However, it does not explain some other crises, especially those in the industrial countries, such as the Exchange Rate Mechanism crisis in Europe in 1992-1993. In these European economies, neither monetary nor fiscal policy had been excessively profligate, nor did inflation or a trade deficit have any role. In this episode, unemployment played the central role. If unemployment continues to increase, the interest rate needs to be reduced to boost employment, a measure that is incompatible with a pegged exchange rate. As soon as the market begins to foresee this outcome, the interest rate needs to be increased to defend the peg, which further increases the unemployment rate and destabilizes the political situation. This causes further intensification of speculative attacks against the peg.

How well do these explanations fit the Asian currency crisis of 1997 and 1998? The answer is, not well. First, the Asian currency crisis was neither driven by fiscal profligacy nor by excessive credit creation or runaway monetary expansion on the part of government. (See Table 1.2 for a comparison of major economic indicators in the affected and nonaffected Southeast Asian and East Asian economies.) The affected economies have had a better fiscal record than the nonaffected economies: all posted modest budgetary surpluses during 1994-1996. Before the crisis, the growth of money supply showed no signs of acceleration. No doubt the growth in broad money was high, averaging about 19 percent per year, yet given that these economies were also growing at extremely high rates, the growth of monetary aggregates was not excessive. The average inflation rate of less than 7 percent per year was relatively moderate, and did not show signs of acceleration. Second, while the affected countries had exhibited a slight slowdown in growth before

Figure 1.8 Weekly Composite Stock Price Indexes: Selected Asian Economies, January 1996-January 1998

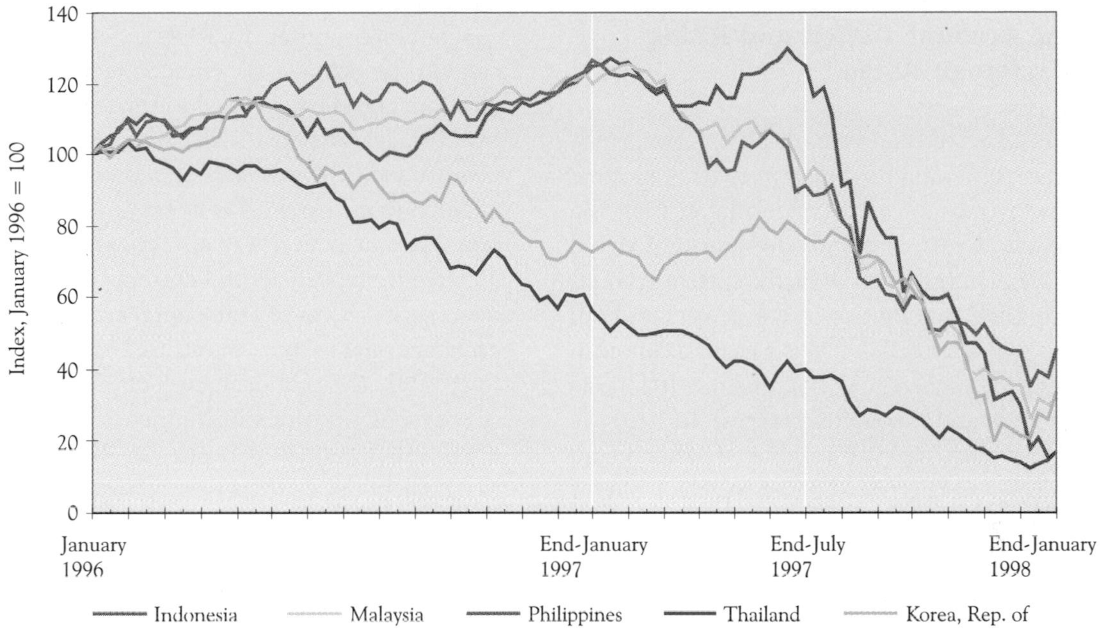

Source: Based on data from BLOOMBERG.

the crisis, they did not suffer from any substantial unemployment. Indeed, all of them had full or near-full employment and some even imported foreign labor to mitigate domestic labor shortages. Therefore, these countries did not have the incentives to abandon their pegged foreign exchange rates to

pursue more expansionary monetary policies to bring real wages and unemployment down.

Indeed, the Asian story is somewhat more complex than those described. Its principal elements include the pegged exchange rate (that eventually contributed to the current account deficits and rising

Table 1.2 Major Economic Indicators: Affected and Nonaffected Economies, 1991-1997 (percent)

Item	Affected economies			Nonaffected economies		
	1991-95	1996	1997	1991-95	1996	1997
GDP growth	7.3	7.0	4.4	6.5	5.7	6.5
Inflation rate	6.1	5.8	5.1	4.9	3.7	2.5
Gross domestic saving/GDP	33.9	33.3	32.8	31.8	31.5	31.3
Current account balance/GDP	-3.0	-5.0	-3.0	4.1	4.9	4.2
Fiscal balance/GDP	0.3	0.4	-0.2	-0.7	-2.0	1.4
Money supply (M2) growth	19.5	18.6	18.5	14.5	9.8	8.1

Note: Affected economies include Indonesia, Korea, Malaysia, Philippines, and Thailand. Nonaffected economies include Hong Kong, China; Singapore; and Taipei,China.

Source: Asian Development Bank data.

real exchange rates), private capital inflows, financial sector imbalances and frailties, and weaknesses in the corporate sector.

Current Account Deficit and Rising Real Exchange Rates

While the affected economies displayed few macroeconomic vulnerabilities, in retrospect, the large and growing current account deficits in Malaysia and Thailand were a significant warning signal (Figure 1.9). During 1991-1995, the current account deficit to GDP ratio averaged 6.4 percent in both Malaysia and Thailand, but was somewhat lower in the Philippines (averaging 3.6 percent), Indonesia (2.3 percent), and Korea (1.3 percent). In 1996 the current account deficits widened further in all affected countries except Malaysia, reaching almost 8 percent in Thailand and about 5 percent in Korea.

The current account deficit was partly caused by structural changes in the "real" side of these economies and partly by appreciation of the real exchange rate. In recent years, countries such as

Malaysia and Thailand have undergone extensive structural changes and faced an erosion in their competitiveness in labor-intensive products, such as garments and footwear, in relation to lower wage Asian competitor countries. In 1996 a sharp cyclical decline in the demand for semiconductors and other electronic products (as well as the slower growth of world trade compared with previous years) further compounded the problem of export slowdown. In addition to the export slowdown, the rise in the current account deficit was also caused partly by an increase in imports (both consumption and investment goods) because of the appreciation of the real exchange rates in these countries. During June 1995-June 1997, the real exchange rate appreciated by 21 percent for the Philippines, 14 percent for Thailand, and 12 percent for Indonesia and Malaysia. Korea also experienced some appreciation, but only by a modest 1.5 percent (Figure 1.10).

The real exchange rate appreciated because of a combination of factors that included higher domestic inflation in relation to the world average; appreciation of the US dollar, to which these currencies were pegged; depreciation of the Japanese

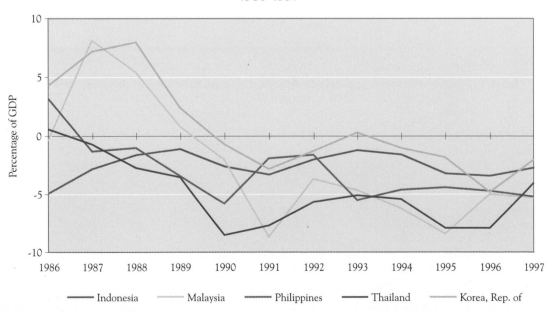

Figure 1.9 Current Account Balances, Selected Asian Economies, 1986-1997

Source: Asian Development Bank data.

yen and many European currencies; and devaluation of the PRC currency, the renminbi, in 1994. The combination of the persistent current account deficits and rising real exchange rates provided a vital ingredient for the financial crisis that ensued.

Private Capital Inflows

Private capital flows from abroad have sustained the combination of increased current account deficits and rising real exchange rates. Indeed, a substantial flow of private foreign capital not only financed the current account imbalances, but for several years also enhanced official reserve positions. Despite large capital inflows, domestic interest rates were kept high through sterilization, which attracted further capital inflows. (Sterilization is an operation undertaken by the central bank—such as buying or selling government bonds—to offset the effects on the money supply of balance-of-payments deficits or surpluses.)

Since the late 1980s, many Asian developing economies have experienced surges in capital inflows (Figure 1.11). Aside from the PRC, the surges were largest in the affected countries. On a cumulative basis, from 1987 through the end of 1996, Korea received $80 billion, Thailand received $75 billion, Indonesia and Malaysia received $68 billion each, and the Philippines received $23 billion. These inflows averaged nearly 12 percent of GDP per year in Malaysia, followed by 7.4 percent in Thailand, 5.7 percent in Indonesia, 5.1 percent in Korea, and 4.3 percent in the Philippines. Only a small fraction of this flow came in the form of foreign direct investment. The remainder came either through portfolio investment or through the banking sector.

Why has this surge of capital flows taken place? This surge is largely due to a combination of "push" and "pull" factors. First, since the beginning of the 1990s, weak growth in Japan and Europe led to a decline in attractive investment opportunities in relation to available domestic savings. Slow growth also led to accommodating monetary policies with low interest rates. All these contributed to a situation where domestic investors in Japan and Europe started to look for lucrative investment opportunities abroad. Second, financial liberalization in the late 1980s and the 1990s in many Asian developing

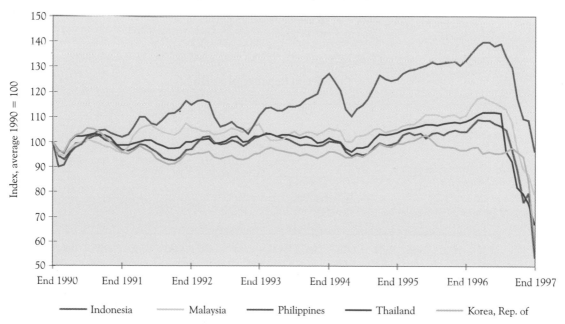

Figure 1.10 Weighted Real Effective Exchange Rates: Selected Asian Economies, 1990-1997

Index, average 1990 = 100

Indonesia   Malaysia   Philippines   Thailand   Korea, Rep. of

Source: Kiel Institute data.

Figure 1.11 Net Private Capital Flows: Selected Asian Economies
1970-1996

A. Southeast Asia

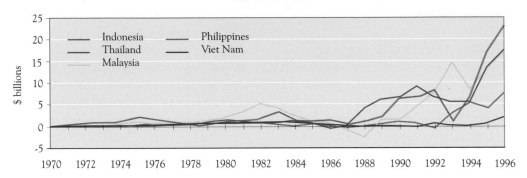

B. South Asia

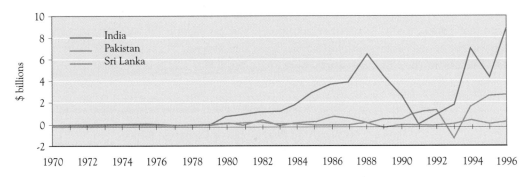

C. PRC and Republic of Korea

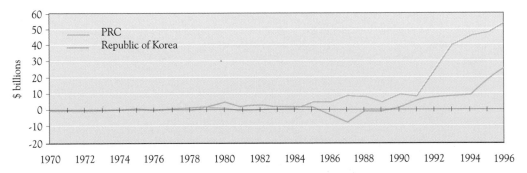

Source: Asian Development Bank data.

countries opened up new investment opportunities for industrial country investors looking for higher returns and greater risk diversification. The rates of return to investments are generally expected to be higher in developing countries with low levels of capital if the factors that complement capital in the production process (such as skilled labor and infrastructure) are not constrained. Returns in emerging markets also tend to exhibit low correlation (that is, they do not move together in sympathy) with those of industrial country equities. In general, by holding an asset whose returns are not correlated to the returns of another asset, investors can raise the overall return on their portfolio without a commensurate increase in risk. The drive for higher returns and greater diversification of risk among industrial country investors received further impetus with recent developments in information technology, which enabled greater efficiency in gathering and disseminating information and in processing transactions. Finally, many of the affected countries maintained high interest rates. This, along with pegged exchange rates, created a false sense of security among many

investors—especially those holding debt instruments—that they could earn relatively high rates of return without any exchange rate risk.

Thus the combination of push and pull factors made the rapidly growing Asian economies a magnet for private capital. While the economic fundamentals of these economies were no doubt an important consideration for this capital inflow, the international capital market often exhibits investment exuberance. Investors often follow each other in investment decisions, a phenomenon known as herding, irrespective of whether the particular investment is warranted by economic fundamentals. (For an explanation of herding behavior see Box 1.5.)

Once the surge of private capital inflows started—driven partly by the economies' fundamentals and partly by investors' herding tendencies—a rampant increase in domestic asset prices ensued. This increase in asset prices, which increases returns to capital, in turn induced further capital inflows, and by mid-1996 private capital flows into these countries had reached an all time high. Some ob-

Box 1.5 Sheep Herd, So Do Investors

Much of the discussion on international capital flows is based on the implicit assumption that the international capital market is efficient. However, the international capital market has exhibited strong deviations that can hardly be reconciled with market efficiency. Capital inflows and outflows often exhibit behavior that implies a stampede, that is, behavior magnified by imitation. Why is that so?

Herding may reflect sheer irrationality: the biases and limitations of human cognition. However, herding does not need to reflect irrationality. Economic theory provides two distinct explanations that are consistent with individual rationality and occur in an environment in which the availability of information is less than perfect. One explanation runs in terms of the so-called bandwagon effect. The bandwagon gets built up because of informational cascade. An informational cascade happens when individuals make particular decisions, having observed the behavior of preceding individuals, without giving adequate consideration to their own private information. To illustrate the idea, assume that three individuals are considering whether or not to invest in Thailand. All of them have some private information about some aspects of the economy. Individual 1 has private information that is positive, individual 2 has information that is neutral, and indi-

vidual 3 has information that is negative. Individual 1 first decides to invest in Thailand. Having observed individual 1, individual 2, who was initially ambivalent, also decides to invest in Thailand. Individual 3, having seen individuals 1 and 2 investing in Thailand, finds an information cascade in favor of investing in Thailand. Individual 3 therefore overrides his own private information and follows the others in investing in the country. Some argue that such bandwagon effects in combination with private information create herding behavior, which explains the phenomenon of "hot money" that causes foreign capital to overreact to national economic prospects.

The second explanation runs in terms of the way money managers are compensated. Money managers are usually compensated based on comparison with other money managers: the median performer. Even when a money manager makes a wrong investment decision in which most other managers commit the same mistake, the chances are that the money manager in question will not be penalized (by being denied a bonus), and may actually be rewarded if his investment portfolio performs slightly better. Thus money managers have strong incentives to act alike even if they have information that indicates that the market's judgment is wrong.

Sources: Banerjee (1992) and Krugman (1998).

servers also argue that some of the rapid rise in asset prices in many of these economies was due to their slow progress in opening up certain sectors of the economy to foreign investors. In a number of countries, foreign capital was channeled into sectors that were open, such as properties and equities, leading to sharp increases in these asset prices.

Financial Sector Imbalances and Frailties

The upsurge of private foreign capital brought about three sets of imbalances in the banking sectors of the affected countries. First, between 1993 and 1996 the foreign liabilities of the commercial banks increased by about 12 percent per year, while foreign assets increased by about 7 percent per year. By contrast, in the nonaffected Asian developing economies, the banking sectors' foreign assets increased at the same rate as foreign liabilities, and the net foreign debt position remained virtually unchanged. Second, much of the collateral that the banking sector accepted for loans was real estate and equities, assets whose prices contained a large "bubble" element. Finally, the maturity structure of the banks' assets and liabilities was imbalanced. As much of the capital inflow was short term, the banks were borrowing short and lending long.

These imbalances made the banking sectors critically vulnerable. Vulnerability implies that if something goes wrong, a lot of other things suddenly start to go wrong. If, for some reason, confidence in the economy shatters and the capital flow reverses, this can result in serious damage to the banking sector. A sudden exodus of capital would lead on the one hand to a depreciation of the currency, which in turn would cause an increase in the banks' foreign liability (as debt contracts are often denominated in foreign currencies). On the other hand, the reversal of capital inflow would also lead to a deflation of equity and real estate prices, which would in turn diminish the value of the banks' collateral. Finally, given the mismatch in the maturities of banks' assets and liabilities, a sudden reversal of capital flow, which was in this case mostly short term, can wreak havoc with banks' balance sheets. This is precisely what happened after the net private capital flows reversed.

In addition to the above imbalances, the financial systems of the affected countries suffered

from two critical frailties, a double "whammy" of moral hazards that were exacerbated by the severe internal and external shocks. While moral hazard and other information problems exist in all countries, when compounded with currency crises, they are often sufficient to bring about a sharp contraction of economic activity and precipitate a financial crisis. (See Box 1.6 for an elaboration of the role of moral hazard and asymmetric information in a financial crisis.) The first moral hazard relates to borrowers. Like in other countries, the financial systems in the affected countries suffer from information constraints in the allocation of credit. As lenders have less information than borrowers about the intended use of credit, this often leads to a moral hazard problem on the investors' part. The second moral hazard relates to lenders. Unlike in many other countries, the financial institutions of the affected countries—such as the Thai finance companies and the Korean banks—believed implicitly that their respective governments guaranteed their financial liabilities. This implicit guarantee was visible in the strong connections between politicians and the owners of these institutions and in government assistance that had previously been provided in times of financial distress. In addition, the supervisory and regulatory authorities in some of these countries did not possess the independence needed to ensure that prudential standards were met, and in some countries standards themselves were inadequate, both of which led to a lack of transparency and lax regulations. This type of environment created an additional type of moral hazard problem on the part of financial institutions to undertake high-risk lending activities. Globalization and the substantial inflow of foreign capital exacerbated the moral hazard problem created by an environment of implicit guarantee.

It may be noted in passing that there is a large economic literature that emphasizes financial sector frailties as the principal cause of economic downturns. Indeed, financial crises have been a common feature in most industrial countries throughout history. In the nineteenth and twentieth centuries, most economic downturns in the US (in 1819, 1837, 1857, 1873, 1884, 1893, 1907, and 1929-1933) can be traced to major financial crises. The situation in Asia in 1997 was in many ways parallel to that in the US during those crises. However, in Asia the financial crisis intermingled with the currency crisis

Box 1.6 The Role of Information in a Financial Crisis

The financial system enables funds to move from economic agents who lack productive investment opportunities to those who have such opportunities. A crucial impediment to the efficient functioning of the financial system is asymmetric information, a situation in which one party in a financial contract has less accurate information than the other party. Borrowers who take loans have much better information about the risks and returns of their planned investments than the lenders do. Asymmetric information leads to two basic problems in the financial system: adverse selection and moral hazard.

Adverse selection is an asymmetric information problem that occurs before the transaction. Those who are potentially the worst credit risks are likely to be the most eager to take out loans, because they are the most unlikely to pay them back. Thus the problem of adverse selection exists when those parties who are most likely to produce an undesirable (adverse) outcome are those most likely to be selected to receive loans. The implication of adverse selection is that the lenders may decide not to make any loans, despite the existence of good credit risks (investment projects) in the marketplace.

Moral hazard is an asymmetric information problem that occurs after the transaction. Lenders run the risk (hazard) that the borrowers have incentives to engage in activities that are not desirable (moral) from the lenders' point of view, because they make it less likely that the loan will be paid back. For example, once borrowers have received the money they have incentives to take on large risks (which have high returns as well as greater risks of default), because they are playing with someone else's money. The borrowers also have incentives to misallocate funds for their personal use or to invest in unprofitable projects that increase their power or stature. Because of this moral hazard problem, many lenders may decide not to lend, and investment would be below the optimal level.

A financial crisis is a nonlinear disruption of financial markets in which adverse selection and moral hazard problems become so intense that the markets are unable to channel funds efficiently to those economic agents who have the most productive investment opportunities. A financial crisis thus prevents financial markets from functioning efficiently, which leads to a sharp contraction in economic activity.

Four factors lead to a financial crisis: increases in interest rates, increases in uncertainty, asset market effects on balance sheets, and bank panics. First, increases in interest rates lead to a higher probability that lenders will lend to bad credit risks, because good credit risks are less likely to borrow at high interest rates. Because of the increase in adverse selection, lenders will make fewer loans, which could lead to a sharp decline in aggregate investments and economic activity. Second, a dramatic increase in uncertainty in financial markets due to the collapse of an important financial institution, political uncertainty, or a stock market crash makes it harder for lenders to separate good from bad risks. The increase in uncertainty makes information more asymmetric and worsens the adverse selection and moral hazard problem. Third, the state of the balance sheets of both nonfinancial firms and banks has important implications for the severity of the financial sector's asymmetric information problems. Deterioration of balance sheets worsens both adverse selection and moral hazard problems in financial markets, and if the deterioration is dramatic enough, it is a major factor behind banking and financial crises. One factor that affects balance sheets in developing countries is unanticipated exchange rate depreciation. Because of uncertainty about the future value of the domestic currency, many banks and nonfinancial firms find that issuing debt is easier if it is issued in foreign currencies. When the debt contracts are denominated in foreign currency, an unanticipated depreciation of the domestic currency increases the debt burden of domestic firms. As assets are denominated in domestic currency, firms' assets do not show a corresponding rise in value. The result is a deterioration in firms' balance sheets, which then leads to a decline in investment and economic activity. Finally, banks play an important financial intermediation role by producing information that facilitates productive investment. Consequently, a financial crisis in which many banks go out of business reduces financial intermediation and leads to a decline in investment and economic activity. Even if banks do not fail but suffer a substantial contraction in capital, it leads to similar economic outcomes.

Source: Mishkin (1997).

---

to create a vicious downward spiral in the economy. A financial crisis, which makes depositors jittery about the quality of banks, can quickly blossom into a currency crisis, as foreign currency deposits run off. Once the devaluation of the currency takes place, it worsens the financial crisis, as the cost of servicing foreign currency debt increases relative to earnings on assets denominated in domestic currency. That was precisely what happened during the last quarter of 1997 in the affected countries.

Weaknesses in Corporate Governance

The governance structure of private companies in the affected countries, in conjunction with company laws and the implicit government guarantee to rescue businesses in trouble, contributed to corporations' high-risk borrowing and investment behavior. In contrast with the industrial countries, ownership and control of both large and small companies are not separated, but are vested in families. This is equally true of the large Korean *chaebols* as of the companies owned by Chinese families in Indonesia and the Philippines. While this coupling of ownership and control often helps address the so-called agency problem (that is, the dissonance between owners and management in pursuing company goals), it also creates corporate vulnerabilities.

To begin with, the coupling of ownership and management no doubt makes decisions to expand and diversify business operations more expeditious, but the diversification may entail expanding the business away from its core competencies. In Korea, for example, such diversification included ventures into high-technology areas. However, this requires complex skills on the part of management, which in family corporations often did not exist.

The coupling of ownership and control of business conglomerates, as in the large Korean *chaebols*, also often leads to a management system that maximizes not the profits of a single firm, but a group of firms. This often entails cash transfers between *chaebol* subsidiaries. Indeed, *chaebols* have routinely guaranteed the debts of their affiliated companies. While such practices can be helpful in overcoming short-term liquidity problems, they also erode the discipline provided by the markets and the careful assessment of investments before embarking on them. (This is why the market disciplining device of the hostile takeover—a change in corporate ownership that the current management and board oppose—can be helpful.)

In addition, in Korea, family-run conglomerates were overextended, with an average debt to equity ratio of 4:1, and in some cases of 10:1. This partly reflects the particular structure of corporate governance—the preference for raising funds by borrowing from banks rather than on the stock market to avoid stockholder interference in the business—and partly the easy availability of credit from banks under the implicit government guarantee.

Finally, in most Asian countries, for example, Indonesia, effective bankruptcy laws to enforce market discipline do not exist. In addition, firms are often able to avoid impending bankruptcy by receiv-

ing an injection of funds. For example, while close to bankruptcy, Jinro, Korea's 19th largest *chaebol*, was able to receive $91 million in emergency rescue funds from banks acting on government directives.

In short, the particular structure of corporate governance, implicit government guarantees, and existing business laws contributed to an environment in which corporations overindulged in investments in risky undertakings. While this type of investment pattern may be sustainable, and may even be a source of dynamism when the economy is on the upswing, it may precipitate a collapse when the economy is declining.

The Main Issues: A Summary

The traditional currency crisis story does not fit the Asian experience. Fiscal and monetary profligacy was generally absent, as was persistent large unemployment. There were few macroeconomic vulnerabilities. The current account deficits were relatively large, but not alarming, and were more than offset by foreign capital inflows, which both added to reserves and led to an appreciation of real exchange rates. Propelled largely by globalization, a large volume of private capital moved to developing Asia through short-term bank instruments, attracted partly by the pegged exchange rates, the high interest rates, and the perception that governments guaranteed financial institutions. However, the financial systems' structural weaknesses led to moral hazard on the part of both banks and borrowers, which resulted in overinvestment in excessively risky projects and in asset bubbles.

While structural reasons account for the slowdown in export growth in the affected countries—such as the eroding competitiveness of Indonesia, Malaysia, Philippines, and Thailand in labor-intensive exports—the trigger that set off the crisis was the 1996 export slowdown. The cyclical downturn in the demand for electronics, in conjunction with a rising dollar and a declining yen, had an adverse effect on export growth, which led to skepticism about the robustness of economic growth in the countries concerned. This threatened the large inflow of foreign capital, which was now badly needed to sustain the increasing current account deficits. This in turn led to market concerns about the prevailing exchange rates and the eventual collapse of the Thai baht. Once the crisis unfolded, investors realized that there were no implicit government guarantees for investment, and asset price bubbles burst. Falling asset prices resulted in insolvency of the financial intermediaries, leading to a full-fledged financial crisis.

ECONOMIC IMPACTS OF THE CRISIS

The most discernible impact of the financial crisis has been a sharp decline in private capital inflows to the five affected countries. According to recent estimates by the Institute of International Finance, the five affected Asian countries suffered net private capital outflows of $12 billion in 1997, compared to net inflows of $93 billion in 1996. Private capital flows from commercial banks exhibited the sharpest decline. At the end of 1997, as investors' confidence was shattered, maturing short-term debts in several economies were not rolled over. This resulted in an estimated outflow through commercial banks of $21 billion, as compared with inflows of about $56 billion in 1996. Foreign direct investment in these economies remained more or less constant at about $7 billion, approximately the same as in 1996. The relatively small role foreign direct investment played in these economies in recent years made them increasingly vulnerable. Portfolio investment suffered a large outflow of as much as $12 billion in 1997, in contrast with an inflow of about $12 billion in 1996. The affected countries' reserves fell sharply, despite official assistance and a narrowing of their combined current account deficit.

The impact of the crisis on the financial sectors of the affected countries has been enormous. Although data on financial distress are still very tentative, they indicate serious problems with respect to nonperforming loans and capital adequacy of financial institutions. However, the full impact of high interest rates, lower domestic aggregate demand, and reductions in external financing on the corporate sector are yet to be reflected in the financial statements of banks. According to some available private estimates, the ratio of nonperforming loans to total loans varies among the affected countries, ranging from 10 percent in the Philippines to 35 percent in Indonesia. This in turn implies that the ratio of nonperforming loans to GDP varies between 7 percent in the Philippines and 40 percent in Thailand. The corresponding official estimates, however, are 3.4 percent for the Philippines and

18 percent for Thailand. In other words, the private estimates imply a much higher degree of financial distress, well beyond that implied by those official estimates. The extent of financial distress indicates the degree of effort that will be required for financial restructuring as well as the likely adverse effect the economy might suffer on account of it.

The financial crisis has also posed a serious liquidity problem for enterprises. Indeed, the credit crunch has been so severe in Korea that, according to one report in the *New York Times* (December 31, 1997), an average of 45 companies a day declared bankruptcy in December. According to some private sector estimates, 30,000 more small and medium enterprises are likely to go bankrupt in 1998 in Korea, and the situation in other affected countries is not significantly different. Ironically, the liquidity problems continue to constrain the ability of enterprises in the affected economies to take full advantage of the depreciation in the currency values. While export orders in these economies have been forthcoming, enterprises are having a hard time obtaining credit with which to purchase inputs and make factor payments. Without a major improvement in the credit situation, enterprises will not be able to fill export orders, and the possibility of an export boom leading these countries out of the crisis will be remote.

Events are unfolding rapidly. Thus an in-depth assessment of the impact of the crisis on the Asian economies' economic growth prospects is difficult. Given that the Asian crisis was not an outcome of macroeconomic imbalances, but was caused principally by structural weaknesses in the financial and corporate sectors, problems that take time to redress, the economic upturn may not follow Argentina's and Mexico's V-shaped recovery following the 1994-1995 so-called Tequila Crisis. Nevertheless, if the governments concerned implement the appropriate policies and reform institutions, the impact of the economic crisis is likely to be moderate, and at worst, medium rather than long term.

GDP growth in the affected economies slowed significantly in 1997, but the brunt of the impact will be felt in 1998, when several of the affected economies, including Indonesia, Korea, and Thailand, are projected to register negative growth rates. Significant reductions in growth are also expected in Malaysia and the Philippines. Growth slowdowns are also likely in Hong Kong, China and

Taipei,China, which have so far weathered the crisis comparatively well. Growth rates in the PRC and in the transitional economies of Southeast Asia will slow as regional demand weakens, foreign investors assess the situation, and the countries lose some export markets to cheaper sources of supply. South Asian growth will suffer somewhat from its rising trend, though not in absolute terms, both because of reduced trade with, and investment from, the affected countries, as well as because of reduced remittances from expatriate workers in these countries. (See Box 1.7 for an assessment of how the crisis has adversely affected the flow of remittances.)

The effect of the reduction in economic growth will vary among different segments of society. The affected economies are likely to experience considerable social turbulence as the social impact of the crisis unfolds. There will be a significant increase in the incidence of unemployment and poverty as these economies go onto a tailspin. In addition, many of these economies lack any social safety net, because they relied on rapid growth and employment for the provision of social security to their citizens. Despite considerable success in poverty reduction in Thailand and Indonesia, a large

segment of the population in both these countries is located near or below the poverty line. This group of poor and near-poor will be particularly vulnerable to the impact of the economic slowdown. This adverse social impact on the affected countries, if not addressed appropriately and in a timely manner, has the potential of generating political turbulence, which will not augur well for their growth. Other countries that are not directly impacted by the crisis yet related by trade, investment, and labor movement to the affected countries are also likely to experience some social impact, although to a much lesser extent than the affected countries. The social impact will, however, be moderated as growth picks up.

A modest recovery is expected in the affected economies in 1999, but recovery to pre-crisis GDP growth rates and per capita income levels will take a number of years. In addition, the situation could deteriorate further if the current currency and stock market crisis widens, for example, to the PRC and Hong Kong, China, or spills over into a full-fledged banking crisis with a run on banks.

Notwithstanding the financial crisis, the longer term outlook for the region is far from bleak. The

Box 1.7 The Effects of the Crisis on Labor Market Integration and Remittances

In recent years, the Asian economies have seen the gradual evolution of an integrated labor market as an important component of the overall economic integration of developing Asia. Since the 1970s, governments in labor-surplus countries in Asia have encouraged their workers, especially the less skilled workers, to go abroad. In recent years, in addition to easing domestic employment problems, these workers' remittances have contributed significantly to national savings and the overall balance of payments of many of these economies. About 4.5 million Filipinos are overseas, and their remittances amounted to some $4.3 billion in 1997, or about 4.3 percent of the country's GNP. Last year, the Hong Kong, China branch of Indonesia's Bank Negara reported that 300 to 400 Indonesian workers sent money home every day. South Asian workers did the same in many countries. While Asian labor migration focused on West Asia in the 1970s, in the late 1980s and 1990s more migrant workers went to East and Southeast Asia.

In the wake of the recent crisis, Korea, Malaysia, and Thailand have announced plans to repatriate foreign workers, which when implemented will further compound the problem of rising unemployment Bangladesh, India,

Indonesia, Myanmar, Pakistan, Philippines, and Thailand, in particular, are facing. To ease the social costs associated with increased unemployment, Indonesia has undertaken a number of safety net programs, but these are limited in both their scope and their sophistication in dealing with the magnitude of problems facing less skilled laborers. In addition, the repatriation programs themselves are a strain on the budgets of the labor-sending economies. The Philippine government, for instance, has allocated about ₱100 million (some $2.5 million) for emergency repatriation of Filipino workers. Greater problems await Bangladeshi workers in Malaysia, who have lost their jobs, but who cannot afford to pay for the trip home.

Ironically, the repatriation plans are likely merely to replace old problems with new ones. The host governments hope that repatriation of foreign workers will open up job opportunities for their own citizens; however, most of the jobs that would be freed up are low-paying manual jobs in sectors shunned by local workers. When domestic workers replace the cheap and compliant foreign workers, these governments are likely to face not only a rise in labor costs, but also an increase in labor disputes.

capacity for resource mobilization (past savings rates exceeded 30 percent), the reasonably good infrastructure, the favorable demographics, the open trading system, and the general commitment to macroeconomic prudence should stimulate growth, which should resume once appropriate adjustment policies are implemented and take effect. Given strong supply-side fundamentals, the challenge will be to ensure that internal and external demands increase fairly rapidly to exploit these supply-side strengths.

How vulnerable are Asian economies other than the five affected countries to a currency crisis? The degree of vulnerability varies. The financial crisis resulted from an unpropitious combination of open capital accounts (implying the free movement of capital), unsound financial systems, and pegged currencies. With the notable exception of Hong Kong, China and Singapore, most other economies in the region do not have open capital accounts. While Hong Kong, China and Singapore have open capital accounts, their financial systems are sound, and they therefore do not run the risk of a currency crisis. In addition, Hong Kong, China has a currency board with sufficient foreign reserves and Singapore has a flexible exchange rate system, both of which make the possibility of a currency crisis remote. Other economies that are relatively insular and have closed capital accounts do not run the risk of this type of currency crisis. However, those insular economies that are profligate in their fiscal and monetary policies (that is, they have large budget deficits and high money supplies), may be subject to the traditional type of currency crisis.

Initially, the current crisis in Southeast Asia was not expected to have much of an impact on the world economy. However, the scene changed quickly as Korea, the world's 11th largest economy and 12th largest in terms of its share of world trade, became embroiled in the crisis. The five affected countries account for about 20 percent of Japan's and Australia's exports, 8 percent of the United States' exports, and 3 percent of Europe's exports. Measured by a more relevant yardstick, exports to the affected countries account for 2.8 percent of Australia's GDP, 1.7 percent of Japan's GDP, 0.7 percent of the United States' GDP, and 0.6 percent of Europe's GDP. Economic forecasts indicate that the total direct impact of the crisis will be to reduce real GDP in countries of the Organisation for Economic Co-operation and Development by around 0.6 percent (0.4 percent for the European Union, 0.6 percent for the United States, and 1.4 percent for Japan). For the world as a whole, including the adverse impact on Asia itself, the reduction in GDP will be around 1.1 percent.

POLICY OPTIONS FOR THE AFFECTED ECONOMIES

The key element required for rapid recovery of the affected countries will not be the traditional austerity measures, but structural reforms to improve their financial systems and corporate governance. No doubt, some recovery in currency values will be important to improve banks' and corporations' balance sheets, but the challenge will be how to accomplish this without using public resources.

The IMF-led reform programs in the affected countries are much more broadly based than traditional austerity programs to ensure macroeconomic balances. They are designed to bring about structural reforms that will strengthen financial systems, increase transparency in both the public and private sectors, and open markets, thereby restoring investors' confidence. To this end, nonviable financial institutions, including banks, are being closed down. Other weak, but viable, institutions are required to produce restructuring plans, including mergers and consolidations, and to comply, within a reasonable time, with internationally accepted best practices in terms of capital adequacy requirements for banks and accounting practices and disclosure rules for companies. Other proposed structural changes include strengthening financial sector regulation and supervision. Together, these policies are intended to create a more level playing field for the private sector and to intensify competition.

To reverse the sharp slide in currency values, the IMF programs also recommend steep increases in interest rates and tight monetary policies to stem the outflow of capital. If monetary policies are not held tight after a massive currency shock, the risk is that the collapse in currency value could be self-fulfilling by inducing further outflows of capital and causing a greater erosion in confidence. Higher interest rates will encourage companies to restructure their finances and move from debt toward equity. At the same time, high interest rates have serious adverse effects on banks and corporate entities and slow down the economy. Therefore a fine balance must be struck between these conflicting policy objectives. The timing and nature of monetary policy adjustment—particularly interest rate adjustment—should reflect the circumstances prevailing in individual economies.

While fiscal profligacy did not cause the crisis, the fiscal positions of the affected countries nonetheless need firming up to deal with the future costs of financial sector restructuring, as well as to handle any current account deficits. Some observers have advocated more expansionary fiscal programs to offset the inevitable slowdown. Here again, the issue of balance between conflicting policy objectives arises. The timing, degree, and composition of fiscal adjustment should be dictated by individual economies' circumstances.

No doubt, the impact of these reforms will be painful. However, the slowdown would have been much more dramatic and the costs to the general population would have been much higher without the IMF-led assistance packages. Indeed the governments in the region are, in general, initiating fiscal, banking, and other reform measures, although uncertainties about the strengths of responses and the political will to carry out the reforms persist. Mexico recovered from the Tequila Crisis of 1994-1995 relatively quickly partly because of the government's decisive political actions in implementing reforms. Indecisiveness in implementing required reforms can only worsen the situation and spread the contagion to other countries.

Experience suggests that managing a recovery is just as difficult and demanding as managing a crisis. Successful implementation of any policy reform or structural adjustment depends on three basic elements: government commitment, political support, and institutional capability. Governments need to be single-minded about reform programs and about implementing them. Such programs should be politically acceptable. Reform programs may result in social costs that place a disproportionate amount of the burden of policy reform and structural adjustment on the poorer segments of society. Thus measures to mitigate social costs are usually helpful to enhance the political acceptability of the reform programs. Institutional capability is critically important for successful formulation, implementation, and monitoring of reform programs.

LESSONS FOR NONAFFECTED ECONOMIES

The recent experiences of Southeast and East Asia indicate that private capital flows can be an important source of development finance. At the same time, if this flow is poorly managed, it can be extremely destabilizing. Thus the important lesson that emerges is that responsible fiscal management, prudent monetary policy, and greater exchange rate flexibility are important elements of a strategy to redress the adverse effects of surges in private capital. However, before opening up the capital account, institutional reforms are needed to improve the soundness of economies' financial sectors to ensure that capital inflows are well managed. In this connection, it may be noted that the timing, pacing and sequencing of reforms are as important as the reforms themselves in building up a robust financial system.

The banking system plays a critical role in allocating capital. The health of this system largely determines whether a country will be able to exploit the benefits of financial integration and avoid its pitfalls. While many Asian developing economies have partially liberalized and deregulated their financial sectors since the early 1990s, their banking sectors are still weak and fragile. These economies urgently need to address the issue of the poor health of their banking sectors to reduce their vulnerability to globalization. Actions are required to (i) reform institutional structures in areas such as regulatory and supervisory frameworks, transparency and disclosure of information, accounting systems, market infrastructure, and risk management; (ii) improve such areas as regulation, supervision, and accounting; and (iii) upgrade the overall governance of the sector to avoid the various financial sector frailties that can lead to a financial crisis.

These economies should also take measures to develop well-functioning capital markets to reduce the risks of potential instability in an integrated world. Actions are required in three major areas: (i) market infrastructure, which comprises the systems and institutions required for trade and custody of securities; (ii) corporate governance, including protection of property rights, especially those of minority shareholders; and (iii) disclosure of market and company information and control of abusive market practices. Reforms of business laws, such as bankruptcy procedures, are also required.

The financial crisis has generated skepticism in many quarters about the benefits of globalization, especially of financial integration with the global economy. As with trade in goods and services, capital flows between countries generally benefit both sending and receiving countries. However, to benefit from globalization, the countries need to prepare themselves for it, so that they can avoid its adverse effects, including the volatility it may sometimes generate. Globalization is a double-edged sword. It rewards good policies and punishes bad ones. The difficulties the affected economies have experienced are not grounds for inaction or for adopting measures that will retard the liberalization process. The benefits of globalization are too large to ignore.

PART II

Economic Trends and Prospects in the DMCs

NEWLY INDUSTRIALIZED ECONOMIES

Hong Kong, China

Republic of Korea

Singapore

Taipei, China

HONG KONG, CHINA

The handover of Hong Kong to the People's Republic of China (PRC) took place smoothly in 1997. While Hong Kong, China, continues to develop as a financial and business services center, the region's economic crisis and high interest rates have slowed economic activity.

RECENT TRENDS AND PROSPECTS

Two events of major importance took place in Hong Kong, China in 1997. The first was the political handover of Hong Kong, China to the PRC in July. At that time Hong Kong, China became a Special Administrative Region of the PRC. (Note that Hong Kong, China and the PRC maintain separate memberships in the Asian Development Bank and are therefore discussed here as separate economies.) The second event was the sharp downturn in stock and property markets that began around the fourth quarter of the year. Whereas the handover took place smoothly against a backdrop of a fairly robust economic environment, the market downturn—which largely reflects the currency and financial crisis engulfing the region—led to a sharp slowdown in economic activity.

During the first three quarters of 1997 consumer and investment spending grew rapidly, influenced by buoyancy in the stock and property markets. As a result GDP rose by 5.2 percent in 1997, an increase over the rate of growth in 1996. Spending on high value consumer goods such as cars and jewelry increased. Retained imports of capital goods showed a large increase, particularly imports of office equipment, industrial machinery for manufacturing, and construction machinery. While the imports of construction machinery were driven largely by a high demand for housing, imports of office equipment and industrial machinery reflected increased demand for information technology and retooling of existing manufacturing activities to increase the capital intensity of production.

From the fourth quarter, however, high interest rates adversely affected financial and property markets. By the end of 1997, the benchmark Hang Seng Index stood 36 percent below its August peak and property prices had dropped by 14 percent since October. The profitability of both financial and nonfinancial firms came under pressure, and along with the sharp falls in asset markets caused a slowdown in consumer and investor spending.

Poorer than expected exports also affected the economy during 1997. While goods exports grew at a moderate pace, exports of services were weak in the second half of 1997. An anticipated pickup in exports did not fully materialize because of a strengthening US dollar (which implied a strong Hong Kong dollar because of the link between the two currencies) and weak import demand in some major industrial country markets, such as Japan and the United Kingdom.

Travel and tourism, which has accounted for more than a quarter of exports of services in recent years, was expected to be a source of robust growth for 1997, especially with the handover ceremonies scheduled in the end of June. However, the number of incoming visitors during the first six months of 1997 was actually lower than in the last six months of 1996. The situation failed to improve after the handover because the regional economic crisis and the continued strength of the Hong Kong dollar discouraged tourism.

Imports of goods grew faster in 1997 than in 1996, with retained imports of capital goods largely responsible for the acceleration. Imports of goods were once again larger than exports, but the resulting deficit on the merchandise trade account for 1997 was balanced to some extent by a surplus on the services trade account.

After tightening during the first three quarters of 1997, labor markets began to reflect the slowdown in consumption and investment expenditures. The labor force grew by 3.9 percent during 1997 as a whole, and robust labor demand until the last quarter resulted in an unemployment rate of around 2.5 percent. Most of the unemployed were semiskilled and unskilled workers from the manufacturing, construction, wholesale and retail sectors. While total employment increased by about 4.6 percent compared to 1996, the trend of declining employment in the manufacturing sector continued with the relocation of labor-intensive production from Hong Kong, China to other economies, particularly the PRC. Whereas manufacturing employment was 46 percent of total employment in 1980, it was down to some 13 percent in September 1997.

Inflation remained under 6 percent. Upward pressures on prices generated by tightening labor markets and property rentals in the earlier part of 1997 were balanced out by subdued imported inflation. In the last quarter the drop in property prices and slowdown in economic activity further reduced any likelihood of accelerating inflation.

Budgetary deficits are the exception rather than the rule in Hong Kong, China and a surplus of some HK$77 billion (around $10 billion) has been estimated for 1997-1998. This will add to Hong Kong, China's healthy official fiscal reserves, which received a major injection of funds when the PRC transferred the almost HK$200 billion (around $26 billion) Land Fund to Hong Kong, China in June 1997. (The Land Fund consisted of revenues from land auctions reserved for the Hong Kong Special Administrative Region agreed on under the 1984 Sino-British Joint Declaration.)

Hong Kong, China's economy is clearly feeling the strains of the regional economic crisis. The combination of high interest rates, sharp contractions in share and property prices, and expectations of a protracted economic slump in the region will continue to dampen consumer and investment spending. External demand for Hong Kong, China's goods and services is also likely to remain weak in 1998, both because of weak demand in some export markets and competition. Unemployment is bound to increase as the economy slows down.

Table 2.1 Major Economic Indicators: Hong Kong, China, 1995-1999
(percent)

Item	1995	1996	1997	1998	1999
Gross domestic product growth	3.9	5.0	5.2	3.0	3.5
Gross domestic investment/GDP	34.8	32.3	34.5	31.0	32.0
Gross domestic saving/GDP	30.5	30.7	30.6	30.0	32.0
Inflation rate (consumer price index)	8.6	6.0	5.7	4.5	5.0
Money supply (M2) growth	14.6	10.9	8.4	9.4	9.6
Fiscal balance/GDP	-0.3	2.2	5.8	0.3	0.1
Merchandise exports growth	14.8	4.0	4.0	2.2	3.5
Merchandise imports growth	19.1	3.0	5.1	1.0	6.0
Service exports growth	10.3	8.7	0.3	4.1	1.5
Service imports growth	11.6	3.6	6.3	1.4	1.0

Sources: Hong Kong Monetary Authority data and staff estimates.

On a positive note, inflationary pressures will remain weak and some fiscal stimulus should result from the cuts in corporate and income taxes announced in February 1998. Moreover, if expectations of moderate growth in the PRC and a stable renminbi are borne out, then the economy can expect some relief from its close links with the PRC. Over the longer term, as regional growth and investments resume, Hong Kong, China's economy should once again pick up as long as it maintains its competitiveness in providing financial and other business services, not just to the PRC, but to Asia as a whole.

CRITICAL ISSUES IN SHORT-TERM ECONOMIC MANAGEMENT

The economy of Hong Kong, China has come under severe pressure as a result of the regional financial and economic crisis. While business exposure to recession-prone regional economies has contributed to the economic slowdown of this extremely open economy, fears of declining competitiveness of Hong Kong, China's products have also taken their toll. With substantial currency devaluations occurring in such advanced Asian economies as Republic of Korea; Singapore; and Taipei,China, some market participants expect Hong Kong, China to follow suit to remain competitive. The linked exchange rate system under which the Hong Kong dollar is pegged to the US dollar has come under heavy speculative attack on a number of occasions as investors sell Hong Kong dollars and buy US dollars in anticipation of a devaluation of the local currency. However, Hong Kong, China's authorities have ruled out a devaluation, and the PRC supports this decision.

The speculative attacks have led to an increase in interest rates in Hong Kong, China. Interest rates rose because the linked exchange rate system entails not only pegging the local currency to the US dollar, but backing local currency by an equivalent amount of US dollars. Thus a speculative exchange of Hong Kong dollars for US dollars by investors anticipating a devaluation reduces the supply of domestic currency, thereby putting upward pressure on interest rates. The loss of US dollars by note-issuing banks constrains their ability to issue new Hong Kong dollars and counter the rise in interest rates.

The main result of the increase in interest rates has been to choke off funds that were flowing into the share and property markets. The steep declines in asset prices in conjunction with the continued high interest rates—the 3-month interbank loan rate at end-January 1998 was about 6 percentage points higher than a year earlier—have taken a toll on business. In addition, the continuation of the peg has caused concerns in the tourism and manufacturing sectors, because the relatively strong Hong Kong dollar makes local goods and services more expensive.

While it may appear that maintenance of the local currency's peg to the US dollar is making Hong Kong, China uncompetitive, this is not necessarily the case for several reasons. First, flexibility of prices and wages can make up for the lack of nominal exchange rate adjustments. Available evidence suggests that wages in Hong Kong, China are quite downward-flexible, and property prices and rentals, major determinants of Hong Kong, China's cost structure, have already fallen. In addition, and in contrast to those Asian economies that have devalued their currencies, adherence to the peg is keeping "imported" inflation in check.

Finally, Hong Kong, China is essentially a service-oriented economy and does not compete directly with those regional economies such as Indonesia and Thailand that have seen devaluations of 50 percent or more. A more relevant comparator for Hong Kong, China may be Singapore, which has seen its currency devalue by 17 percent in relation to the US dollar (and hence the Hong Kong dollar). While a devaluation of this magnitude is not trivial, the competitiveness of high-end services such as finance, insurance, and other related business services that Hong Kong, China is increasingly providing is not as sensitive to prices as, say, low-technology manufactured goods. However, tourism is somewhat more sensitive to prices than other services. Perhaps more important, Hong Kong, China has a strategic position as the chief provider of services to the PRC. Thus as long as growth in the PRC does not slow down dramatically during the next year, the economy of Hong Kong, China should continue to benefit.

In sum, a devaluation of the Hong Kong dollar would be of no obvious overall benefit to the economy. Its value in increasing competitiveness is questionable, and it might, perversely, only add to the instability both in Hong Kong, China and in the region. Hong Kong, China's current economic slowdown should be seen not as a result of the decision to maintain the linked exchange rate system, but as the inevitable consequence of an extremely open economy operating during a period of regional slowdown.

POLICY AND DEVELOPMENT ISSUES

Structural changes in Hong Kong, China's economy during the last 15 to 20 years have made it one of the most service-oriented economies in the world, with services now accounting for around 85 percent of GDP. The resulting decline in the importance of manufacturing has caused concern among some observers that too much of the manufacturing base has been lost. Observers are also concerned about the paucity of high-technology industries within the manufacturing sector. As a result, some have called for setting up a high-technology industrial park, introducing tax breaks for multinationals, and establishing a venture capital fund for domestic firms attempting to establish high-technology businesses.

However, the loss of the manufacturing base within Hong Kong, China itself need not be viewed with particular alarm. Since the early 1980s, Hong Kong, China's manufacturing facilities have increasingly been relocated to the PRC as Hong Kong, China companies contract out all or part of their production processes to companies in the PRC to take advantage of the abundant supply of low-cost labor. In parallel with this, offshore trading and exports of professional and other business services that service the relocated manufacturing facilities have grown in importance. Thus while Hong Kong, China's own manufacturing sector has diminished in importance, its service sector is not bereft of a manufacturing base.

The economy has benefited from its increased service orientation and is likely to continue to do so. In the last 15 years the PRC has attracted some $200 billion as foreign direct investment, of which around 55 percent has flowed through Hong Kong, China. Moreover, the Asian and Pacific region is expected to generate a huge demand for infrastructure upgrading once it is back on a firmer economic footing. This will lead to a rise in the demand for investment funds and professional support services, and Hong Kong, China is in a good position to play

a key role as a provider of financial and business services.

However, two factors may constrain further development of financial and business services, namely, a human resource constraint and a possible deterioration in the business environment.

Currently, aside from those in the finance sector, many of Hong Kong, China's service sector jobs tend simply to be "front office" operations for low-skill-intensive manufacturing firms. Moreover, even within manufacturing, much of the activity takes place under contract production, so firms tend not to be involved in higher end research, design, and market promotion activities. Thus the concern is that Hong Kong, China's workforce is not adequately equipped to make the transition to more skill-intensive manufacturing and to high-end services.

Government efforts to upgrade the human resource base have included providing vocational and retraining programs and encouraging greater enrollment in tertiary education. Some progress is apparent. For example, the percentage of the population aged 17 to 20 enrolled in tertiary education increased from about 5 percent in 1984 to about 18 percent in 1994-1995. In addition, universities and training centers are stressing communication and computer skills, both of which are essential when providing high-end services. Nevertheless, room for improvement still exists. For instance, enrollment in tertiary education remains low by industrial country standards, and recently there have been complaints about declining proficiency in English, a crucial language in international business.

As concerns the business environment, it is currently characterized by openness, low taxes, high standards of corporate disclosure, and generally well-policed capital markets. Moreover, the overall policy stance has been and continues to remain one of positive nonintervention by the state, whose activities are essentially limited to providing prudential regulation and supervision. Hong Kong, China has prospered under this framework, and there is no reason why it should not continue to do so.

Recent events in East and Southeast Asia have demonstrated the importance of maintaining high standards of prudential regulation and supervision and ensuring transparency in economic transactions. While the record of Hong Kong, China on this front is among the best, its close ties with business in the region suggest that it cannot rest on its laurels. Whereas business in Hong Kong, China has so far been based foremost on clear-cut market considerations, business elsewhere in the region tends to take place in the shadow of government and market. This generates the potential for lack of transparency, corruption, and political interference. While these can obstruct the efficient working of markets, they can be particularly devastating for financial markets as the regional economic turmoil has revealed. For Hong Kong, China's future competitiveness as an international center for financial and business services, its business environment must not be allowed to deteriorate.

REPUBLIC OF KOREA

A loss of confidence in its financial markets led the Republic of Korea (henceforth referred to as Korea) to ask the International Monetary Fund (IMF) for a bailout. In the meantime, contractionary monetary and fiscal policies and an extended recession are expected, and the government should strictly implement overall economic reforms.

RECENT TRENDS AND PROSPECTS

Korea grew steadily during the 1990s, reached a peak of 8.9 percent in 1995, and then began a steady slowdown, declining to 7.1 percent in 1996 and 5.5 percent in 1997. The 1996 slowdown was caused by a slackening of external demand, falling prices of semiconductors, and sluggish capital investments. In 1997, even though exports experienced growth in real terms, the downward trend of the previous year continued in other major sectors. Investment in equipment decreased throughout 1997 because of excess capacity and high uncertainty. Investment in construction stayed at much the same level as in 1996, even though infrastructure-related construction remained robust. The growth of consumer spending dropped steeply because of concerns about job security and the wave of corporate bankruptcies. As an outcome of slower economic growth, the unemployment rate rose from 2 percent in 1996 to 2.6 percent in 1997.

However, the slackening of economic growth did not give rise to serious concern until the third quarter of 1997. Even when the Southeast Asian countries had already experienced the financial and currency crisis, the Korean economy was in relatively good shape. For the first three quarters of the year, the inflation rate remained at 3.8 percent, and the ratio of the current account deficit to GNP was 3.7 percent.

At this time, a series of insolvencies of large business conglomerates or *chaebols* led to an accumulation of bad loans by financial institutions that undermined their soundness. At the same time, instability in international financial markets because of the currency crisis in Southeast Asia had a contagion effect. This led to a deterioration of Korea's creditworthiness in international financial markets and reduced inflows of capital. Finally, in December 1997, the government sought help from the IMF in the form of a bailout package totaling $57 billion, which included assistance from the IMF itself, from the World Bank, and from the Asian Development Bank. In accordance with the standby arrangement, Korea undertook a number of measures to strengthen its economy and pledged to continue implementing more reform policies in the coming years.

Budget expenditure increased by 12.4 percent in 1997, resulting in a budget deficit of around 0.5 percent of GDP. As concerns monetary policy, the stance was contractionary. The growth rate of the targeted money supply (a slightly broader definition than M2) decreased throughout 1997 except for December. This mainly reflected a recession, and therefore a decrease in demand for liquidity. It was also affected by a structural change unrelated to a liquidity condition, that is, shifts between financial assets. In December, the money supply increased more rapidly, reflecting the Central Bank's efforts

Table 2.2 Major Economic Indicators: Republic of Korea, 1995-1999
(percent)

Item	1995	1996	1997	1998	1999
Gross domestic product growth	8.9	7.1	5.5	-1.0	3.1
Gross domestic investment/GDP	37.0	38.2	34.6	26.4	29.4
Gross domestic savings/GDP	36.8	35.2	34.5	34.9	33.9
Inflation rate (consumer price index)	4.5	4.9	4.5	9.8	7.2
Money supply (M2) growth	15.6	15.8	14.7	13.1	13.2
Fiscal balance/GDP	0.5	0.0	-0.5	-0.9	-1.0
Merchandise exports growth	31.5	4.1	7.2	5.8	5.6
Merchandise imports growth	32.1	12.2	-2.3	-12.3	14.0
Current account balance/GDP	-1.8	-4.8	-2.0	6.9	3.4

Sources: International Monetary Fund (1998), National Statistics Office (1997), and staff estimates.

to ease the credit crunch created by the shaky financial markets.

The increase in the growth of consumer prices dropped slightly to 4.5 percent in 1997, down from 5 percent in 1996. The prices of agricultural, forestry, and marine products showed unstable movements, recording higher increases than in 1996. Charges for services slowed, reflecting a steep rise in 1996, as well as stability in the prices of private services. The prices of manufactured goods showed a large increase in the first quarter of 1997 because of the rise in the prices of petroleum products and in the fourth quarter of 1997 because of depreciation. Producer prices rose 3.9 percent during 1997, which was higher than the 2.7 percent recorded in 1996. The pace of wage increases, which have affected economic performance, fell from 12.2 percent in 1996 to 7.5 percent in 1997.

The balance of payments deteriorated significantly in 1996; however, exports reversed their downward trend in the second quarter of 1997 and expanded strongly in the third quarter. Exports increased by 7.2 percent during 1997, in contrast to the 4.1 percent growth registered in 1996. This was helped by the sharp pickup in exports of heavy industrial and chemical products, such as semiconductors and refined petroleum products. Meanwhile, export prices fell, partly because of the steady weakening of semiconductor prices. Imports showed a slight decrease of 2.3 percent in 1997, down from a

12.2 percent increase in 1996, largely in response to sluggish consumption and the decrease in investments. The trade balance registered a deficit of $2.8 billion during 1997. Overall, the current account improved quarter by quarter in 1997. It recorded a deficit of $8.8 billion, or 2 percent of GDP, far less than the 4.8 percent in 1996.

The Korean won depreciated by 15.4 percent, on average, in nominal terms in 1997, and by 43.5 percent year-on-year in response to the crisis. As concerns exchange rate policy, the authorities widened the band for daily movement from 2.2 percent to 10 percent, and then finally abolished it as of 16 December 1997.

The IMF agreement demands extreme contraction in both fiscal and monetary policies. The main objective of monetary policy is to maintain inflation at 9 percent in 1998 and to limit downward pressure on the won. The targeted money supply indicator was further broadened to M3 in 1998, and is projected to increase by only 13 percent, compared with 16.5 percent in 1997. The government will maintain tight fiscal policy to alleviate the burden on monetary policy and to provide for the still uncertain costs of restructuring the financial sector. To this end the government has increased special excise tax and transportation tax rates. It has also widened the bases of the value-added tax, corporate taxes, and income taxes by curtailing or abolishing tax exemptions or reductions, which were, in any case, inconsistent with international standards. On the expenditure side, the government will make major cuts in infrastructure outlays and defense expenditures. As a result, the fiscal deficit is likely to be about 1 percent of GDP in 1998.

These policies imply that the economy will contract, and expectations are that it will take longer than two years for it to return to its potential growth path. Provided that the government implements the IMF agreement faithfully, the GDP growth rate is expected to decline to -1.0 percent in 1998 and rise to 3.1 percent in 1999. The unemployment rate will increase to 4.3 percent in 1998 because of the contractionary policies and the restructuring of the economic system. Even if replacement investment is active, new investment is likely to be suspended or reduced. Thus total investment in real terms is expected to decrease by 28.7 percent in 1998, and then to increase by 12.3 percent in 1999. Consumption in real terms will decrease by 4.2 percent in 1998 because of greater fears of future unemployment as well as actual high unemployment, but will then increase by 1.6 percent in 1999.

Reflecting the lagged effects of the steep depreciation of the Korean won on input costs in 1997, both consumer and producer prices are expected to rise by around 10 percent in 1998, higher than the initial target set by the government and the IMF. Nominal wages are likely to stay at their 1997 level in the coming years, or even to decrease, in response to contractionary policies and corporate restructuring.

Exports will grow by 5.8 percent while imports will decline by 12.3 percent in 1998, mainly because of the depreciation of the won in 1997. The trade balance is expected to record a surplus of $22.4 billion. The steep depreciation of the won in 1997 and the extended economic recession will help improve the trade balance in the next few years. The current account balance is expected to yield a large surplus of $21.1 billion in 1998 and $11.4 billion in 1999. However, a decrease in the imports of investment goods is likely to have a negative effect on the economy in the longer run.

POLICY AND DEVELOPMENT ISSUES

After the economy slowed down in 1996, concerns were voiced about the "high-cost and low-efficiency economic system." The government's reaction was swift and focused on structural adjustments. While the government rapidly reached consensus about some policy measures and started to implement them, it needed more time to reach agreement on other issues, such as financial reforms.

The government's economic reforms turned out to be insufficient to protect the economy from the financial and currency crisis, even though they were generally in line with the IMF package. The effect of the financial crisis and the IMF package was to provide the momentum for reforms that were broad in scope and immediate in implementation. As such, the distinction between short-term and long-term policy issues disappeared and prioritization was difficult. The issues discussed in the following sections are the most urgent and have the greatest impact on the economy.

Financial Market Reform

In terms of international competitiveness, the financial sector is far behind the real sector. The key source of the financial sector's weakness was the predominantly state-led distortion in credit allocation. This practice deprived the financial sector of its primary function of screening and monitoring, and led to excessive risky investments by the corporate sector, and eventually to the current crisis.

The government became aware of this problem, and in response established the Financial Reform Committee in January 1997. The committee produced a report in June; however, the crisis hit before the government implemented full-scale reforms that reflected the report's recommendations. The IMF package, which shared many ideas with the report, called for restructuring financial institutions to construct a sound and competitive financial industry. Measures to be taken included protecting deposits, closing troubled merchant banks, resolving nonperforming assets of banks and merchant banks, facilitating mergers, and strengthening prudential supervision standards. To strengthen supervision of the financial sector, three agencies responsible for supervising banking, security, and insurance institutions were consolidated into the Financial Supervisory Commission. In addition, the Central Bank was given greater autonomy.

While to date the financial reforms appear to have touched on all major issues and to comply with market mechanisms, they will confront many challenges, mainly because of the unprecedented business environment characterized by competition. The government can no longer avoid the challenge of competition by resorting to protection. Instead, autonomy of and accountability by each financial institution can enhance the efficiency of the financial sector.

Trade and Capital Account Liberalization

The IMF agreement required the government to set a timetable for trade liberalization in line with World Trade Organization commitments; and the government promised to shorten the timetable for abolishing trade-related subsidies, restrictive import licensing schemes, and its import diversification system. The government opened stock and bond markets wider and ahead of schedule, promised to liberalize money market instruments, increased the ceiling of domestic bank shares that foreign banks could acquire, and allowed domestic corporations to borrow long-term loans from overseas.

One question in this context is the extent to which these measures will help protect financial markets against volatile capital movements. Considering the high interest rate target of more than 20 percent, capital account liberalization could stimulate hot money movements and cause the performance of already highly leveraged domestic firms to deteriorate. It will also increase interest rate risk, exchange rate risk, and credit risk and hamper the development of long-term capital markets. To mitigate this undesirable situation, the interest rate target needs to be lowered to a level that the weak corporate sector can manage. At the same time, sufficient monetary policy instruments need to be developed so that the Central Bank can stabilize interest rates.

Corporate and Labor Market Reform

Much of the blame for the crisis has fallen on the *chaebols,* because of their excessive capacity expansion and industrial diversification. The government has recently encouraged the restructuring of corporate finances, including measures to reduce corporations' high debt-to-equity ratios and to facilitate mergers and acquisitions. To achieve these goals, the government has prepared legislation that would require corporations to prepare financial statements on a consolidated basis. Another item of legislation would gradually reduce the cross-debt payment guarantees among group affiliates that had enabled the *chaebols* to take on excessive debt.

The *chaebol* problem is intimately related to labor market rigidity. Because trade unions have developed through confrontations with *chaebol* management, labor market flexibility could be greatly improved if promoted at the same time as corporate reforms. The IMF package provided a good opportunity for labor, government, and industry representatives to form a committee to examine and discuss the current crisis, especially in relation to layoffs and how to maintain workers' living standards. While providing a sufficient social safety net is a good idea, given its high costs it will be possible only after the crisis is over. In addition, more transparent corporate management would help workers regain confidence in their employers.

To the extent the crisis originated from a loss of confidence, strict implementation of the economic reforms is crucial for the recovery of foreign investment. One of the main features of the crisis is that it is a private sector problem, and therefore involves a complicated combination of vested interests of many firms and financial institutions. Thus to keep the reforms on track, the emphasis should be on transparency and accountability.

SINGAPORE

While Singapore withstood the region's financial crisis better than its neighbors in 1997, the region's crisis is likely to affect future growth. Industrialization policy remains active, and the financial sector is poised for expansion.

RECENT TRENDS AND PROSPECTS

Except for its currency and stock market, Singapore was only mildly affected by the region's economic crisis in 1997. The economy surged ahead with 7.8 percent growth in GDP as world demand for computer-related electronics, especially semiconductors, rebounded. Manufacturing output rose by 4.3 percent, spurred by chemicals, petroleum, and electronics. Electronics account for roughly half of manufactures, which in turn account for more than three quarters of exports, and Singapore now has the world's largest disk drive industry. While the petrochemicals subsector expanded significantly as new plants came on stream, commerce, and in particular tourism, suffered somewhat from reduced regional demand.

High salaries and property prices relative to those in neighboring countries have taken their toll on Singapore's manufacturing base, particularly for lower value-added and labor-intensive manufacturing, much of which has migrated to Malaysia. While the remaining manufacturing sector has maintained increasing productivity, it has become more concentrated on electronics. The services sector now accounts for more than 66 percent of GDP, while industry accounts for 34 percent. Financial and business services, particularly foreign exchange activity and provision of business hub services, grew by 11 percent in 1997, assisted by tax breaks. The steady rise in net services income has

played an important role in the current account surplus, although this was tempered somewhat in 1997 by the slowdown in tourism resulting from the financial crisis and the haze that affected the region following the forest fires in Indonesia.

The construction industry benefited from public investment in infrastructure in 1997, which included expansion of the mass rapid transit system and port facilities and land reclamation. It expanded by 13.3 percent and led employment growth. Public and private housing projects contributed to the sector's robust growth. Growth in such spending generally offset the slower growth in machinery and equipment, resulting in fixed investment growth of nearly 10 percent.

Activity in the property market remained subdued as restrictions imposed in 1996 to prevent overheating remained generally in force (except for a stamp duty on sellers of properties held for less than three years, which was removed), and property demand from neighboring countries diminished. The resulting glut of private housing prompted the government to halt land sales in late 1997 and extend the time granted to developers to construct their projects.

The labor market remained tight, with unemployment running at less than 2 percent. The concentration on electronics manufacturing has increased the demand for engineers and technicians, and resulting wage increases have been only partially constrained by importing skilled foreign workers.

Table 2.3 Major Economic Indicators: Singapore, 1995-1999
(percent)

Item	1995	1996	1997	1998	1999
Gross domestic product growth	8.7	6.9	7.8	3.0	4.5
Gross domestic investment/GDP	33.7	35.3	37.4	32.0	33.0
Gross domestic saving/GDP	51.0	51.2	51.8	50.0	50.0
Inflation rate (consumer price index)	1.7	1.4	2.0	3.2	3.3
Money supply (M2) growth	8.5	9.8	10.3	8.6	7.5
Fiscal balance/GDP	7.6	6.8	3.3	1.7	na
Merchandise exports growth	21.0	6.4	-3.1	2.0	4.0
Merchandise imports growth	21.6	5.4	0.1	2.0	4.0
Current account balance/GDP	17.0	15.4	15.2	12.9	10.3

na Not available

Sources: International Monetary Fund (1997a), Ministry of Trade and Industry (1996), and staff estimates.

Real wage increases have, in turn, supported private consumption, although such increases are likely to moderate because of the regional slowdown. Public sector consumption remained strong in 1997, increasing by 8.6 percent.

The Monetary Authority of Singapore (MAS) practices a managed floating exchange rate system, with a target of a trade-weighted currency basket. As the MAS only adjusts the weights every three to five years, the region's currency turmoil and changing trade patterns may require the MAS to reassess this target. The sensitivity of the small, open economy to trade and capital fluctuations necessitates a focus on monetary stability. Money supply (M2) growth averaged 10.3 percent for the year, and inflation was just 2 percent, aided by lower prices for imported food from neighboring countries with depreciated currencies. Meanwhile, prices for administrative charges, transportation, communications, water, health care, and housing increased. Singapore pledged to assist in the bailout packages for neighboring Indonesia and Thailand led by the International Monetary Fund.

The high savings rate (equivalent to roughly half of GDP), fiscal surplus, current account surplus, limited foreign debt, and the world's highest per capita foreign reserves helped the country come through the regional currency and financial turmoil less affected than its neighbors. While the Singapore dollar depreciated about 17 percent relative to the US dollar, it appreciated substantially more relative to most regional currencies.

In recent years the emphasis on outward direct investment has increased, and successive current account surpluses and substantial inward bound foreign direct and portfolio investment have led to steady growth in international reserves. With the low level of foreign debt, which consists primarily of long-term borrowing by the private sector, and substantial exports, the debt-service ratio is less than 1 percent.

External demand typically contributes more to Singapore's growth than domestic demand. Singapore's merchandise exports to Southeast Asia may be relatively unaffected by the slowdown there, as many of them are intermediate goods with end markets ultimately in Europe or North America. Of greater significance is the steep depreciation of the Korean won, as the Republic of Korea produces and exports electronic goods that compete directly with those of Singapore.

While the region's difficulties had some negative impact on Singapore's exports, robust future economic activity in Europe and North America is likely to more than offset this. Of Singapore's five largest markets (the European Union; Hong Kong, China; Japan; Malaysia; and the United States), the financial turbulence has affected only Malaysia. Exports declined slightly in US dollar terms in 1997, but are expected to recover in 1998. Slow growth in imports is expected to compensate to a large extent for the reduced growth in exports, and the current account surplus is expected to decline slightly as a percentage of GDP, but to remain substantial.

Slower regional growth is expected to affect hub-related services, such as entrepot trade, and shipping services, such as freight, insurance, and port charges, leading to slower growth and rising unemployment in 1998. The appreciation of the Singapore dollar relative to other regional currencies is also likely to affect net tourism and retail receipts negatively. In addition, reduced residential construction in 1998 is expected to contribute to slower investment growth. Projections indicate that GDP growth will fall to 3 percent before recovering somewhat to 4.5 percent in 1999.

Given the government's commitment to increasing spending on education and infrastructure, such spending is expected to continue to rise, although at a more moderate pace in 1998 and 1999. The government has maintained its operating expenditure near a constant 20 percent of GDP. Development expenditure is expected to remain high because of upcoming infrastructure projects, including land reclamation, communications facilities, a new rapid transit line and extension to Changi Airport, and light rail projects.

POLICY AND DEVELOPMENT ISSUES

The financial crisis in much of Southeast Asia have brought to the fore a nexus of issues that will affect Singapore's future prospects. Prominent among these are the country's industrial policy and development of the financial services industry.

Industrial Policy

Singapore maintains a concerted effort to broaden and deepen its economy, particularly in relation to the Southeast Asian subregion. The government emphasizes low land-intensity operations, and uses tax incentives, investment allowances, training, research and innovation programs, and capital assistance schemes to steer investment toward higher value-added activities. The objective is to attract foreign investment, promote and develop service sectors, and develop small- and medium-size enterprises. Within the services sectors, the focus is on serving regional business headquarters (approximately 2,000 of which are located in Singapore), logistics, education and health care services, and communications and media. The authorities also devote substantial effort to promoting financial services.

Infrastructure and technological innovations are necessary to boost productivity and attract foreign investment. The government's Manufacturing 2000 program aims to maintain manufacturing at 25 percent of GDP and 20 percent of employment, but these goals may come into conflict with the expansion of business and financial services. The government is devoting more resources to research and development (R&D) and to technical training of the labor force. Singapore's gross expenditure on R&D has been growing rapidly, expanding at a rate of 19 percent per year over the last five years, but remains lower in relation to GDP than in other industrial countries. The small size of Singapore's population may limit the amount of R&D that can be done domestically.

Singapore is a prominent investor in other countries in Asia, including PRC, India, Indonesia, Myanmar, and Viet Nam. To some extent this is patterned after the Swiss model of obtaining substantial national income from foreign investments. In this effort, the sharp depreciation of other Asian currencies in 1997 may create a buying opportunity for Singapore's regional investment objectives.

The Singapore ONE (One Network-for Everyone) plan to link every home by computer and turn Singapore into an "intelligent island" is intended to help establish Singapore as a regional financial and product design center. Singapore ONE aims to bring multimedia services with a broadband network and high-speed links to other economies to most Singaporeans by the end of 1998. Companies that participate in developing products and services that facilitate or use the new network are eligible for income tax exemptions, tax deductions for R&D expenditures, funding from the National Science and Technology Board, and preferential telecommunications tariffs.

The Economic Development Board's Innovation Development Scheme has been allotted S$500 million to offer companies grants for half their costs in such areas as product and process design. Innovation Development Scheme funding is also available for companies that participate in Singapore ONE for up to 70 percent of development costs.

In addition, the authorities are promoting biotechnology. In 1997 the National Science and Technology Board started an incubator unit for infant biotechnology firms at the Bioprocessing Technology Centre, which makes laboratory space and equipment available for rent.

The concentration of fiscal incentives to benefit particular sectors reflects a government commitment to industrial policy that is likely to deepen. While Singapore appears to be moving toward an industrial policy in which the private sector takes the lead, that transition appears to be some way off. While one could argue that Singapore's industrial policy has been successful at picking industries for promotion, one could also argue that it may have been more a matter of the industries picking Singapore based on comparative advantage. Yet Hong Kong, China succeeded in many of the same sectors with much less government intervention. Some of the industries, such as electronics, that the government has promoted may have made Singapore's economy particularly susceptible to the regional export slowdown in 1996. In addition, some sectors, such as biotechnology, have received considerable promotion with limited results. Whether Singapore can continue to guide the market as well as in the past remains to be seen as the economy expands, diversifies, and moves increasingly into services, and as other examples of national industrial policy (such as in the Republic of Korea) appear less successful in hindsight. Fortunately, Singapore maintains a high degree of transparency in its policy implementation.

Development of Financial Services

The limited size of the domestic market implies that to maintain rapid growth financial activity must be externally oriented. To promote its efforts to expand as a regional financial center, the government has initiated a review of the banking and financial sector. The sector is considered sound, and Singapore maintains an open capital account. The capital adequacy ratio for banks is set at 12 percent, substantially above that recommended by the Bank for International Settlements, but most banks maintain even higher ratios, all in assets that have the lowest risk. While this ensures that banks are well capitalized, it reduces the sector's return on equity. In 1997 estimates indicated that less than 3 percent of loans were nonperforming, but this ratio may increase as events unfold in Indonesia and Malaysia, with which Singapore has close economic links. The MAS estimates that offshore loans are roughly three times the value of domestic loans. The large banking sector comprises both domestic and foreign institutions, but the former are limited in size. The four largest domestic banks are either family or government controlled, and are too small to compete effectively in financing most of the region's large infrastructure projects. Foreign banks are currently restricted from owning more than 40 percent of any local bank's capital, thereby limiting the prospects for mergers to increase the size of domestic banks to internationally competitive levels. Transparency is also limited as, among domestic banks, only the government-owned bank reveals information about bad loans or provisions made against these loans to the public.

In 1997 the financial services sector benefited from greater foreign exchange trading and volatility-induced trading in the stock market, although Singapore's stock market fell by more than 40 percent, which reduced the benefits for domestically listed financial service firms. The foreign exchange market is active, and a futures exchange has been set up. There are no restrictions on forward exchange transactions. Forward exchange rates of up to one year's term are available for most major and regional currencies, and foreign currency futures are traded at the Singapore International Monetary Exchange. Plans to expand the financial services sector may, however, have to be scaled back if the region's setback results in reduced foreign borrowing from Singapore's banks, as seems likely.

In its July 1997 budget the government introduced a set of tax breaks for income earned from overseas activities of banks, income earned by fund managers in managing nonresident funds, income earned in managing initial public offerings in shares denominated in foreign currency, income earned from trading foreign currency shares, and income earned from credit ratings of foreign currency denominated securities issued in Singapore. In addition, offshore bond issues no longer need to be underwritten locally to qualify as tax exempt, and the authorities raised the limit on tax deductible bank provisions against unforeseen losses by 50 percent. The number of seats on the stock exchange offered to foreign brokerage houses is expected to increase, fixed commissions on stock sales may be abolished, and the Singapore dollar is likely to be gradually internationalized by eased restrictions on foreigners lending Singapore dollars.

Market reaction has been muted, partly because of skepticism about the government's willingness to ease its traditionally tight control of the country's finances. This control is still apparent in the concentration of national savings in the Central Provident Fund, the large budgetary surpluses, the substantial deposits of government agencies in the government-controlled savings bank, and a host of regulations covering relatively minor details of foreign bank branch operations. The 1998 budget aims to ease some of this control. Pressure from the United States and the World Trade Organization to liberalize the sector further is likely. However, in November 1997 the government announced that in future, the MAS will focus on supervision rather than on strict regulation of financial markets, and that listing requirements on the stock exchange would be eased. These modest efforts are in the right direction, but more can be done. The success of the government's efforts to establish Singapore as a regional financial center will depend critically on the government's willingness to cede more of its control over national savings.

TAIPEI,CHINA

The region's financial crisis has left Taipei,China largely untouched. Reforms in the banking and financial sectors are to continue. Policy to encourage high technology, which will bring about a number of structural changes, remains active, but needs to gain momentum.

RECENT TRENDS AND PROSPECTS

In a year of unprecedented turmoil in Asia's financial markets, Taipei,China has managed to avoid a major financial crisis. Not only has it survived this turbulent period, but its economy grew at 6.8 percent during 1997, slightly faster than in the previous two years. This was largely due to sustained growth in finance, insurance, real estate, and social services. While the manufacturing sector is still recovering from its previous slowdown, the recovery is noticeable, and the growth rate is a little more than 4 percent.

Despite the higher growth rate and only a modest increase in the labor force, unemployment rose to 2.7 percent, a little higher than in 1996. However, the current rate is still relatively low by international standards, and future unemployment rates are not expected to be much higher.

Gross domestic investment as a percentage of GDP increased slightly compared to 1996. This was due mainly to an increase in private investment, as investment in public enterprises grew only slightly, and several public investment projects fell far behind schedule. Government investment increased by less than 2 percent. By contrast, the growth rate of private investment more than doubled in 1997, compared with 1996, to just under 13 percent. The primary cause was the optimism generated by the stock market boom.

With the strong growth in income tax collection, overall government current revenues rose by 10.6 percent in 1997, but government current expenditures grew only 5.8 percent. Nevertheless, total revenues still fell short of total expenditures by about 5.7 percent of GDP, largely because of the implementation of government investment projects that had fallen behind schedule in previous years.

Slow growth of the money supply (M2) at 7.2 percent was largely an outcome of the Central Bank's anti-inflationary policy and weak demand for bank financing by the construction industry. The former has proven successful to the extent that consumer price inflation was about 1 percent, the lowest rate since 1987. The depreciation of the Japanese yen, which reduced the prices of imports from Japan, helped keep the inflation rate down.

Exports grew by more than 5 percent in 1997, with exports of heavy industrial products holding up particularly well. In sharp contrast, agricultural and processed agricultural exports continued their slowdown, shrinking by as much as 19 and 34 percent, respectively. Livestock epidemics explain some of this slowdown, but it also reflects a general decline of the agriculture sector.

The value of imports rebounded in 1997, growing by about 10 percent after stagnating in 1996. The principal imports were machinery, electrical equipment, and chemicals, which together accounted for more than 45 percent of total imports in 1997. As in 1996, imports of consumer goods grew more rapidly than imports of capital goods and raw materials. This may reflect an increasing consumerist orientation in a maturing economy.

As a result of the faster growth of imports, the current account balance declined to a surplus of 2.7 percent of GDP, a marked fall from the 4 percent surplus in 1996. Under pressure from a strong US dollar, the New Taiwan dollar depreciated an average of 15 percent. Despite the depreciation, the trade surplus did not increase further in 1997.

After a slight decline to 5.8 percent in 1998, real GDP growth is expected to recover in 1999. Accordingly, government current revenues are also projected to pick up in 1999. In an attempt to bring down the budget deficit, the government's capital expenditure will be more conservative. Projections indicate that the ratio of government expenditure to GDP will decrease by 3 percentage points over the next two years, down from 28 percent in 1997. By contrast, because tax revenues will exhibit stable growth, the overall deficit to GDP ratio will decrease by less than one percentage point in 1999.

The money supply will grow slightly faster in 1998 and 1999 than in 1997, with a growth rate of about 7.4 percent. The Central Bank's anti-inflationary policy and the direct financing of businesses supported by the stock market will be responsible for the low monetary growth.

With aggregate demand increasing as a result of sustained growth of the economy, depreciation of the New Taiwan dollar, and continuing steady growth in service prices, the consumer price index is expected to grow at 3.2 percent in 1998 and 2.2 percent in 1999.

CRITICAL ISSUES IN SHORT-TERM ECONOMIC MANAGEMENT

Taipei,China has been relatively insulated from the region's currency turbulence. However, the continued emphasis on advertising the economy's successes has raised some concerns that the government has not paid sufficient attention to how Asia's financial crisis might affect the domestic economy and what adjustment strategies it should pursue. Two areas in particular deserve attention.

The first is the domestic economy. Current projections of both private consumption and investment growth for 1998 may turn out to be overly optimistic. At the same time, fears of creeping inflation may lead to tight monetary and fiscal policies. Given that the economy is not at present overheated, some flexibility in short-term macroeconomic management, including the provision of adequate liquidity through the banking system, would seem to be prudent.

The second area is the external economy. Taipei,China should maintain its open trading system even in the face of a declining trade surplus. In

Table 2.4 Major Economic Indicators: Taipei,China, 1995-1999
(percent)

Item	1995	1996	1997	1998	1999
Gross domestic product growth	6.0	5.7	6.8	5.8	6.2
Gross domestic investment/GDP	23.7	21.2	21.8	22.6	23.4
Gross domestic saving/GDP	25.6	25.1	24.7	24.9	25.2
Inflation rate (consumer price index)	3.7	3.1	0.9	3.2	2.2
Money supply (M2) growth	9.4	9.1	7.2	7.4	7.4
Fiscal balance/GDP	-7.4	-7.4	-5.7	-5.3	-4.8
Merchandise exports growth	20.0	3.8	5.2	6.8	7.0
Merchandise imports growth	21.2	-0.1	10.1	9.5	10.0
Current account balance/GDP	2.1	4.0	2.7	1.5	0.8
Debt-service/exports	0.1	0.1	0.1	0.1	0.1

Sources: Directorate-General of Budget, Accounting and Statistics data; Wu (1997); and staff estimates.

this respect 1998 will be a crucial year. Even without a devaluation of the People's Republic of China's (PRC's) renminbi, Taipei,China's exports will slow down. Maintaining a free trade stance will be crucial for the future of not only the domestic economy, but also of free and open trading in the region.

POLICY AND DEVELOPMENT ISSUES

The economy is still undergoing considerable structural transformation, in particular, the industry sector is continuing to experience major structural changes. Light and labor-intensive manufacturing activities are declining in importance, and efforts to increase the share of capital-intensive and high-technology activities are under way. In the changing global trade environment, promoting specific industries in which the economy may have distinct comparative advantages continues to be a major challenge.

To make the process of structural transformation as smooth as possible, two policy areas deserve particular attention, namely, liberalizing financial and capital markets in the face of the continuing turmoil in the region and continuing with the plan to convert Taipei,China into a regional center for financial and high-technology-based economic activities. Successful implementation of these two related sets of policies could go a long way toward ensuring the economy's transition to a high-technology base. However, the problems involved could also be formidable.

Capital markets are being liberalized with the introduction of new financial instruments and the pledge by monetary authorities to lift capital controls by 2000. However, the ad hoc committee, which consists of Ministry of Finance and Central Bank representatives, has suggested strengthening financial institutions along with carrying out further liberalization. The recent currency crisis seems to have strengthened the position of those who argue for a slower pace of reforms. Historically, Taipei,China's financial liberalization has been gradual; too slow according to some critics. However, such a step-by-step policy may be defensible, as it probably played a major role in protecting the economy from the financial turmoil of 1997.

Reforms under discussion include allowing commercial banks to become involved in investment banking by entering the securities and bond markets. The authorities also launched a domestic futures exchange, thereby giving companies the option to hedge risks without going offshore. In addition, the central government has taken steps to privatize state-run banks, a plan that was boosted by constitutional reforms passed in July 1997 that shrank provincial governments and stripped them of their substantial assets.

The objective of ensuring smooth maturation and playing a significant role in the next century has led to the formulation of a scheme—the Asia-Pacific Regional Operations Center plan—to turn Taipei,China into a regional financial and economic center. The idea is to attract private capital flows, especially to high-technology industries, such as microchips and semiconductors.

For a comprehensive plan of this type to succeed, a number of developments will be necessary. To begin with, it will require free mobility of goods, services, capital, human resources, and information, which will call for institutional and regulatory reforms. Furthermore, physical infrastructure will need to be improved to support the movement of productive factors into increasingly sophisticated activities. At the same time, specific supporting sectors, such as financial services, telecommunications, and air transportation, would have to be liberalized further.

Along with the push for high-technology industries, Taipei,China is also aiming for stable relations, and even direct business and transport links, with the PRC. Positive developments in this direction will help improve the general business climate. In particular, the environment for implementing the objectives of the Asia-Pacific Regional Operations Center plan will be more favorable. To sum up, from a long-run perspective Taipei,China is continuing the transition from labor-intensive activities to capital-intensive and high-technology activities. Such a transition has posed complex problems of competitiveness, skill bottlenecks, and internal and external balance. Nevertheless, an export-driven, high-technology future appears to be attainable. However, to realize this vision, the challenges noted must be tackled boldly and imaginatively through flexible, short-term, macroeconomic policies and strategies for long-run transformation.

PEOPLE'S REPUBLIC OF CHINA
and
MONGOLIA

PEOPLE'S REPUBLIC OF CHINA

The economy of the People's Republic of China (PRC) grew by 8.8 percent in 1997, driven partly by strong exports. Moderately tight monetary and fiscal policies, along with consecutive years of bumper grain harvests, contributed to abating inflation to 2.8 percent. The financial turmoil in Southeast and East Asia has thus far not spread to the PRC. Economic growth is predicted to slow down to about 7 percent in 1998 and 1999. Reforms of state-owned enterprises (SOEs) and the financial sector are expected to gather new momentum in coming years.

RECENT TRENDS AND PROSPECTS

The PRC's economy maintained its strong growth momentum in 1997, growing by 8.8 percent. The moderate slowdown from 9.6 percent in 1996 reflects the continuing tight fiscal and monetary policies.

The growth in industrial output, which accounts for about half of the GDP, decelerated further from 12.1 percent in 1996 to 10.8 percent in 1997. SOE industrial production continued to grow at a slower pace than that of nonstate enterprises, and its share in total industrial output declined to 47 percent from 48.5 percent in 1996. The agriculture sector grew at an annual rate of about 5 percent in 1995 and 1996 because of a number of factors, such as higher public investment in agriculture, good weather conditions, upward adjustments in procurement prices, and various other supportive measures introduced since 1995 under the government's Grain Bag Policy. In 1997 GDP from agriculture grew at a lower, but still robust, rate of 3.5 percent. The rapidly growing and modernizing economy has generated a huge demand for financial, accounting, legal, wholesaling, retailing, and other support services, and the service sector grew by 8.2 percent.

A combination of administrative controls on new investments; a slowdown in net lending by the People's Bank of China, the Central Bank; the tighter project screening by commercial banks; the high real interest rate; and the excess capacity in some industries kept investment growth in check.

The Ninth Five-Year Plan, which envisages balancing the budget by 2000, continued to guide the government's budgetary policies. Revenues increased by 18.5 percent in 1997, and the share of revenues as a percentage of GDP increased to around 12 percent from 10.8 percent in 1996. Fiscal reforms introduced since March 1994 are gradually relieving strains on the government's budgetary position. Value-added and consumption taxes collected by the central government grew by 19.3 percent, which is 4.7 percentage points higher than the growth of those collected by local governments, resulting in a rise in the central government's share in the total to 56.5 percent, an increase of 0.9 percentage point from that in 1996.

Government expenditures increased by 18 percent in 1997, despite the continued strict control over nonpriority expenditures and the downsizing of the SOE sector and of the civil service. The budget deficit remained unchanged at around 0.8 percent of GDP. There has been a substantial shift in the financing of the deficit to noninflationary sources. Since 1994 government borrowing from the People's Bank of China has contracted and that from commercial banks and the public has increased.

The government kept monetary policy tight for the fourth consecutive year. In 1997 broad money supply (M2) grew at 17.3 percent, or 7.7 percentage points less than the official target. With the tight monetary policies having helped the government achieve a soft landing of the economy, pressure to ease credit has been growing.

Tight monetary policy, good agricultural harvests that have persisted for three consecutive years, excess capacity in some industrial sectors, and weak consumer demand enabled the country to reduce inflation significantly. The consumer price index fell to 2.8 percent from 8.3 percent in 1996 and 17.1 percent in 1995. At 0.8 percent the retail price index, which excludes services, was even lower. With the easing of inflationary pressures, the People's Bank of China has started slowly loosening its monetary policy in recent months by cutting interest rates. A notable institutional development in monetary policy was the State Council's formation of the Monetary Policy Committee in April 1997, which reflected the government's resolve to pursue a more independent monetary policy.

Exports grew by 20 percent, about 2 percentage points more than in 1996. Import growth remained subdued, at 2.5 percent, because of weak domestic demand. Consequently, the PRC achieved a record trade account surplus of more than $40 billion and a current account surplus of $20 billion. On the capital account, the PRC received around $45 billion in foreign direct investment (FDI). These large inflows of foreign capital, along with the current account surplus, enabled the PRC to strengthen its foreign exchange reserves further. These reserves reached $140 billion by the end of 1997 and provided more than 11 months of import cover.

The PRC ranks second among all countries in terms of FDI inflows and first among all developing countries. Initially, most FDI went into low-technology, assembly-type operations, primarily for export, that took advantage of the PRC's low labor costs. This situation is changing, however. In 1997 most FDI inflows were invested in industries whose products cater to the domestic market, including the service sector. In the last two years large inflows of FDI were directed toward telecommunications, electric power, transportation, banking, and insurance. The liberalization of the service sector and the rapid increases in real household incomes account for this changing pattern of FDI inflows.

Table 2.5 Major Economic Indicators: People's Republic of China, 1995-1999
(percent)

Item	1995	1996	1997	1998	1999
Gross domestic product growth	10.5	9.6	8.8	7.2	6.8
Gross domestic investment/GDP	40.2	39.2	39.8	39.0	39.0
Gross domestic saving/GDP	41.9	41.4	42.6	39.0	39.0
Inflation rate (consumer price index)	17.1	8.3	2.8	4.0	6.0
Money supply (M2) growth	29.5	25.8	17.3	20.0	22.0
Fiscal balance/GDP	-1.0	-0.8	-0.8	-0.6	-0.5
Merchandise exports growth	24.9	17.9	20.0	3.0	3.0
Merchandise imports growth	15.5	19.5	2.5	12.0	12.0
Current account balance/GDP	0.2	0.9	2.2	0.9	0.4
Debt-service/exports	9.9	10.1	9.8	11.0	11.0

Sources: State Statistical Bureau (1997), International Monetary Fund (1998), and staff estimates.

Figure 2.1 Net Foreign Direct Investment:
People's Republic of China, 1990-1996

A. Committed and Utilized Net FDI

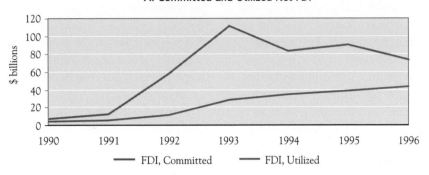

B. PRC's Share in FDI Flows to Developing Countries

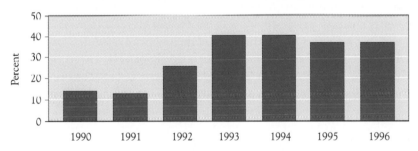

Sources: State Statistical Bureau (1997) and World Bank data.

An important initiative in foreign exchange system reform that occurred in 1997 was allowing large domestic enterprises to open foreign exchange accounts in state commercial banks. Previously only foreign-funded enterprises had been permitted to do so. This put domestic enterprises on the same footing as foreign-funded ones. The measure also helped reduce the foreign exchange risks the government was facing when all foreign exchange was sold to the Central Bank.

The financial crisis in Southeast and East Asia have thus far not spread to the PRC. The renminbi appreciated marginally against the US dollar during 1997. The following factors explain the strength of the renminbi compared to the currencies of the PRC's neighboring countries. First, the PRC's capital account is still not convertible. Second, the bulk of foreign capital inflows during the first half of the 1990s went into productive sectors as direct investment as opposed to portfolio investment. Third, the PRC has adopted prudent policies with regard to external borrowing, with about 82 percent of its external debt being medium and long term, and its debt to GDP and debt-service ratios being significantly below the thresholds at which the International Monetary Fund expresses concern. Finally, because of massive foreign capital inflows and strong export performance, the PRC maintained a robust external position, with foreign currency reserves exceeding total foreign debt.

The economic turmoil prevailing in Asia and its ramifications for the world economy make an accurate assessment of the PRC's economic prospects for the coming years difficult. However, given weakening domestic demand, excess capacities in some industries, and a possible decline in export growth, the economy is expected to grow at about 7 percent per year in 1998 and 1999. The industrial sector is likely to feel the main effects of the slowdown. In contrast, the government's increased emphasis on the agriculture sector should result in continuation of the 3.5 percent annual growth rate. To stimulate economic growth, the government is planning major infrastructure expenditures.

The recent depreciation of the currencies of Southeast and East Asian countries is likely to reduce the competitiveness of some of the PRC's exports. The expected slowdown of the world economy, including Japan and the United States, could also adversely affect the country's export prospects. In the interests of the region's recovery from the currency turmoil, a competitive devaluation of the renminbi is unlikely. However, the government is taking some measures to stimulate exports, such as improving the tax rebate system. Taking all these factors into account, a reduction in annual export growth from 20 percent in 1997 to about 3 percent per year in 1998 and 1999 is forecast. Coupled with the weakening domestic investment brought about by excess capacity in some industries, the slower growth in exports is likely to result in a slowdown of the industrial sector's growth to 8 percent in 1998 and 7 percent in 1999.

The government's efforts to encourage growth of the service sector to absorb surplus labor in agriculture and SOEs will lead to continued expansion of this sector over the medium term. Recent measures to liberalize the financial sector, particularly banking and insurance; to open the retail and wholesale sectors to foreign investment; and to expand transport and communication services to alleviate bottlenecks will help the sustained growth of the service sector. The slowdown in the industrial sector would, however, reduce the demand for services, and hence dampen the growth of the service sector. Taking these two opposite influences into account, the service sector is forecast to grow by 7.5 percent in 1998 and 8.4 percent in 1999.

The slowdown in economic growth and the overall deflationary trends in Asia should keep domestic prices from rising significantly. The government may, however, ease monetary policy to counter the possible economic slowdown. However, given the inflationary consequences of an expansionary monetary policy a few years ago, the government is likely to be cautious in easing money supply and credit. On balance, therefore, inflation is forecast to remain moderate, but be somewhat higher during the next two years.

Import growth will pick up in 1998 and 1999 because of the recent, and possible further, reduction in tariffs and other trade barriers, and because of increased imports from Asian countries that have depreciated currencies. Coupled with a slowdown in exports, this will reduce the trade and current account surpluses. The contraction in committed FDI inflows is anticipated to continue, reflecting a correction to their unprecedented levels in the 1990s, the gradual withdrawal of preferential policies previously granted to FDI, and the adverse impact of the financial crisis in Southeast and East Asia on the supply of FDI. Given these developments, the government is expected to take a more cautious approach toward implementing the convertibility of the renminbi on the capital account.

The central government's fiscal situation in the medium term will depend on revenue performance and the extent to which the authorities implement SOE reforms. As the new tax measures and the tax collection system become more entrenched, revenue buoyancy should increase the tax-GDP ratio. Expediting SOE reforms will also reduce subsidies channeled through the budget, which in recent years amounted to 4 to 5 percent of total government revenues.

POLICY AND DEVELOPMENT ISSUES

Despite the PRC's recent resilience to the region's economic crisis, it may not be immune to future shocks. While the threat of a crisis may not be immediate, the country needs to draw lessons from the ongoing Asian crisis and take the necessary steps to prevent a similar crisis from disrupting its economic stability. While the economic situations of the countries affected by the crisis and the PRC are different, there are also some similarities that point toward the need for vigilance. In this context, two of the most pressing issues facing the government are the weak financial sector in general, and the banking system in particular, and an ailing state enterprise sector.

Strengthening the Financial Sector

One of the crucial factors that triggered the Asian crisis was weak governance of the financial sector. Weaknesses in the PRC's financial sector need to be addressed in a timely and prudent manner to avoid the problems other countries in the region are experiencing (see Box 2.1).

The government is aware of the problems in the financial sector and is taking action to address them. Reforming the financial sector is now a priority in the economic policy agenda. In December 1997 the government announced that it would abolish the directed lending quotas applicable to state commercial banks as of 1 January 1998. It will use a set of financial indicators—such as the capital adequacy ratio, the deposit-lending ratio, the lending portfolio, and the cash reserve requirement—to control credits indirectly and, together with other macroeconomic management instruments, to maintain appropriate levels of monetary aggregates. This is a significant step toward establishing a financial system that operates on the basis of sound commercial principles and strict prudential norms.

To reduce the amount of nonperforming loans, Y30 billion (about $3.6 billion) in bad debt was taken off the banks' balance sheets in 1997, another Y50 billion (about $6 billion) will be taken off the balance sheets in 1998, and a further Y60 billion (about $7.2 billion) will be taken off in 1999 and 2000. In February 1998 the Standing Committee of the Eighth Congress of the PRC approved issuance by the Ministry of Finance of Y270 billion (about $32.5 billion) in bonds to help recapitalize the four state commercial banks. The government's objective is eventually to reach the 8 percent capital adequacy ratio, and it is committing substantial amounts of financial resources to achieve this objective. The government is also taking serious measures to tackle rural credit funds and unofficial security exchange centers and to strengthen the regulation and supervision of nonbank financial institutions.

However, reform of the financial sector faces many challenges, some of which need to be given special attention. First, the legal and regulatory framework for the financial sector needs to be strengthened. Second, the government needs to pay continuous attention to the problem of nonperforming assets of the key financial institutions, and to ensure the timely implementation of the recently announced bank recapitalization program. Third, prudential norms and risk management procedures guiding the financial sector need to be tightened. Fourth, competition in the banking sector should be promoted by easing entry barriers and by further reducing the government's role in directing the banking sector's resources. Fifth, the government should clearly define its role as the owner of banks and as the regulator of the banking system with the objective of transforming the state-owned banks into genuine commercial banks. Finally, the capital market needs to be broadened and deepened, along with increasing the market's efficiency and transparency. Promoting associated industries, such as pension, insurance, and mutual funds, should form an integral part of the development of the capital market.

Reforming SOEs

Many of the financial sector's problems arise from an ailing state enterprise sector. The PRC currently has more than 300,000 SOEs. The proportion of loss-making SOEs grew from around 10 percent of the total in 1985 to 47 percent in 1997. In the first quarter of 1997 the SOE sector as a whole was operating at a loss. The support of loss-making SOEs is a major reason for the high proportion of nonperforming loans in the banking system. A radical restructuring and reform of these enterprises is needed to improve industrial efficiency, maintain the economy's growth momentum, and improve the banking sector's balance sheet.

The main reason for the SOEs' poor performance is their weak governance structure. SOEs do not have fully market-based management autonomy, are not subject to strict financial discipline, and do not face a credible threat of bankruptcy. In addition, monitoring and supervision by the government, the sole capital owner, has often been ineffective. The weak governance has led to poor responses to market signals, excessive and inefficient investment, and a lack of incentives to undertake technological innovations. These weaknesses, coupled with the

Box 2.1 The Weak Financial Sector in the PRC

Weaknesses in the PRC's financial sector are related to the banking sector, capital markets, and nonbank financial institutions.

The Banking Sector

There are a number of problems in the banking sector. First, the level of nonperforming loans is high. According to government estimates, of the total loans of state commercial banks, around 25 percent are nonperforming and between 5 and 6 percent are nonrecoverable. The main sources of nonperforming loans are the large financial losses of the SOEs, which the state banks were directed to lend to. Second, the financial performance of the state commercial banks has been deteriorating. The banking sector as a whole operated at a loss in 1996, and the situation is believed to have continued in 1997. This deterioration has occurred even though many banks treated accrued (but often unpaid) interest as paid income and made negligible provisions for bad debts. Third, the level of equity capital is low. During the last decade the total assets of the state banking sector increased by more than 25 percent per year, while equity capital increased only by 18 percent each year. The different growth rates led to a fall in the capital adequacy ratio from more than 10 percent in 1986 to less than 6 percent in 1996, which is low by international standards. Because of the accumulation of bad debt in recent years, the state banking sector's effective equity capital is even smaller. This has put the banking sector in a vulnerable position and caused external credit rating agencies to downgrade its credit ratings recently.

Capital Markets

Weaknesses in the capital markets are also a major source of potential financial risks. Like many other emerging markets, stock markets in the PRC suffer from limited disclosure, a bunching of public offerings, weak regulation, and a circumscribed role for competitive underwriters and primary dealers. Compounding these shortcomings is the limited participation by wholesale and institutional purchasers of securities. A credit plan sets quotas on how much equity can be issued in primary markets in a given year. The primary market for equity is then distributed by region. The government's shares, which usually account for more than 80 percent of the total capitalization of a listed company, cannot be traded. Listed companies often fail to perform up to expectations, partly because of limited exposure to market forces in the stock market. A study of 178 companies listed in 1994 found that net assets per share of these companies declined, on average, by around 70 percent from 1994 to 1997. The quota controls on equity, which limit capital market access, led to the emergence of many unofficial security exchange centers. These unofficial exchange centers provide much needed capital for the nonstate sector, which in recent years has received only about 15 percent of total state bank lending. Because these entities fall outside the oversight of any government regulatory institutions, their nonstandard practices could weaken the financial system.

Nonbank Financial Institutions

The excessive growth in the number of nonbank financial institutions and their indiscriminate business operations constitute another potential threat to the financial system's stability. In recent years thousands of rural credit funds have emerged. These funds have developed rapidly, mainly because of the underdeveloped rural capital markets. Village and township governments in rural areas are responsible for providing social services and public goods, but do not have sufficient funds to do so. By attracting deposits from local residents and paying a slightly higher interest rate than the commercial banks offer, these funds provide a convenient and cheap way to raise funds. Many rural credit funds are now operating virtually as banks in that they take deposits and provide lending beyond their regional boundaries; however, they remain outside the government's regulatory control, and could become sources of financial instability.

The PRC currently has about 250 trust and investment companies. Because of their indiscriminate business operations, nonstandard practices, and lack of effective regulatory supervision, many of them have a disproportionate structure of assets to liabilities and are facing the threat of bankruptcy, which could generate systemic shocks.

SOEs' responsibility for providing employment and performing social functions for urban populations, have made them vulnerable to competition both from foreign imports and the nonstate sector.

In September 1997 the Fifteenth Party Congress endorsed a strategy of radical SOE reforms aimed at clarifying property rights and responsibilities, separating ownership from management, and building up an enterprise system with a diversified ownership structure. Under this strategy the government will (i) corporatize large- and medium-size SOEs, with the state remaining as sole or majority shareholder for enterprises that are of strategic importance; (ii) restructure more than 250,000 small

SOEs by means of joint shareholding, leasing, contract operation, and employee and management buyouts; and (iii) encourage mergers, bankruptcies, and sell-offs to deal with the worst performing SOEs and to accelerate the reform process.

Since 1994 the government has been experimenting with bankruptcies, mergers, and corporatization in pilot cities, whose number had increased from 18 in 1995 to 111 by May 1997. During 1997 the government liquidated 675 SOEs, merged 1,022 SOEs, and took action to increase efficiency by reducing the number of redundant workers in 789 SOEs. The government has offered incentives to SOEs willing to take on the debts, assets, and workers of poorly performing enterprises to make for a more gradual increase in redundancies. The pace of corporatizing large and medium-size SOEs accelerated in 1997. The government's long-term goal is to concentrate state resources into building a core group of 1,000 companies that will dominate the PRC's major economic sectors and compete on a global scale. The last few years have witnessed a spontaneous movement to transform small SOEs through employment and management buyouts and sell-offs.

The transformation of enterprises into corporations, however, cannot on its own ensure greater operational efficiency. Concomitant changes in other areas are essential, including enforcing a hard budget constraint by commercializing the banking sector; allowing unprofitable enterprises to declare bankruptcy; and developing competitive markets for goods, factors of production, and management talent. Similarly, the transfer of decisionmaking to managers does not guarantee the efficient use of resources. In the absence of an effective mechanism to monitor managers' performance, the transfer may simply provide them with a license to pursue personal objectives. SOE reform will be a long, drawn-out process. Supporting changes that are under way in banking, capital markets, taxation, labor markets, and social security are equally important for improving SOE performance.

The immediate challenge facing the government in reforming SOEs is redeploying redundant workers to avoid increasing urban unemployment. Estimates indicate that between 10 and 20 million SOE workers would need to be redeployed between 1996 and 2000. While the government has made substantial efforts to reduce unemployment among retrenched SOE workers by introducing reemployment programs, it should seek new ways to do so, such as setting up enterprise funds to support small, private enterprises and self-employment, which have the potential to absorb a large number of redundant workers.

MONGOLIA

During 1997 economic growth recovered and inflation declined. The foreign exchange rate stabilized after March, and the 17 percent depreciation experienced during 1997 was the smallest decline in the last five years. Forecasts for 1998 indicate that GDP will increase by 4.5 percent.

RECENT TRENDS AND PROSPECTS

Real GDP growth increased from 2.4 percent in 1996 to 3.3 percent in 1997; however, continuing problems in the banking sector and energy shortages constrained growth. The service sector, which grew by 5.3 percent, provided the main impetus for the improved economic performance. Mongolia achieved higher growth, together with a marked decline in inflation, despite continued weakness in international copper and cashmere prices. The 1997 economic performance reflects successful macroeconomic stabilization and could mark the beginning of a period of sustained noninflationary growth.

Agricultural output, which accounted for almost 37 percent of GDP, grew by 2.6 percent. The weakening of domestic meat prices and lower international prices of cashmere moderated the overall impact of increased livestock herds and higher cashmere output. Despite the 4 percent reduction in land area sown, crop harvests improved in response to an improved policy environment, liberalization of wheat prices, and favorable weather conditions.

The industry sector recovered, with 2.3 percent growth in 1997, compared with 0.5 percent in 1996. Manufacturing output rose by 2.8 percent, with the private sector playing the lead role, stimulated by the government's ambitious privatization program, under which some small businesses and agro-enterprises were privatized. Construction output contracted by 6 percent, primarily because of a slowdown in public sector activity. Gold production from privately-owned mines increased from 5.4 tons in 1996 to 8 tons in 1997, thereby increasing foreign exchange reserves.

Private enterprises dominate the service sector. Services related to trade, transport, communications, hotels and restaurants, and tourism improved in 1997, aided by the stability of the exchange rate, the initiation of bank restructuring and reforms, and the abolition of price controls.

The number of those officially registered as unemployed reached 63,700, or 7 percent of the labor force. This was 15 percent higher than the 1996 level, but probably underestimates the actual level of unemployment. Unemployment resulting from problems related to state-owned enterprises (SOEs) increased during 1997. Money wages and salaries increased by 25 percent, leading to an increase in real wages of about 5 percent, the first increase since 1993. On the whole, total income per household improved in real terms during 1997.

Tax revenue collection improved, particularly of income and corporate taxes, because of the major tax reforms implemented in May 1997. Import tariffs were abolished, except on alcohol and tobacco products. To avoid further revenue losses, the authorities replaced these tax cuts with new revenue measures, including extending the coverage of domestic sales tax to about 300 additional enterprises by broadening the tax base to include the food, construction, and communication sectors; doubling excise taxes on petroleum products and alcoholic spirits when they were converted from local currency to foreign currency rates; and introducing a new excise tax on passenger vehicles. These new measures increased tax revenues by about 2 percentage points of GDP.

Expenditures and net lending remained at about 40 percent of GDP, with increases in both current and capital expenditures. The increase in current expenditures was a result of (i) an increase in civil servants' wages and salaries, (ii) the clearance of domestic arrears of both the central and local governments, (iii) the interest payments on bank restructuring bonds, and (iv) an increase in pensions. Interest payments increased from Tug4 billion ($7 million) in 1996 to Tug22 billion ($28 million) in 1997.

The net result was that the overall fiscal deficit deteriorated in 1997. While total revenues increased from 28 percent of GDP in 1996 to 30 percent in 1997, total expenditures and net lending increased from 36 to 38.8 percent of GDP in 1997. The current budget balance was 2.3 percent of GDP, compared with a target of 1 percent. However, the 1997 result was only half the 1996 level, and the overall fiscal deficit was contained at 8.6 percent, compared with the target of 10 percent.

Money supply (M2) grew by 36 percent in 1997. Time saving deposits rose by 27 percent, compared with a contraction of 8.7 percent in 1996. This reflects improvements in the banking sector resulting from restructuring undertaken in late 1996 and stronger supervision by the Bank of Mongolia. The growth in currency in circulation slowed to 23.3 percent, down from 57.6 percent in 1996. Net credit to the government from the banking sector fell sharply; credit to public sector enterprises remained constant; and credit to private enterprises rose, but not enough to sustain the required rate of capacity expansion in the manufacturing sector. The real rate of interest on bank credit was high, more than 40 to 50 percent per year, making the use of debt financing for capital investment difficult. Thus the next challenge for monetary policy is to encourage banks to reduce their lending rates while ensuring credit quality and improving recovery ratios.

Following the price decontrol and adjustments in 1996 and sharp increases in fuel and electricity prices during the first quarter of 1997, monthly inflation was as high as 5.8 percent by April 1997. In addition, the authorities removed subsidies from water rates, accommodation rents, and transport fares; however, declining meat and vegetable prices helped offset these increases. The Bank of Mongolia's tight monetary policy effectively restrained further price increases, resulting in price deceleration in the second half of 1997. Annual inflation was estimated at about 20 percent, a

Table 2.6 Major Economic Indicators: Mongolia, 1995-1999
(percent)

Item	1995	1996	1997	1998	1999
Gross domestic product growth	6.3	2.4	3.3	4.5	5.0
Inflation rate (consumer price index)	56.8	49.6	20.0	15.0	10.0
Money supply (M2) growth	32.9	25.8	36.0	20.0	17.0
Fiscal balance/GDP	-3.8	-8.2	-8.6	-8.6	-7.0
Merchandise exports growth	32.3	-12.8	8.9	2.0	5.0
Merchandise imports growth	32.0	4.5	-1.5	6.0	7.5
Current account balance/GDP	5.5	-10.0	-5.6	-11.5	-10.0
Debt service/exports	12.0	11.5	9.0	9.8	10.5

Sources: Bank of Mongolia, National Statistics Office, and staff estimates.

significant improvement over the 49.6 percent recorded in 1996.

Total export earnings reached about $461 million, an increase of about 9 percent from 1996 levels. The value of copper exports, which accounted for about 43 percent of total exports, rose by 14 percent following increased production. Other principal exports were cashmere, leather garments, gold, live animals, and animal products. Although Switzerland nominally accounted for the largest share—32 percent—of Mongolia's exports, these actually represented copper concentrate that was re-exported to the People's Republic of China (PRC) and Russia. The PRC was the second largest market for Mongolia's exports, accounting for 22 percent of total exports, followed by the Republic of Korea with 11 percent. Imports declined by 1.5 percent. Primary imports included machinery, chemicals, and energy. Russia, at 36 percent, was the largest source of imports, followed by the PRC with 14 percent. The trade deficit shrank and the current account deficit improved to around 6 percent of GDP. The inflow of concessional external finance was substantially larger in 1997 than in 1996, and was sufficient to finance the current account deficit and build up net foreign exchange reserves to $89.9 million by the end of 1997.

The Bank of Mongolia responded decisively to the sharp depreciation of the tugrik in early 1997 by tightening monetary policy and intervening in the foreign exchange market. As a result, the exchange rate stabilized in March 1997, and over the year averaged Tug794 to the US dollar. The exchange rate at the end of the year was Tug813 to the US dollar. This 17 percent depreciation was broadly in line with annual year-on-year inflation. This is the smallest depreciation rate in the last five years, and reflects the successful implementation of macroeconomic stabilization measures.

Forecasts indicate that GDP will increase by 4.5 percent in 1998, while inflation will fall to 15 percent. Services will continue to lead growth performance. A likely reduction in real interest rates for bank credit and greater inflows of foreign capital into the mining sector will result in higher investment growth. In addition, more foreign companies are likely to invest in oil exploration and production projects. The private sector will lead growth in both manufacturing and services, with the government's role increasingly focused on providing physical and social infrastructure. An accelerated program of SOE privatization will encourage private sector expansion.

Fiscal stability will continue over the medium term, with the government bringing down the tax burden on the economy. Total revenues will decline as a percentage of GDP in 1998, but will then stabilize. Privatization receipts will contribute about 1.5 percent of GDP to total revenues. The government will reduce its expenditures to lower the overall deficit to a level that will not require exceptional financing from concessional foreign sources.

Exports are expected to increase by about 2 percent in 1998, despite the expected softening of international copper prices. The increase is likely to come from higher gold and cashmere exports. Imports could increase by 6 percent, resulting in a larger balance of trade and current account deficit of about 11 percent of GDP in 1998. The inflows of official concessional financial assistance already in the pipeline will cover the current account deficit. Mongolia's external debt, all of it long-term and on concessional terms, is just over half of GDP. Given the concessional nature of the debt, the servicing requirement is well within prudential limits at less than 10 percent of exports.

POLICY AND DEVELOPMENT ISSUES

The government has successfully introduced a broad range of reforms that are achieving macroeconomic stability. It has undertaken structural reforms that are encouraging private sector-led growth, implemented a bank restructuring and reform program, is streamlining public administration, has accelerated privatization programs, is implementing tax reforms, and has made its trade regime such that it is one of the most liberal in the world. With the major structural reforms either completed or well under way, the government is now beginning to address the issues pertinent to long-term development prospects and poverty reduction. This will require identifying Mongolia's comparative advantages and adopting policies that will encourage private sector-led investment to build on these comparative advantages.

About 36 percent of the population, mostly in the provincial capitals, is living below the poverty line. Poverty has increased following the withdrawal of budgetary subsidies and the closure of SOEs. The government has initiated some labor-intensive public works programs to mitigate the unemployment and poverty situation, but rapid, sustainable economic growth and the restructuring of industrial capacity are required to solve the two related problems of unemployment and poverty. At present, however, the agencies involved in poverty alleviation lack the ability to coordinate their efforts, thereby making the formulation of a comprehensive poverty alleviation strategy difficult. Given its resource constraints and the substantial number of people living in poverty, Mongolia cannot afford inefficiency in its poverty alleviation efforts, and cooperation across agencies would facilitate the targeting of specific goods and social services for poverty alleviation.

CENTRAL ASIAN REPUBLICS

Kazakstan

Kyrgyz Republic

Uzbekistan

KAZAKSTAN

While Kazakstan's postindependence economic trauma may have come to an end, much deeper reforms in policy and governance structures are now needed to accelerate growth. In addition, prudent management of the country's natural resource wealth will be critical.

RECENT TRENDS AND PROSPECTS

Following independence, Kazakstan was pre-occupied with crisis management. On the dissolution of the former Soviet Union (FSU), Kazakstan's trade collapsed; income support from Moscow was severed; and its inherited economic and legal institutions, forged within a centrally planned system of production and distribution, were completely ill-suited to its new circumstances. Moreover, as a fledgling state Kazakstan lacked many of the institutions of modern government.

Against this backdrop, the country's output collapsed, and by 1996 output was only half what it had been five years earlier. Output declines were arrested in 1996. In that year GDP growth of 0.5 percent was recorded, and in 1997 moderate GDP growth of 2.0 percent was achieved. Two years of positive output growth have buttressed confidence in the view that the era of postindependence economic depression may now have ended. However, the economy is still narrowly based: a few export-oriented sectors—oil and gas and some nonferrous metals—dominate. These sectors have benefited from the shifts in the terms of trade since independence, and the bulk of foreign direct investment (FDI) has been directed toward these sectors.

Agriculture depends heavily on rainfed grain. While wheat and related crops have now recovered from a poor harvest in 1995, to date, signs of any underlying growth in productivity are few. Most crops other than grain show continuing production declines, but at more moderate rates than in earlier years. The reported livestock population has also declined, but with the ongoing privatization of farms some underreporting of livestock populations is possible.

Industry has tended to move away from processing raw materials toward primary, extractive activity. This trend reflects the shifts in the terms of trade that have occurred since independence, the cessation of subsidies from the FSU that had sought to encourage industrialization, and the concurrent collapse of traditional markets and supply relationships with FSU enterprises. For example, while the production of metals has grown, the machinery sector's output has declined. Similarly, the production of woolen textiles has contracted by almost twice as much as the production of raw wool. The oil sector, however, has exhibited considerable expansion. In recent years, investment in oil and gas has represented approximately one third of all FDI. Fuel and energy now account for just under 40 percent of total industrial output, up from 15.5 percent in 1990.

There is evidence that the service sectors are buoyant. In some urban centers, such as Almaty and Shimkent, the number of retail trade outlets and restaurants has increased markedly and a significant number of new hotels and service centers for vehicles, appliances, and computers have sprung up. The FSU economy had severely restricted the development of many of these services.

Figure 2.2 Growth of Money Supply (M2) and Consumer Price Index: Kazakstan, 1991-1997

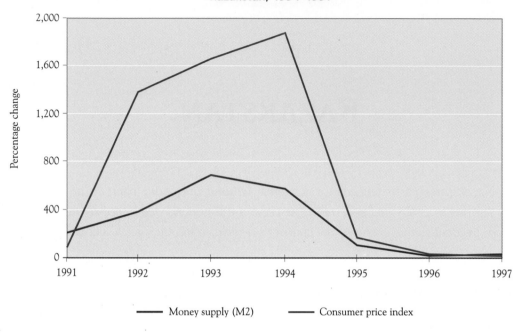

Sources: Asian Development Bank (1997b) and staff estimates.

In mid-1997, 4.7 percent of the registered labor force was unemployed; however, a much larger number of people are thought to be unofficially unemployed or underemployed. In addition, real wages have fallen dramatically, and the payment in-kind of many wage obligations reflects the weakening of traditional payments systems. These in-kind payments are often of little utility to the workers and their families, thereby reducing disposable income severely. Wage arrears running to many months are also common: in mid-1997 the wage arrears of state enterprises were about $600 million, which posed serious political problems for the government.

A deterioration in the social indicators of well-being reflects the extent of economic dislocation. Estimates suggest a sharp increase in both the incidence and depth of poverty. In 1996 more than one third of households lived below the official poverty line. Pensioners and children have been particularly badly affected by the weakening of social support. Rapid inflation and a decline in the real value of pensions have destroyed the savings of the elderly, while the health, nutritional, and educational status of children in poor households has worsened dramatically as public services have contracted along with the resources available to the government.

The need to mitigate hardship has led to demands for the government to do more, but at the same time the resources available to the government have shrunk. As a result, maintaining fiscal balances has proven extremely difficult: in 1997 the deficit was over 4 percent of GDP. Efforts to collect revenues have been hampered by the poor economic situation of larger enterprises in the formal, registered economy and administrative difficulties in taxing smaller enterprises in the informal economy. In addition, the need to create public sector institutions in the wake of independence has strained expenditure control systems.

The government has, however, made significant headway in controlling inflation. In 1997 inflation was 20.4 percent, but in 1994 it was almost 2,000 percent. This reduction in inflation has been the outcome of much tighter monetary control and an improving fiscal position. Financial sector reforms have also helped promote monetary stability. Some banks have been restructured, others have had their licenses revoked, and the weakest banks have been allowed to fail. With lower inflation, capital market development has proved easier. Securities transactions have deepened, interbank credit and settlement systems for commercial banks have been developed, and investors are eager to acquire Treasury bills.

Large trade and current account deficits persist. In 1997 the current account deficit stood at more than 4 percent of GDP. The development of new markets for Kazakstan's output has been slow, and the Russian Federation remains as Kazakstan's largest trading partner. The lack of restructuring and reinvestment in farms and state enterprises and Kazakstan's locational disadvantages thwart the penetration of new markets. Inward capital flows, especially those related to the large foreign investments in oil and gas, mining, and metallurgy, continue to finance current account deficits.

Over the next two years, output growth of 3 percent is achievable. The oil and gas sector is expected to continue to show strength, but the current dependence on pipelines controlled by the Russian Federation restricts large increases in export sales of oil and gas. The construction of other pipelines to markets either in Europe or in the People's Republic of China is planned, but considerable political and administrative problems need to be resolved before construction begins, oil flows, and public revenues rise. Output from the minerals sector should also increase.

The squeeze on public resources will continue during the next few years, especially given the need to restore an adequate social safety net; to clear wage, pension, and social assistance arrears; to provide support for pension reform; and to finance a broader program of public capital investment. The last item is particularly important. The failure to increase public investment, particularly for infrastructure rehabilitation, will increasingly place farms and enterprises at a competitive disadvantage. The decision to move the capital from Almaty in the southeast to Akmola in the north-central region will place further pressure on public resources, as this relocation has necessitated large-scale construction of new public buildings, residences, and infrastructure facilities in a comparatively short period. As a result of these fiscal pressures, the fiscal deficit is expected to increase to more than 5 percent of GDP in 1998.

Although fiscal policy will ease to some extent, the government is likely to maintain a tight monetary stance. As a consequence, inflation is expected to continue to moderate, and could be as low as 10 percent in 1998. Faster economic growth is, however, anticipated to make further containment of the current account deficit difficult. As a proportion of GDP it is likely to remain at around its 1997 level.

POLICY AND DEVELOPMENT ISSUES

In the short run, the main challenge for economic policy is to consolidate the progress made toward macroeconomic stabilization while providing strong foundations for future growth. At the same time, the government must develop safety net mechanisms that can assist the most needy and ease some of the pain of poverty.

Future progress on macroeconomic stabilization will rest on three pillars, namely: the government must persist with its anti-inflationary monetary stance, it must strengthen its revenue mobilization efforts so that fiscal balances improve, and it must take steps to support the development of a modern and robust financial system. The banking sector remains weak and unable to provide attractive savings facilities and meaningful intermediation for loanable funds. It also has limited capacity for commercial risk assessment for evaluating loan portfolios.

Achieving sustainable growth over the longer run will require restructuring of and reinvestment in the operations of farms and firms. In most sectors, enterprises are handicapped by a set of interlocking disadvantages: they continue to operate with obsolete equipment from the Soviet era for which spare parts are often difficult to obtain; managers who possess basic business skills are in short supply; most enterprises are heavily indebted, owing suppliers and the government (for tax payments and pension contributions); deteriorating utility and infrastructure services, especially electricity, hamper enterprises' operations; and enterprises lack financing for either trade or investment credit. To date, privatization has resulted in the formal transfer of some assets, but not the development of entrepreneurs willing to take risks, new investment, and competitive markets.

Unreconstructed enterprises are a source of considerable inefficiency for the economy and jeopardize fiscal stability. In 1996 government subsidies to loss-making firms amounted to 2 to 3 percent of GDP; however, it has demonstrated some willingness to tackle this complex problem. It has shut down some nonviable operations, and retrench-ments have occurred in others as part of restructur-ing. Nevertheless, more determined efforts are needed. While Kazakstan's location means that for-eign investors are unlikely to be attracted to more than a few sectors, the role of foreign investment in providing needed capital and technological, mana-gerial, and institutional know-how is still likely to be important. However, even where foreign take-over of enterprises has occurred, effective restruc-turing has been fraught with difficulties. Above all, foreign investors require a predictable legal and policy environment, which in turn necessitates even-handedness and consistency in implementing rules and regulations. Without improved governance structures, particularly in government-private sector relationships, kindling growth is likely to prove hard.

While natural resources will be an important future source of income for Kazakstan, the manage-ment of these resources will present challenges. Looking to the longer term, the development of manufacturing industries often seems to be prob-lematic in resource-rich economies like Kazakstan, partly because an abundance of natural resources automatically tends to shift the terms of trade against the manufacturing sector. To the extent that the manufacturing sector is where most productivity gains are realized, economic dynamism is then lost.

In addition, large resource rents often seem to present difficult problems for public sector manage-ment, especially in economies where governance capacities are weak. Despite these difficulties, some economies have managed their natural resource wealth well. These economies have actively pro-moted economic diversification, partly through pro-cessing before export, but also through policies of openness to FDI and trade and wise investment of their resource windfalls. They have struck a judicious balance between investment and consumption uses of rents. Kazakstan could benefit from looking at these experiences.

Kazakstan faces a number of other difficult challenges. For a landlocked and remote country such as Kazakstan, regional transport and commu-nications systems are particularly important. Regional cooperation aimed at harmonizing and coordinating investment in transboundary trans-portation and distribution would be one way to ease the constraints of geography. Regional cooperation might also help to develop markets, making invest-ment feasible in sectors that might otherwise not be viable. While the difficulty of overcoming the dis-advantages of physical isolation should not be underestimated, the process of integration in the global economy is likely to be easier if integration starts close to home.

KYRGYZ REPUBLIC

Following severe economic dislocation, growth in the Kyrgyz Republic has recovered, supported by growth in both the agriculture and industrial sectors. However, the transition to market institutions required for long-term growth still has a long way to go.

RECENT TRENDS AND PROSPECTS

The breakup of the former Soviet Union brought political freedom to the Kyrgyz Republic, but also dislocated the production, trade, and financial networks on which its centrally planned economy rested. As a result, GDP declined by about 50 percent from 1990 through 1995, external trade was disrupted, inflation accelerated, and fiscal deficits increased sharply. In response to these difficulties, the government adopted a comprehensive program of macroeconomic stabilization and structural reforms. It is now committed to developing an economy that is based much more on market institutions and much less on state direction.

After six difficult years, some signs of economic recovery are now apparent. Real GDP has grown for two consecutive years: by 5.6 percent in 1996, and by an impressive 10.4 percent in 1997. Solid growth in the agriculture sector has helped this turnaround in economic performance. Agriculture is the largest sector in the Kyrgyz economy, accounting for around 50 percent of GDP. In the past two years, agricultural output has grown by an average of 10 percent, assisted not only by favorable weather conditions, but also by economic reforms. These reforms have allowed private sector farmers to respond to market incentives more easily, and despite a continuing lack of essential farm inputs, the output of key crops has increased in response to growing urban demands.

The spurt in GDP growth in 1997 was largely due to a leap in industrial production, which expanded by a massive 46.8 percent. Much of this is attributed to the commencement of production from the newly completed Kumtor gold mine. Stronger industrial growth has also been assisted by a recovery in food processing activity. Input supplies to food processing have expanded with the growth in agricultural production. Demand for industrial output has also increased as the economies of former Soviet Union partners have begun to stabilize.

Compared with agricultural and industrial production, activity in services seems to have been somewhat sluggish. Official statistics estimate the output growth in services to be about 1 percent in 1996. However, measuring the output of services is somewhat difficult, and some market activity probably goes unrecorded. In particular, the number of private businesses engaged in the urban retail trade and in other services has expanded rapidly in recent years, but is underreported in official statistics.

Despite recent output growth, the employment situation shows few signs of improvement. The overall unemployment rate at the beginning of 1997 is estimated to have been about 22 percent. Difficult labor market conditions, exacerbated by the deteriorating quality and delivery of social services and the erosion of the social safety net, have increased the incidence of poverty. The proportion of households below the official poverty line rose from 40 percent in 1993 to 49 percent in 1996. Those in

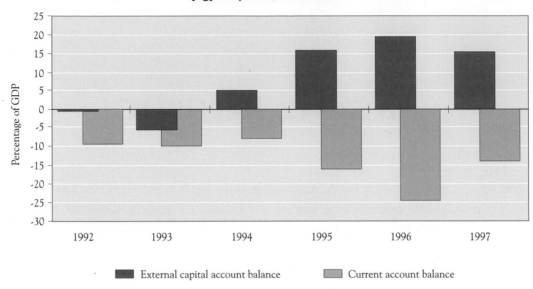

**Figure 2.3 External Capital and Current Account Balances:
Kyrgyz Republic, 1992-1997**

■ External capital account balance   ☐ Current account balance

Sources: Asian Development Bank (1997e) and staff estimates.

rural areas, pensioners, young people, and those in large families have been affected particularly badly.

Economic expansion has eased fiscal pressures, and fiscal consolidation is proceeding slowly, but steadily. Budgetary and civil service reforms have contributed to reduced government spending. The authorities have also taken measures to strengthen tax administration and increase tax revenues. As a consequence, in 1997 the budget deficit fell to 4.5 percent of GDP, down from 5.6 percent in 1996.

Inflation has improved markedly, declining to 25.5 percent in 1997 from nearly 300 percent in 1994. The successful containment of monetary growth helped to subdue domestic inflationary pressures, as did greater nominal exchange rate stability in 1997, which followed a sharp depreciation in 1996.

External balances remain fragile, although some improvement is detectable. The importation of capital goods needed to develop the Kumtor mine has, to some extent, exacerbated current account deficits, but structural weaknesses are also apparent. In 1997, despite a slowdown in capital goods imports, the current account deficit was still around 11 percent of GDP. To finance its current account deficits, the Kyrgyz Republic continues to rely largely on official transfers. Notwithstanding the Kumtor

project, foreign direct investment remains small. One reason for this is that the country faces a competitive disadvantage compared with its neighbors, as it lacks Kazakstan's large energy and mineral resources and Uzbekistan's larger markets.

Since 1990, output and incomes have fallen precipitously. While the recent growth is welcome, the country still has a long way to go to restore previous standards of living. The potential for growth in the medium term is good. Output from the Kumtor mine project should again bolster growth in 1998 and 1999, and reforms in the agriculture sector should improve productivity. Overall economic growth of around 7 percent per year is expected. Improvement on other fronts is also likely, namely, a steady reduction in the fiscal deficit through 1999; more disciplined monetary control resulting in reduced inflation rates; and a decrease in the current account deficit, partly as a result of revenues from the Kumtor mine.

POLICY DEVELOPMENT AND ISSUES

Agriculture is the most important sector of the Kyrgyz economy and is likely to remain as such for the foreseeable future. Productivity gains in agriculture will, above all, determine the economy's medium-term development prospects. Accordingly, the authorities must make determined efforts to address the pronounced policy and institutional inefficiencies that still exist in the structure of agricultural production and organization. While they have made some progress, a long agenda of unfinished reforms remains to be dealt with. In the medium term, agricultural policy and institutional reforms should focus on developing the legal framework for private farms and privatizing the remaining state and collective farms. Promoting the efficiency of the supply of inputs will also be necessary to alleviate input shortages. Other measures that would help agriculture include improving efficiency in the use of irrigation water and providing agricultural credit on a commercial basis.

The state has retained either full or partial ownership of the key medium and large industrial enterprises. These firms are, by and large, moribund. Inefficient enterprises survive only through subsidized loans and income transfers from the govern-

ment. The ability of these firms to compete in international markets is limited, and they show little institutional or technological dynamism. Enterprise reform is thus essential, both to stabilize macroeconomic balances and, more generally, to promote a healthy market economy. Where enterprises can be maintained as going concerns, they should be sold off in such a way that the state receives a fair price for its assets. Where enterprises are effectively insolvent and are beyond resuscitation, they should be closed with the recovery of whatever salvage value remains. To win the political and social consensus for these bold measures, some kind of social safety net is likely to be needed. However, safety net provisions must be well targeted; kept within the government's fiscal means; and, to the extent possible, support the development of human capabilities. Failure to take tough decisions on state enterprise reform will not only deprive the truly needy of resources, but will jeopardize everyone's future living standards.

UZBEKISTAN

While the worst of Uzbekistan's macroeconomic troubles seem to be over and growth has become more broadly based, domestic savings must increase if the country is to narrow its large resource gap. In addition, foreign exchange management remains weak.

RECENT TRENDS AND PROSPECTS

Like the other Central Asian republics, Uzbekistan has had to cope with severe economic dislocation since it gained independence from the former Soviet Union in 1991. Following the dissolution of the Soviet Union, Uzbekistan's output declined, external trade was disrupted, and inflation and fiscal deficits rose sharply. In response to these difficulties the government adopted macroeconomic stabilization and structural reform programs whose objectives have been to contain the decline in output and to lay the foundations for future growth. These initiatives now appear to be bearing some fruit.

After persistent declines in output from 1990 through 1995, the economy showed tentative signs of recovery in 1996. Economic performance in 1997 was even more encouraging: GDP grew by 5.2 percent. The recovery in income was reasonably broadly based. Agricultural output increased by about 5.8 percent in 1997 following a sharp contraction in 1996. Production of cotton, the country's principal agricultural crop and export commodity, expanded by about 9 percent. Industrial production also picked up following the start-up of several large joint ventures. In aggregate, industrial output grew by 6.5 percent in 1997. Although official estimates of output growth in the service sector do not exist, scattered evidence suggests a healthy expansion of activity. Private sector activity in urban retail

trading, restaurants, bars, hotels, and taxi services seems to have grown significantly.

Uzbekistan's official unemployment rate was less than 1 percent in 1997, but this number masks considerable labor market dislocation. A large number of enterprise employees have been on forced leave without pay, and many other unemployed people have not been officially registered. In rural areas alone, estimates indicate that hidden unemployment amounted to more than 1 million people in mid-1997.

During 1997 the government continued its efforts to mobilize revenues by undertaking new tax measures. The most important measures included raising the basic value-added tax from 17 to 18 percent; increasing property, land, and mining taxes by 50 percent; introducing a new ecological tax on the assets of all nonagricultural enterprises; and introducing a tax on enterprises' gross sales. On the expenditure side, the government continued to reduce its spending on defense, state administration, and water and electricity subsidies. As a result of these measures, Uzbekistan's consolidated state budget deficit was about 3 percent of GDP in 1997. Despite fiscal constraints, the government has earmarked additional budgetary resources for capital expenditures and social services. It views the completion of some public sector investment projects as crucial for broader economic recovery, and remains committed to maintaining the delivery of social services and an effective social safety net.

In recent years, monetary discipline has been lacking. The broad money stock (M2) expanded by a staggering 114 percent in 1996, which far exceeded the government's target. Money supply targets were breached largely as a consequence of large state loans to the agriculture sector. However, in 1997 some monetary tightening occurred, and the growth of the broad money stock slowed to an estimated 24 percent.

Inflation is declining steadily, albeit from an extremely high level in earlier years. In 1997 inflation fell to 30 percent from more than 64 percent in 1996. The government's tighter fiscal stance, an expansion in agricultural output, and a general easing of shortages and bottlenecks all helped to reduce inflation.

After difficulties in 1996, the balance-of-payments situation improved slightly in 1997. The current account deficit declined from 7.9 percent of GDP in 1996 to about 6 percent of GDP in 1997. Despite the overall improvement in the current account, a deficit persists in the merchandise trade account. Uzbekistan's official external debt is climbing steadily, reflecting the persistent underlying current account deficits. At the end of 1997 total debt was estimated to be $2.8 billion, with $0.5 billion accumulated in 1997 alone. The ratio of the stock of debt (at the end of 1997) to GDP was about 25 percent. As most debt is of a medium- or long-term nature, Uzbekistan's debt-service ratio is currently manageable, and in 1997 was 10 percent.

Uzbekistan's rich natural resource endowments (oil, natural gas, and gold) and its relatively well-developed human skills base are its two major assets. Harnessed appropriately, these can provide a solid foundation for future growth. With an improving policy environment, GDP growth of between 4 and 5 percent per year is attainable over the next two years. Weakened fiscal resolve or reduced monetary discipline would, however, undermine this potential. Projections indicate that export growth is likely to pick up in the next two years, thereby easing the trade deficit. Current account deficits will decline slowly over the medium term as production of energy and of manufactured exports increases, but at the same time steady import growth is also envisaged. Unemployment will remain a concern as the deepening of agricultural reform and the restructuring of enterprises will lead to the closure of many inefficient collective farms and industrial enterprises, and thus to job losses.

POLICY AND DEVELOPMENT ISSUES

Macroeconomic stabilization is a prerequisite for restoring sustained growth of productivity, employment, and income. Although Uzbekistan has made some progress in moving toward macroeconomic stabilization, the stabilization process remains partial and fragile. Currently savings remain low, and this has created a large savings-investment gap. The financing of this gap through foreign sources on a recurrent basis is not sustainable, as eventually it would pose serious difficulties for the balance-of-payments situation. However, in the absence of substantial foreign support, a large savings-investment gap will persist.

Thus policies that promote saving are needed to ensure a more stable macroeconomic environment in the medium term, and a number of measures are required to support saving and mobilize domestic resources. First, the government must build upon past achievements in reducing inflation. This will require somewhat more disciplined monetary policies than it has pursued in the past, in particular, it must try harder to restrain bank liquidity. The government should also contain monetary financing of its deficits. The Central Bank, for its part, should ensure that its refinancing rates move in line with inflation to ensure positive real interest rates. In addition, mobilization of private savings will require deeper financial sector reforms.

While the authorities have taken the initial steps to establish a modern banking system, it remains underdeveloped and weak: many banks have limited experience in commercial operations, and rural financial institutions are still largely used as conduits for extending subsidized government loans to the agriculture sector. Much work needs to be done to strengthen banking regulations and supervision, which will require broad institutional strengthening and capacity building. In particular, the managerial and technical capacities of those who work in the financial sector must be improved. In addition to these measures, banks saddled with poor loan portfolios will have to be restructured. Banks that are insolvent and whose prospects for improvement are few should be closed, but where viable

Figure 2.4 Composition of GDP: Uzbekistan, 1991 and 1996

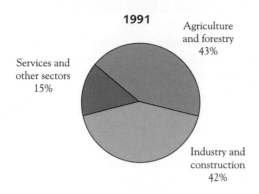

1991

Agriculture and forestry 43%

Services and other sectors 15%

Industry and construction 42%

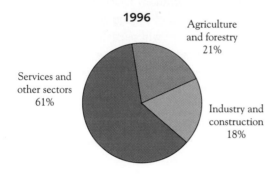

1996

Agriculture and forestry 21%

Services and other sectors 61%

Industry and construction 18%

Source: Asian Development Bank (1997g).

concerns face liquidity difficulties, the government should consider such actions as mergers and recapitalization. Over the longer term the authorities should pursue the development of broader and deeper securities markets, but the immediate priority should be to build a robust banking system that can allocate resources efficiently and monitor their use capably.

Increased public savings would also help close Uzbekistan's resource gap. One way in which the government might increase its revenues is to reduce the scope for tax exemptions, which are currently quite broad. More generally, revenues would be bolstered by further strengthening of tax administration and collection. Given the government's commitment to maintaining public expenditures on social services and protection for vulnerable groups, it will have to control current expenditures by (i) restraining the growth of public sector wages, including undertaking civil service reform to reorient

and downsize the bureaucracy; (ii) phasing out remaining subsidies through administered price adjustments; (iii) limiting transfers to loss-incurring state-owned enterprises; and (iv) targeting social protection benefits more accurately. Privatizing state-owned enterprises' assets would also help the government's financial situation, both on its current and capital accounts.

In addition to taking the measures needed to close the resource gap, Uzbekistan should continue the broader process of structural reform necessary to create competitive market conditions. The government has already made progress in such areas as liberalizing prices, privatizing small-scale enterprises, and opening the service sector to private activity. However, the large-scale reform agenda under way still needs to be fulfilled. In addition to the reforms needed in the financial sector, the government will need to devote special attention to reforms in agriculture, foreign trade systems, and exchange settlement procedures.

Agriculture plays a pivotal role in the overall economy, accounting for 21 percent of GDP, 60 percent of exports, and 40 percent of employment. Currently sectoral inefficiencies are constraining rapid and sustainable agricultural growth, namely: cotton yields have declined since 1991, and grain yields are low by international standards; farms owe substantial debts to their suppliers and to their employees; efficiency is unlikely to improve without appropriate incentive and support structures; and the state still plays much too dominant a role in the sector.

The steps the government should take to promote a more efficient agriculture sector include phasing out the state order systems for cotton and wheat. In addition, it should dismantle the monopolies in domestic marketing, processing, and foreign distribution of agricultural commodities. At the enterprise level farms need to be restructured. Farmers need security of land tenure as an incentive to invest in land. Also needed for improved farm efficiency are pricing and management systems that would encourage better utilization of water resources.

A liberalized foreign trade system and a flexible exchange rate regime are among the major objectives of the structural reform program. However, in the face of increasing balance-of-payments pressures, in late 1996 the authorities introduced a number of restrictions on foreign trade and exchange to protect international reserves. These policy actions have resulted in a breach of the program targets under the standby arrangement provided by the International Monetary Fund. As a result, the Fund suspended disbursements under the standby arrangement in December 1996. As the authorities continued to maintain the foreign exchange restrictions in 1997, the parallel market exchange rate continued to depreciate more rapidly than the official exchange rate. This led to a further widening of the spread between the two exchange rates from about 60 percent in January 1997 to some 140 percent in December 1997.

Foreign exchange restrictions have three adverse effects. First, they tend to result in a general misallocation of resources; in particular, an over-valuation of the local currency tends to divert resources from the traded to the nontraded sector of the economy. Second, restrictions significantly reduce the private sector's access to foreign currency. This hinders domestic private investment and inflows of foreign direct investment. Third, multiple currency practices, which have emerged following the foreign exchange restrictions, contribute to growing speculative activities in the exchange market. This leads to inefficiency in the utilization of scarce foreign exchange resources. For all these reasons, the government should consider removing the trade and exchange restrictions, re-unifying the exchange markets, and restoring convertibility on the current account. Ultimately, foreign exchange controls may be as likely to exacerbate balance-of-payments difficulties as to ease them.

SOUTHEAST ASIA

Cambodia

Indonesia

Lao People's Democratic Republic

Malaysia

Myanmar

Philippines

Thailand

Viet Nam

CAMBODIA

Cambodia's economy has exhibited a general slowdown in growth. Areas that require atten-tion include tax reform, budgetary discipline, administration of the Foreign Investment Law, and poverty alleviation. In addition, to promote capital formation the authorities need to de-dollarize the economy and reform the financial sector.

RECENT TRENDS AND PROSPECTS

The economy's performance in 1997 was far from promising. GDP growth was 2 percent, the in-flation rate was 9.1 percent, and budget revenues were 9.3 percent of GDP. These numbers fell con-siderably short of the government's targets of 7 per-cent real GDP growth, an inflation rate of less than 5 percent, and budget revenues of 10 percent of GDP. Agriculture, which is the largest sector in the economy, did show a respectable growth rate of 4.9 percent in 1997, after growing at only 1.8 percent in 1996. However, both the industry and service sectors experienced drastic slowdowns, reporting 0.6 percent and -0.4 percent growth, respectively, for 1997. The labor force grew by 3 percent in 1997, which translated into a need for around 135,000 new jobs, 100,000 of them in rural areas. The agri-culture sector absorbed some 75 percent of the workforce.

Trade reform and exchange rate liberalization have had positive effects on trade volumes since 1992. Both export and import volumes reported respectable increases from 1992 to 1995, but expe-rienced negative growth rates from 1995 to 1997. The trade deficit was around $388 million in 1997. Foreign direct investment amounted to about $240 million in 1996, but substantially fell in 1997. The main areas of investment include the textile and

garment industries, construction, and tourism. The recent declines in trade volume and investment re-flect the general slowdown in economic activity. The 1997 national budget targeted a shift from defense and security expenditures to social expenditures, while the expenditure to GDP ratio declined to 13.9 percent. Operational outlays by the civil admin-istration, which include the bulk of social spending, were targeted to increase by 0.5 percent of GDP; however, actual social expenditures decreased by 0.18 percent of GDP compared with 1996. Overall expenditures still reflect strong demand from the defense and security sectors. In 1998 Cambodia will need $21 million to fund elections, of which more than 60 percent will have to be financed by foreign assistance.

Increasing political instability in the coalition government culminated in the violent political events of early July 1997, when Prime Minister Hun Sen toppled his co-prime minister, Prince Norodom Ranariddh. The July event severely disrupted econo-mic performance and slowed the economy's regional integration. Not only did tourism slump, but more important, trade and customs duty receipts fell sharply (customs duty receipts provide, on average, about 70 percent of annual government tax rev-enues). To make things worse, some bilateral donors suspended their programs and Cambodia's planned membership in the Association of Southeast Asian

Nations was put on hold. In addition, the International Monetary Fund suspended budgetary support because of the government's failure to meet formally agreed performance conditionalities, particularly as concerned the management of nontax proceeds from logging and other forestry practices.

If confidence in the Cambodian economy by the international community and domestically is restored fairly rapidly following new elections, GDP growth may reach as much as 3.5 percent in 1998 and 7 percent in 1999. Inflation is projected to rise to 9.6 percent in 1998, but to drop to 6 percent in 1999.

CRITICAL ISSUES IN SHORT-TERM ECONOMIC MANAGEMENT

The major critical issue in short-term economic management is the need for tax reform and budgetary discipline. Fiscal policy has to aim at managing the government's budget more efficiently through restructured revenue and expenditure measures, so that the authorities can meet budget targets without increasing the money supply. From the revenue side, the main thrust of fiscal policy has been tax policy. By adopting the Law on Taxation in February 1997, the government intended to expand its revenue base by further improving tax administration and by introducing a value-added tax. In this context, the main priority at this point is to speed up the implementation of this new law. Another priority relates to discipline with respect to the approved budget: the implementation of the 1997 budget did not achieve its main targets. In addition, the weak budget position will undermine efforts to contain inflation.

POLICY AND DEVELOPMENT ISSUES

Financing its development will inarguably be Cambodia's most important objective in years to come. About 40 percent of government expenditure is financed by foreign aid, which amounts to $200 million to $300 million a year. In September, the International Monetary Fund decided to freeze a $120 million, three-year Enhanced Structural Adjustment Facility program to the country. Hun Sen's takeover also led the United States to suspend all but humanitarian aid and Germany to cut all assistance, both of which reduced total foreign aid

by 10 percent. Thus restoring international confidence in the country is the key to Cambodia's recovery. Nevertheless, political commitments, economic development, and domestic policies to implement programs that ensure more effective management of natural resources, especially forestry, would immediately lead to marked improvements in national income.

Financial Sector Reform and Foreign Investment Policy

Further reform of the financial sector is essential to promote capital formation by increasing domestic savings and investment. It will also raise the potential for more effective monetary policy as increased formal transactions through banks enhance the economy's responsiveness to monetary instruments. At the same time, the government must accelerate de-dollarization of the economy by continuing to denominate all its transactions in riels and restoring confidence in the currency through a commitment to both macroeconomic and political stability.

The authorities also need to address the lack of banks in rural areas. While existing rural credit programs by nongovernment organizations have proved useful, they are limited in both geographical coverage and the scope of local participation. In addition, interest rates in some nongovernment organization programs are based more on an estimation of clients' ability to pay than on market determined rates of interest. The development of a sustainable rural credit system will require liberalization of interest rates. Furthermore, the government needs to strengthen Central Bank supervision of commercial bank lending practices, particularly in the areas of credit risk analysis and debt recovery. In general, increased coverage of rural credit must be based on sustainable financial service provision to the poor and must be consistent with national financial stability. However, if the Central Bank is to take on the necessary supervisory tasks, it must first completely end its direct involvement in the commercial banking sector, and then introduce appropriate market-oriented monetary instruments, such as Treasury bills.

Given Cambodia's current stage of economic development, external financing will have to play a much more active role than at present. While political stability; social security; sound institutional, financial, and legal frameworks; macroeconomic stability; and appropriate physical and social infrastructures will gradually have to be instilled in the economy, a more direct way to improve the domestic investment environment is major improvement in the administration of the Foreign Investment Law. The latter incorporates liberal provisions for profit remittances, exemptions from duties, limited tax holidays, and a ceiling of 9 percent corporate tax on foreign investors. However, to be effective it requires strengthening through further simplification of approval procedures and elimination of inconsistencies pertaining to royalties. In addition, the authorities should develop a monitoring system to track everything from the number of queries by foreign investors, to the number of formal applications and the number of approved investments that are actually implemented. The monitoring system would involve regular reporting on the operation of foreign investment policy so that any necessary changes could be implemented efficiently.

Poverty Alleviation

Cambodia must focus on alleviating poverty: 30 percent of the population fall below the poverty line. In developing Asia, Cambodia has one of the lowest life expectancies at birth, one of the highest infant mortality rates, and lowest calorie intake per person, facts which all indicate the existence of widespread poverty. Implementation of the reforms already mentioned will certainly promote economic growth, and thereby contribute to alleviating poverty, but policies that directly address poverty are also needed. These efforts would include providing basic social support services, improving access to basic education and training, and creating job opportunities.

To facilitate the targeting of poverty reduction initiatives the government must rely on external assistance. Given its current fiscal constraints, without any external assistance the government has little capacity to identify and design effective delivery mechanisms to protect vulnerable groups. The facts are daunting: even with an annual growth rate of 7 percent, the target growth rate for GDP set by the government, the economy may not be able to absorb more than 250,000 low-skilled, unemployed workers and simultaneously create jobs for 135,000 new entrants into the labor force each year. Neither could it absorb the 30,000 workers likely to be displaced as a result of initial public sector restructuring. The task of poverty alleviation is going to be long and arduous, but it is certainly one that the government cannot afford to postpone.

INDONESIA

Despite its sound macroeconomic fundamentals, Indonesia suffered some of the worst conse-quences of the recent regional financial crisis. As a result, Indonesia is pursuing a comprehen-sive and credible economic reform program to address the economy's various weaknesses. The risk of stagflation in 1998 remains real. In the long run, one of the pressing politico-economic problems that the country will have to address is the economic disparity that is prevalent both among income groups as well as between regions.

RECENT TRENDS AND PROSPECTS

In terms of the extent of its currency depreciation, Indonesia is the most serious casualty of Asia's financial crisis. This is paradoxical, given the sound-ness of Indonesia's economic position in 1996 and the economy's good performance during the first half of 1997, which was supported by tight fiscal policies, prudent monetary policies, and an adequate ex-change rate policy. The end result is that the crisis that has afflicted Southeast Asia since mid-1997 has radically changed Indonesia's economic position, with the rupiah suffering a severe depreciation of 80 percent between July 1997 and January 1998. As the private sector's creditworthiness fell concomitantly, many foreign creditors stopped renewing debt to Indonesian companies and capital inflows declined, thereby putting further pressure on the exchange rate.

The strong economic performance before the crisis was not, however, without its problems, and the apparent creditworthiness of Indonesian borrow-ers, coupled with low interest foreign commercial loans, increased their exposure to unhedged short-term external debt. The growth of non-oil exports had slowed, and oil exports grew sluggishly. The rupiah began to weaken in the second week of July 1997, immediately following the floating of the Thai baht. GDP growth for 1997 declined to slightly less than 5 percent. Growth in the manufacturing sec-tor slowed to 6 percent because of liquidity con-straints; the drought brought about by El Niño hampered agricultural performance, causing agricul-tural prices to rise; and at the same time, the forest fires in Sumatra and Kalimantan imposed severe costs on the economy and reduced tourism, the country's third largest export industry.

The steep decline in the rupiah's exchange rate since July 1997 affected the inflation rate. The con-sumer price index climbed 11.6 percent year-on-year by December (an annual average of 6.6 percent) de-spite tight monetary policy. Following the currency's depreciation, the prime lending rate reached 30 per-cent, compared with 20 percent in 1996.

Exports grew by 11.2 percent in 1997. Imports, after registering a growth rate of about 8 percent in 1996, decelerated to 4.8 percent in 1997. Most of the decline was in consumption goods. Capital goods imports slowed little, given the persistence of strong investment until mid-1997. Imports of intermedi-ate goods also showed little in the way of a slow-down. Notable exceptions were synthetic fibers and some chemical products that are essential for the textiles industry, primarily because domestic textiles production increased. The current account showed a reduced deficit of 2.7 percent of GDP, and total

Table 2.7 Major Economic Indicators: Indonesia, 1995-1999
(percent)

Item	1995	1996	1997	1998	1999
Gross domestic product growth	8.2	8.0	4.6	-3.0	1.0
Gross domestic investment/GDP	31.9	30.8	31.6	25.0	27.0
Gross domestic savings/GDP	30.6	30.2	31.0	24.0	25.0
Inflation rate (consumer price index)	9.5	7.9	6.6	20.0	15.0
Money supply (M2) growth	27.6	29.6	27.7	25.0	26.1
Fiscal balance/GDP	0.4	0.8	-0.2	0.0	3.0
Merchandise exports growth	18.0	5.8	11.2	5.0	7.0
Merchandise imports growth	26.6	8.1	4.8	-5.0	2.0
Current account balance/GDP	-3.2	-3.4	-2.7	-1.6	2.5
Debt service/exports	30.9	29.5	30.0	28.0	30.0

Sources: Bank Indonesia data, Bank Indonesia (1997), International Monetary Fund (1998), World Bank (1997d), and staff estimates.

external debt was 61 percent of GDP in 1997, of which the private sector accounted for half. The debt-service ratio was approximately 30 percent. International reserves are estimated to be $20 billion, including $3 billion drawn from the International Monetary Fund (IMF) standby facility in November 1997. In 1996 foreign reserves amounted to 5 months worth of imports, and by May 1997 had risen to 5.5 months worth of imports. Thus, the balance of payments showed few signs of any major weaknesses immediately prior to the currency crisis.

The exchange rate policy was designed to respond to increased capital inflows, including short-term portfolio capital and private debts. Since 1993 the monetary authorities have opted for a strategy of periodic widening of the nominal exchange rate band. In announcing the increase from 2 to 3 percent in December 1995, the monetary authorities stated that the move was meant to improve the effectiveness of monetary control and the stability of the exchange rate to anticipate future growth of capital flows. In 1996 they widened the band twice, the last of which was in July 1997, when it was increased from 8 to 12 percent (but this was short-lived since the rupiah was floated on 14 August).

Given the magnitude of the crisis, projections indicate that Indonesia will take about three years to recover fully. The most likely outcome is a decline in GDP of around 3 percent in 1998, followed by stabilization in 1999. Given the depreciation of the rupiah, inflation is projected to increase to 20 percent in 1998. Exports are expected to grow by 5 percent and imports to decline by 5 percent in 1998. The growth of non-oil exports is forecast to be around 12 percent in 1998, which is rather a low increase given the extent of the rupiah's depreciation. In 1998 oil exports are expected to stagnate; however, the prospects for export growth will be harmed unless the country can secure some form of international guarantee for its letters of credit.

CRITICAL ISSUES IN SHORT-TERM ECONOMIC MANAGEMENT

Even as the crisis unfolded during mid-1997, Indonesia's economy appeared robust. However, after the baht fell, the rupiah entered a phase during which international financial markets expected a rapid depreciation, and the rest was a self-fulfilling prophecy. The crisis did, however, magnify the adverse consequences of past policy mistakes.

In end-October 1997, Indonesia reached agreement with the IMF, which, with the participation of the Asian Development Bank, the World Bank, and various nations, came up with an economic assistance package of $23 billion. The package was linked to a three-year IMF adjustment program whose tenets are fiscal and monetary discipline, banking sector restructuring, and acceleration of deregulation and trade reforms. A major step related to the agreement was the decision in November to liquidate 16 banks. After a few days of shake up, it soon became clear that market confidence had not been restored. The rupiah continued to fall and the stock market plummeted. The government revised the Letter of Intent to the IMF in January 1998, spelling out a deeper and wider reform program and a stronger macroeconomic agenda in response to the continuing economic crisis. This projects, among other things, zero growth in 1998; a year-on-year inflation rate of 20 percent; and a budget deficit of 1 percent of GDP, assuming an exchange rate of Rp5,000 per US dollar. However, given that this is an optimistic exchange rate, inflation could well end up in the neighborhood of 40 to 50 percent. Key reforms include restructuring and consolidating the banking sector, reducing import and export tariffs, removing trading monopolies for some key staple foods, allowing foreign companies to set up their own distribution wholesale outlets, dismantling monopolies, and imposing greater transparency. In addition, the government postponed or canceled several expensive infrastructure projects, especially energy and road projects.

Indonesia currently faces three related short-term problems. The first is the dual task of stabilizing the rupiah and bringing it to a new and more realistic level. In early February 1998 Indonesia announced its intent to establish a currency board. Under this arrangement, Indonesia would peg the rupiah at a fixed exchange rate (the level under discussion is around Rp5,500 per US dollar). If this were done, Indonesia's base money supply would be backed by dollar reserves at the fixed exchange rate. The most important economic policy implication is that the country would automatically lose its ability to use monetary policy. The advantage of such a scheme is that it would bring monetary and fiscal discipline to the country; for example, the government could not print money to finance a budget deficit unless it were backed by an equivalent amount of dollars at the fixed exchange rate. However, many observers believe that Indonesia does not currently meet the requirements for a currency board, because to succeed, the government would have to respect the currency board's two key features, namely, a com-

mitment to exchange domestic currency for dollars at a fixed rate, and a commitment to issue currency only if it were backed by dollars. In addition, from a technical point of view, the country must have a sound banking system. The issue is that given the present level of political uncertainty, investors might perceive that the government would not keep its commitments. Also, Indonesia does not have a sound banking system. However, some of the banking system's problems are a result of the currency crisis and cannot be resolved without stabilizing the exchange rate. At the end of February the IMF and the government agreed to postpone the implementation of a currency board.

The second problem is the banking sector crisis. Although some issues are still unresolved, the IMF package outlines how the banking sector should be restructured, and the government has announced the establishment of the Indonesian Bank Restructuring Agency, which is to help restructure or take over troubled banks. The objective is to have fewer, more efficiently managed banks. The number of state banks will be reduced from 7 to 4, and the remaining 144 private banks will also have to face mergers and consolidations. The government has announced the provision of a guarantee to all depositors and creditors of locally incorporated banks for at least two years. Deregulation will also take place to encourage foreign participation, including granting permission to start full branching and removing the 49 percent cap on foreign ownership of publicly listed banks. Finally, the Central Bank will need to undergo institutional changes in light of its weaknesses in bank supervision. Reforms of the Central Bank will be the cornerstone of a healthy banking system.

The third problem—which is related to the stabilization of the rupiah—is the private sector debt crisis. Without a stable currency the foreign debt burden of the corporate sector will keep mounting, and without serious prospects for debt reduction, the currency will continue to be under pressure. So far no satisfactory solution has been found. The recent announcement of a voluntary, temporary freeze on corporate foreign debt repayments should ease pressure on the currency in the short term. However, this is not a durable solution. Uncertainty surrounding the resolution of the debt crisis means that investor sentiment will remain volatile. Because the private sector is responsible for most of the debt, ascertaining what role the government might play is difficult. To date, attempts to register the amount of private debt and coordinate efforts between the government and private sector debtors have not succeeded. Indonesia must avoid defaults to prevent its international credibility from being eroded even further.

POLICY AND DEVELOPMENT ISSUES

While Indonesia has made impressive strides in poverty reduction in the last 30 years, the financial crisis has undone some of these gains. In January 1998, three quarters of the companies in Indonesia either had already or were in the process of having a large part of their workforce retrenched. The majority of these companies were in export sectors, such as textiles, garments, and shoes, that employ mostly women. According to some estimates, an additional 3 million workers will be unemployed in 1998, which would place the unemployment rate at 11 to 14 percent of the workforce of 95 million people. Those most likely to be most severely affected are the urban lower-middle-class, for whom little in the way of social safety nets is available. The increase in unemployment may fuel social unrest. The unemployment problem, which has been exacerbated by the recent financial crisis, is likely to be a major challenge for policymakers for some time to come.

Although the country has had some success in alleviating poverty, income distribution has been a pressing problem throughout the 1990s. The problem has perhaps been further compounded by the financial crisis, whose impact has been far from symmetrical across various social groups. The future challenge for policymakers will be to maintain macroeconomic balances, while at the same time improving the distribution of income to ensure that disadvantaged segments of society do not bear the brunt of the economic crisis.

Public expenditures directed at providing health, nutrition, and education to those in lower income groups could help address problems of inequality. Indeed, much has been done in this regard in the past; however, more needs to be done in the future in terms of policy changes and institutional reforms. The government needs to undertake supportive measures to promote small businesses. It also needs to correct major policy distortions in the economy that have arisen from the absence or lack of enforcement of antimonopoly laws and to introduce various institutional reforms to ensure that all segments of society have equal access to public resources.

Another long-run policy challenge is to address development imbalances between regions. Despite the strong economic growth of the last two decades, Indonesia has not achieved regionally balanced development. For example, disparities in economic development between Java and the rest of the country and between the eastern and western regions are considerable. The eastern region is generally less developed. Its lack of infrastructure and a sizable pool of skilled labor are frequently cited as factors hindering the region's further growth. Lack of geographical proximity to central levels of power in a system dominated by excessive bureaucracy may also have contributed to its backwardness.

The economic structure of the eastern region is quite different from that of the western region. In the 1990s, more than half of the gross regional domestic product in the eastern region still originated in the agriculture sector, compared with a mere 18 percent in the western region. Similarly, at 10 percent of GDP, manufacturing's share in the eastern region is less than half that in the western region. Furthermore, the eastern region has 21 percent of the country's small agricultural estates, but only 0.6 percent of large estates. Likewise, the eastern region has 6.7 percent of small and home-based manufacturing industries, but 2.6 percent of the country's medium and large industries. With a low level of industrialization, virtually all provinces in the eastern region have a low level of urbanization. Social indicators further demonstrate the relative deprivation of the eastern region: even though its share of the total population is 13.2 percent, it has 16.5 percent of the nation's poor. In many cases, isolation and difficult geographic conditions have left villages with inadequate transportation, communication, and other services.

All these differences between the two regions indicate an imbalance in regional development. The removal of the numerous regulations and unnecessary red tape and the nurturing of a market-friendly environment would have a considerable impact on the development of the eastern region. However, that may not be enough. The government may have to adopt special programs and policies in favor of the eastern region to redress the persistent regional imbalance.

LAO PEOPLE'S DEMOCRATIC REPUBLIC

The Lao People's Democratic Republic (Lao PDR) continued its steady growth of the 1990s through 1997. The crisis in Thailand, however, affected Lao PDR's trade and currency. Membership in the Association of Southeast Asian Nations (ASEAN) is expected to increase trade liberalization and facilitate foreign investment, as is the promise of Most Favored Nation (MFN) trading status from the United States.

RECENT TRENDS AND PROSPECTS

Flooding in 1996 took its toll on GDP growth, which slipped to 6.9 percent. In 1997 more favorable weather conditions and increased government incentives to farmers resulted in improved agricultural performance, which contributed to GDP growth of 7.2 percent. Agriculture continues to account for more than half of GDP, but slow growth in agriculture has meant that manufacturing, construction, and services (including tourism) have been the driving forces behind the strong growth of the 1990s. Industry accounts for about 22 percent of GDP and services for 26 percent.

As a landlocked country heavily dependent on trade with its neighbors, particularly with Thailand, Lao PDR has not escaped the effects of the Southeast Asian currency turmoil. Thailand has been the largest investor in Lao PDR, accounting for more than a third of foreign direct investment through August 1997. Information on domestic savings and investment is not available, but they are believed to amount to relatively small shares of GDP. The economic dominance of subsistence agriculture and a correspondingly low level of monetization buffered the real economy from the regional crisis to some extent, but inflationary pressures remain a significant danger, both from the floods' effects on agricultural prices and from events in Thailand.

Following the rapid depreciation of the Thai baht, uncertainty spread to the Lao kip. The kip continued to depreciate, especially in the second half of 1997, to a level roughly 50 percent lower than at the beginning of the year, relative to the US dollar. The financial system remains fragmented, and the interbank market for kip is small. With the baht's status as the principal currency for cross-border trade between Lao PDR and Thailand, inflation has been largely imported. This has resulted both from the baht's depreciation and the August increase in the Thai value-added tax, which appears to have been passed on to Lao consumers. Estimates indicate that inflation reached more than 19 percent during 1997.

Widespread use of the Thai baht and the US dollar hampers the central bank's implementation of effective monetary policy. Foreign currency deposits account for roughly 40 percent of broad money and one third of loans to the private sector. As the kip depreciated, the authorities restricted the use of foreign currency for imports. The resulting monetary expansion was somewhat erratic, as consumers tended to hoard dollars and release them only gradually to the banking system. The foreign currency restrictions thus had the perverse effect of decreasing the amount of dollars available to the banking system and further undermined public confidence in the government and banks. At the same time, the restrictions had a limited effect on reducing

Figure 2.5 Direction of Trade: Lao People's Democratic Republic, 1996

Exports: $348 million

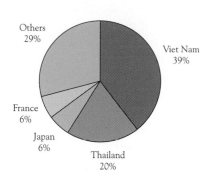

Imports: $681 million

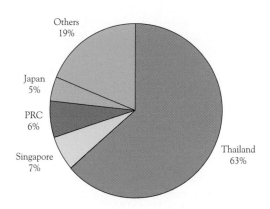

Source: Asian Development Bank (1997b).

imports because of the porous nature of the country's long border. They did, however, restrict imports of goods that earn high import duties, thereby affecting government revenues negatively. They also restricted imports of materials and equipment crucial for export production. At present, wood products remain the largest source of export earnings, followed by electricity sales. Expansion of hydroelectric projects has resulted in increased logging, contributing to export receipts, and future electricity sales should eventually reduce reliance on foreign aid.

Despite some improvements in tax collection, particularly in timber royalties and income taxes, the tax base needs to be broadened further to reduce reliance on customs revenues. The ratio of fiscal revenues to GDP remains low, but limits on expenditures in 1997 led to current fiscal surpluses and a declining trend in the overall fiscal deficit. Capital spending is widely financed by external assistance, and domestic debt has been reduced. Substantial foreign assistance and investment has strengthened the capital account and reserve position.

The 1996/97 budget increased current expenditure allocations on social sectors by 10 percent in an effort to raise the level of human resources in the country, and future increases are planned. The budget for 1997/98 aims to increase revenues and

decrease expenditures (as a percentage of GDP) further, thereby raising the current surplus and reducing the overall deficit. Inflation is expected to remain in double digits in 1998, and the large trade deficit is likely to exert continued downward pressure on the kip. Growth is expected to pick up somewhat in 1998.

POLICY AND DEVELOPMENT ISSUES

As a relatively small, low-income, landlocked country, Lao PDR is heavily dependent on other countries for opportunities and resources for its development. In recent years the government has taken major steps to expand such links, which has increased both risks and opportunities.

In 1997 Lao PDR became a member of ASEAN. Membership will result in further trade liberalization in preparation for the ASEAN Free Trade Area. The scheduled lowering of tariffs will also motivate fiscal reform, because currently some 20 percent of revenue is derived from tariffs. The regular schedule of numerous ASEAN meetings, however, is likely to tax the country's limited English-speaking human resources severely, and substantial capacity building efforts are required. ASEAN membership also confirms the shift in external relations in recent years to broader commercial ties in hopes of stimulating trade and investment. While Thailand remains the principal source of imports by a large margin, since 1994 Viet Nam has been the leading destination for Lao PDR's exports.

The United States has promised to grant Lao PDR a MFN status in the near future. As a requirement for MFN status, Lao PDR has adopted a legal framework that should also facilitate accession to the World Trade Organization. In addition, MFN status will increase the attractiveness of Lao PDR for foreign investors who wish to produce for export. Capitalizing on this potential will require the authorities to reduce bureaucratic delays in customs procedures, increase transparency in granting licenses, and address infrastructure inadequacies.

Access to the outside world is increasing: Japan has agreed to fund a second bridge across the Mekong River and has donated an international direct dialing system, agreement was reached on new Thai-Lao border passes, and renovation of the Vientiane airport has begun. However, as Thailand is the main source of Lao PDR's imports and foreign direct investment and a principal destination of exports, the slowdown in the Thai economy may temper the expansion of foreign trade and investment. Thailand's agreement with the International Monetary Fund may require Thailand to reopen talks with Japan on the planned 50-50 financing of the proposed third Mekong River bridge.

Before the regional currency turmoil, Lao PDR manufacturing workers were generally considered to be less productive, but to be paid more, than competitors in Cambodia, PRC, or Viet Nam. To the extent that the kip has now depreciated further than the currencies of these other countries and foreign currency restrictions have eased, Lao PDR's export prospects may improve. Cross-border infrastructure and trade links are expanding, which should help, but recovery in Thailand would have the biggest effect.

MALAYSIA

Financial turbulence reduced economic growth in 1997 and a more marked decline is likely in 1998. The potentially favorable impact of the depreciation of the ringgit on exports requires complementary measures, and stronger and broader responses to the financial crisis may be necessary.

RECENT TRENDS AND PROSPECTS

Currency instability and asset market disruption buffeted Malaysia's financial and corporate sectors in 1997. A massive depreciation of the ringgit, combined with plunging stock market values, seriously eroded the financial standing of many Malaysian businesses. After some initial hesitancy, the Malaysian government responded to these events by paring back public expenditures on prestige projects, tightening monetary policy, and taking measures to strengthen the financial system. Although asset values plummeted in 1997, the effects of the crisis have yet to register fully on incomes.

The financial crisis that unfolded during the second half of 1997 took its toll on economic performance. Economic growth for the year slowed to 7.5 percent from 8.6 percent in 1996. All components of aggregate demand grew more slowly, largely because of diminished confidence in markets and the loss of purchasing power associated with large reductions in the capital value of assets. The fiscal and monetary measures introduced in the latter part of the year in response to the crisis held back growth still further.

Notwithstanding difficulties in other sectors, agriculture performed well. Output grew by a strong 3.5 percent in 1997. The growth in output was broadly based, with palm oil, sawlogs, and livestock output all growing. However, rubber and cocoa production declined, largely because of the conversion of land to other uses and labor shortages.

Manufacturing output growth eased, particularly because of the weak performance of the electrical and electronics industry. This industry dominates Malaysian manufacturing and has been hard hit by the slowdown in the growth of global demand in this sector. Growth in the construction sector also slowed. Measures taken to limit lending to the property sector and a general slackening in demand for office space, condominiums, and retail outlets affected construction activity. The service sector was comparatively buoyant based on strong performance of the transportation, storage, and communications subsectors. However, finance, insurance, real estate, and business services, as well as wholesale and retail trade, and hotel and restaurant services, recorded lower growth. This was attributable to the instability in the financial markets and to the haze problem that resulted from the Southeast Asian forest fires caused by the drought associated with El Niño. This led to a downturn in tourism.

Despite the moderation in economic growth, Malaysia's unemployment rate remained low at 2.5 percent in 1997. This was the sixth year in a row that the economy was virtually at full employment. As a result, upward pressure on wages grew, and wage increases again outpaced productivity gains. Unskilled foreign workers continue to provide

Table 2.8 Major Economic Indicators: Malaysia, 1995-1999
(percent)

Item	1995	1996	1997	1998	1999
Gross domestic product growth	9.5	8.6	7.5	3.5	4.5
Gross domestic investment/GDP	43.5	41.5	42.0	40.5	41.5
Gross domestic savings/GDP	39.5	42.6	43.8	42.0	42.5
Inflation rate (consumer price index)	3.4	3.5	4.0	5.0	4.5
Money supply (M2) growth	24.0	20.9	18.5	18.0	20.0
Fiscal balance/GDP	0.9	0.7	1.8	0.9	1.4
Merchandise exports growth	26.6	7.3	6.0	8.0	10.0
Merchandise imports growth	30.4	1.7	7.0	6.0	7.0
Current account balance/GDP	-8.4	-5.0	-5.3	-4.9	-3.8
Debt-service/exports	6.2	na	na	na	na

na   Not available.

Sources: Ministry of Finance (1997), International Monetary Fund (1998), and staff estimates.

an important reservoir of labor that is used to meet local demands. Estimates indicate the presence of more than a million documented foreign workers in 1997 and another million undocumented migrants.

Malaysia continued to finance its development expenditure through public savings to avoid borrowing and tried to minimize increases in both operating and development expenditures. Although public sector operating and development expenditures increased, so did public sector revenues. The government maintained the overall public sector surplus at 2.1 percent of GNP.

Inflation picked up slightly during 1997. Consumer prices increased by 4 percent during the year. Strong credit growth in the first half of 1997 helps explain some of the acceleration.

The direction of monetary policy in the second part of 1997 was tentative as Malaysia struggled to find a way to stop the hemorrhaging of the ringgit and the collapse of its stock market. Foreign exchange controls, which were introduced in August, quickly proved counterproductive, as they led to an exodus of investors from the stock market and further weakened the ringgit. As a consequence, the government abandoned these measures. Interest rate policy also lacked clear direction. The government relaxed an initial tightening of interest rates

as equity prices declined, but comparatively low interest rates made stemming the tide of the ringgit's depreciation more difficult. Subsequently, the government tightened monetary policy again as part of an overall policy response to the crisis.

Merchandise exports increased by only 6 percent in 1997. While this is only slightly less than the increase in 1996, it is far below the double-digit export growth that Malaysia has routinely posted in the past. The dominance of electronic and electrical goods production has left Malaysia particularly prone to the vagaries of global demand in this sector. Unfortunately, exports of textiles, clothing, and footwear—traditionally the second largest foreign exchange earner among manufactured goods—have also been languishing. Stiffer competition from lower cost countries is now adversely affecting growth in these sectors. The performance of other exports was mixed. Commodity exports increased by slightly less than 1 percent, led by higher export volumes of palm oil and palm kernel oil. However, export earnings from crude petroleum declined by 1.7 percent as global prices softened. Led by exports of liquefied natural gas, "mining" exports registered strong growth.

Capital goods imports accounted for much of the 7 percent expansion in merchandise imports in

1997. Some of these imports, particularly ships and commercial aircraft, are needed to offset Malaysia's long-standing service account deficit. Imports of intermediate and consumption goods grew more moderately because of the ringgit's depreciation. The faster growth of imports relative to exports caused Malaysia's trade surplus to contract in 1997. Together with the deficit on the income and service account, this contributed to a widening of the current account deficit to 5.5 percent of GNP.

Projections indicate that growth will slow abruptly in 1998. The growth of GDP will be somewhere between 3 and 4 percent, the slowest growth in more than a decade. As a result of the depreciation of the ringgit, the collapse in asset values, and the tighter fiscal and monetary policies, domestic demand will fall markedly. In 1999, as the government eases its restrictive policies somewhat and net exports respond favorably to the currency depreciation, growth may pick up to about 4 to 5 percent. However, private investment is likely to remain subdued for some time.

On the production side, slower growth is anticipated in all sectors. Agricultural output is expected to grow by only 2 percent in 1998 because of anticipated weakness in international commodity prices and competition from lower cost countries. Short-term growth in the manufacturing sector is likely to be weak. Intermediate goods will cost more, foreign direct investment (FDI) may falter, and global demand conditions in the electronic and electrical goods sector are not expected to strengthen much. Some firms may find obtaining new credit difficult. The construction sector will also experience lower growth in the face of excess capacity in residential and office space, high interest rates, and the measures introduced to dampen speculation in the property market. Beyond 1998, manufacturing growth should recover as restocking of inventories occurs and manufacturers begin to feel the benefits of the ringgit's depreciation. A favorable supply response depends, however, on the containment of domestic inflationary pressures, as well as on external market conditions.

Service activity will also be badly hit in 1998. The finance, real estate, and business service sector will bear the brunt of asset and currency market dislocation. Consumer services will also suffer as real income growth slows. The hosting of the Commonwealth Games in September 1998 should help buoy services and, provided the haze does not return, tourism may pick up as a consequence of the currency depreciation.

Inflationary pressures emanating from a weaker ringgit will put upward pressure on consumer prices. Despite sluggish domestic demand, consumer price inflation could accelerate to about 5 percent in 1998. As the economy adjusts to the new exchange rate regime and labor constraints loosen, continued fiscal and monetary discipline should succeed in easing price increases in the latter part of 1999.

Exports are expected to pick up in 1998 as a result of the ringgit's depreciation. Subdued import growth will lead to a larger trade surplus. To moderate import growth, the government is planning to establish a RM1 billion ($250 million) fund for small and medium-scale manufacturers to spur local production. Companies with paid-up capital of less than RM50 million will be able to avail themselves of this fund. With service payments for freight and insurance and FDI income repatriation growing more slowly, the service account deficit is projected to narrow somewhat. Thus the current account deficit is expected to decline to 5 percent of GNP in 1998.

By 1999, exports should respond strongly to a more favorable exchange rate and should outpace import growth even more. While the trade account surplus will continue to increase, this will likely be more than offset by a persistent deficit on the service account. Consequently, the current account will remain in deficit, although it is projected to ease somewhat. External borrowing by public enterprises is expected to be less in 1998 than in 1997. Malaysia should maintain a relatively comfortable international reserves position, although some short-term capital outflows are likely to persist.

CRITICAL ISSUES IN SHORT-TERM ECONOMIC MANAGEMENT

Malaysia is exposed to a number of short-run economic risks, of which the most immediate is its current account position, which remains fragile. There is no prospect for anything other than marginal improvement in 1998. Indeed, the deficit may even widen because of lumpy imports (for instance, for aircraft, ships, and infrastructure projects), lower export growth, and continued increases in net service payments. At the same time, financing the

Figure 2.6 Banking System Loans to Major Sectors: Malaysia, March 1996-March 1997

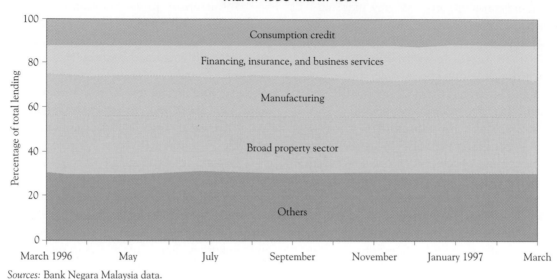

Sources: Bank Negara Malaysia data.

deficit could become a problem if FDI flows decline, particularly in the electrical and electronics industry as a result of excess capacity. While lower FDI would also reduce capital imports, the net effect on the balance of payments will be negative. To mitigate risks, Malaysia should focus on re-evaluating the economic returns of planned large infrastructure projects, maintaining a restrictive monetary stance, and encouraging long-run capital inflows whenever possible.

Malaysia also faces the difficult challenge of reining in its overheated property sector. Although the growth of the broad construction sector appears to be slowing, the banking system's exposure to the property market remains high at nearly 26 percent of total loans in early 1997. Bringing this exposure down to the target limit of 20 percent or less will require a strong and resolute effort. While the authorities have instituted measures to restrict the supply of credit to the sector, the momentum of credit growth and activity in the construction sector cannot be halted overnight.

Malaysia's financial sector would benefit from more prudent supervision and tighter regulation. In this regard, the government's plan to undertake a broad review of the supervisory and regulatory system is appropriate, and should result in long-term benefits if follow through on the outcome of the review is appropriate. A stronger regulatory and supervisory framework should improve loan quality and standards of asset management, leading to a more healthy and robust financial sector. Fuller and more timely disclosure of information would be a critical component of improved regulation. In this connection, the Bank Negara's recent initiatives to increase transparency in the conduct of monetary policy are a welcome move.

POLICY AND DEVELOPMENT ISSUES

To promote a solid platform for long-term growth, Malaysia must devote more resources to investing in the development of relevant skills for its labor force. Secondary education and curricula need to be strengthened further, as do tertiary-level technical and vocational education programs. Indeed, the need to invest in the domestic provision of education has become more urgent as the foreign exchange costs of educating Malaysians overseas have now risen sharply. The development of a modern and responsive education system is an objective worthy of consistent support, even during troubled times.

The need to upgrade Malaysia's industrial base in a way that is responsive to its shifting comparative advantage raises broader questions. While, as part of its strategy to deal with the current crisis, the government has put the recruitment of foreign workers on hold, it needs to work out a longer term vision that is not only sensitive to the needs of immigrant workers, but also meets national economic objectives. Given the structure of migrant flows to Malaysia, these issues could perhaps be usefully considered within the broader framework of the Association of Southeast Asian Nations.

Malaysia's New Economic Policy has helped lift many from poverty. For some time the policy also seemed to succeed in reducing income inequality; however, income distribution appears to have worsened since the mid-1980s, both between and within ethnic groups, and especially within the Malay group. At the same time, regional inequalities seem to be on the rise. East Malaysia and the eastern states of Peninsular Malaysia have not benefited from growth to the same extent as parts of west Peninsular Malaysia. To the extent that poor and comparatively uneducated Malays are disproportionately concentrated in those regions that are lagging, regional and ethnic inequality are related. For distributional reasons, and with a view to easing congestion and related costs, especially in the Klang Valley, Malaysia might consider policies to promote more balanced growth across its regions, for example, by supporting existing initiatives on growth areas with a more balanced spatial apportionment of resources for education, and for infrastructure more generally.

MYANMAR

Myanmar is continuing to implement market reforms. Its integration with the region's econo-mies will improve following its recent membership in the Association of Southeast Asian Nations (ASEAN). However, the existence of a dual exchange rate system continues to undermine the efficient functioning of the economy. Long-term growth prospects depend on the extent to which Myanmar can improve its openness and competitiveness and overcome infrastructural bottlenecks.

RECENT TRENDS AND PROSPECTS

Myanmar is continuing the slow process of implementing a market economy. While the government has already partially liberalized foreign direct investment (FDI), trade, and agricultural prices, the legacy of central planning continues to hamper development. In 1997 GDP grew by 5 percent. Nevertheless, Myanmar continues to suffer from structural problems, such as inefficient state enterprises that continue to require budget subsidies and an underdeveloped financial system. These are preventing the economy from growing more rapidly. With the recent financial crisis in the region, a realignment of the fixed exchange rate has become imperative. Myanmar has yet to implement the measures needed to achieve greater openness and competitiveness, such as providing more infrastructure in areas like transportation, shipping, ports, and utilities. The country's political status and international relations have yet to be resolved, and information about Myanmar remains limited.

Despite being to a large extent a closed economy, Myanmar felt the impact of the financial crisis in East and Southeast Asia. In the last few years, despite its economic and political problems,

Myanmar has managed to achieve fairly respectable growth rates. However, the mini-boom has begun to fade, and the financial crisis has highlighted both the country's economic frailty and policy short-comings.

Inflation has generally remained in the 20 to 30 percent range in recent years. However, in mid-1997 serious flooding in the south and in the Irrawaddy delta region destroyed 1.2 million hectares of rice. This drove up food prices and increased inflation from 30 to 35 percent in April 1997 to more than 40 percent by the end of the year. In early September the situation forced the government to appeal to the United Nations for emergency food relief.

Gross investment stood at 16.8 percent of GDP in 1997, while national savings amounted to 8.3 percent. Total foreign investment rose to $6 billion by April 1997, up from $5.3 billion in December 1996. The United Kingdom was the largest inves-tor, with around $1.3 billion, followed by Singapore with $1.2 billion and Thailand with $1 billion. Despite a highly publicized pullout by Western investors, investment continues to flow in from Asia.

Growth is expected to remain at 5 percent in 1998 and 1999. This is lower than in previous years

1997 refers to fiscal year 1997/98, ending 31 March.

because of adverse factors that will affect agricultural production, such as a lack of inputs and continued government intervention in production decisions. Gross investment is expected to decline slightly to 16 percent of GDP, and national savings to a little under 8 percent of GDP. Fiscal deficits and lax monetary policy will keep inflation high. Although financing problems will moderate import growth, weak export growth will keep the current account in a substantial deficit.

CRITICAL ISSUES IN SHORT-TERM ECONOMIC MANAGEMENT

The single most critical problem Myanmar faces relates to the management of the exchange rate system. Myanmar's dual system of an official exchange rate and one determined in a parallel market was cause for concern well before the recent regional currency depreciations. In the last few months, the influence of the fixed official exchange rate in restricting the country's ability to maintain growth, investment, and trade and to hold inflation at bay has become even more apparent. The official exchange rate continues to be fixed at MK6 to the dollar. However, at the beginning of the region's financial crisis, the kyat's rate of exchange in the parallel market fell by nearly 100 percent. At one point it traded at more than MK300 to the dollar.

In June and July 1997, as foreign exchange became scarcer, confidence collapsed. The government then resorted to printing kyat to buy dollars at the parallel rate, but this generated inflation. These events reflect the fragility of Myanmar's economy and its lack of resources to react to current events in the region. While the authorities are well aware of the exchange rate problem, they consider that a devaluation will not only increase inflation, but will also increase the amount of kyat necessary to repay foreign debt that is denominated in foreign currency. While the authorities have made some attempts to depreciate the kyat by shifting transactions from the fixed official rate to the parallel exchange market, about a third of external transactions, all related to the public sector, still use the official rate. Most private sector external transactions are now conducted in the parallel market. However, the complex set of foreign exchange and trade regulations still needed to maintain the dual exchange system has reduced transparency and undermined the efficiency of other measures taken to orient Myanmar toward a market economy.

The second important problem that Myanmar needs to resolve is the recurrent large fiscal deficits, which result from a small revenue base. Budget revenues declined from about 8.4 percent of GDP in the early 1990s to 5.1 percent in 1996. Despite a significant reduction in government expenditures from about 10 percent of GDP to 6.6 percent during the same period, the nonfinancial public sector deficit (that of the central government and state enterprises) remains at some 5 to 6 percent of GDP. These deficits are routinely financed with credit from the Central Bank and contribute to inflationary pressures. During the first six months of 1997 the amount of net credit to the public sector increased sharply. At the same time, credit to the private sector also began to expand rapidly, growing by 45 percent (albeit from a small base).

POLICY AND DEVELOPMENT ISSUES

Myanmar's long-term growth prospects depend on the extent to which it succeeds in introducing greater openness and competitiveness, improving infrastructure, accelerating market reforms, liberalizing trade, and increasing its capacity to attract FDI. Myanmar must encourage FDI as a way to obtain foreign technology, but this will be difficult as long as current distortions persist.

As concerns integration into the world economy, probably the most important event in 1997 was Myanmar's entry into ASEAN. This is expected to lead to substantial inflows of investment from neighboring countries. Myanmar is a resource-rich nation and possesses a large, low-cost workforce, which makes it potentially attractive as a production base for industrializing ASEAN members, such as Malaysia, Singapore, and Thailand. Myanmar will also join the ASEAN Free Trade Area and has been given until 2008 to complete the tariff reduction process.

PHILIPPINES

Despite the currency crisis, economic performance in the Philippines was satisfactory in 1997. The current account deficit was kept manageable, supported by high receipts in the service sector, particularly from remittances of overseas contract workers, and inflation was unexpectedly low. However, the full impact of the currency turmoil will become apparent in 1998.

RECENT TRENDS AND PROSPECTS

The Philippine economy performed satisfactorily in 1997 despite disruptions caused by the regional currency turmoil in the latter half of the year. GNP and GDP registered relatively high growth rates of 5.8 and 5.1 percent, respectively, in 1997, which were, however, lower than the 6.9 and 5.7 percent, respectively, achieved in 1996. The difference between GNP and GDP was largely due to the remitted earnings of overseas Filipino workers, and the convergence of their growth rates in 1997 reflects the stabilization of these earnings. The industry and service sectors recorded reasonable growth rates of 5.7 and 5.6 percent, respectively. Notwithstanding pessimistic expectations based on the El Niño phenomenon, which caused adverse weather conditions, including severe droughts, the agriculture sector posted a growth rate of 2.8 percent, which was better than anticipated.

Overall aggregate employment growth slowed down to around 2 percent in 1997, with the agriculture sector affected most severely. The labor force grew similarly, but with 40 percent of the labor force employed in agriculture, the unemployment rate is estimated to have risen marginally to 8.7 percent in 1997.

Gross national savings as a percentage of GNP have tended to hover around 15 to 19 percent in the 1990s, with 1997 being no exception at around 19 percent. Private savings accounted for roughly 60 percent of total savings. Gross domestic investment fluctuated within a band of 20 to 24 percent of GNP during 1990-1996. After sluggish performance in 1995, investment activity picked up significantly in 1996, and this trend continued right up to the third quarter of 1997, when the high interest rates that prevailed at that time because of the currency turmoil dampened investment activity. Gross domestic investment as a percentage of GNP was 24 percent in 1997, with public investment accounting for roughly one fifth.

The government has succeeded in its efforts to achieve budget surpluses since 1994, and the trend continued in 1997. However, the public sector as a whole posted a deficit because of deficits in government corporations.

Broad money (M2) grew by about 20.5 percent in 1997, up from about 16 percent in the preceding year. Nevertheless, inflation was kept in check at 5.1 percent in 1997, mainly because of satisfactory output growth early in the year.

Export growth has been strong in recent years, increasing from a mere 4.7 percent in 1990 to 29.4 percent in 1995. Some slowdown in export growth was evident in 1996 as a result of slackening global demand for electronic components; however, 1997 saw a resumption of high export growth of 22.8 percent. Imports had maintained even higher growth rates throughout the 1990s, but slackened

Table 2.9   Major Economic Indicators: Philippines, 1995-1999
(percent)

Item	1995	1996	1997	1998	1999
Gross domestic product growth	4.8	5.7	5.1	2.4	4.0
Gross domestic investment/GNP	21.6	23.3	23.9	20.0	22.0
Gross national saving/GNP	16.8	18.8	19.2	17.0	19.0
Inflation rate (consumer price index)	8.1	8.4	5.1	10.0	8.0
Money supply (M2) growth	25.2	15.8	20.5	17.0	17.0
Fiscal balance/GDP	0.6	0.3	0.1	0.2	0.3
Merchandise exports growth	29.4	17.7	22.8	21.0	21.0
Merchandise imports growth	23.7	20.8	14.0	9.0	10.0
Current account balance/GDP	-4.4	-4.7	-5.2	-3.8	-1.3
Debt-service/exports	15.8	12.0	10.4	11.4	11.0

Sources: Bangko Sentral ng Pilipinas (1998a,b); National Statistical Coordination Board (1997, 1998); Department of Budget and Management, Fiscal Planning Service data; and Bureau of Treasury data. Projections are entirely staff estimates.

in 1997, when merchandise imports rose by 14 percent.

The trade deficit increased during 1990-1996, rising from $4 billion in 1990 to 11.3 billion in 1996. In 1997 the trade deficit was virtually unchanged at $11.4 billion. The increase in the trade deficit could have been lessened had the appreciation of the real exchange rate not been so significant. Between 1990 and September 1997, the real effective exchange rate appreciated by 28 percent against the currencies of major trading partners and by 20 percent against competing countries' currencies.

The current account deficit was kept at manageable levels in the 1990s, with the highest deficit reaching 5.5 percent of GDP in 1993. In 1997 the figure was 5.2 percent. This was largely a result of high receipts in the services sector, particularly remittances from overseas contract workers. Even though the major share of remittances is from outside the region, some slowdown is likely in the medium term if overseas workers in other Asian countries are retrenched as a result of the regional economic contraction that has followed on the heels of the currency instability. This highlights the fact that the Philippines cannot rely on such remittances as a sustainable source of support for bolstering the current account.

The Philippines has experienced large capital inflows in recent years: net capital inflows increased from $1.8 billion in 1990 to $8.6 billion in 1996. Following the currency instability, foreign investment inflows and capital inflows to commercial banks dropped sharply, and in 1997 the resulting capital account surplus could not cover the current account deficit. The overall balance-of-payments deficit exceeded $3 billion, financed through a drawdown of reserves, which dropped to $8.8 billion by the end of 1997.

GNP growth will slow down considerably to 2.9 percent in 1998, and will be accompanied by a significant rise in unemployment. High liquidity growth and rising import costs will be evident in 1998, and the inflation rate is likely to reach double digits. The savings rate is likely to fall as higher debt-service costs and inflation affect the savings capability of both the public and private sectors. The current account deficit is projected to improve to 3.8 percent of GDP in 1998, largely because of a reduced trade deficit.

As lower GDP growth will likely affect government revenues in 1998, they are unlikely to grow much beyond the levels achieved in 1997. Thus the national budget is not expected to yield a significant surplus in 1998. Expenditure will be trimmed to match available revenues, and as the government is unlikely to reduce its current operating expenditures significantly in an election year, cuts are expected in maintenance and capital expenditures that will probably affect the public sector development program in 1998.

The full impact of the monetary expansion, the peso depreciation, and the El Niño weather phenomenon will be felt with a lag in 1998. In addition, unemployment is likely to rise in 1998 as agricultural employment falls further. The government's ability to maintain public investment levels will be an important determinant of economic performance in 1998. With conditions stabilizing in the rest of the region, recovery is expected to begin in 1999.

CRITICAL ISSUES IN SHORT-TERM ECONOMIC MANAGEMENT

The year 1998 is likely to be crucial for the Philippine economy. Successful containment of the economic impacts of the currency turmoil and the pace of eco-

nomic recovery will depend on such policies as maintaining aggregate investment levels, preventing disruption in banking and financial services, managing corporate indebtedness, enabling the export sector to take maximum advantage of the opportunities created by the currency depreciation, and effecting a smooth political transition after the elections. The continuation of economic reforms is crucial and will be closely monitored by foreign investors.

With high interest rates prevailing to stabilize the currency, private investment demand is likely to be sluggish. Unless public investment levels are maintained, overall investment and growth will be severely affected. Rising interest and debt servicing costs as a result of the sharp depreciation of the peso; the lack of flexibility in major items of current expenditure, such as salaries; and absence of buoyancy in revenue generation because of reduced growth are going to pose a challenge to government efforts to sustain public development expenditures.

The possibilities of corporate defaults and consequent difficulties for the banking sector are likely,

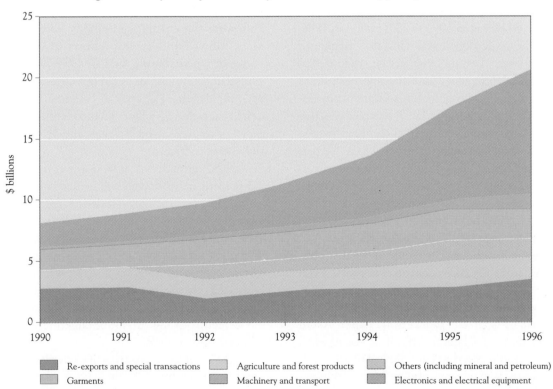

Figure 2.7 Exports by Commodity Classification: Philippines, 1990-1996

Re-exports and special transactions   Agriculture and forest products   Others (including mineral and petroleum)
Garments   Machinery and transport   Electronics and electrical equipment

Source: Bangko Sentral ng Pilipinas (1998b).

and need careful attention. Official estimates of the banking sector's exposure to the real estate sector have been revised upward, and currently stand at 13.7 percent of total loans. The current estimate of the share of nonperforming loans is 4.7 percent; however, this will rise given the much greater excess capacity in the real estate sector likely to be experienced in 1998. The capabilities of the Bangko Sentral ng Pilipinas (the Central Bank) and the Philippine Deposit Insurance Corporation to supervise the banking system, and of the Securities and Exchange Commission to supervise the corporate sector need to be enhanced, and policy measures should be put in place to allow these agencies to play a more effective supervisory role. In addition, the monetary authorities need to develop effective hedging instruments to protect those with foreign currency loans.

POLICY AND DEVELOPMENT ISSUES

Despite its improved economic performance since the mid-1990s, the Philippine economy exhibits several weaknesses, namely: the domestic savings rate remains low and stagnant; the growth in agricultural production has been weak and variable, and is subject to large output fluctuations as a result of weather changes because irrigation remains insufficient; the industry sector's technological progress has been slow, especially in small and medium enterprises; the integration of manufactured exports with local manufacturing has been weak, which has prevented the surge in exports from having a significant impact on local industry; and the physical infrastructure needs considerable upgrading. The high rate of population growth has reduced the gains that resulted from economic growth, and GNP per capita growth was negative from 1990 to 1993. However, since 1994 GNP per capita has shown some improvement. The provision of social services is still inadequate, especially in health and education. In addition, the distribution of the benefits of growth has also been uneven across income classes and regions. Concerted action to overcome these weaknesses is necessary for sustained development.

The major medium-term policy concern is to address the economic vulnerabilities exposed by the current currency turmoil and to find ways to improve the economy's resilience in the context of its further globalization. This involves implementing further reforms in the financial and capital markets, promoting the sustainability of export growth, and reappraising the exchange rate policy.

Reform in Financial and Capital Markets

Central to the reform process are measures to boost domestic savings and to restore the confidence of foreign investors. Reforms under way on the equity side of the capital market include improving the functioning of the stock market, increasing transparency, ensuring the protection of shareholders' interests, introducing international standards and practices, and ensuring better supervision and regulation.

In addition, further development of the debt market is necessary. Treasury bills dominate the bond market; corporate debt is confined mainly to short-term commercial paper; municipal and project bonds are largely underdeveloped; and domestic institutional investors, such as pension funds and insurance companies, prefer to hold risk-free government paper. Reforms are needed to enable all these entities to play a more meaningful role in augmenting savings. In addition, considerable policy and institutional reforms are required to develop the domestic debt market to cater to the economy's long-term investment needs. These measures include changing the tax treatment of and regulations concerning debt instruments; strengthening secondary market and credit rating institutions; and building the capacity of agencies, financial institutions, and local governments.

Export Development

Although the export growth the Philippines has experienced is among the most impressive in the region, the authorities need to take steps to ensure that the growth performance is sustainable over the long term. These include paying more attention to traditional exports that have not experienced much buoyancy, such as garments and food processing, and trying to diversify manufactured exports and increase their local content, particularly of electronics exports. Accomplishing this calls for a wide array of policy and capacity building measures in the areas of trade, foreign investment, and industry. These include upgrading the skills of the work force, improving the technology base of the economy, removing infrastructural bottlenecks, paying greater attention to credit provision for exports, promoting small- and medium-size enterprises, and adopting specific capacity building measures for government agencies concerned with export promotion.

The exchange rate policy should be viewed not only in the context of assisting exporters, but also of overall macroeconomic management. Although the Bangko Sentral maintains that the exchange rate is determined by the market with only occasional limited intervention to provide indicative guidance,

before the onset of the currency turmoil the peso-dollar nominal exchange rate had experienced unusual stability. However, despite some depreciation of the nominal effective exchange rate, the real effective exchange rate had witnessed a steady appreciation. The gains from the current steep nominal depreciation of the peso could similarly be quickly reversed unless fiscal and monetary policy were used effectively to keep inflation under control. The attainment and maintenance of appropriate real effective exchange rates is necessary to sustain the momentum of growth in exports and output.

THAILAND

Thailand's recent era of high growth ended in 1997. The financial crisis spread throughout the economy, underscoring its fragility. Accustomed to double-digit growth rates, Thailand saw negative growth in 1997, and 1998 is expected to be worse with the onset of stagflation. The short-term priority is to resolve the financial crisis that is strangling business. In the medium to long term, Thailand must rethink its growth strategy, emphasize those sectors that have a long-term growth potential, and enhance education.

RECENT TRENDS AND PROSPECTS

By the first quarter of 1997, the Thai economy was showing clear signs that it was in trouble. Speculative attacks on the baht and the closure of several finance companies constituted the prelude to financial turmoil of unprecedented magnitude. The currency depreciated from B26 to the US dollar in July 1997 to more than B50 to the dollar by January 1998. Negative growth occurred in 1997, and the political consequences included the prime minister's resignation in November 1997.

The lack of liquidity caused by the financial crisis had serious repercussions on manufacturing. While production declined only slightly during the first seven months of 1997, with growth running at 5.1 percent compared with 7.1 percent during the same period of 1996, the last three months of 1997 saw a decline in production of more than 5 percent compared with the same period of 1996. Capacity utilization fell to around 70 percent in such industries as automotive assembly and sales of motor vehicles fell 73 percent from the previous year's figures. This will undoubtedly adversely affect the future growth of the petrochemicals, glass making, rubber, and steel sectors.

Private investment expanded moderately by 4.1 percent in July 1997, but only by 2.5 percent in

August 1997, from the levels during the corresponding months in 1996. This reflected the economic slowdown and the excess capacity prevailing in many industries, particularly the real estate sector. Private consumption fell by approximately 5 percent in real terms because of declining real incomes.

Thailand's fiscal position further deteriorated in 1997, with the budget deficit as a proportion of GDP reaching 0.9 percent in 1997. This was caused by a shortfall in revenues because of a decline in funds collected from the value-added tax and from customs duties. In contrast, expenditures remained as budgeted.

Liquidity conditions in money markets remained tight during the year. In August 1997 the interbank rate climbed to an average of 15.4 percent, up from 12.1 percent in December 1996, in an attempt to counteract the outflows of capital and the persistent excess demand for US dollars in the foreign exchange market.

Inflation accelerated during the second half of the year, because of the increased costs of imports following depreciation of the baht, as well as the increase in the value-added tax from 7 to 10 percent. By December 1997, the year-on-year inflation rate was 7.7 percent. This must be seen as a significantly low, even puzzling, increase in prices given the large fall in the value of the baht. Likely reasons why inflation has not shot up to date is the contraction of the domestic economy; the decrease in imports; the cutting of salaries, especially of annual bonuses; and the selling off of inventories.

After the 1996 slump, exports began showing signs of recovery around March 1997, and further minor improvements were observed throughout the year. Medium-technology exports, such as automobiles and parts, as well as electrical products and resource-based products, performed well. Exports grew by 3.2 percent during 1997, a slight improvement on the decline of almost 2 percent the previous year. Imports, by contrast, declined by about 9 percent. Imports of motor vehicles fell by 50 percent in the first ten months of 1997, while sales of brand-label clothing and leatherwear fell by 30 to 40 percent during the same period. Despite the improvement in the current account deficit, the ratio of external debt-service to exports doubled from slightly more than 12 percent in 1996 to 25 percent in 1997.

Projections indicate that the economy will register a negative growth rate of around 3 percent in 1998. Signs of a mild recovery will appear in 1999, with growth of around 1 percent. Further declines in private consumption by 9 percent in 1998 and 1.5 percent in 1999 are predicted. Inflation is projected to be 15 percent in 1998, but the exact figure will depend partly on the extent of the depreciation of the baht and the increase in import prices. Finally, exports are expected to grow at 5 percent, while imports are expected to continue decreasing. With this pattern the current account balance will show a surplus of around 3.4 percent of GDP. An increase in unemployment is also forecast for 1998.

CRITICAL ISSUES IN SHORT-TERM ECONOMIC MANAGEMENT

The interaction of two factors contributed in important ways to the Thai financial crisis. The first was Thailand's exchange rate policy, which tied the baht to a basket of currencies heavily weighted by the US dollar. The appreciation of the dollar in 1995 made Thai exports uncompetitive. The second was the lack of effective regulatory control over the private financial sector, whose lending policies were imprudent. The crisis has therefore raised questions about the conduct of Thailand's economic policy as well as the adequacy of its institutional and sectoral structures. Consequently, in the short to medium term, Thailand must address the problems of the liquidity constraint created by the closing of private banks and finance companies, and must restructure its financial sector. The latter is required to avoid future misallocation of foreign capital to speculative assets and to projects with inadequate rates of return.

Table 2.10 Major Economic Indicators: Thailand, 1995-1999
(percent)

Item	1995	1996	1997	1998	1999
Gross domestic product growth	8.8	5.5	-0.4	-3.0	1.0
Gross domestic investment/GDP	41.6	41.7	35.0	26.0	29.0
Gross domestic saving/GDP	33.6	33.7	31.0	31.4	32.0
Inflation rate (consumer price index)	5.8	5.9	5.6	15.0	9.0
Money supply (M2) growth	17.0	12.6	16.4	6.8	7.5
Fiscal balance/GDP	3.0	0.9	-0.9	-2.0	-1.0
Merchandise exports growth	24.8	-1.9	3.2	5.0	8.0
Merchandise imports growth	31.9	0.6	-9.3	-15.0	3.0
Current account balance/GDP	-7.9	-7.9	-4.0	3.4	2.0
Debt-service/exports	11.4	12.2	25.0	15.0	15.0

Sources: Asian Development Bank (1997f), Bank of Thailand (1997), International Monetary Fund (1998), and staff estimates.

The substantial volume of nonperforming loans, the depreciation of the baht, and a run on deposits have weakened the capital base of Thailand's financial institutions. Together with sluggish economic activity, this could increase the incidence of corporate bankruptcy. A fall in inflated property prices could further depress the commercial banks' balance sheets. With monetary policy no longer constrained by a fixed exchange rate, the baht has depreciated substantially since July 1997 in response to the perception that the authorities might have decided to rescue the economy and the banking system by printing money. In the absence of a comprehensive reform package for the financial sector, the international capital markets' fears of a banking crisis are likely to keep the baht under pressure.

The establishment in October 1997 of the Financial Restructuring Agency and the Asset Management Company was an important step forward. The Financial Restructuring Agency will supervise the overall rehabilitation of the financial sector and will help viable companies merge and/or raise capital, while the Asset Management Company will oversee the liquidation of unviable companies. In December 1997 the government announced that it would liquidate all but 2 of the 58 suspended finance companies in a move to restore investor confidence and to reduce selling pressure on the baht. The government has also decided to allow foreigners to hold controlling interests in the banking sector. In addition, the Central Bank has lifted most remaining foreign exchange controls, for example, local financial institutions can now resume their baht trading with nonresidents, and foreigners are no longer restricted from transferring baht offshore after selling Thai stocks and bonds. Finally, the government now prohibits banks and the remaining finance companies from lending for nonproductive purposes, for instance, consumer spending and real estate development. The restructuring costs will be large: around 15 percent of GDP.

In August 1997 Thailand negotiated a $17 billion line of credit with the International Monetary Fund (IMF) in exchange for implementing an austerity plan. The initial plan called for increasing the value-added tax from 7 to 10 percent, which has already been implemented; reducing the current account deficit to 3 percent by 1998; low but positive growth; capping inflation at 9.5 for 1997 and 5 percent for 1998; maintaining foreign exchange reserves equivalent to more than four months' worth of imports; implementing fiscal policies to generate a budget surplus of 1 percent of GDP in 1998; and restructuring the financial sector. However, six months after the implementation of the IMF program the economy showed few signs of improvement. This called into question the feasibility of targets negotiated with the IMF, in particular, the requirement for a budget surplus, and has created uncertainty about the final policy mix the authorities are scheduled to adopt.

Sectors of Thai society have questioned the appropriateness of the IMF program. The combination of anti-inflationary policies with reductions in the money supply and in government spending could deepen a crisis generated by private sector debt. These concerns led the IMF and the Thai government to revise previous agreements, and toward the end of February 1998, they issued a third Letter of Intent that set more realistic objectives, such as a negative GDP growth rate for 1998, higher inflation, and a budget deficit. Likewise, the government backtracked on some previous privatization commitments. On the financial side, the government aims to reduce its stake in four recently nationalized banks.

POLICY AND DEVELOPMENT ISSUES

Thailand's industrialization process began accelerating in the mid-1980s. Given its relative abundance of labor, the country specialized in producing and exporting labor-intensive products. However, after only a little more than one decade, this comparative advantage has ended. Thailand is currently caught between the newly industrialized economies, against which it cannot yet compete in medium- to high-technology products, and countries such as People's Republic of China, Indonesia, and Viet Nam, which can produce a wide variety of labor-intensive products at lower labor costs.

Bias in the Pattern of Industrialization

Compared with countries at a similar level of development, Thailand's industrial structure is biased toward light industries that produce consumer goods, in particular, toward food and beverages, textiles, and apparel. This bias is partly explained by the economy's natural resource base. The industrial sector processes natural resources and manufactures labor-intensive products. Intermediate and investment goods are imported. Thailand depends heavily on demand in the industrial countries to which it exports. This pattern of trade and industrialization lies at the core of Thailand's balance-of-payments problems.

As concerns Thailand's policy options, one short-run strategy would be to reduce the prices of exports to stay competitive. This would probably be reflected in real wage cuts and the adoption of capital-intensive technologies. A second, longer term option would be to develop the domestic market rather than relying on exports. Either strategy or a mix of the two should be combined with investment and research in more technologically advanced sectors. To achieve product diversification and improve product quality, Thailand will have to raise its current level of human capital and its capacity to adopt and adapt advanced technologies.

Given Thailand's economic structure and natural endowments, the sectors that offer the most promising possibilities for the future are food processing and tourism. Thailand has plenty of scope for continuing to develop a competitive and world-class food processing industry. Thai producers must constantly adapt to changing tastes: wealthier societies may consume less regular rice, but spend more on first-class (and well-marketed) mangoes, aromatic rice, and oven-ready frozen foods. These are goods for which, as income grows, the demand for them grows more than proportionately. The businesses that make and export such items can use increasingly sophisticated production technologies and management methods to increase agricultural productivity and raise incomes.

Thailand also has considerable potential for developing its tourism industry further. In 1997, 6 million tourists visited Thailand. This figure could be increased by targeting tourists with high purchasing power. The Tourism Authority of Thailand has prepared the "Amazing Thailand" campaign for 1998/99 to try to make the best of the currency depreciation by increasing tourist arrivals to 7.7 million in 1998 and 8.3 million in 1999.

The appropriate development strategy is for Thailand to focus on the factors that are likely to give the country a longer term comparative advantage. Thus from a policy perspective, the important question is to be able to move to higher stages of development, avoiding the types of shocks the economy is currently experiencing. To accomplish this Thailand must work on three fronts. The first is intra-industry restructuring, implementing changes within existing industries, such as textiles and food processing, to improve production methods and attain best practice standards. The second front is relocating labor-intensive activities in the country's poorer regions for reasons of both efficiency and equity. The third front is intrasectoral restructuring. This involves making the transition from low-productivity, low-skill, labor-intensive industries to higher productivity industries, such as information technology. The first two are medium-term strategies and the third is a long-term strategy.

Lack of Competitiveness and the Role of Education

Thailand has a weak human capital base. Until recently, it lagged far behind other Asian countries in terms of the enrollment ratio at the secondary school level. While enrollment at the primary level was satisfactory, more than half of those who finished primary school did not go on to secondary education. This is partly because a large share of the population was still engaged in agriculture. A low value placed on education plus difficult access to schools made secondary education unattractive.

In the past five years, however, the situation has improved, and currently the transition rate from primary to secondary education is close to 90 percent. While Thailand currently has only 6 years of compulsory education, plans exist to raise this to 9 years in the near future and to 12 years by 2007. The government plans to achieve almost universal lower secondary education by 2000 or so and virtually universal upper secondary education around 2020.

Today, 80 percent of Thailand's labor force of around 33 million has no formal education or only a primary education. These workers have little access to better jobs and frustrate Thailand's hopes of moving up the development ladder. Four reasons account for the prevailing situation. The first is access: institutions of higher education tend to be concentrated in the capital, Bangkok, thereby putting rural populations at a disadvantage in terms of their access to higher education. Second, curricula do not match employers' needs. This is due, in part, to the predominance of course offerings in the humanities and arts at the expense of scientific and applied education and training. While education of the latter kind is more costly to deliver, it is likely to have greater linkages with the economy's needs and thereby have greater benefits, particularly in the longer term. Moreover, the quality of the system is low, it does not encourage creativity, and it does not emphasize research at the university level. Efforts must be made to increase agricultural research in particular. This could not only raise the sector's productivity by providing new and improved inputs, methods of cultivation, and machinery, but could have a far-reaching effect on the job situation in rural villages as higher incomes increase demand for goods and services. Third, teachers are underpaid and undertrained, as reflected in the quality of teaching. Finally, the physical infrastructure of many schools is extremely poor.

Thailand needs a radical, sustained, and far-reaching reform of its national education system to face the economic challenges of the 21st century and the technology age. However, even if such a reform program is implemented immediately, there may not be any significant effect on the economy in the short run. The reform, which should be directed toward improving the quality of education across various levels and increasing enrollment ratios, particularly at the secondary level, will take at least a decade to bear fruit and contribute toward enhanced growth and structural transformation of the economy.

VIET NAM

The rapid speed of recent growth is likely to moderate as Viet Nam is affected by events elsewhere in Asia. One weak spot that must be closed is the country's huge resource gap. In addition, to invigorate the private sector, reforms are needed in a wide range of areas.

RECENT TRENDS AND PROSPECTS

In recent years Viet Nam has been one of the world's fastest growing economies. Its stellar growth has been combined with comparatively low inflation and with exemplary fiscal prudence. However, if Viet Nam is to sustain its growth, the government must extend its progress on reforms; in particular, it must transform moribund state enterprises into vibrant, competitive firms and lay the foundation for a modern, robust financial system.

GDP growth was 9.2 percent in 1997, maintaining the pace of earlier years. Both the agriculture and industrial sectors stayed strong and services maintained good momentum.

In 1997 industrial growth escaped the worst effects of the regional crisis. Vigorous growth in the private sector spearheaded growth in industrial output, but weaknesses continue to be apparent in the state-owned enterprise (SOE) sector. SOEs are increasingly encountering difficulties in selling their output, because the goods they produce are often of low quality and are not competitively priced. As a result, many SOEs have accumulated unwanted inventories and are now cutting back on production.

Services output grew a little more slowly in 1997 than in 1996. However, aggregate performance masked wide differences among subsectors. Those services provided by the public sector, including those related to social expenditure, showed strong growth, but other subsectors performed less well. In

particular, the SOEs' problems have spilled over into the financial system. Viet Nam's state banks carry a heavy burden of nonperforming SOE loans. Institutional weaknesses that have reduced confidence in its ability to discharge basic transactions and intermediation functions have also bedeviled the financial sector.

Viet Nam's agriculture sector again posted strong growth in 1997. Rice, the staple food, dominates agricultural activity, and Viet Nam is a net exporter of rice. Viet Nam's crop was spared the worst of the El Niño effect, and agricultural output grew by 4.9 percent.

Viet Nam has made remarkable headway in promoting price stability. In 1997 inflation was slightly lower than in 1996. The prices of consumer goods and services increased by only 3.2 percent during the year. The price of rice and other foodstuffs fell in the first half of the year, thereby helping the overall inflation picture. Tight monetary policy also helped contain inflation. Growth in the broad stock of money has been slowing for a number of years, but its rate of expansion rose slightly in 1997. Although the rate of growth of the money stock remains a little faster than that of Viet Nam's nominal GDP, some increase in the ratio of the broad money stock to GDP would be expected in a fast-growing, low-income economy with an underdeveloped financial system.

Government saving declined slightly as a proportion of GDP in 1997, falling to 5 percent, compared to more than 7 percent in 1996. Saving might have contracted further but for reductions in the growth of recurrent expenditure. The overall fiscal deficit also increased in 1997, up 2 percent of GDP from 1996. The authorities have agreed in principle on the implementation of far-reaching tax reforms that should broaden the tax base, but details have yet to be worked out. These reforms will, in any case, not be implemented until 1999.

Viet Nam's rapid growth has been propelled by a surge in investment. In 1997 the investment to GDP ratio was 25.4 percent. While the savings ratio increased, it has not been able to keep pace with investment demands. The weak financial position of many SOEs, along with a poorly developed and regulated financial system, have held back saving: in 1997 gross domestic savings amounted to 17.7 percent of GDP. The conjunction of high rates of investment but modest saving has spawned a yawning resource gap that amounted to 7.7 percent of GDP during the year.

On the heels of the blistering 41 percent growth in 1996, export growth slackened slightly to 22.2 percent in 1997. Some of this slowdown in growth is attributable to factors that adversely affected specific export markets, particularly those in agriculture. However, slower regional growth and large devaluations in the currencies of several Asian economies may also have adversely affected export performance. Import growth also slowed in 1997 for a number of reasons. The depreciation of Viet Nam's currency, the dong, raised import prices; a softening of foreign direct investment (FDI) reduced the demand for capital imports; and in an attempt to redress some of the problems of its SOEs, the government banned imports of a number of goods in 1997. Throughout 1997 Viet Nam maintained adequate foreign exchange cover. Its external debt service ratio was about 11 percent of export earnings.

While official estimates indicate that the unemployment rate was around 3.5 percent of the labor force in 1997, actual unemployment was probably somewhat higher. In rural areas a considerable number of workers are underemployed, and in some of the larger urban centers unemployment is as high as 7 percent. In those areas growth has bypassed, unemployment rates are much higher.

Ongoing turmoil in the region is likely to dampen Viet Nam's short-run economic prospects. In the near term, Viet Nam will increasingly find itself at a competitive disadvantage in some key export markets. Although pressure for further depre-

Table 2.11   Major Economic Indicators: Viet Nam, 1995-1999
(percent)

Item	1995	1996	1997	1998	1999
Gross domestic product growth	9.5	9.3	9.2	5.0	6.5
Gross domestic investment/GDP	27.1	27.9	25.4	23.0	25.0
Gross savings/GDP	17.0	16.7	17.7	16.0	18.0
Inflation rate (consumer price index)[a]	12.7	4.5	3.2	4.0	4.0
Money supply (M2) growth	22.6	22.7	24.0	15.0	15.0
Fiscal balance/GDP[b]	-1.3	-1.2	-3.2	-0.5	0.0
Merchandise exports growth	28.2	41.0	22.2	15.0	16.0
Merchandise imports growth	43.8	39.0	-1.6	5.0	5.0
Current account balance/GDP[c]	-10.1	-11.2	-7.7	-7.0	-7.0
Debt service/exports	6.3	8.7	11.0	12.0	12.0

[a] End of period.
[b] On cash basis, excluding interest arrears from expenditures; excluding grants.
[c] Excluding official transfers.

Sources: Asian Development Bank (1997h), General Statistical Office (1997), and staff estimates.

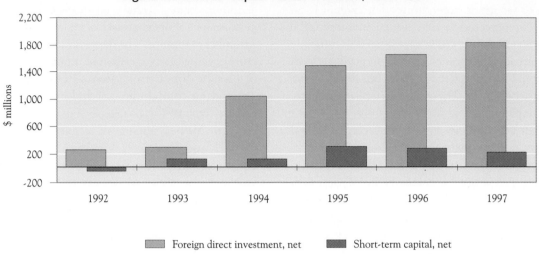

Figure 2.8 External Capital Flows: Viet Nam, 1992-1997

Foreign direct investment, net   Short-term capital, net

Sources: State Bank of Viet Nam data; and staff estimates.

ciation of the dong is building, the currencies of some competitors have depreciated by much more than the dong. In addition, with slower growth across the region, demand for Viet Nam's exports is likely to soften. Viet Nam is particularly vulnerable to a slow-down in FDI. Most of Viet Nam's FDI is currently sourced from other Association of Southeast Asian Nations (ASEAN) countries, Japan, and Republic of Korea, all of which may pare back their FDI in response to their own financial difficulties. Internally, even if the authorities can bring about meaningful reforms, they are unlikely to be able to resolve quickly the structural difficulties that beset SOEs and the financial sector. The confluence of all these factors may mean that GDP growth will slow to about 5 percent in 1998. This is likely to exacerbate underlying unemployment problems and could further aggravate regional imbalances. Inflation should, however, moderate in the face of weaker demand.

POLICY AND DEVELOPMENT ISSUES

Viet Nam's achievements in controlling inflation and mobilizing government savings are laudatory. Al-though needed SOE reforms would help the gov-

ernment mobilize revenues, government saving is already high. Viet Nam's Achilles' heel is its exter-nal account. Few economies have managed to sus-tain current account deficits of more than 5 percent of their GDP for long, and Viet Nam's current ac-count deficit is higher than this level. To date this deficit has been financed largely by FDI and official flows. Short-run capital inflows have been relatively unimportant. However, the FDI resources needed to close the resource gap may begin to dry up in the near future. While reduced FDI flows should also reduce the demand for capital imports, and so nar-row the current account deficit, private savings may still be insufficient to cover residual foreign exchange needs.

If FDI and growth slow down, Viet Nam will have to tighten both fiscal and monetary policy to mitigate balance-of-payments risks. In particular, it should reconsider the scope and magnitude of its public sector investment programs. In prioritizing projects, the government should pay careful atten-tion to comparative social returns. It may also wish to take immediate steps to raise additional revenues. However, the only viable, long-run solution to the resource gap is to mobilize more private savings, which, among other things, will require major financial sector reforms and the development of better banking infrastructure, particularly in rural areas. Import reduction measures of the kind undertaken in 1997 are, at best, only a short-term palliative. If Viet Nam were to persist with such policies it would not only delay its entry into the World Trade Organization, it would also find it more difficult to make the adjustments needed to comply with its obligations under the common effective preferential tariff of the ASEAN Free Trade Area.

A second step that Viet Nam could consider to help close its resource gap would be to permit greater flexibility of its exchange rate. Although the nominal value of the dong depreciated slightly in 1997, it has nevertheless appreciated in real terms against the currencies of its major trading partners for most of the 1990s. Thus the dong now seems to be overvalued in real terms. To peg its nominal value, Viet Nam will have to sacrifice valuable foreign exchange. A managed depreciation of the dong would have the advantage of boosting net exports and eventually narrowing the resource gap. The authorities would have to weigh the benefits of a managed depreciation against the risks of it igniting inflationary pressures and exacerbating Viet Nam's somewhat fragile debt position. Tighter fiscal and monetary policy would ease these risks.

The path to a fully fledged market economy is now becoming increasingly difficult to traverse in Viet Nam. The remarkable economic growth of the past will ultimately amount to little if the country cannot sustain growth well into the future. Experience elsewhere suggests that the private sector can provide the needed dynamism in the long term. Thus the lack of progress in private sector development during the 1990s is a concern. Indeed, official estimates suggest that the private sector's share in both GDP and industrial output has declined steadily in recent years. Part of the reason for this could, however, be the underreporting of private sector incomes.

A number of interlocking policy, institutional, and legal constraints hinder private sector development. Institutional arrangements in the financial sector restrict private sector access to credit and erode business trust and confidence. The tax system strongly discourages entrepreneurship and business owners squander resources to evade taxes. In addition, state monopolies and preferences do not allow private enterprises to compete on an equal footing, while a variety of other legal and bureaucratic obstacles not only raise costs, but also increase risks. These impediments and institutional weaknesses combine to encumber private sector growth and hold back economic modernization. To build a lasting foundation for long-term growth pending reforms of the banking sector, the trade system and state enterprises must remove the barriers that now hobble private enterprise. The stalled progress on many of these fronts is a source of concern.

SOUTH ASIA

Bangladesh

Bhutan

India

Maldives

Nepal

Pakistan

Sri Lanka

BANGLADESH

While economic growth has accelerated, inflation has slowed down, and fiscal and current account balances have improved, unemployment has remained high. Despite the currency turmoil in Asia, Bangladesh's taka has remained relatively stable.

RECENT TRENDS AND PROSPECTS

The most striking macroeconomic development in 1997 was the upturn in economic growth, with much lower inflation and improved fiscal and current account balances. GDP grew by 5.7 percent in 1997, the highest rate in the 1990s to date. The agriculture sector performed impressively, with a growth rate of 6 percent. The services sector also performed well, growing by 6.2 percent. The weakness in the economy was the industry sector, whose growth was sluggish and was the lowest in the decade, mainly because of supply bottlenecks in the power sector and low private investment. The slow pace of financial sector reforms and further deterioration in the performance of state-owned enterprises were further factors that hindered the growth rate.

The savings rate rose from around 6 percent of GDP in 1992 to 9 percent in 1997, a reflection of better control over current government spending and improvements in private saving. However, this was less than in 1994 and 1995, when savings was about 13 percent of GNP. Despite a drastic decline in inflows of foreign finance, the country was able to maintain the steady increase in the investment rate, which rose from 12.1 percent of GDP in 1992 to 17.4 percent in 1997. Part of this was due to increased private investment in response to the government's efforts to encourage private sector activities.

Although the open unemployment rate based on official statistics is low, estimates indicate that about 40 percent of the labor force is underemployed. While Bangladesh's labor costs are probably among the lowest in Asia, this cheap labor cannot be matched by adequate capital investment, and labor productivity is low.

While the overall fiscal deficit remained high, it showed some improvement in 1997. The collections of major tax revenue items, including customs duties, value-added tax, and income tax, largely met targets. On the expenditure side, revenue expenditure slightly exceeded the budget target because of unexpected interest payments on domestic debt and increased subsidies to public enterprises. However, this increase was largely offset by below target capital expenditures caused by slow progress in aid disbursement and project implementation. As a result, the overall budget deficit was 5.5 percent of GDP in 1997, about half a percentage point lower than in the previous year.

The money supply expanded modestly, with broad money supply (M2) growing by 10.8 percent in 1997, up from 8.2 percent in 1996. Net credit to the private sector rose by only 12.6 percent, compared with an average of 22.8 percent per year in 1995-1996, partly reflecting the crowding out effects

1997 refers to fiscal year 1996/97, ending 30 June.

of the rapid expansion of credit to the government, and also the commercial banks' more cautious approach toward extending new credit, as well as their increased efforts to recover overdue loans.

Sufficient food crop production and moderate monetary expansion kept inflation under control. Food prices only increased by a modest 1.3 percent. The inflation rate was 3.9 percent during 1997, lower than the 4 percent recorded in 1996. Transport, communications, and health care prices recorded the largest price increases.

Since 1990, measures to liberalize trade and payments have included reducing tariff and nontariff barriers, simplifying import procedures, introducing export incentives, and liberalizing foreign exchange controls. The authorities lowered the unweighted mean tariff from 89 percent in 1991 to 23 percent in 1997, and reduced the number of items subject to quantitative restrictions from 315 in 1990 to 23 in 1997. As a result, the external trade position has improved considerably in recent years. Export earnings remained buoyant in 1997 at $4.4 billion, although growth commodity was varied. Ready-made garments exports contributed more than half of the earnings, and grew by 14.8 percent. Imports grew slowly at 3.0 percent, mainly because of a decline in foodgrain purchases. Worker remittances from abroad surged by 21 percent. These factors brought down the current account deficit from 5.2 percent of GDP in 1996 to 2.6 percent of GDP in 1997.

However the deterioration in the capital account outweighed these improvements. Food and commodity aid decreased and many project aid disbursements were behind schedule. Net private capital outflow amounted to $120 million, and consisted largely of an outflow of foreign portfolio investments.

Despite the recent turbulence in Southeast Asian currency markets, the taka has so far remained relatively stable. The following factors contributed to this stability: (i) the taka's convertibility on the current account rather than on the capital account; (ii) the government's pursuit of a flexible exchange rate policy (from June 1996 to the end of 1997 the exchange rate devalued by more than 11 percent); (iii) the relatively low current account deficit compared with that of other Southeast Asian countries; and (iv) the foreign capital inflow to Bangladesh, which to date has been minimal, so that the subse-

quent outflow has not had any major financial consequences.

Nonetheless, the recent currency turbulence in Southeast Asia could have some adverse impact on Bangladesh's economy in the future. The economy is particularly vulnerable in the following areas: (i) its official foreign reserves stood at an uncomfortably low level of $1.6 billion in December 1997, equivalent only to 2.4 months of imports of goods and services; (ii) the competitiveness of Bangladesh in labor-intensive exports such as garments and frozen foods could be reduced because of the sharp depreciation of currencies in Southeast Asia; (iii) the level of potential foreign investment from East and Southeast Asian countries into Bangladesh could be depressed because of these countries' financial problems; and (iv) the demand for Bangladeshi overseas workers could be reduced, which would dampen workers' remittances to the country.

The medium-term outlook also depends critically on the pace of economic reforms. Based on the assumption that the government implements major structural reforms in a timely manner and maintains macroeconomic stability, projections indicate that GDP growth will rise slightly from 5.7 percent in 1998 to 6 percent in 1999. While the growth in agriculture may slow down somewhat compared to its impressive achievement in 1997, the industry sector could rebound from its disappointing performance. However, to achieve this, adequate infrastructure, including energy, roads, ports, and telecommunications, must be developed. This growth scenario assumes substantial increases in the domestic savings and investment rates, which in turn depend on timely implementation of comprehensive banking sector and capital market reforms, as well as further fiscal consolidation. Efforts to attract investments from the private sector, both domestic and foreign, need to be intensified through accelerated implementation of reforms in infrastructure and public enterprise restructuring.

As a result of the expected increase in tax collection, the fiscal deficit is forecast to decline from 5.5 percent of GDP in 1997 to about 5 percent in 1999. It will remain high in 1998, as the recent pay increase for the public sector will raise public expenditure. In line with the general expansion of economic activities, the money supply will increase by around 12.2 percent per year. Appropriate restructuring of the banking system and capital markets will be needed to ensure that adequate funds are available to the private sector. The inflation rate is projected to average just over 5 percent during 1998 and 1999.

In the next two years, the government should intensify its efforts to maintain robust exports. Export growth is projected at 15 percent in 1998 and 16 percent in 1999. The current account deficit is forecast to be about 3 percent of GDP in the next two years. An increased amount of foreign investment is expected in power generation, gas exploration, telecommunications, and cement production.

CRITICAL ISSUES IN SHORT-TERM ECONOMIC MANAGEMENT

Bangladesh must weather the adverse economic winds set in motion by the crisis in Southeast Asia. Despite improvements, its macroeconomic stability remains fragile. The two areas of short-term economic management that are particularly important are fiscal and monetary policies and external trade and the balance of payments.

Fiscal and Monetary Policies

To maintain macroeconomic stability Bangladesh must reduce its budget deficit. At the same time it must mobilize resources for funding essential public services and productive investment. Therefore, the government must adopt appropriate policies to reduce nonessential expenditures, especially as the implementation of the National Wage Commission's recommendations will lead to substantial increases in expenditures. In addition, hidden deficits arise from loss-making public enterprises and banks that must be eliminated. On the revenue side, given the low tax-to-GDP ratio, there is much scope for raising tax revenues by enforcing income tax laws, expanding the base of value added tax, and making customs administration more transparent and efficient.

While monetary policy should be noninflationary, the supply of credit to the private sector could increase somewhat from the 12.6 percent rate in 1997. Greater provision of credit and liquidity to promising and soundly managed firms is necessary to maintain the growth momentum. However, for such monetary and credit policy to be a realistic option, the government must carry out the financial reforms discussed below without delay.

External Trade and the Balance of Payments

Bangladesh's policies of trade liberalization and export promotion have so far been relatively

Table 2.12 Major Economic Indicators: Bangladesh, 1995-1999
(percent)

Item	1995	1996	1997	1998	1999
Gross domestic product growth	4.4	5.4	5.7	6.0	6.2
Gross domestic investment/GDP	19.1	17.0	17.4	17.2	18.0
Gross domestic saving/GDP	12.8	7.5	9.0	8.6	8.8
Inflation rate (consumer price index)	5.2	4.0	3.9	5.5	5.0
Money supply (M2) growth	16.0	8.2	10.8	12.0	12.5
Fiscal balance/GDP	-5.1	-5.9	-5.5	-5.5	-5.0
Merchandise exports growth	37.2	12.2	13.7	15.0	16.0
Merchandise imports growth	39.4	17.8	3.0	8.0	10.0
Current account balance/GDP	-2.7	-5.2	-2.6	-3.1	-2.7
Debt-service/exports	10.3	12.1	11.4	10.7	10.5

Sources: Asian Development Bank (1997c), Bangladesh Bureau of Statistics, Bangladesh Bank, and staff estimates.

successful; however, the export base remains narrow. This, together with the possible slowing of the inflow of emigrants' remittances, means that the balance-of-payments position remains fragile. The temporary assurance of garment exports in major markets through quotas and the Generalized System of Preferences agreements should not lead to a false sense of security. (The Generalized System of Preferences is an agreement to give preferential access to the markets of certain of the industrial economies of exports of some low-income countries.)

The export processing zones can continue to play an important role in promoting trade and attracting foreign investment. With the establishment of new export processing zones and the intensification of the activities of existing ones, continuing to improve the balance of payments without substantial depreciation in the value of taka should be possible.

POLICY AND DEVELOPMENT ISSUES

Bangladesh's primary challenges into the next century will be to reduce poverty and improve living conditions. In this context, three significant areas of ongoing policy efforts are of strategic importance: financial sector reforms, governance reforms, and environmental protection. Together, these policies can bring Bangladesh closer to maintaining a sufficient and sustainable growth rate to achieve its development goals, barring the impact of any adverse developments in the world economy.

Financial Sector Reforms

For many years, inefficiency, poor quality intermediation, and a lack of accountability have characterized Bangladesh's financial system. To facilitate adequate economic growth Bangladesh must accelerate improvements in the efficiency and flexibility of financial markets. Without efficient financial markets the mobilization of additional resources for development will slow down. Therefore, the implementation of comprehensive capital market and banking reforms should have the highest priority.

In terms of banking sector reform, supervision and regulation by the Central Bank—reported to be lax, particularly in enforcement—must be brought up to international standards. Capital

adequacy requirements, criteria for asset classification, and prudential regulations must be implemented quickly and uniformly. The authorities should vigorously accelerate loan recovery, restructure private banks, and privatize weak nationalized commercial banks. In addition, they should implement strong loan recovery measures, such as the amended Financial Loan Court Act, impartially.

The problems of the capital market are deep-rooted. The Securities and Exchange Commission is largely an ineffective regulatory and supervisory agency. In operation only since 1993, it has not had a well-established system of monitoring and surveillance. Partly because of this, the stock market shows excessive volatility.

If Bangladesh is to attract domestic and foreign savings through its equity and bond markets, the government must exert considerable efforts to develop a fair, transparent, and efficient capital market. The recently reorganized Securities and Exchange Commission should have wide discretionary powers of surveillance. Separation of the management of stock exchanges from the brokers must be maintained without exception. In the future, improved prudential regulation and incentives for channeling capital to productive enterprises will enable the financial sector to facilitate investment better.

Governance Reforms

After initial steps such as reviewing the size and functions of government departments and setting up the Efficiency Unit in the prime minister's office, the reform process should accelerate.

The Public Administration Reform Commission needs to be reorganized and given adequate support for carrying through reforms to enhance the efficiency of public sector management and administration. A new incentive structure based on merit and productivity is needed. The strategic emphasis should be on establishing mechanisms to improve transparency and accountability in all areas, including budgeting, the regulatory environment, and the government's day-to-day operations.

In terms of devolution of power, local governments should be strengthened and given financial powers to use local resources. The development of human resource and technical capacities at the local level is also urgently needed.

Environmental Protection

Finally, the government must pay attention to maintaining environmental quality. Air and water pollution and other environmental problems need to be monitored and actions taken to prevent further deterioration. The environmental issue must be addressed immediately if sustainable development is to be a realistic goal. The reduction of public expenditures should not mean abandoning preliminary efforts in this direction. On the contrary, by making the environment a priority, gains from public sector reforms could more easily be used to contain ecological damage and improve the environment.

Some specific areas where the government needs to sustain and deepen its efforts are providing protection from floods and cyclones, managing forestry, reforesting mangrove swamps, restocking fish populations, and improving environmental management in the industry sector. With international support the government should be able to take further steps toward implementing the National Environment Management Action Plan.

BHUTAN

Bhutan is continuing its cautious policy of modernization and accelerated growth while maintaining its commitment to preserving its environmental and cultural heritage. Although the public sector still plays a dominant role in the economy, the government is committed to reducing its presence in certain areas while still concentrating on the provision of infrastructure. Bhutan must maintain its efforts to diversify the economy and reduce poverty, which is still high.

RECENT TRENDS AND PROSPECTS

Bhutan initiated a cautious policy of modernization in the mid-1960s, but remains a predominantly agriculture-based economy. Growth in 1996 was 6.1 percent, partly because of the construction of a ferro-alloy plant and expenditures to increase the capacity of the power and cement industries. In 1997, however, despite the absence of such new projects, growth was slightly higher at around 6.6 percent.

Fiscal policy has been prudent during the last few years. Recently commissioned power projects, together with adjustments in electricity tariffs to India, increased fiscal revenues. These have helped the government cover its increasing recurrent expenditures brought about by a 25 percent increase in civil service pay at the beginning of 1996 and another 20 percent raise in early 1997. These wage increases were intended to help reverse the erosion of real wages that has occurred since the last general wage increase in 1988. Development expenditures also increased significantly in 1997, and these were mainly financed by foreign grants and loans. Tax revenues have increased gradually because of

improved administration. Nevertheless, the tax ratio of 8 percent of GDP caused by an extremely narrow tax base remains low compared with other countries at similar income levels. The government is continuing its tax reform policy introduced earlier, and is also attempting to strengthen nontax revenues by expanding user fees and improving cost recovery. However, despite these measures and a strong inflow of grants, Bhutan recorded an overall budget deficit of 5 percent of GDP in 1997. With gross domestic savings at 30 percent of GDP and gross domestic investment at 47 percent, the resource gap was 17 percentage points.

In 1997 the money supply (M2) grew by 20 percent and inflation was kept to 7 percent. The government has implemented policies to increase the efficiency of the financial sector. These include liberalizing rates for deposits above Nu5 million, introducing a government securities auction, and converting the Unit Trust of Bhutan into a second commercial bank.

Bhutan is continuing its cautious policy of modernization and accelerated growth while maintaining its commitment to preserving its environmental and cultural heritage. Although the public

---

1997 refers to fiscal year 1996/97, ending 30 June.

sector still plays a dominant role in the economy, the government is committed to reducing its presence in certain areas while still concentrating on the provision of infrastructure. Bhutan must maintain its efforts to diversify the economy and reduce poverty, which is still high. The external balance deteriorated in 1997: while exports grew at 8.5 percent, this was more than offset by a 25 percent increase in imports. As a result, the current account deficit, which in 1996 amounted to $48 million (or 14 percent of GDP), increased to $79 million (22 percent of GDP) in 1997. At the same time the country's external debt increased from 35 to 45 percent of GDP. However, the debt-service ratio halved from 24 percent in 1996 to 12 percent in 1997. At the end of 1997 Bhutan's reserves stood at $180 million, enough to cover imports for 17 months.

The short- and medium-term economic prospects for Bhutan are favorable. Assuming that the reform measures and investment projects announced for the Eighth Plan (1997/98-2001/02) will be realized, GDP growth is projected at 5 percent for 1998 and some 7 percent for 1999. To improve revenue prospects, the government should focus on broadening the tax base; introducing user fees; improving cost recovery; and preventing any deterioration in the fiscal situation, while safeguarding such expenditures as those on social services and operations and maintenance.

Projections indicate that the agriculture sector, which contributes 40 percent of GDP and employs 90 percent of the workforce, will grow about 2.5 percent in 1998, mainly because of productivity gains and horticultural development. Higher growth of around 12 percent is projected for manufacturing in 1998, while the figure for energy is 7 percent.

Although external assistance will continue to finance capital investments, domestic revenues will cover recurrent costs completely. The upward trend in the budget deficit is expected to continue during 1998 and 1999, with deficits reaching 9 and 12 percent of GDP, respectively, because of the implementation of a number of major projects.

The growth rate of exports is expected to decline slightly to around 6 percent in 1998, while in 1999 it will be around 9 percent. The growth rate of imports during the same period will be around 7 to 9 percent. Projections indicate that the current account deficit will reach 30 percent of GDP by 1999. Reserves will continue increasing to reach a level that could finance 18 months worth of imports. The debt-service ratio is expected to stay at around 15 to 16 percent during 1998 and 1999, while the country's external debt will continue to increase to more than 65 percent of GDP. Inflation will remain at around 8 percent, and the resource gap will continue at around 17 percentage points.

CRITICAL ISSUES IN SHORT-TERM ECONOMIC MANAGEMENT

Bhutan's growth and development prospects for the next five years depend largely on the success with which the government implements the Eighth Five-Year Plan. This plan retains the overall objectives of earlier plans, namely, accelerated growth and improved living standards, and is also committed to preserving Bhutan's environment and cultural heritage.

While the public sector continues to dominate the economy, the Eighth Plan emphasizes strengthening the private sector's contribution to economic activity. Thus the government is committed to reducing the state's role in the commercial sectors of the economy through such means as privatizing public sector enterprises, which should improve telecommunications and transportation; allowing the state to focus on providing infrastructure, including addressing the various structural and institutional constraints; strengthening the legal framework; introducing tariff reform; implementing financial, industrial, and trade liberalization; helping small businesses, including cottage enterprises; and decentralizing government decisionmaking. If these measures are implemented successfully, they will lay the foundations for future sustained growth.

Bhutan needs to increase the amount of domestic resources mobilized for investment. Finally, if plans to establish a free trade zone among the seven members of the South Asian Association for Regional Cooperation between 2000 and 2005 materialize, this could provide a major boost to Bhutan's development.

POLICY AND DEVELOPMENT ISSUES

Bhutan continues to be a poor country, with one of the lowest per capita incomes in the world. Some 80 percent of the population live in rural areas. Adult illiteracy remains high. The fertility rate is high, with an average of 5.6 births per woman. The maternal mortality rate has decreased to 380 deaths per 100,000 live births.

Since Bhutan began opening its borders to the world in the 1960s, it has established a series of long-term development objectives. These include promoting self-reliance, encouraging sustainability, preserving the country's culture and traditions, ensuring balanced development as well as national security, promoting industrialization, developing institutional and human resources, and focusing on integrated rural development. The country needs to continue its efforts to escape from the poverty trap and to achieve sustainable growth. To this end, Bhutan has rapidly expanded its expenditure on primary education and health services during the past few years. These policies will greatly enhance its development potential, as such investments have a high rate of return in countries at low levels of development. Bhutan also needs to improve its transportation network. In a country of such breathtaking beauty, tourism could play an important role in generating foreign exchange. At present, however, road access is extremely difficult and air connections are limited. As access expands, a delicate balance will have to be maintained between preserving cultural heritage and enjoying the benefits of globalization.

INDIA

While the fallout from Asia's crisis has been limited, economic growth slowed down in 1997 because of weather-related factors and subdued demand. Infrastructure bottlenecks also played a role and will need to be alleviated to enhance India's future growth prospects.

RECENT TRENDS AND PROSPECTS

After a strong performance in 1996, when real GDP grew by 7.5 percent, growth slowed to 5 percent in 1997. Agriculture, which accounts for a little more than a quarter of GDP, grew at a robust rate of nearly 8 percent in 1996. However, delayed monsoons in some areas and unseasonable and heavy rainfall in much of the country resulted in a dramatic fall in agricultural growth, which stood at just 2.5 percent in 1997.

Industrial growth remained disappointing in 1997 at 6.5 percent, well below the target of 12 percent. Manufacturing growth fell for the second consecutive year, dropping to 5 percent, compared with 7.9 percent in 1996. Once again, both consumer goods and capital goods industries were affected. Continued slow growth in consumer demand, subdued export demand, and worsening infrastructure constraints—which by raising the costs of production have played a role in limiting demand—were the main factors responsible for the slowdown in industrial growth, although heightened political uncertainty was also a factor.

The government's 1997 budget was designed to continue the process of fiscal consolidation, while at the same time giving a strong push to growth, particularly in industry. In addition to substantial cuts in direct taxation, the budget also included a range of other measures designed to boost savings and investment and revive the capital market. With government expenditure held constant in real terms, the budget also envisaged a further reduction in the fiscal deficit from 5 to 4.5 percent of GDP. This was based primarily on assumptions of improved tax buoyancy, although measures to improve tax compliance, as well as increased income from the disinvestment of government holdings in public enterprises, were also expected to contribute to the improved budget outcome.

However, with the economy, especially industry, failing to respond to the budgetary stimulus, revenues fell well short of the target, despite the success of the government's tax amnesty scheme. In addition, the government had to cut back its plans to sell off its holdings in public enterprises because of the downturn in global stock markets in the latter half of 1997. At the same time, the government's decision in July 1997 to grant major pay increases in excess of those recommended in the Fifth Pay Commission Report pushed expenditures well above budgeted levels. Even allowing for the impact of the government's supplementary budget, introduced in September to deal with the revenue shortfall, the fiscal deficit is expected to have risen rather than fallen in 1997. The increase in civil servants' pay will also contribute to the intense pressure on state governments' finances, because they are more or less

1997 refers to fiscal year 1997/98, ending 31 March.

Table 2.13 Major Economic Indicators: India, 1995-1999
(percent)

Item	1995	1996	1997	1998	1999
Gross domestic product growth[a]	7.2	7.5	5.0	6.7	7.0
Gross domestic investment/GDP	26.2	27.1	26.6	27.1	29.0
Gross national saving/GNP	24.4	25.6	25.5	25.6	27.1
Inflation rate (consumer price index)	10.0	9.2	6.5	7.0	7.2
Money supply (M3) growth	13.7	15.9	16.5	16.7	15.0
Fiscal balance/GDP	-7.1	-7.0	-6.7	-6.7	-6.5
Merchandise exports growth	20.8	4.1	5.0	7.5	7.8
Merchandise imports growth	28.0	5.1	8.2	9.9	11.2
Current account balance/GDP[b]	-1.8	-1.0	-1.2	-1.5	-2.0
Debt service/exports	37.3	41.9	31.8	29.9	28.9

Note: All data are on a fiscal year basis.

[a] Based on constant 1980 factor cost.
[b] Excluding official transfers.

Sources: Central Statistical Organisation (1998), Reserve Bank of India (1997), and staff estimates.

obliged to follow salary revisions made by the central government.

On a more positive note, the release of the *Government White Paper on Subsidies* in May 1997 has initiated more open debate on the subsidy issue and is expected to prompt substantial reform in the next few years. Total budgetary subsidies, both at the central and state levels, amounted to a massive 14.4 percent of GDP in 1994. Only about a quarter of these subsidies could be justified on the grounds that the market by itself would not provide the right level of output. Another important development was the government's announcement in the 1997 budget that, despite its continued fiscal pressures, as of 1 April 1997 it would discontinue the system of ad hoc Treasury bills as a means of automatic financing for the budget deficit. This move was designed to strengthen fiscal discipline while providing greater autonomy to the Reserve Bank of India (RBI) in its conduct of monetary policy.

Monetary policy was further eased in 1997 in an effort to complement the fiscal stimulus given to the economy by the budget and to prevent the rupee from appreciating as a result of strong capital inflows in the first half of 1997. Measures taken included further cuts in the cash reserve ratio and the bank rate, which, with controls lifted on almost all deposit and lending rates, was reintroduced especially to signal the policy stance of the Central Bank. Despite the fall in lending rates, the amount of credit taken up by the corporate sector remained subdued because of lack of business confidence and the continued high real costs of domestic borrowing. Another factor was the persistent caution on the part of banks in appraising the riskiness of loans, a result of the stricter requirements of the RBI's new prudential norms. As business confidence began to pick up in the latter part of the year, credit uptake also began to increase. However, this may have been partially offset as the RBI tightened monetary policy in an effort to ease downward pressure on the exchange rate toward the end of the year.

While the scope for further improvements in credit appraisal and loan recovery is substantial, the banking system's performance continued to improve in response to financial sector reforms. The 27 public sector banks posted an aggregate profit of $950 million in 1996, compared with a loss of $110 million in 1995. The RBI intensified its supervision of nonbank financial institutions during 1997, particularly those that were sponsored by or had close links with particular corporate groups. In December the government appointed the Second Financial Sector Committee to review the progress of financial sector reforms. The committee is expected to pay particular attention to the role and operations of all-India development financial institutions and nonbank financial institutions. The continued fall in inflation was one of the main bright spots of 1997, with inflation as measured by the consumer price index falling to 6.5 percent.

After rapid growth in both exports and imports between 1992 and 1995, the rate of growth fell sharply in 1996 and 1997. Exports are estimated to have increased by just 5 percent in 1997, while imports are estimated to have risen by 8.2 percent, although in both cases these growth rates are higher than in 1996. The major cause of slow export growth in 1997 was the fall in exports of primary products and garments. As in 1996, the slow growth in imports primarily reflected the continued slow growth of the industry sector, and hence reduced demand for imported capital goods. However, it also reflected a fall in crude oil imports because of increased domestic production. The current account deficit is estimated to have increased marginally to 1.2 percent of GNP.

Inflows of foreign direct investment (FDI) increased to around $4 billion, almost 50 percent more than in 1996, while FDI approvals reached $17 billion, compared with $8.7 billion a year earlier. Although foreign portfolio investment in 1997 increased marginally over the previous year, net outflows of portfolio investment occurred in both November and December 1997 as a result of the worsening Asian currency crisis and the loss of confidence in the region's stock markets.

The economy is expected to grow by between 6.7 and 7 percent during 1998 and 1999 based on a recovery in both agriculture and industry. While the potential for a stronger recovery in industry exists, infrastructure constraints are becoming increasingly binding. With exports rising more slowly than imports, the trade deficit will widen, leading to a substantially wider current account deficit. In view of this, and in light of the Asian currency crisis, the authorities must try to ensure that India's exchange rate remains competitive.

CRITICAL ISSUES IN SHORT-TERM ECONOMIC MANAGEMENT

Apart from efforts to boost economic growth, particularly industrial growth, concerns about the exchange rate dominate economic management. While concerns in the first half of 1997 revolved

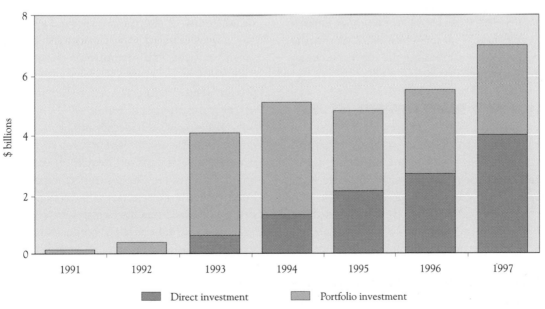

Figure 2.9 Foreign Investment Inflows: India, 1991-1997

Sources: Reserve Bank of India (1994-1997) and staff estimates.

around the upward pressure on the rupee resulting from the then strong capital inflows, the focus of concern since around the fourth quarter of 1997 shifted to limiting the contagion from the Asian currency crisis. The RBI's initial welcoming of the weakening of the rupee in August and September 1997 was not surprising. However, from mid-December onward, the RBI began to intervene to defend the currency. The RBI introduced measures to defend the rupee after it hit an all-time low of Rs39.93 to the US dollar, and responded even more vigorously when the rupee fell below the psychologically important rate of Rs40 to the US dollar. As a result, the rupee appreciated to around Rs38 to the US dollar by the end of January 1998.

However, whether further weakening of the rupee would be undesirable is not clear. Given the massive devaluations that have occurred in Indonesia, Republic of Korea, Malaysia, Philippines, and Thailand, the rupee is now significantly overvalued compared with these countries' currencies. While relatively few of India's exports compete directly with those of these countries, the currency depreciations have also increased their attractiveness as locations for FDI and tourism. Some further depreciation of the rupee may therefore be necessary to maintain India's external competitiveness. Moreover, some of the measures adopted to contain the rupee's slide, such as the increase in the cash reserve ratio by 2 percent in January, could choke off an industrial recovery by dampening business enthusiasm to borrow funds for investment. These considerations suggest that the authorities will need to weigh carefully the costs and benefits of supporting the rupee if it comes under renewed pressure during 1998.

POLICY AND DEVELOPMENT ISSUES

Although India has already made substantial progress in implementing economic reforms in recent years, the government will need to enhance both the scope and pace of economic reforms if it is to sustain the improved economic performance of the last few years. Among the many areas that need attention, infrastructure development is one of the most critical.

Serious infrastructural deficiencies present a major impediment to sustainable growth of the Indian economy, and are among the major contributors to the slowdown in growth in the last two years. Estimates indicate that the level of investment in infrastructure needs to be increased by almost 50 percent in real terms during the next decade if India is to maintain GDP growth of at least 7 percent. Given the pressure on government capital spending, the private sector will have to come up with the bulk of the additional requirements. Projections suggest that the level of private investment would need to increase almost sevenfold per year, to some $23 billion by 2007. Substantial scope for private sector participation also exists in industrial parks, ports, power, roads, telecommunications, and urban infrastructure.

However, the commercialization of infrastructure faces several major constraints, including the absence of an appropriate, long-term framework and policy incentive mechanism for private investment; the poor policy coordination among different government agencies in the implementation of large infrastructure projects; and a shortage of long-term funding. Although recent years have seen some progress, a number of critical issues need resolution.

Governments in developing economies have traditionally provided infrastructure services below supply costs, and India's government has been no exception. In the case of the power sector, net subsidies in India have been estimated to be around 1 percent of GDP. Even though the costs of private sector operations may be lower because of better efficiency, greater cost recovery though increased user charges is essential to ensure the viability and sustainability of the private sector. Unfortunately, any adjustment of prices and tariffs remains a sensitive issue, and setting user charges that are sufficiently high to provide adequate returns to the private sector, while ensuring that users do not perceive the charges as unfair, will be important.

Because of such factors as high costs, long gestation periods, and irregular revenue flows, infrastructure investments rely heavily on long-term debt financing. However, in contrast to equity markets, India's debt markets are not well developed and constrain infrastructure financing. One critical problem with the debt market is the thinness of the secondary market, which makes it difficult for holders of long-term debt to convert it into more liquid assets. This has served to reduce the attractiveness of holding long-term debt. One factor constraining liquidity is the stamp duty states impose on the issuance and trade of financial instruments. Stamp duties are an important source of revenue for state governments and cannot be abolished. However, exempting the trade of financial instruments, particularly those relating to infrastructure funding, from these duties should be made possible in order to develop secondary markets.

In addition, institutional investors with a long-term investment horizon, such as insurance companies, provident funds, and pensions funds, are critical sources of long-term funding. Opening up this sector to greater competition and allowing the entry of foreign institutional investors will widen the investor base. Attempts to do this have, however, met with setbacks. The government had to back off from its initial moves to introduce competition into health insurance because of opposition in Parliament, and the opening up of the insurance sector, especially to foreign companies, remains constrained.

While the private sector must increasingly take the lead in infrastructure development, it will be some time before the appropriate legal and regulatory frameworks are in place. In addition, public investment in basic infrastructure, as well as a strong public-private partnership in infrastructure development, are needed to increase private investment. Given the vital role that the public sector continues to play, any further cuts in public sector capital expenditure need to be carefully evaluated.

MALDIVES

The Maldives consolidated its growth during 1997, and growth is projected to continue at 6 percent per year in 1998 and 1999. The economy continues to depend heavily on fishing and tourism, and the authorities should ensure that future development does not damage the environment, on which these industries depend. The policy priorities for the future are to liberalize and modernize the financial sector; to reduce the government's role in the commercial sector; and to develop human resources, so that the economy can become less dependent on foreign workers.

RECENT TRENDS AND PROSPECTS

Real GDP growth was approximately 6 percent in 1997. Tourist arrivals in the first half of the year amounted to almost 177,000, 6 percent higher than during the corresponding period of 1996. This was associated with an increase of nearly 2 percent in total hotel bed capacity and an increase in the occupancy rate from 75 to 78 percent. Fisheries' output declined in volume in 1997, but the total value of production remained relatively stable because of a significant increase in the price of fresh fish. Construction activity was brisk as work started on several new tourist resorts scheduled to open in 1998 and 1999, and continued on some key economic and social infrastructure (ports, schools, hospitals) in the atolls outside Malé. Transportation and communications also grew rapidly, while retail and wholesale trade remained relatively stable.

Inflation was about 8 percent in 1997, somewhat higher than the 6.2 percent registered in 1996. Higher fish prices caused by the low catch and the increased demand from the brisk construction activity were the main reasons behind the rise. Monetary growth was about 20 percent in 1997, compared with 24 percent in 1996. Credit expansion was a modest 3 percent, reflecting a decline in net credit to the government. However, credit to the private sector and public entities increased. Foreign workers increased by 17 percent in response to stronger demand for labor in the face of a relatively stable domestic labor supply. Foreign labor, both skilled and unskilled, now accounts for nearly a quarter of the labor force. Consequently, job opportunities for nationals are likely to be plentiful in the future if the present growth momentum continues and domestic workers can upgrade their skills.

The Maldives continued to pursue a prudent fiscal policy in 1997. The modest deficit was financed through concessional foreign loans, eliminating, for the second consecutive year, the need to resort to monetary financing from the Monetary Authority. While more than 90 percent of government revenues are still derived from import duties and tourism tax receipts, some diversification is expected in 1998 with the introduction of a rental income and business turnover tax.

In the first half of 1997 the trade deficit deteriorated to $86 million, compared with $75.8 million during the same period of 1996. The increase in fish prices partly offset the reduced catch, while tourism receipts compensated for the growth in imports. As a result, the overall balance-of-payments position improved. At the end of 1997 international reserves stood at about four months worth of imports, despite the repayment of a balance-of-payments support loan contracted earlier.

The outlook for 1998 and 1999 remains bright, with growth rates projected at 6 percent. As Asian tourists account for approximately 20 percent of arrivals in the Maldives, the recent currency crisis in East Asia may lead to a modest decline in tourism. In addition, the increase in resort construction in 1998 and 1999 may result in some inflationary pressures and in a further increase in the foreign labor force.

CRITICAL ISSUES IN SHORT-TERM ECONOMIC MANAGEMENT

The macroeconomic stabilization measures implemented in 1994 succeeded in eliminating the excessive budget deficits and high inflation that characterized the early 1990s. They have, however, left a legacy of high domestic debt contracted by the Treasury with the Monetary Authority. Macroeconomic policies should continue to be cautious to facilitate noninflationary growth. Somewhat greater flexibility than in the recent past may be advisable in the management of the exchange rate, especially in light of the substantial depreciation of the Southeast Asian currencies. There is still a need for structural reform in the financial sector. The scope for liberalizing and modernizing the financial sector by shifting from direct to indirect instruments of monetary control is considerable. A prerequisite for this course of action would be gradually to retire outstanding government debt, followed by securitization of the balance. A gradual reduction in the role of public enterprises is also needed, as is the improvement of the legal and regulatory framework (particularly commercial and bankruptcy laws) in order to foster private sector development.

POLICY AND DEVELOPMENT ISSUES

The Malé atoll suffers from both population and environmental pressures. To relieve these, the government will have to ensure that growth and infrastructure development are more widely distributed among the atolls. The government has started to respond to these issues and has identified growth centers in the north and south where investment in infrastructure is being concentrated. However, the government will have to attempt to maintain a balance between developing the economy and preserving the environment to avoid undermining the sustainability of tourism and fisheries, the two pillars of the economy.

The Maldives will also need to respond to two main challenges in relation to human resource development. First, the successful implementation of a number of social policies has resulted in such achievements as the virtual eradication of malaria, nearly universal literacy rates, and greatly improved life expectancy. However, the population growth rate, at nearly 3 percent per year, is still one of the highest in the world, and if this is sustained it will lead to considerable pressures on the country's natural resources, including land. Thus the government needs to adopt more effective policies to reduce population growth. The second challenge is to continue the expansion of educational opportunities at all levels, especially for girls and women. Those who acquire secondary and postsecondary education will be able to compete for relatively high-paying jobs currently occupied by foreign workers. This is necessary if the country is to sustain its current level of growth and dynamism.

NEPAL

Growth will continue to be weak, while inflation should remain moderate. Structural weaknesses relate to external trade, resource mobilization, and fiscal imbalances.

RECENT TRENDS AND PROSPECTS

GDP growth declined to 4.3 percent in 1997, compared with 6.1 percent in 1996. The slowdown was evident in all sectors, particularly the nonagriculture sectors. Although the rapid growth of nonagriculture sectors in recent years reduced the share of agriculture in GDP from about 50 percent in 1990 to 41 percent in 1997, agriculture is still the single most important determinant of overall economic performance. About 80 percent of the total labor force depend on agriculture for their livelihood. Aided by the favorable monsoons, agriculture grew 4.1 percent in 1997, close to the average annual growth rate of the sector for the past two decades.

Industrial growth slowed from 5.9 percent in 1996 to 3.2 percent in 1997, mainly because of slow growth in construction. Although manufacturing grew by a respectable 5.7 percent, this was lower than in 1996. The major obstacles to further industrial development are limited infrastructure, power shortages, and a lack of skilled human resources. The public sector has reduced its involvement in many areas, and private sector participation has been enhanced since 1992 through privatization, institutional reforms, and economic liberalization. In addition, in September 1997 amendments to the Industrial Enterprises Act reduced distortionary tax holiday incentives.

The service sector grew by 5.0 percent in 1997, down from 7.9 percent in 1996. This reflected a significant slowdown in finance, real estate, and community and social services. Increasing concerns about environmental pollution, natural disasters such as flash floods and landslides, malaria in India, and political disturbances had an adverse effect on tourism. Unemployment stood at about 23 percent of the total labor force in 1997 and underemployment remains widespread.

Total budgetary revenues grew by almost 12 percent, less than half the government's target, and remained at about 11 percent of GDP in 1997. Tax revenues have gradually increased their contribution to 80 percent of total revenues (excluding grants), and grew from less than 7 percent of GDP in 1992 to 9 percent in 1997. The continued weakness in revenue collection since 1995 reflects reduced growth of imports and changes in import composition toward low tariff commodities. Imports account for almost 30 percent of tax revenues through custom duties, and sales tax generates another 20 percent. In September 1997 the government amended the Customs Act to improve customs valuations in preparation for the introduction of an automated customs system at the international airport.

With low revenue collections and lower than expected foreign grants, the government's fiscal performance would have deteriorated in 1997 if not

1997 refers to fiscal year 1996/97, ending 15 July.

Table 2.14 Major Economic Indicators: Nepal, 1995-1999
(percent)

Item	1995	1996	1997	1998	1999
Gross domestic product, growth[a]	2.8	6.1	4.3	3.7	4.0
Gross domestic investment/GDP	23.4	23.2	23.4	24.9	25.0
Gross national saving/GNP	15.2	10.3	12.5	13.1	13.0
Inflation rate (consumer price index)	7.6	8.1	7.8	7.5	8.0
Money supply (M2) growth	16.1	14.4	10.7	12.0	12.0
Fiscal balance/GDP[b]	-4.6	-5.6	-5.3	-5.6	-5.8
Merchandise exports growth	-9.6	1.7	10.3	4.0	6.0
Merchandise imports growth[c]	21.9	9.0	10.3	5.0	6.0
Current account balance/GDP	-7.8	-12.8	-7.2	-8.7	-8.8
Debt-service/exports	7.9	8.4	8.2	8.4	8.2

Note: All data are on a fiscal year basis.

[a] At factor cost.
[b] Including grants.
[c] Cost, insurance, and freight.

Sources: Asian Development Bank (1998); Central Bureau of Statistics (1997a, b); Ministry of Finance data; and staff estimates.

for a significant shortfall in development expenditures, which rose just 6 percent rather than the 33 percent envisaged in the budget. This was partly due to a slowdown in project implementation resulting from political disturbances and staff changes after local elections. The fiscal deficit (including foreign grants) improved slightly to 5.3 percent of GDP in 1997.

Money supply (M2) growth slowed to 10.7 percent, down from about 14 percent the previous year. Net domestic assets, which account for more than 90 percent of the change in money supply since 1995, rose by 17 percent in 1997. Domestic credit grew by 13 percent, and credit to the private sector posted a relatively modest, but still respectable, increment of 18 percent.

The auction of Treasury bills and securities from the Central Bank is now an integral part of the monetary program. Open market operations are a principal instrument for controlling domestic liquidity. In addition, the authorities took steps to reduce the government's automatic recourse to the Central Bank's overdraft facilities, which had compli-

cated the conduct of monetary policy in the past, by placing a binding annual limit on its annual overdraft of NRs1 billion as of the beginning of 1998. The commercial banking system was strengthened through the recapitalization of the two government-owned commercial banks—Nepal Bank Limited and Rastriya Banijya Bank—which account for about 65 percent of total deposits. The government reduced its ownership in Nepal Bank Limited to 40 percent in early 1997 as part of its privatization efforts. The Rastriya Banijya Bank is undertaking major restructuring and is high on the government's priority list for privatization.

Inflation declined from 8.1 percent in 1996 to 7.8 percent in 1997, reflecting moderate price changes. Because of the open border trading with India, price developments in Nepal closely reflect those in India.

The exchange rate was relatively stable in early 1997, with the Nepalese rupee depreciating about 3 percent against the US dollar, and thereby exerting little inflationary pressure on the economy. The currency's depreciation since July 1997 reflects adjustment of the Indian rupee as well as the alignment of the real effective exchange rate to maintain the competitiveness of Nepalese products.

Exports continued to recover, with an increase of more than 10 percent in 1997, compared with 1.7 percent the previous year. Imports showed a similar increase, up slightly from 9 percent in 1996, thus maintaining the trade deficit at 23 percent of GDP. Nepal generally has a large trade deficit because of its low export base and high import levels. Remittances from overseas workers were an important source of earnings. Higher investment income also contributed to the improvement in the current account. As a result, the current account deficit (excluding grants) improved by 38 percent to $354 million, or 7.2 percent of GDP. Inflows of official grants and concessional aid continued to finance a substantial portion of the current account deficit. By the end of 1997, the balance of payments had registered a surplus of $161 million and foreign exchange reserves had grown to $812 million, equivalent to more than six months' worth of imports of goods and services.

Projections indicate that in 1998 real GDP growth will be 3.7 percent, with increased crop production and continued normal growth trends in the financial, manufacturing, and service sectors. With implementation of the Agriculture Perspective Plan, revitalization of reform efforts, and favorable weather, real GDP growth may reach 4 percent in 1999; however, agricultural growth is expected to decelerate to 2.0 percent following unfavorable weather conditions during the first quarter of 1998.

The government continues to encourage private sector development in industry by pursuing macroeconomic stability and removing distortions in prices and regulations. The industry sector is therefore forecast to grow by 4.6 percent in 1998 and 4 percent in 1999. Hydropower development should also improve Nepal's long-term development prospects through power exports to India. In 1997 Parliament ratified the Mahakali Integrated Development Treaty between India and Nepal, a joint hydroelectric, irrigation, and flood control project, and an agreement was also signed between the two countries for possible investment in and financing of hydroelectric projects by the private sector and lending agencies. More development projects in sectors like power, transportation, and irrigation would support a gradual recovery in construction activi-

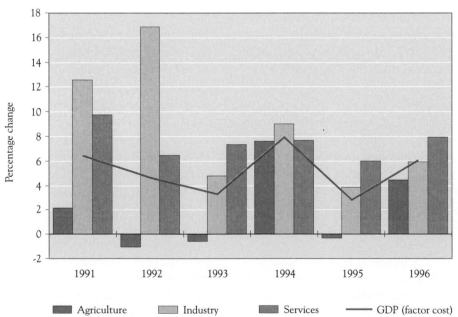

Figure 2.10 GDP Growth by Sector: Nepal, 1991-1996

Agriculture ■ Industry ■ Services — GDP (factor cost)

Source: Central Bureau of Statistics data.

ties. The strength of export demand for carpets and garments will largely determine the prospects for manufacturing.

Increased tourist arrivals and trading and financial activities will support growth in services, although at a lower rate than in the past. Providing the necessary legal framework and continuing economic liberalization efforts will foster greater private sector participation. Service sector growth is expected to exceed 4 percent in 1998 and 1999.

While forecasts indicate that domestic savings and investment will increase in 1998 and 1999, the resource gap is likely to widen. Economic liberalization programs have not only helped to open up new investment opportunities for investors, but have also encouraged consumption and savings mobilization, particularly through the establishment of rural financial institutions. Therefore, the government's commitment to continue its efforts to improve resource mobilization will be crucial, including major tax reforms and measures to ensure efficiency in the financial sector and revitalize the capital market.

The 1998 budget includes programs to facilitate development activities and improve the stagnant revenue performance by strengthening tax collection and administration. The value-added tax introduced in November 1997 will further enhance domestic revenues by expanding the tax base. While the full impact of proposed tax reforms and revenue mobilization measures will not be apparent for a few years, government expenditures are expected to increase in 1998, mainly because of adjustments in civil service salaries and the implementation of major projects. Thus despite the anticipated increase in domestic revenues, the fiscal deficit as a percentage of GDP is likely to deteriorate in 1998. Net domestic borrowing in 1998 will be contained at about 1 percent of GDP if revenue targets and anticipated foreign grants and loans are realized.

Merchandise exports and imports are likely to grow at roughly the same rate in 1998 and 1999, and the current account will stabilize at just under 9 percent of GDP, compared with 7.2 percent in 1997. The expected increase in tourist visits as a result of the "Visit Nepal Year 1998" campaign and the operation of international flights by private sector airlines could raise net service receipts during the next two years. However, the increase in the service and transfer accounts surplus will not be sufficient to cover trade deficits. Official capital inflows should increase substantially in 1998 and subsequent years, reflecting improved use of external aid. Net transfers are projected to increase temporarily because of the return of a large number of Gurkha soldiers formerly stationed in Hong Kong, China. Increased remittances can also be expected from the increasing number of Nepalese workers in the Middle East and India. The government's total outstanding external debt will increase to more than 55 percent of GDP in 1999, but the debt-service ratio will remain below 9 percent of exports during the next two years, as most foreign loans are on concessional terms and substantial repayments are not due to begin for some time.

POLICY AND DEVELOPMENT ISSUES

Even assuming favorable results from economic policies to increase private sector participation, substantial government support will be needed to boost overall development in the next few years. However, the extent of government support will be constrained by its limited capacity to mobilize domestic resources and the country's weak implementation and monitoring capabilities. Measures are needed to address the economy's structural weaknesses, particularly in the areas of external trade, resource mobilization, and fiscal imbalances.

Reducing fiscal expenditures will be difficult without further cuts in operation and maintenance expenditures and/or local counterpart funds for new development projects. However, the country cannot afford any slippage in its fiscal targets, particularly in revenue mobilization and domestic borrowing, unless it accepts lower growth and/or higher inflation and external imbalances. Under these circumstances, the government will need to tackle the structural weaknesses that are at the root of the fiscal imbalances. This should include efforts to reduce public service overstaffing, contain the burden of loss-incurring public enterprises, prioritize development expenditures effectively to avoid project underfunding, and find new sources of revenues.

PAKISTAN

In addition to a declining growth rate and stagnant production, investment and savings performance continues to be weak, export growth is decelerating dramatically, and governance is weak and inefficient.

RECENT TRENDS AND PROSPECTS

GDP growth was only 3.1 percent in 1997. Agriculture grew by just 0.7 percent because of low productivity coupled with untimely rainfall and cotton viruses. Manufacturing showed poor growth of 1.8 percent, largely as a result of negative growth in the large-scale manufacturing subsector, which made up three quarters of total manufacturing. This can be attributed to limited financial resources, reduced exports, and outdated equipment. Growth in the service sector also fell in 1997. During 1996 and 1997 foreign exchange reserves were at a precarious level, equivalent to an average of only about four weeks worth of imports.

Two factors are responsible for the low growth and the accompanying high macroeconomic instability. The first is the political situation, which has included frequent changes of government and an unstable law and order situation in Karachi. Although the three-month-long political crisis ended in December 1997, its economic consequences have persisted. The second factor is structural bottlenecks, such as persistent fiscal imbalances, limited financial resources, and inadequate infrastructure. Lengthy legal procedures and poorly organized regulatory systems aggravate the situation. To deal with these weaknesses, the government has undertaken a series of broadly based policy reforms that include adopting major tax and tariff reforms in March 1997, which substantially lowered tax and tariff rates across the board. The purpose of reducing tax and tariff rates was to boost private sector industrial activity, enhance productivity, and promote new production techniques. Furthermore, a wide range of financial sector reforms that cover capital markets, the central banking system, and commercial banks are either under way or on the drawing board. Although these reforms have produced some favorable outcomes in recent months, such as a small increase in exports, major effects may not be visible for one or two years.

In 1997 investment and saving rates remained extremely low. Total investment as a percentage of GNP fell to 18.4 percent in 1997 because of financial and foreign exchange constraints, low growth in exports, policy conflict with the International Monetary Fund (IMF), and frequent government changes. The continued decline in national savings since 1994 exacerbated the effect of these factors on investment.

Official unemployment was reported at 2 million, or 5.4 percent of the labor force, in 1997. However, given the definition of employment in the labor force survey, that is, a person who works for at least one hour during the reference period is considered employed, actual underemployment is substantially higher.

1997 refers to fiscal year 1996/97, ending 30 June.

Budgetary deficits have long impaired efforts to achieve macroeconomic stability. In an effort to reduce the deficit, in 1997 the government streamlined development plans and projects and cut the Public Sector Development Plan budget by 19 percent. It also restructured the tax system to tax agricultural income more efficiently. However, these efforts met with limited success, as the consolidated budget deficit remained at 6.3 percent of GDP, the same as in 1996. This led to substantial domestic borrowing from financial markets, which financed more than 80 percent of the deficit.

Government borrowing for budgetary support is a main contributor to domestic credit expansion. The banking and financial sector also suffers from extensive levels of loan defaults, which by 1997 amounted to 7 percent of GDP. The authorities pursued a tighter monetary policy in 1997 and the rate of M2 growth decelerated to 13.1 percent. However, inflation was 11.6 percent, about 2.6 percentage points above the government's target, as a result of fiscal laxity in 1996.

Commodity exports declined by 2.7 percent in 1997, mainly because excessive rains curtailed cotton production. Other major products whose exports suffered included raw leather, medical instruments, and chemicals and pharmaceuticals. Persistent inflation, a low-technology industrial base, and a shortage of financial resources hindered any recovery in exports. Imports were 5 percent lower than in 1996. The rise in capital goods imports was offset by the decline in imports of food (except for wheat and rice), chemicals, and metals. As a result, the trade deficit improved marginally in 1997. And despite the widening of the deficit on the services account because of increased debt servicing, the current account deficit narrowed to 6.5 percent of GDP. However, there was a significant drop in the capital account surplus, which led to a considerable decrease in foreign exchange reserves.

If the government continues both its economic and governance reforms and no severe natural disasters take place in the next two years, Pakistan's macroeconomic prospects are likely to improve. GDP growth is projected to be a little more than 5 percent in both 1998 and 1999. The agriculture sector, after its minimal growth in 1997, is forecast to grow faster. With the government's support for private

Table 2.15   Major Economic Indicators: Pakistan, 1995-1999
(percent)

Item	1995	1996	1997	1998	1999
Gross domestic product, growth[a]	5.2	4.6	3.1	5.1	5.5
Gross domestic investment/GNP	18.3	18.7	18.4	20.0	22.0
Gross national saving/GNP	14.2	11.6	11.4	12.5	13.5
Inflation rate (consumer price index)	13.0	10.8	11.6	10.0	10.2
Money supply (M2) growth	16.6	14.9	13.1	14.2	15.0
Fiscal balance/GDP[b]	-5.5	-6.3	-6.3	-5.0	-5.0
Merchandise exports growth	16.1	7.1	-2.7	6.0	9.0
Merchandise imports growth	18.5	16.7	-5.0	0.5	10.0
Current account balance/GDP[c]	-4.1	-7.1	-6.5	-5.1	-5.2
Debt-service/exports	34.9	33.9	37.0	35.0	34.0

Note: All data are on a fiscal year basis.

[a] At constant factor cost.
[b] Based on consolidated federal and provincial accounts and including surplus of autonomous bodies.
[c] Excluding official transfers.

Sources: Economic Adviser's Wing (1997); State Bank of Pakistan (1997, 1998); Asian Development Bank (1997b); and staff estimates.

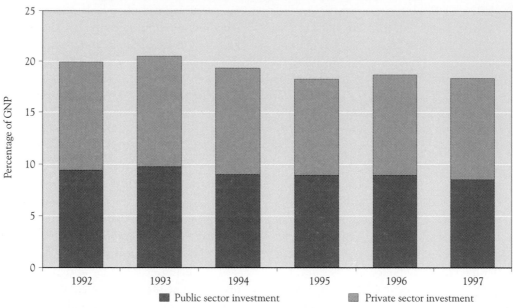

Figure 2.11 Gross National Investment: Pakistan, 1992-1997

Sources: State Bank of Pakistan (1997) and staff estimates.

sector-led industrialization, industrial output is also expected to increase. Likewise, the service sector is projected to grow because of a gradual recovery in the financial sector. Projections also indicate that exports will increase because of improved industrial activity in 1997 and that imports are likely to increase only marginally because of increased imports of petroleum products and chemical products. Therefore, the current account deficit is expected to decline further to a little more than 5 percent of GDP in 1998 and 1999.

CRITICAL ISSUES IN SHORT-TERM ECONOMIC MANAGEMENT

Pakistan suffers from a number of macroeconomic imbalances and structural problems, which in the past were frustrated by slippages in policy implementation. As a consequence, in October 1997 the IMF approved SDR1,137.3 million ($1,558 million) under two of its programs (the Extended Fund Facility and the Enhanced Structural Adjustment Facility) for macroeconomic adjustments and reforms. Under these programs Pakistan is to rein in the inflation rate and current account deficit.

An important issue in short-term economic management relates to the government's ability to

meet the accompanying IMF macroeconomic targets. A critical issue in this context is revenue collection. According to estimates by independent tax experts, revenues are expected to fall some 15 to 20 percent short of the target during 1997. Thus to adhere to the budget deficit target prescribed by the IMF the government needs to broaden the tax base, revamp tax administration, and rationalize government expenditures.

The level of foreign exchange reserves has also been a source of concern. This will probably reduce Pakistan's ability to import capital and intermediate goods, thereby prolonging the industrial recession of 1996 and 1997, when 4,000 factories closed down. A high priority is the need to increase the growth of exports and rationalize imports.

POLICY AND DEVELOPMENT ISSUES

Economic growth has barely kept pace with population growth, and the debt-service ratio reached 37 percent, the highest in Asia. To revive economic dynamism, Pakistan must promote investment and exports.

The two 1997 IMF programs require a number of medium-term reforms needed to revitalize the economy. To promote growth the government is to strengthen the private sector and rationalize the public sector. The privatization program is to be given a new impetus by privatizing public assets in the manufacturing, power and gas, and telecommunications sectors. This program is to be extended to the financial sector, complemented by efforts to strengthen supervisory and regulatory institutions. Although the two IMF programs focus on fiscal and balance of payments areas, education, health care, population welfare, and family planning are also addressed. Therefore expenditures on the social sectors will rise in the near term.

Promoting Investment and Saving

Gross national investment has been low: as a percentage of GDP it stood at around 18 percent during 1995-1997, while such high-performing Asian countries as Indonesia and Malaysia were investing more than 30 percent of their GDP. To achieve a growth rate of 6 percent per year will require an investment ratio of about 25 percent, which implies that the savings rate must rise. However, a low savings rate is one of Pakistan's major problems. The national savings rate hovers at about 12 percent of GNP, one of the lowest levels in Asia. Pakistan's financial sector, which is dominated by nationalized banks, is ineffective in mobilizing savings. The 360 national savings centers are primarily designed to help finance public sector deficits. Specialized private savings institutions are nonexistent, the insurance industry is small, and the growth rate of quasi-money is far slower than in other Asian economies. The result is that financial institutions have developed little in the past two decades. If this situation is remedied, savings performance will improve.

As households with fewer dependents save more and family size is gradually declining in Pakistan, the savings rate may rise in the medium term. An increase in the real interest rate would also improve savings performance. Evidence from other Asian economies indicates that a relatively small rise in the interest rate can lead to a large increase in savings.

Encouraging Exports to Revive the Economy

As noted earlier, exports contracted in 1997, causing low utilization of industrial capacity. The decline in Pakistan's exports can be attributed in part to an unfavorable commodity composition. Most exports are either primary, for instance, rice, for which demand has not been growing rapidly, or manufactured products, for which market access is limited, for example, the Multifibre Arrangement currently restricts Pakistan's textile exports. Export promotion policies should therefore address production as well as marketing.

The potential for upgrading the major export industries is vast. For instance, local firms should be encouraged to capture some of the world's fashion garments and leather product markets by developing joint ventures with firms in the industrial world. As concerns textiles, the emphasis should be on producing ready-made textiles and high-end fabrics. There is a large market in Asia and Africa, as well as in the industrial economies, for embroidered cloth, lace, and so on. By developing a large production base of such high value-added items (which are also labor-intensive), Pakistan could develop a reasonably large export market. To this end, the government should not only encourage appropriate incentives, but should ensure the presence of the physical and institutional infrastructure necessary for a smooth supply of required imported materials and other inputs.

SRI LANKA

Despite the prolonged ethnic strife, Sri Lanka's economic fundamentals continue to improve, although the regional currency crisis may have some indirect impact on future prospects. Foreign direct investment increased in 1997 and contributed to a balance-of-payments surplus of more than $400 million.

RECENT TRENDS AND PROSPECTS

GDP growth accelerated to 6.3 percent in 1997, a significant increase from the 3.8 percent growth in 1996. This was primarily due to recovery in the agriculture sector, which grew by 5.4 percent in 1997 as fair weather resulted in good crops. Manufacturing remained the most dynamic sector in 1997, growing at around 9 percent, stimulated by buoyant demand for Sri Lanka's manufactured exports such as garments and rubber goods. Growth in the services sector was also robust, particularly in the communications, banking and finance, and tourism-related sectors. Despite continuing civil conflict, tourist arrivals recovered strongly from the 1996 slump, increasing by more than 20 percent.

Investment was about 26 percent of GDP and domestic savings ran at 17 percent in 1997, slightly up on 1996. Increased business confidence and a decline in interest rates translated into higher private domestic investment. The reduction of the budget deficit and the use of privatization proceeds to retire public debt also stimulated private investment by reducing public sector claims on available financial resources. Local investors and a high demand for plantation sector shares dominated activity on the Colombo Stock Exchange. Foreign investors continued to remain cautious because of the turbulent situation in Asia.

Unemployment declined to about 10 percent of the labor force, a moderate fall from the 1996 figure. Real wages continued to decline in industry, commerce, and services in 1997, but remained substantially unchanged in agriculture. To correct distortions in relative salaries, the government raised civil service wages and allowances by an average of 12 percent in 1997, with a further 15 percent increase planned for 1998.

The 1997 budget was designed to continue fiscal consolidation and achieved the target of limiting the budget deficit to 4.9 percent of GDP. Government revenues were up nearly 15 percent in nominal terms, reflecting increased tax collection from improved corporate profits, and government expenditures did not increase significantly. The recent decline in wheat prices resulted in savings on subsidies. The privatization of 35 percent of Sri Lanka Telecom was finalized in August 1997, and yielded $225 million to the government, a large share of which the government used to retire Treasury bills. This reduced government debt and the interest payment burden. The sale of government-held convertible debentures for the National Development Bank raised an additional $73 million, further easing public budget constraints. Over time, the fall in interest rates and the partial shift in government borrowing from short-term to medium-term debt should have a positive impact on the budget's interest component.

Monetary policy was eased considerably in 1997, with broad money growing by 14.7 percent, and the statutory reserve ratio was lowered in two steps. Combined with greater fiscal discipline, these measures helped reduce interest rates considerably. The yield on one-year Treasury bills fell to 10 percent in 1997 from 17 percent in 1996, and the prime lending rate declined from 18 to 12 percent. Given the relatively long duration of deposits, deposit rates did not fall by as much, creating temporary pressure on bank intermediation spreads and profitability.

The inflation rate declined from 16 percent in 1996 to 9.6 percent in 1997. Annual average inflation was on a declining trend since the start of the year because of improved supplies of rice, vegetables, coconut, and other food crops and the lower cost of money as a result of declining interest rates.

Imports grew by 7 percent in 1997 in dollar terms, while exports increased by approximately 13 percent. Investment and intermediate goods led the recovery of imports, followed by consumer products. Industrial exports, particularly clothing, leather, and rubber products, led export growth. Agricultural exports also rose because of favorable tea and coconut prices, and a modest expansion in volume. In the first ten months of 1997 tourist arrivals were 22 percent higher than in 1996 and tourist earnings were 29 percent higher, resulting in an improved services account. Overseas remittances increased by 9 percent and the current account deficit fell to 2.1 percent of GDP in 1997, down 3 percentage points from 1996.

The capital account balance was positive in 1997, reflecting a 27 percent increase in long-term foreign aid inflows and more than $550 million of foreign investment. Large-scale privatization of Sri Lanka Telecom and the National Development Bank contributed to these inflows. The balance of payments closed with a $400 million surplus at the end of 1997, increasing reserves to approximately five months worth of imports. The exchange rate depreciated by nearly 7 percent in nominal terms during 1997, with the depreciation rate accelerating in the last two months of the year. In real terms, the exchange rate remained relatively unchanged.

Projections indicate that the economy will continue to grow at a rate of between 5 and 6 percent in both 1998 and 1999. In the absence of

Table 2.16 Major Economic Indicators: Sri Lanka, 1995-1999
(percent)

Item	1995	1996	1997	1998	1999
Gross domestic product growth[a]	5.5	3.8	6.3	5.6	6.0
Gross domestic investment/GDP	25.7	24.2	25.8	26.7	27.6
Gross domestic saving/GDP	15.3	15.5	16.5	17.5	18.0
Inflation rate (consumer price index)	7.7	15.9	9.6	10.0	9.0
Money supply (M2) growth	19.2	10.8	14.7	14.0	13.0
Fiscal balance/GDP	-9.6	-8.9	-4.9	-5.7	-4.0
Merchandise exports growth	18.7	7.9	13.0	9.0	10.0
Merchandise imports growth[b]	11.6	2.5	7.0	10.0	9.0
Current account balance/GDP[c]	-6.3	-5.3	-2.1	-4.2	-4.0
Debt-service/exports	11.6	12.9	11.4	11.2	11.0

[a] At constant 1982 factor cost.
[b] Cost, insurance, freight.
[c] Excluding official transfers.

Sources: Central Bank of Sri Lanka (1997); Siripala (1997); Ministry of Finance and Planning (1997); and staff estimates.

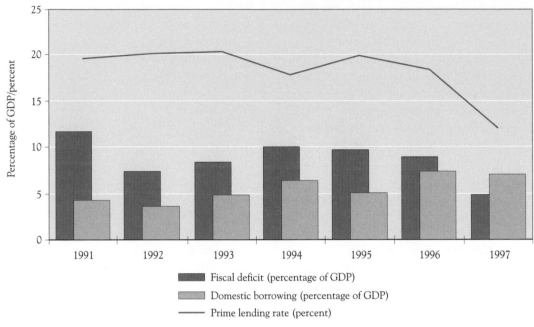

Figure 2.12 Fiscal Deficit, Domestic Borrowing, and Interest Rates: Sri Lanka, 1991-1997

■ Fiscal deficit (percentage of GDP)

■ Domestic borrowing (percentage of GDP)

— Prime lending rate (percent)

Sources: Central Bank of Sri Lanka (1997) and Siripala (1997).

adverse weather conditions, expectations are that the agriculture sector will grow 3 percent per year in both years. Tea is likely to perform well in the next two years, with stable or growing output and prices, while rubber prices are likely to recover moderately. The industry sector is forecast to grow by around 8 percent in 1998 and 1999. Stronger price competition by Southeast Asian countries in Sri Lanka's export markets and a possible reduction in foreign investment flows will partially offset the positive impact of the incentives included in the 1998 budget. The services sector is anticipated to grow by more than 5 percent in 1998 and 1999, reflecting increased tourism, greater activity in the retail and wholesale sector, and growth in the banking and finance subsectors.

Savings and investment patterns will depend on the general health of the economy, on the government's ability to reduce the budget deficit, on the continuation of privatization, and on success in containing the impact of the Asian currency turmoil on Sri Lanka. Gross domestic investment is projected to increase to about 27 percent of GDP in 1998 and 28 percent in 1999. Private sector invest-

ment, stimulated by a decline in interest rates, is expected to expand and support growth. As the public sector's financing requirements decrease, a reorientation of the private sector's savings should take place from traditional saving deposits and investment in government securities to other financial instruments.

The 1998 budget envisions a deficit reduction to 6.5 percent of GDP in 1998 and 4 percent by 2000. The improvement in government accounts in 1998 is to be achieved through lower real current expenditures and an expansion in capital expenditures, matched by increased revenues. The revenues from privatization in 1998 are projected to be $125 million, or one third of those in 1997. Defense expenditure remains as a potentially destabilizing component in the budget, although the government has asserted that it will not exceed defense targets.

Also included in the 1998 budget are a number of investment promotion measures to which the business community has reacted favorably. These measures include accelerated depreciation and investment tax credits, duty exemptions for imports of advanced technology machinery and equipment, and extended tax holidays for investment and employment creation in backward areas. The budget also introduced a goods and services tax that will replace the business turnover tax.

The government will have to manage monetary policy prudently to accommodate growth without fueling inflation. Inflation in 1998 and 1999 should remain at, or slightly above, the 1997 rate of 9.6 percent. Interest rates will be influenced by the extent of fiscal consolidation and the strength of economic growth and monetary expansion.

Exports and imports are expected to grow by some 9 to 10 percent in 1998 and 1999. Improved agricultural exports will reflect increased export demand and higher prices. Manufactured exports will face stronger competition from some Asian countries whose exchange rates have depreciated sharply. Duty exemptions granted in the 1998 budget will sustain import growth. Services receipts are expected to increase as the tourist industry recovers and economic activity strengthens generally, and the current account deficit will remain at some 4 percent of GDP. Private capital inflows are likely to moderate, particularly in 1998, as the international climate becomes more cautious and economic adjustment takes place in some economies that have been traditional sources of foreign direct investment.

POLICY AND DEVELOPMENT ISSUES

Maintaining fiscal discipline remains a critical economic policy issue. The public deficit (as a percentage of GDP) has declined for three consecutive years, and the authorities have set targets to continue on this path. The use of privatization revenues to retire public debt sent an important signal to markets. The government should define its ratio-nale for a second wave of privatization clearly, and should continue to pursue the privatization and/or commercialization of public enterprises with attention to the development of an appropriate regulatory framework. Structural measures on pensions, on the size and efficiency of the civil service, and on other relevant expenditure and revenue items will continue to be needed to achieve the government's target of a budget deficit equivalent to 4 percent of GDP by 2000.

Reducing the deficit and the government's financing requirements would also have beneficial effects on the financial market. The immediate impact would be lower interest rates, which would reduce the crowding out private sector investment has experienced and generate a virtuous cycle of lower budget outlays for public debt service and still lower deficits. This would permit lengthening the maturity of government debt, which would free the government from frequent renewal of short-term debt and would provide useful benchmarks for developing the long-term debt market, which is currently extremely thin. This should be accompanied by other interventions to strengthen governance in the financial sector, such as improved accountability by and performance of the two state-owned commercial banks and more stringent prudential regulations and banking supervision.

The status of the ongoing civil conflict is a key determinant of the country's long-term development prospects. Successful conclusion of the conflict would increase investor confidence, reduce the drain of defense expenditures on the budget, free resources for investment and economic growth, and lead to a resurgence in tourist arrivals. This would lead to an upward revision of the growth outlook and offer the potential for sustained growth.

PACIFIC ISLANDS

Cook Islands

Fiji

Kiribati

Marshall Islands

Federated States of Micronesia

Papua New Guinea

Samoa

Solomon Islands

Tonga

Tuvalu

Vanuatu

FIJI

After achieving an average growth rate of 2.7 percent during 1990-1996, Fiji's economy continued to weaken during 1997 because of major changes in global currency and commodities markets. The devaluation of the currency in early 1998 and the continuation of economic reforms aimed at stimulating growth through private sector initiatives are expected to improve economic performance in the medium term.

RECENT TRENDS AND PROSPECTS

Fiji is one of the most developed of the Pacific island economies and has the standard of living of a lower-middle-income developing country. In the past decade economic growth has been low. After growing 3.1 percent in 1996, economic activity contracted by about 1 percent in 1997. A decline in sugar production caused by cyclones and industrial disputes and a decrease in investment because of the continued uncertainty about the renewal of leases for land used for sugarcane farming adversely affected the agriculture sector. The decline in gold prices had a negative impact on the mining industry. Activity in the building and construction sector was weak, and garment production faced increased competition from other Asian exporters. Tourism, however, continued to make a strong contribution to the economy, with substantial increases in visitor arrivals. Overall, investment remained low, reflecting the weaknesses in the economy and low investor confidence. Both private and public enterprise investment fell to around 4 percent of GDP. Government capital expenditure decreased to less than 3 percent, while operational expenditure remained at around 23 percent of GDP. Consumer prices rose by 2.9 percent in 1997. Weak domestic demand and excess capacity in the economy, a relatively stable exchange rate, and sub-

dued inflationary pressures in the economies of major trading partners contributed to the low inflation rate.

Fiscal performance deteriorated significantly. The budget deficit rose from 0.7 percent of GDP in 1995 to 5.7 percent in 1996 and to around 9.2 percent in 1997. In 1997, for the first time in more than a decade, government revenues did not cover operating expenditures. The government approved two supplementary budgets in 1997, including one for the Commodity Development Framework (CDF), which provides large-scale support to the agriculture sector. The increase in the budget deficit was partly caused by the decision to fund a restructuring program for the National Bank of Fiji, a government-owned commercial bank, which in 1995 had become essentially insolvent. Government debt increased from 41 percent of GDP in 1996 to 48 percent in 1997. About 90 percent of this debt was financed from domestic resources. The balance of payments switched from a surplus in 1996 to a deficit in 1997, largely because of a turnaround in the current account. Foreign reserves continued to remain at high levels, equivalent to almost five months of imports.

The exchange rate of the Fiji dollar is linked to a weighted basket of currencies of the country's main trading partners. Faced with a weak economy and a deteriorating medium-term outlook, the government devalued the currency by 20 percent in

January 1998 in an attempt to increase the competitiveness of Fiji's products and to protect incomes and jobs. In the months ahead inflation is expected to rise substantially to up to 9 percent, but to decrease to lower levels by 1999. Much will depend on the response of wage setters to the devaluation. A strong increase in exports is forecast, with economic activity growing by 2 to 3 percent in 1998 and beyond. The enactment of the new constitution in 1997 that gives more rights to native Indians and the subsequent readmission of Fiji to the Commonwealth is expected to lead to a recovery of domestic and foreign direct investment and to a decline in the rate of emigration.

CRITICAL ISSUES IN SHORT-TERM ECONOMIC MANAGEMENT

The 1998 Budget Address, delivered in November 1997, emphasized the government's efforts to adopt financial management policies that are consistent with promoting economic growth. This is to be achieved by consolidating revenue collection—

including improving tax compliance and reducing concessions and exemptions—and by controlling operating expenditures. Revenues are projected to grow in 1998, with half of the growth expected from the sale of government assets. Total expenditure is to rise only marginally, largely because of the completion of the restructuring program at the National Bank of Fiji in 1997. Capital expenditure is also forecast to increase only slightly, yet operating expenditures will rise to more than 26 percent of GDP. The government needs to adopt bolder reforms for reducing the budget deficit and debt levels, and to focus government expenditure on areas that encourage growth and development. Consistent fiscal policies would also help increase private sector investment levels.

In the near future the government will need to direct major efforts toward controlling inflationary pressures resulting from the devaluation. The government promised to exercise monetary policy with a view to containing inflation, and urged that productivity increases should be the only consideration in negotiating wage increases. The prices of

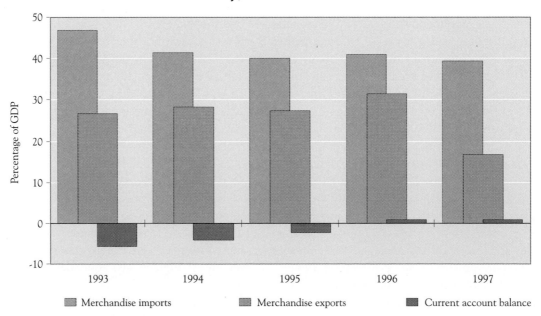

Figure 2.13 Exports, Imports, and the Current Account Balance: Fiji, 1993-1997

■ Merchandise imports   ■ Merchandise exports   ■ Current account balance

Source: Supplement to the 1998 Budget Address.

many consumer items are now rising. With one in four households below the poverty line, the price increases of basic food items are a particular concern.

The Asian crisis will affect Fiji indirectly by dampening growth prospects in its main export markets, and by strengthening competitiveness effects on the tourism and garment industries. Global trade liberalization policies are likely to have an adverse effect on exports under preferential trade arrangements, such as the South Pacific Regional Trade and Economic Cooperation Agreement and the Sugar Protocol under the Lomé Convention of the European Union. The implementation of structural adjustment policies and more effective utilization of resources is therefore crucial for achieving sustainable growth rates in the short to medium term.

POLICY AND DEVELOPMENT ISSUES

Land tenure issues relating to the expiration and renewal of sugar land leases are proving to be a major problem in Fiji. During the period 1997-2005, some 5,345 leases are due to expire. The National Land Trust Board has indicated that most of the landowners want the sugar land back from the lessees to grow sugar themselves, because they think that their returns will be higher than what they would obtain by leasing the land to others. The authorities are developing proposals for more flexible leases in the future that will help avoid the current bunching problem and that can provide more secure tenure. However, they do not appear to be working on policy measures to resolve the problem of a possible displacement of a large number of leaseholders during a short period.

Land tenure and the protection of property rights are also major issues for foreign investors, particularly those with large-scale investments as in the tourist sector. Recent attacks on resorts, disputes with landowners, and perceptions that legal means to redress such problems will be ineffective are important disincentives for foreign investors.

Inconsistencies and uncertainties with respect to government policies discourage private sector investment. The CDF, the government's involvement in the construction of a major new hotel resort, and the escalation of tariff rates in the 1998 budget are important examples of government initiatives that are inconsistent with its stated aim of reducing its level of involvement in the economy. The CDF initiative was incorporated in a supplementary budget in 1997. While the original budget did not consider agricultural development as a central priority, the CDF was subsequently developed and given the status of an essential government activity. The program involves a range of functions, such as research, extension services, marketing, and quality control, which are considered to be government functions essential for supporting economic growth. However, the CDF also involves direct production and investment by government entities, which are inconsistent with the government's stated policy objectives and framework. In addition, critics have raised doubts about the government's ability to follow through on all these activities.

The medium-term economic outlook is not encouraging. The fiscal burden of the National Bank of Fiji's failure and lack of progress in curbing nonessential government expenditures will mean persistent budgetary pressures. Commitments of additional support for the National Bank of Fiji, the possibility of further government support for a major hotel development, and an infrastructure project for the sugar industry will keep pressure on the budget for several years. These pressures suggest that the government is unlikely to achieve its medium-term fiscal target of a balanced budget by 2000.

PAPUA NEW GUINEA

While economic growth has picked up, it is likely to slow. The terms of trade have deteriorated, the exchange rate is likely to come under pressure in 1998, and the banking system is suffering from a major liquidity overhang. In addition, measures taken to ameliorate the recent drought were inadequate.

RECENT TRENDS AND PROSPECTS

Economic growth recovered in 1996 but sharply declined to -6.5 percent in 1997. Completion of the Lihir mine, pre-election expenditures, and rising incomes from agricultural crops all contributed to GDP growth. However, a major drought, and a fall in gold and copper prices affected growth during the second half of 1997. In addition, Papua New Guinea (PNG) was affected by another bout of political instability. Rain recently provided some relief in certain areas of the country, although the current coffee and cocoa outputs are still expected to be some 20 percent less than in 1997. Therefore, GDP growth is likely to decelerate in the future.

The rate of inflation fell to 3.9 percent in 1997. After a period of relative stability, further weakening of the currency was evident in late 1997 despite a buildup of substantial foreign exchange reserves, which amounted to some K768 million ($1,061 million) by mid-1997, or 5.8 months of import cover. The weakness in the currency reflects the following: a recent decline in the terms of trade, the significant food imports as a result of the drought, the prospective decline in volumes of agricultural and mining exports, and the reduced confidence in the economy and in government policies. The terms of trade declined by 10 percent in 1997 because of declining copper, gold, and timber prices.

The banking sector poses an additional problem. Demand deposits in banks have grown rapidly in recent years. As these deposits can be converted on demand to foreign exchange in PNG, the existing level of reserves, while not low, is not necessarily comfortable. To ward off any possibility of mass conversion of demand deposits into foreign currency, the authorities have reacted by allowing the currency to weaken rather than face eventual pressure on reserves.

Interest rates have been pushed up in response to possible pressure on foreign exchange reserves. The Treasury bill rate increased from 9 percent in September 1997 to 13 percent by early December. A small budget deficit was recorded in 1997.

The mining sector's contribution to economic activity and export revenue is likely to fall sharply in 1998. Both major mines have become victims of the drought because of the lack of water for processing. One of them completely stopped shipments in August 1997, while the other operated at 12 percent of capacity. Tax revenues generated from the mining sector are also expected to be considerably lower in 1998 than in 1997.

CRITICAL ISSUES IN SHORT-TERM ECONOMIC MANAGEMENT

Managing a buildup of liquidity in the banking system, maintaining a prudent approach to fiscal

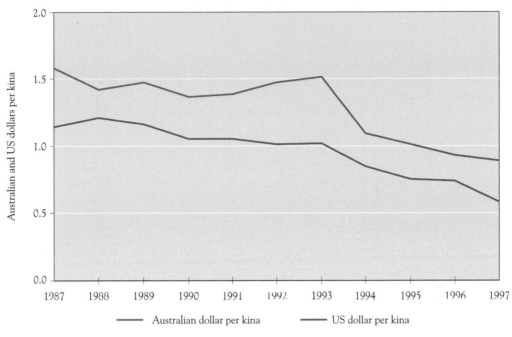

Figure 2.14 Australian Dollar and US Dollar per Kina Exchange Rates: Papua New Guinea, 1987-1997

Australian dollar per kina ——   US dollar per kina ——

Source: Bank of Papua New Guinea data.

policy, managing the exchange rate, and responding effectively to the drought are the key short-term issues. The monetary system accumulated excessive liquidity during the period of fiscal expansion in 1993 and 1994. By late 1997 the government was running a small surplus.

Although recent rains have provided some respite, many communities still face a desperate situation because of record drought. Food shortages are likely to occur in 1998, and estimates indicate that up to 650,000 people will need food aid for several months in early 1998, and a monthly cost of K6 million ($8.29 million).

POLICY AND DEVELOPMENT ISSUES

The economy is beset with long-standing structural problems. The key constraints are a serious and widespread law and order problem, formal and informal institutions that are ineffective in facilitating economic development, poor workforce skills, and inadequate infrastructure. Together these constraints lead to an environment that is not conducive to broadly based economic growth. The structural

adjustment program that is currently being implemented contains a range of measures to liberalize the economy through trade and tax reforms, improve the management of forestry resources, restore fiscal stability, increase public investment, and improve social services. While the government has been able to deliver on some key macroeconomic targets that were part of the structural adjustment program, little fundamental reform has taken place. No progress has been made in improving the government's efficiency and effectiveness, and the privatization program has stalled.

A supply bill was introduced in November 1997, and the government announced a delay in the implementation of the value-added tax to 1999. The delay is a problem, because tariffs have already been reduced, and this has left the government with a revenue shortage. The supply bill increased the top income tax rate to 47 percent and created three new tax brackets. On the one hand, this is not likely to raise much revenue, and on the other, it is likely to discourage foreign investors.

Public governance suffers from major weaknesses and the entire government system exhibits a pervasive lack of accountability for performance. A major long-standing issue is that government policy generally tends to be ad hoc and highly politicized. Effective medium-term fiscal planning and fiscal responsibility legislation are lacking, policy reversals are common, and large gaps between announced policies and actual implementation are frequent.

Under the new constitutional law, government decentralization is to be promoted and the importance of provincial and local governments is to be enhanced. To this end, a large array of programs and services are being developed that provincial and local governments are to implement. The budget has earmarked funds to meet the financial requirements of the provincial and local governments. However, fund transfers have not taken place to date, creating tension between the provincial and local governments and the central government. The new division of responsibilities is not absolutely clear-cut, and a good deal of confusion exists about the revised roles of central government departments and provincial and local government departments. To further complicate the situation, under the new scheme most central government departments were to be restructured, but progress with the restructuring has been limited. The provincial governments have their own restructuring-related problems in that they are short of administrative and technical manpower. Given these problems, doubts have been raised about whether the reforms will work. Critics increasingly believe that the intended improvement in governance will be difficult to accomplish.

Cook Islands, Kiribati, Marshall Islands, Federated States of Micronesia, Samoa, Solomon Islands, Tonga, Tuvalu, and Vanuatu

The year 1997 was a tough one for the Pacific developing member countries (DMCs). Most experienced contractions in their real GDP growth rates, and some even registered absolute declines in their GDP. Inflation stayed subdued in most of these countries, while large trade and current account deficits remained a common feature of their external accounts.

Most of the economies of the Pacific DMCs are highly dualistic, consisting of a subsistence sector on which a large segment of the population depends for its basic livelihood and a predominantly urban sector that accounts for the bulk of measured GDP and for most formal employment. The Pacific islands vary widely, however, in terms of their size, resource endowments, economic growth potential, and institutional capacity for economic management. The smaller Pacific island economies tend to have extremely small resource bases. Manufacturing is generally limited, and public sector budgets tend to account for high proportions of GDP and stay in deficit. Six of the Pacific DMCs have no national currency, which constrains their choice of policy instruments. The Cook Islands uses the New Zealand dollar, the Marshall Islands and the Federated States of Micronesia use the US dollar, and Kiribati and Tuvalu use the Australian dollar.

Most of the Pacific DMCs found 1997 to be a challenging year. Their GDP growth slowed, and they ran large current account deficits. Sluggish demand for the Solomon Islands' commodity exports contributed to its current account deficit in 1997. For Cook Islands, Samoa, Tonga, and Vanuatu, tourism receipts continued to be a principal source of

foreign exchange. In the case of the Marshall Islands and the Federated States of Micronesia, official transfers from the United States persisted as the main source of external income.

COOK ISLANDS

The Cook Islands are still dealing with the aftermath of the 1995 fiscal crisis. Growth is recovering, but remains weak, and privatization has been slow. While tax reforms are under way, tariff reform is needed.

After recording steady growth for most of the 1980s and early 1990s, the economy contracted sharply starting in mid-1994, and exhibited continued weakness in 1995 and 1996, with output falling by around 5 percent per year in both years. The contraction in GDP in 1995 was caused largely by a currency crisis and a fall in tourism. In 1996 the cause was a fall in expenditure as the government cut the pay of civil servants and continued with a substantial retrenchment of staff. These measures were necessary because the government had financed much of its earlier expenditure, which had been a major factor in driving growth, by borrowing, which proved to be unsustainable.

For the Cook Islands, 1997 refers to fiscal year 1997/98, ending 31 March; for Samoa and Tonga, the fiscal year ends on 30 June; and for the Marshall Islands and the Federated States of Micronesia, the fiscal year ends on 30 September. All other references are to the calendar year.

However, some recovery occurred in 1997, with a growth rate of 0.5 percent. Small-scale activity increased as many of the displaced public servants established small businesses. Tourism, the largest private sector activity, performed well in the first half of 1997 before weakening somewhat in the second half. The first three quarters of 1997 saw a 5 percent rise in visitor arrivals compared with the same period a year earlier, and hotel occupancy rates rose from 57 to 61 percent. The sale of two resorts to the private sector will further improve the sector's prospects. The value of pearl exports for the first six months of 1997 was $1 million, almost the same as for the entire year in 1996. While a major cyclone late in the year devastated the main pearl producing island, significant damage was confined to infrastructure, and the pearl crop was not damaged. In any case, the main farmers had reportedly established substantial reserves.

The reduced public sector employment is being partially offset by a rise in informal and formal employment in the tourism, agriculture, and marine sectors. However, the scale of the reduction in public sector employment has been massive, and many people have left the country. Estimates indicate that since the restructuring began in 1995, some 2,000 people, or a little more than 10 percent of the population, have moved away.

Inflation was negative in 1996 and 1997, and the fall in prices was fairly broadly based across such sectors as food, clothing, housing, and transport.

While external accounts have been problematic in the 1990s, improvements have taken place since 1992-1993. The current account for 1997 is estimated to show a small surplus.

The land under tillage is increasing, and the agriculture sector should continue to contribute to exports. Copra exports have recommenced, and both the pawpaw and mango industries have seen positive developments since the privatization of the pawpaw heat treatment plant in 1996 and the agreement on protocols for re-establishing mango exports to New Zealand in late 1997. However, agriculture is not likely to become a major source of income given the limited amount of land available. While the islands currently do not export fish, foreign interest in establishing joint ventures has been expressed.

The ratio of government expenditure to GDP remained at around 50 percent. Even though further expenditure cuts are planned, a high govern-

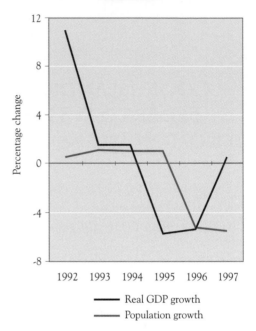

Figure 2.15 Growth of Real GDP and Population: Cook Islands, 1992-1997

Source: Ministry of Finance and Economic Management data.

ment debt means that the community will have to bear the cost of previous poor budget management for some time. Excluding the stalled Vaimaanga Hotel project, external debt was $63 million in late 1996, and would more than double if the hotel were included. Debt servicing costs for fiscal year 1997 were projected to be 19 percent of GDP. Aid is still the single largest source of funding, but internal sources are projected to account for 72 percent of revenues in 1997.

Projections indicate that growth will pick up in 1998 and 1999 to levels of around 4 to 5 percent. Key assumptions underlying this prediction are that investment for more new hotels will be available and that pearl exports will continue to increase as the result of developments on two new pearl farming islands. Over the next few years the current account is expected to move into a modest deficit from a small surplus in 1997 as imports rise in line with economic recovery. Income from remittances from islanders living abroad and more of readily available opportunities to migrate to Australia and New Zealand will also help to maintain income standards. Inflation should remain low, reflecting developments in major trading partner countries, and fiscal and external balances should remain manageable.

Building on the recovery that was under way in 1997, maintaining prudent fiscal policies, tax reform, and the facilitation of private sector activity are the critical short-term economic performance issues. Because of the earlier financial crisis, the government can no longer borrow and must run a balanced or nearly balanced budget. Given the current economic situation and projected revenues, the estimated deficit without adjustments to the 1998 budget is nearly 2 percent of GDP. Further reductions in government expenditure will be needed to ensure a balanced budget.

Privatization and tax reform have been key aspects of the strategy to promote private sector activity, but overall progress on privatization has been disappointing. As of mid-1997 the government had sold about NZ$12 million worth of assets, including some tourist resorts, the Broadcasting Corporation, the Printing Office, and the Housing Corporation. In addition, by August 1997 the government had made substantial progress in finalizing the sale of the Rarotongan and Rapai hotels. However, it is reluctant to accommodate extensive foreign involvement, and the privatization of transport, power, and telecommunications operations faces difficulties because of concerns about foreign ownership and monopoly power. The government is still committed to privatization, but is considering the design and implementation of a Trade Practices Act to deal with market power and other trade practice issues.

Recent major reforms of the tax system are an important feature of the government's development objectives. Prior to the reforms the Cook Islands had almost 300 different income tax rates that ranged from 7 to 37 percent. Now there are only four tax bands with a top tax rate of 30 percent. A value-added tax of 12.5 percent has replaced the old turnover tax.

The new system will reduce the tax rate for foreign-owned companies from 27.5 to 20 percent, will allow immediate deduction of the full cost of capital equipment, and will not issue any new concessions for economic development. The new company tax will also remove the double taxation of dividends, as it will only levy taxes on net profits less dividends, therefore only taxing dividends once at the personal level.

These tax reforms will create a more efficient and equitable system. The initiatives to allow immediate deductions for all capital equipment and remove concessions for economic development should prove particularly effective. However, the tariff (import levy) system still needs to be reformed. The existing tariff system has had distortionary and protective effects and has generally contributed to a higher cost structure than in other countries. The government has maintained the import levy as a safety net because of uncertainty about the levels of value-added tax revenues. It has, however, agreed to reduce tariff rates if the revenue collected from the tax exceeds the target level.

Most local producers of products that compete with imports receive a protective tariff of at least 20 percent. Commodities covered include coconut milk, printed T-shirts, fresh fish, fresh vegetables, soft drinks, ice cream, cut flowers, coffee, pawpaws, pineapples, and citrus fruits and their juices. There are also numerous anomalies in the levy rates that reflect the lack of a consistent, guiding rationale for setting rates and problems related to the exemptions that apply when a good is imported for private use.

Given the government's emphasis on encouraging efficient private sector development, tariff reform is particularly important. Industries that can only be sustained through protection will harm the economy in the long term, and if the economy is to expand, it must do so through its export goods sector, which is generally hindered by high and distortive tariffs. High average tariff rates on business inputs raise costs, and thereby reduce competitiveness. The tourism industry faces the biggest problem because of its high dependence on imports. The pearl industry is also at a disadvantage because of the levies on some of its equipment.

The new value-added tax and direct tax systems could serve as a model that other Pacific island countries could aspire to. However, a sound design is not in itself sufficient to ensure a well-performing tax system. It must also be well implemented and supervised.

KIRIBATI

Although weak growth has become a long-standing economic feature, the devaluation of the Australian dollar has benefited the economy in several ways. Key development strategies include reforming the public sector and public enterprises, facilitating foreign investment, and reallocating development expenditure.

Real GDP growth averaged a little more than 7 percent per year from 1994 through 1996. This is an improvement over the average for the early 1990s and reflects a shift to expansionary fiscal policies. The key productive sectors—fishing and copra—have contracted though, because of poor climatic conditions. Inflation has been declining broadly in line with that of Kiribati's major trading partners, particularly Australia, whose currency is used as legal tender. The estimated growth rate for 1997 is 3 percent.

Domestic lending by the Bank of Kiribati has remained relatively low. Lending rates have been generally stable, while deposit rates have declined slightly in line with Australian conditions. Increased government expenditures have been largely financed by a more aggressive drawdown of funds from the Revenue Equalization Reserve Fund (RERF), which is an accumulation of long-term budget surpluses estimated to be about A$460 million in December 1997. These funds are invested in several different international capital markets, which provides Kiribati with steady interest and dividend income.

One of the government's objectives is to maintain the real per capita value of the RERF. This objective was at risk prior to the recent devaluation of the Australian dollar; however, its devaluation in late 1997 and early 1998 by about 12 percent has substantially increased the RERF's value, as much of the portfolio is in currencies other than the Australian dollar. However, devaluation of the Australian dollar will raise the cost of imports, given Australia's importance as a source of imports, but export revenues in Australian dollars should rise as the devaluation increases exports, the most important of which is copra to Bangladesh. License fees for foreign fishing are also an important source of revenues, and most are customarily paid in US dollars. Thus the overall impact of the currency devaluation on the RERF, as well as on the economy, has been positive. The budget should revert to a small surplus in the near future.

Weak growth, government domination, and cautious macroeconomic management have been long-standing features of the economy. The typical approach to macroeconomic management has been to rely on domestic taxes and revenues to cover recurrent expenditures and to use the RERF to cover unexpected shortfalls. A capital budget has been largely funded by external assistance in the form of concessionary loans or direct grants from donor countries.

For most of the past ten years Kiribati maintained large fiscal surpluses that contributed to the objective of expanding the RERF. However, in 1995 a new government adopted a more active fiscal policy stance to encourage faster growth. It increased recurrent expenditures substantially to finance a large public sector wage increase and to form two new ministries. This increased the fiscal deficit substantially in 1995. And while the deficit declined in 1996, it rose again in 1997. While current expenditure has increased relative to GDP in recent years, development expenditure has been halved. This is bound to have an adverse effect on future growth prospects.

While the expansionary fiscal stance in 1995 and 1996 may have supported higher growth, this impact is only likely to be temporary. If the government is to improve long-term prospects, it needs to avoid a steep rise in its recurrent expenditures, even

Figure 2.16 Sectoral Shares of GDP: Kiribati, 1992-1996

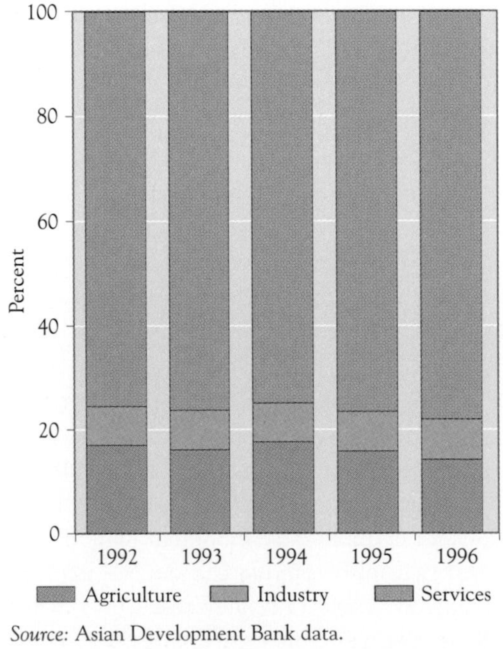

Source: Asian Development Bank data.

if the RERF continues to increase in value. Ensuring that as any surplus develops it is spent on development activities that facilitate private sector development and public sector reform is important. Also, the RERF's resources need to be deployed more as productive investment and less as government expenditure.

Kiribati is one of the poorest Pacific island countries and one that faces large challenges in its efforts to sustain economic and social development. Kiribati consists of 33 coral atolls with a total land area of only 810 square kilometers spread over 3.5 million square kilometers. Most islands are narrow and low lying, and have limited agricultural potential because of corralline soils and periodic droughts.

The population is nearly 80,000 but is concentrated on the South Tarawa atoll, where some 30,000 people live, mostly in extremely unsanitary conditions. Increasing environmental health problems, especially diarrhea, have been linked to groundwater and lagoon pollution. Infant death rates of 65 per 1,000 are the highest of all the Pacific island economies and about triple the average for Fiji, Samoa, and Tonga. Unless the pressure on the natural environment is reduced or the authorities commit substantial expenditures to expanding and maintaining water and sewerage systems, further health problems are inevitable.

Most people are employed in subsistence activities. The public sector, which accounts for more than two thirds of GDP, dominates formal sector activity. The production base is narrow, with copra and fish being the principal exports. The National Development Strategy has adopted a new approach of formulating a strategic framework for development rather than setting out a comprehensive development plan. The specific measures taken under the strategy are (i) reducing and reforming the public enterprise sector, (ii) attracting foreign investment, and (iii) restructuring the budget in favor of private sector development to reduce the public sector's dominance over the economy. The government will focus on providing social services and infrastructure and on establishing an enabling investment environment. Nongovernment organizations help with developing human resources and providing social support systems. Donors are expected to continue to play an important role in developing infrastructure and providing technical assistance.

The budget is expected to return to surplus as the economy benefits from increased production in the copra and fisheries sectors and from higher remittances, fishing license fees, and investment income as a result of the weaker Australian dollar. However, the long-term outlook is not as encouraging. Kiribati faces daunting environmental, economic, and social development challenges. In addition, its isolation and cultural factors are likely to slow the extent to which the government can implement development strategies effectively.

MARSHALL ISLANDS

While grants under the so-called Compact agreement have financed a massive level of government expenditure, the economy has been contracting since 1996. Two critical challenges are reducing the government's overall involvement in the economy and development of private sector activities.

The economy contracted substantially after 1996 because of major reductions in government expenditure. Estimates indicate that real GDP declined by about 5 percent per year in 1996 and 1997, partly because of tight lending conditions and lower copra production because of bad weather.

The Compact of Free Association with the United States, which provides for substantial financial and technical assistance from the United States for a 15-year period that ends in October 2001, dominates the economy. Total financial assistance for the entire period is estimated to be $790 million. The most important part of this assistance is the base grant, but federal grants and access to in-kind assistance are also available. Significant reductions in the base financial grant occurred in 1992 and 1997. Explicit payments declined from 70 percent of GDP in the late 1980s to less than 50 percent in 1997. These grants have financed a massive level of government expenditure. The fiscal situation is also dominated by the availability of foreign grants under the Compact. The budget deficit before grants averaged nearly 70 percent of GDP in the first half of the 1990s, but after the grants this was down to about 15 percent.

The overwhelming reliance on grants from the United States without any conditions attached to ensure effective use of the funds has had pervasive and damaging effects on the Marshall Islands' ability to develop a productive economic base. The problem has now reached crisis stage because the government borrowed heavily against all future Compact resources. Recent budgets have recognized the need to make urgent and substantial adjustments. Measures have included reforming the public sector; cutting real wages; reducing the size of the civil service; lowering subsidies for public enterprises; implementing an across-the-board increase in import duties; and increasing duties on petroleum, alcohol, cigarettes, cars, and other luxury items.

The external position also reflects the substantial dependence on Compact funds. Excluding official transfers, the current account deficit averaged 60 percent of GDP in the first half of the 1990s. As the government had borrowed heavily against future Compact funds, substantial capital outflow occurred during the mid-1990s. External debt stood at $141 million in 1994-1995, or 134 percent of GDP, with debt service at the alarming level of more than 40 percent of exports.

The rate of inflation during 1996 was 6 percent, falling slightly to 4 percent in 1997.

The current program of fiscal stabilization initially emphasized expenditure cuts along with revenue raising measures designed to have a greater impact during 1997-2000 than previously. Tax reforms have included raising income taxes and introducing a value-added tax in late 1998. The government is also considering making complementary changes to the income tax to help offset the regressive effects of the value-added tax and has taken steps to improve the independence and effectiveness of the tax administration. These planned changes to the tax system will provide the Marshall Islands with one of the most economically efficient tax policy environments in the Pacific. Merely returning the budget to a balanced position in the next few years will not be sufficient. Substantial fiscal surpluses that average more than 20 percent of GDP are needed each year until 2001, largely to meet principal repayments. While the government has already made substantial adjustments, further adjustments will be needed for several years

Incomes in urban centers are much higher than in rural areas, but considerable inequality is apparent within urban centers. Although civil servants who lose their jobs will bear much of the brunt of adjustment, cuts in government services, higher charges for utilities, and steeper indirect taxes will also affect other segments of society. Under the Com-

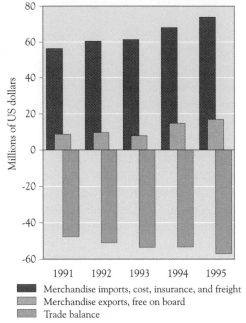

Figure 2.17 Balance of Payments: Marshall Islands, 1991-1995

■ Merchandise imports, cost, insurance, and freight
▨ Merchandise exports, free on board
▨ Trade balance

Source: Asian Development Bank (1996b).

pact, Marshall Islanders are entitled to work in the United States until 2001. Emigration is likely to increase in the short term as employment opportunities diminish. In time, remittances from abroad could become an important source of income as is the case for several other Pacific Island countries.

Agriculture and fisheries have traditionally been the mainstay of the productive economy. The contribution of agriculture increased in the first half of the 1990s, largely because of increased copra production. Increased subsidies and improved transportation were key factors in enhancing incentives to produce more copra. While further expansion of the copra industry is possible, for the industry to be sustainable, it must be developed efficiently, in particular, in a manner that eliminates the need for future direct support in the form of subsidies. Development efforts should focus on atolls that have relatively good resource potential and access to Majuro. Currently, the most critical factor in expanding production of copra, as well as of other commercial crops, is interisland freight.

With an exclusive economic zone of more than 2 million square kilometers of ocean and a relatively low level of resource exploitation, fisheries are the sector with the best prospects for generating large-scale export income and becoming the lead sector in the development of the economy. However, this sector suffers from several long-standing problems, including limited surveillance capabilities with respect to foreign fishing fleets, lack of skills, high domestic costs, and inappropriate government investment decisions. Foreign license fees average only 5 percent of declared catch values.

In the past, government policy was couched within a framework that established a clear role for the government in undertaking commercial projects that the private sector was not interested in. However, the consensus now is that the public sector cannot operate direct fisheries investments profitably. The future success of the fisheries sector lies in the government withdrawing from direct involvement in fishing and restricting itself to providing support infrastructure for longline fleets operating in the Western Pacific. To this end, the government has prepared a fisheries strategy that emphasizes developing Majuro as a base for servicing foreign and domestic fishing fleets, with fisheries business activities carried out by the private sector. The new strategy also aims to increase the returns from fisheries by improving bilateral and multilateral access arrangements.

The tourism sector is underdeveloped, and of the 5,000 visitors a year during the mid-1990s, only about 700 were tourists. The government has recently completed the construction of the 150-room international standard Outrigger Hotel in Majuro, with the management contracted out to a major Hawaii-based hotel operator. A number of other tourism projects are being developed or considered, including niche projects, such as a diving venture at Bikini atoll. While the prospects for small-scale tourism that takes advantage of the Marshall Islands' military history and fishing and diving opportunities are reasonably good, significant development is unlikely. The most effective role the government can play in promoting tourism is to establish a transparent and consistent policy and regulatory environment to encourage foreign investment and to ensure that supporting public infrastructure is in place. The government also needs to deal with the environmental pollution around Majuro.

FEDERATED STATES OF MICRONESIA

The so-called Compact program of financial assistance will cease in 2001. The outlook for economic growth and development in the medium term is grim.

Economic performance has been poor, with real GDP registering negative growth in 1997. The decline in output in recent years is largely attributable to low growth in tourism and fisheries and agriculture, the key export sectors.

A major source of government revenues in the Federated States of Micronesia (FSM) has been a program of financial assistance that the country has received from the United States under the Compact of Free Association (the Compact) since 1986. This is due to be phased out in 2001, and the rundown in funding is taking place in three stages. The first occurred in 1991, when external grants fell by 20 percent. This was followed by a further 15 percent reduction in grants in October 1996. The final stage in 2001 will mean a significant reduction in government revenues, and is necessitating a major reassessment of government expenditures. The 1996 grant reduction led to staff retrenchment and wage cuts, and the government has introduced a wide-ranging program of adjustment and retrenchment. In January 1998, the restructuring of the government itself began.

Of major concern is the continued weakness of the government's consolidated budgetary position, despite its efforts to reduce expenditure, particularly capital spending. The overall position swung from a surplus of 3.4 percent of GDP in 1995 to deficits of a little more than 2 percent in 1996 and 1 percent in 1997. Tax revenues are low, and account for only about 8 percent of GDP. The FSM must find other sources of government revenue. To this end, the government introduced the new Customs Act, which became effective in October 1997 and is projected to increase revenues from customs duties by approximately 35 percent. Its most important features are a shift from a free on board to a cost, insurance, and freight basis for valuation; the elimination of a large exemption; and major improvements in collection, enforcement, and penalties.

While the FSM does not have an official consumer price index, with imports equivalent to more than 60 percent of GDP, domestic prices are heavily influenced by price movements in the United States, the main source of imported goods. Estimates indicate that inflation has been around 4 percent per year in recent years.

Merchandise exports grew strongly during 1991-1994, principally because of rapid expansion of fish exports. That growth leveled off in 1995 and declined slightly in 1996, partly because of the completion of certain bilateral fishing agreements, although a new agreement with the Republic of Korea commenced in mid-1996.

The importance of official transfers for the balance of payments is demonstrated by the fact that if these transfers are excluded, the current account deficit in 1997 was a substantial 56 percent of GDP. However, once these transfers are included, the current account records a surplus of 6 percent.

External debt is also high: at the end of 1995 outstanding debt amounted to 55 percent of GDP, and its servicing was equivalent to 18 percent of goods and services exports. Consequently, the government has been progressively drawing down on its cash reserves, which by the end of 1996 were estimated at the equivalent of two months worth of imports.

The present weak fiscal and current account positions indicate a need for substantial adjustments in the economy following the cessation of the Compact in 2001. This concern has dominated government policy in the last few years and will continue to do so.

The outlook for economic growth and development in the medium term is not encouraging. Export growth is estimated at around 2 percent for 1997, and is expected to continue at this rate during 1998 and 1999. The step-downs in the Compact require a level of fiscal adjustment and reduction in living standards that are unlikely to be made quickly enough and that will be unpopular with the nation's voters. Furthermore, while private sector investment in sectors such as tourism, manufacturing, and agriculture and fisheries could ease the fiscal adjustment, such investment is likely to be slow in coming, while large infrastructure projects normally have long gestation periods. Consequently, the FSM will rely heavily on external resources well into the post-Compact period. Even then, overall living standards are likely to decline, unemployment—which is already high, particularly among the young—is likely to increase, and growth is almost certain to remain low for some years.

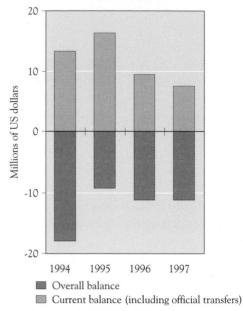

Figure 2.18 Current and Overall Balances: Federated States of Micronesia, 1994-1997

Millions of US dollars

Overall balance

Current balance (including official transfers)

Sources: Asian Development Bank (1996a) and staff estimates.

The overriding economic issue is the adjustment to the Compact funding step-downs by both the national and state governments. The national government has formulated a structural reform program aimed at restoring macroeconomic stability, promoting sustainable development, and ensuring external viability in the post-Compact era. It has also endorsed strategies to reduce the public sector's size and cost, and to promote private sector activity. However, it has made little progress in implementing such reforms, even though funding of $10 million for the Public Sector Reform Program became available during 1997. At the same time, the government must find ways to increase revenues in the immediate future, for instance, through tax reform. Fiscal adjustments should also focus on generating the overall fiscal surpluses necessary to meet debt-service obligations and to rebuild the government's financial holdings.

Despite the cessation of the Compact, the FSM will continue to rely heavily on external resources for the foreseeable future. Technical assistance, grant aid, and concessional loans will all be required to support continued development efforts. In addition, the government has proposed the establishment of a trust fund to help support its operations in the post-Compact era.

For sustained economic growth in the future, the FSM must reduce its reliance on public sector employment and encourage the rise of a vibrant private sector. Developing the private sector calls for implementing a consistent and transparent regulatory framework, reforming the land tenure system, and simplifying foreign investment policy. Expanding tourism will also require developing infrastructure and services.

Foreign investment has the potential to support private sector development and the fiscal adjustment process. To facilitate such investment the government needs to provide appropriate policies and support. In the past, the approval process for foreign investment was cumbersome, because both the national and state governments had to approve each proposal. However, the new Foreign Investment Act, in effect since 1 January 1998, is expected to help liberalize foreign investment.

Future prospects depend on a broadening of the economic base. Tourism is one sector that could contribute significantly to investment, exports, and employment, and consequently, to economic growth. Again, foreign investment and the private sector should lead the development of tourism. To support the development of tourism the government will need to review such restrictions as those on which airlines can fly into the country.

As the FSM has no central bank and uses the US dollar as the unit of currency, it is unable to implement independent monetary policy. This limits the financing options available for addressing fiscal deficits, while any attempts to set interest rates administratively are unlikely to be sustainable because of the likely impact on capital flows. The inability to use monetary policy effectively presents a policy dilemma for which no ready solution is apparent.

SAMOA

Real GDP increased by just under 10 percent in 1995 and a further 6 percent in 1996. This growth was largely generated by the private sector, with tourism, agriculture, and several manufacturing activities all performing well. Growth fell to 3 percent in 1997.

In the wake of the natural disasters of the early 1990s, Samoa's government was forced to make sizable expenditures to restore the economy's productive potential and provide basic services. As a result of a fall in revenues, significant foreign aid was required, but even this was not enough, and the government had to run significant budget deficits during 1992-1995. The budgetary situation improved thereafter, and after two years of surplus, a small budget deficit is estimated for fiscal year 1997/98.

Money supply (M2) growth slowed markedly in 1996, but increased again in 1997. Overall credit to the private sector increased by about 11 percent in 1996, but by mid-1997 private sector credit outstanding was 20 percent higher than a year earlier. Inflation has shown considerable volatility over the years, and was 8 percent in 1997.

The current account had been in deficit for most of the 1990s, but by 1996 this deficit had shrunk to less than a quarter of its nominal value in 1992 because of strong growth in net services trade (mainly tourism), an improvement in the merchandise trade deficit, and sustained high levels of private transfers. The current account deficit for 1997 improved slightly compared with 1996. The real exchange rate appreciated by some 4 percent in 1996, and with the nominal effective exchange rate showing stability in the first half of 1997, further real appreciation of around 4 percent is expected for 1997 as a whole. The government will need to monitor carefully the implied loss in competitiveness.

The Samoan economy depends largely on agricultural production, which has generally been patchy for most of the 1990s, mostly as a result of a significant decline in the production of beef cattle and taro. (In 1994, leaf blight disease destroyed taro, which was the main export crop.) In contrast, fish production increased dramatically in 1996, and together with an expansion in copra, led to an overall increase in agriculture and fisheries production of 23 percent.

Industrial production has grown significantly since 1991, and is based mainly around coconut processing. The restarting of the local oil mill in 1996 has injected cash into rural households through the purchase of coconuts nationwide, and exports of copra, coconut oil, and coconut cream for the first half of 1997 were nearly 40 percent higher than for the same period of 1996. Other significant industries include beer, cigarettes, soft drinks, concrete

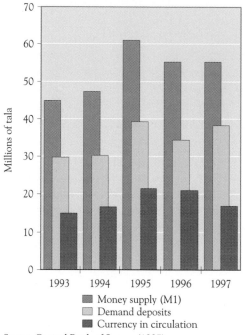

Figure 2.19 Composition of Money Supply (M1): Samoa, 1993-1997

Millions of tala

■ Money supply (M1)
▫ Demand deposits
■ Currency in circulation

Source: Central Bank of Samoa (1997).

products, and sawn timber production. A large assembly operation that produces electrical wiring harnesses for motor vehicles (the Yazaki factory) was established in the early 1990s and is the country's largest private sector employer.

Despite the strength of economic activity in recent years, by 1997 real income per capita was still only at about the same level as in 1987-1989. The economy has long been characterized by weak growth, a large public sector, and strong dependence on remittances from overseas. However, there has also been a long-standing problem in the calculation of accurate national accounts, and living standards are probably higher than official statistics indicate.

The short-term outlook is relatively good, although growth could slow somewhat in 1998 if fish exports weaken. Provided the government is able to maintain a prudent approach to fiscal policy and achieve success with its public sector reform program, slight growth in GDP per capita is expected for the next few years. This projection is predicated on stable terms of trade, the absence of major cyclones, continued support from remittances, and

modest growth in exports of goods and tourism. Inflation should remain at moderate levels in line with that of Samoa's trading partners, and foreign reserves should remain healthy. Exchange rate management will be an important issue in the light of the currency's real appreciation in 1996 and the first half of 1997, and the recent depreciation of the Australian dollar. Although the new emphasis on the private sector could raise living standards, where the growth will come from is not clear, given Samoa's isolation and narrow production base.

Despite three decades of development plans, sectoral strategies, technical assistance, and aid-funded capital projects, Samoa's economy remains dependent on foreign aid, foreign loans, and remittances from expatriate Samoans. While the increase in travel receipts is a welcome sign, the government has recognized the need to put Samoa's economy on a more dynamic path by redefining the government's role, implementing a privatization policy, and creating an economic environment that facilitates private sector economic activity. While the government has declared its commitment to reforming public enterprises for several years, it has made only modest progress. The Bank of Western Samoa has been fully privatized, some government services have been contracted out to the private sector, and some other public enterprises have been fully or partially privatized. However, some see the failure of two recently privatized companies as confirmation of the failure of the entire program, when a possible explanation is that the companies were not viable without the support of significant government resources. The government should make greater efforts to privatize and reform public enterprises effectively so as to achieve sustainable economic growth.

A central element of public sector reform is the implementation of a performance budgeting framework that entails a focus on delivering specified outputs and clear accounting of the costs of producing the outputs. Performance budgeting was first introduced in the 1995/96 fiscal year and extended to all departments in the 1996/97 fiscal year. The performance budgeting framework has involved integrating the old recurrent and development budgets, and defining and classifying outputs. Extensive training in the use of effective accountability arrangements will be needed to ensure the success of the new system. The authorities are continuing to simplify the number of outputs, establish budget plans early in the fiscal year, and develop rolling three-year estimates of specific outputs to assist in long-term planning. The introduction of performance budgeting will allow greater devolution of responsibility to government spending agencies than the previous system of line item budgeting, but the authorities must take care that the degree of decentralization of decisionmaking does not outstrip the accounting system's ability to cope with these changes. However, the development of a medium-term budgetary framework, the provision of appropriate staff training, and the preparation of performance contracts would ensure that the activities of individual departments reflected the government's overall priorities. The adoption of performance budgeting should enable the government to achieve its objective of reducing its overall involvement in the economy.

SOLOMON ISLANDS

After growing by an average of 5.4 percent per year during 1990-1995 and an estimated 3.5 percent in 1996, the economy of the Solomon Islands contracted by 1 percent in 1997. This decline in economic activity was an outcome of declining production of major commodities (induced partly by the weather), falling commodity prices, lower construction activity, and a fiscal contraction. Moreover, rapid population growth has meant that per capita income was appreciably lower in 1997 than in 1996. Average real income in 1995 was only 11 percent higher than in 1980.

In the 1990s successive governments have incurred large budget deficits and have relied on the Central Bank to finance these. In addition to creating balance-of-payment difficulties and inflationary pressures, the deficits have crowded out private investment and have caused a serious problem for the financial system. With Central Bank loans and advances to the government going well beyond the legal limit in 1995, the Central Bank was forced to suspend dealing in government securities. The government began accumulating interest arrears on its domestic debt, postponing its contributions to the National Provident Fund, and suspended most of its external debt servicing.

The Solomon Islands has been a high inflation economy relative to its trading partners. Infla-

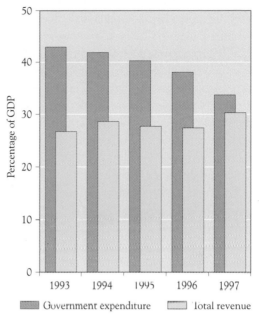

Figure 2.20 Total Revenue and Government Expenditure: Solomon Islands, 1993-1997

■ Government expenditure   □ Total revenue

Source: Ministry of Finance (1996) and staff estimates.

tion was around 12 percent in 1997. The nominal effective exchange rate was devalued at an annual average rate of 9.7 percent during 1986-1996 to help maintain competitiveness. Further downward pressure on the exchange rate is likely as long as inflationary pressures are higher in the Solomon Islands than in its trading partners.

The cycle of frequent devaluation and persistent inflation has proven difficult to break, because it has been driven by persistently irresponsible fiscal policies. The devaluations have meant continued increases in import prices, but the prices of local items have also increased because of demand pressures resulting from fiscal expansion and associated large public sector wage rises. The current account is expected to continue to record small surpluses during 1997 and 1998.

The overriding issue for the Solomon Islands is its alarming financial crisis. Mounting domestic and external debt-service payment arrears, falling revenues and growing expenditures, and declining public and private investment, along with an overexposed financial sector, threaten the nation's economic and financial stability. Remedial action is urgently needed, otherwise the payments system is under serious threat and a currency crisis is likely.

Attention to servicing official debt and the renegotiation of debt repayment are pressing issues. In 1996 the country paid only a little over one fifth of the principal and interest payments on its official debt. The government's borrowing requirements have grown too large to be accommodated by the already highly exposed domestic financial system. The virtual collapse of the securities market as government borrowing exceeded the legal limit for borrowing from the Central Bank means that monetary policy is inoperative and that economic corrections will rely heavily on fiscal policy.

During the 1990s external reserves have covered two weeks to two months worth of imports. In June 1997 the cover was not quite two months, but if government arrears are allowed for, the cover dropped to around one month. Given the country's heavy dependence on log exports and the chance of further price declines for logs, the government confronts the prospect of a balance-of-payments crisis developing during 1998. The government devalued the currency by 20 percent in December 1997 in an effort to preempt such a crisis, yet the low foreign exchange import cover and likely balance-of-payments pressures remain a serious concern, particularly in terms of the potential to support the currency and external payments system.

The growing budget deficit is also a pressing issue. Part of the reason for the increase in the budget deficit is the sharp decline in revenues as a result of a contraction in real GDP.

Declining private investment reflects a growing crisis of confidence and the urgent need to address the many complex financial issues the country faces. Attempts at debt restructuring must be accompanied by a firm commitment to undertake credible policy reform and establish a consistent track record of implementation. The authorities should also support foreign investment by applying simplified, consistent, and transparent requirements for such investment.

In October 1997, shortly after coming to power, the government initiated a comprehensive policy and structural reform program. The immediate focus is on renegotiating domestic and external debt, along with strengthening revenue collection and controlling expenditure. These efforts need to be intensified, and the nation's trading partners and aid donors need to support them. The government has developed the organizational structure and a broad reform agenda, with a focus on macroeconomic and microeconomic policies, to achieve stability, enhance productivity, facilitate public sector reform, and promote private sector-led growth.

Nonetheless, the short- to medium-term outlook remains poor. The uncertainty about export commodity prices, the country's serious financial position, the recent declines in public and private investment, and the rapid rate of population growth all imply that recovery will be slow. In the longer term—beyond the next five years—the outlook is better, provided that the government addresses fiscal imbalances and debt as a matter of urgency. To facilitate future development, the government must also renew run-down infrastructure and enhance labor skill levels.

The growth of the Solomon Islands' economy in the long term depends critically on the performance of merchandise exports based on its natural resource sectors. The realization of the nation's economic potential depends largely on careful management of these resources, on the extent to which Solomon Islanders' capture the profits from this resource exploitation, and on how these profits are divided between consumption and investment. For example, in the commercial fisheries sector, which comprises harvesting and processing of an extensive tuna resource, the estimated biologically sustainable catch is 120,000 tonnes per year, while the largest recent catch was 56,000 tonnes in 1995. Thus an effective national strategy for expanding the tuna industry is urgently needed. Some of the issues that the government will need to address include how much access to give to foreign purse seiners in areas away from the main group archipelago, how to allocate quotas and manage resources, and what the role of private investment in the expansion of the tuna industry should be.

In contrast to the fisheries sector, which has considerable scope for expansion, forest resources are being rapidly depleted. The forestry sector has provided about half of the economy's foreign exchange, and 20 to 30 percent of government revenues for the past four years, but current harvest levels are two to three times the estimated sustainable yield. If present extraction rates continue, the commercial resource will likely be depleted by the end of the next decade. Furthermore, the monitoring of both the price and harvesting of this resource is virtually nonexistent, with the result being uncertainty about the value and volume of the resource being exported.

Maximizing the capture of the value of these resources, reinvesting the resultant cash flows prudently, and placing timber harvesting on a sustainable basis are urgent policy needs. In addition, the government should re-establish the Timber Control Unit to improve price and harvest level monitoring.

TONGA

After several years of good growth performance, Tonga recorded slower growth in 1996. The growth of previous years had been fueled by a rapid increase in the production and export of squash and in construction activity. However, disease; marketing problems; soil depletion; and increased foreign competition, particularly from Latin America, had an adverse impact on the squash industry. Despite a recovery in squash production in 1997, prices were about half the level of the previous year's prices, and thus export values continued to decline. Nevertheless, GDP growth recovered to about 3 percent in 1997.

The decline in the value of squash exports has also had a substantial impact on external accounts. The current account balance moved into a substantial deficit of about 28 percent of GDP in 1994, in contrast to smaller deficits experienced in earlier years. However reduction in the current account deficit has taken place since, mainly as a result of a significant fall in imports. Revenues from the sale of passports to foreigners and lease payments by such entities as Bell South in New Zealand from a telecommunications satellite Tonga purchased relatively cheaply several years ago also helped to relieve pressures on the current account.

Monetary policy tightened in 1996, squeezing credit growth. The government increased the required reserve ratio for banks from 5 to 10 percent in February 1996, thereby slowing net domestic credit growth to 8 percent in 1996, compared with 25 percent a year earlier. The bulk of the impact was on private credit, but this has since resumed to grow in the 8 to 10 percent range. More than half the outstanding credit has gone for housing and other personal expenditures.

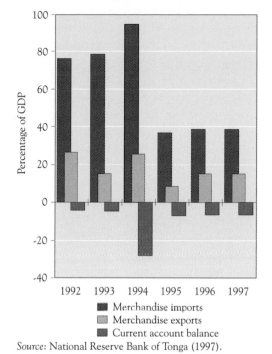

Figure 2.21 Balance of Payments: Tonga, 1992-1997

■ Merchandise imports
▨ Merchandise exports
■ Current account balance

Source: National Reserve Bank of Tonga (1997).

The 1997 budget restrained recurrent expenditure to 1996 levels, but provided for a further increase in development expenditures, which led to an overall deficit of about 3 percent of GDP. The 1998 budget reduced government current expenditure on goods and services and capital spending, and as a result the deficit is estimated to contract to less than 0.5 percent of GDP. External financing of the deficit has been mainly on concessional terms, so the debt-service burden has remained relatively low.

Increased demand associated with the growth in private credit mainly spilled over into imports. Inflationary pressures subsequently picked up somewhat in 1996, but inflation is currently estimated to have stabilized at less than 2 percent. Interest rates for both deposits and lending have been stable. By mid-1997 the base rate for lending was 9 percent and the passbook savings rate was 4.2 percent.

In terms of sectoral developments, the main features in 1997 were weaknesses in agriculture and fisheries, a substantial decline in construction activity, continued weakness in the restaurant and hotel sector, dramatic growth in transport and communications, and modest growth in most other sectors. Telecommunication services have expanded substantially following the introduction of mobile phones and electronic mail services.

Tonga has achieved reasonably good economic growth in the past decade, but its performance has at times been erratic, reflecting the narrow production base. There are now clear signs of a narrowing in the niche opportunities for squash and vanilla, which have provided the basis for good growth in the past. This highlights the need to diversify the economic base. Growth in communication, transport, and tourism activities is, however, expected to offset weaknesses in the agriculture sector. A target growth rate of at least 3 percent per year is desirable, particularly in light of the growing unemployment among young people. This will require either increasing squash export revenues or diversifying into other exports and implementing reforms that entail a greater role for the private sector. The 1998 squash crop is expected to be good, and competition from Latin America is expected to be weaker because of the effects of El Niño.

Restoring economic growth while containing the budget deficit within prudent levels is the dominant short-term economic performance issue. Tonga has no significant macroeconomic imbalances, and the scope for expansionary fiscal or monetary policy to restore growth in the short term is limited, as the main impact of such policy is likely to be a deterioration in the external account. A strategy that is more likely to have enduring benefits would be to continue efforts to redefine the role and improve the performance of the public sector and gradually to increase the contribution of the private sector. Expected benefits from such a strategy would include improved public sector efficiency and public expenditure effectiveness and greater scope for taxation reform, including a taxation environment that would be more conducive to business.

Tonga's high dependence on remittances is a major structural weakness of the economy, and has led to recommendations to pursue diversification in agriculture and fisheries, and in tourism. However, Tonga should not purse diversification for its own sake, and should instead base it on a careful assessment of economic returns and consideration of the impact on the environment. Moreover, for diversification to succeed, it would have to be carried out through public sector reform, facilitation of private sector development, improved management of public debt, and human resource development.

The first step in operationalizing the public sector reform strategy should be consideration of the core roles of government. Tonga currently has a large and diverse public enterprise sector that generally does not require subsidies, but pays neither taxes nor significant dividends. The government would do well to increase the rate of privatization. At the same time, the scope for government involvement in developing its human resources is considerable. Public spending needs to be reprioritized to focus on improving the quality of basic education and providing preventive rather than curative health care. Public spending may also have to entail assistance for displaced civil servants and the development of appropriate training programs.

In its efforts to encourage greater private sector dynamism, Tonga will have to improve the general environment for private sector activity by reforming its tax system and providing more secure property rights. The tax system has undergone numerous studies in recent years and various detailed proposals have been prepared, but little effective reform has taken place. The tax system is characterized by large discretionary exemptions under the Industrial Development Incentives Act, exemptions for the entire public sector, and heavy reliance on trade taxes. In particular, the act provides tax incentives as well as tax holidays, duty exemptions, and special depreciation provisions to approved enterprises. Because of its discretionary and discriminatory nature, the act's actual operations have introduced distortions and encouraged unproductive activity. Surveys of the private sector have confirmed that it would prefer nondiscriminatory measures, such as lower taxes or more generous depreciation allowances applicable to all businesses.

TUVALU

Analyzing recent trends in Tuvalu's economy is difficult because of lack of comprehensive, up-to-date social and economic data. Nevertheless, estimates indicate that growth in 1997 was similar to the average growth rate during 1990-1995, when GDP grew at an average annual rate of just under 2.9 percent, while GDP per capita increased at an average annual rate of 1.8 percent. These rates have been among the best in the Pacific islands in recent years.

Subsistence or nonmarket production arising mainly from the agriculture and fisheries and forestry sectors accounts for about one third of GDP. Growth in these sectors matched the growth in population of 1.1 percent per year during 1990-1995. The public sector is the main provider of marketed output, which grew at an annual average rate of 3.7 percent during the same period.

The private sector remains relatively small and depends largely on the provision of services to the public sector. With forestry and agriculture and fisheries remaining stagnant, growth has been driven by the public utilities and government-owned enterprises in the finance, real estate, trade, and hospitality sectors, together with community and personal services. General government, the economy's largest sector, grew by 13 percent during 1990-1995.

The ratio of gross domestic investment to GDP averaged 52 percent during 1990-1995. However, given the growth of GDP at less than 3 percent per year, this suggests a low capital productivity or inefficient use of investment. This partly reflects Tuvalu's development constraints and the concentration of investment in infrastructure.

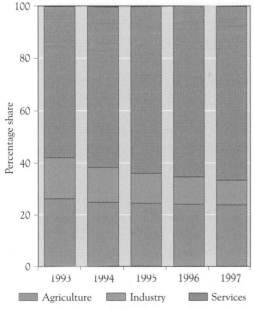

Figure 2.22 Sectoral Shares of GDP: Tuvalu, 1993-1997

GDP does not fully reflect income growth. While no official GNP figures are available, national income is likely to exceed GDP because of significant net remittances from Tuvaluans employed abroad, for example, in the maritime industry, and net interest income receivable from assets owned overseas. Remittances grew at an estimated annual rate of 4.8 percent between 1988 and 1995, totaling 14 percent of GDP in 1995. These data do not reflect remittances in kind, but in other Pacific island countries estimates indicate that such remittances amount to at least 30 percent of official cash remittances.

Aid, remittances, and investment income underwrite Tuvalu's large trade deficit, which reflects the limited opportunities for merchandise exports. The bulk of investment income is derived from overseas assets held by the government. The nation's overall external position is sound, in that Tuvalu does not have an external debt problem. However, continuation of this situation relies on the maintenance of grant aid at existing levels.

Fiscal policy has been sound, with real revenues and expenditures normally growing at average annual rates of about 2 percent. The recurrent budget showed a small surplus from 1980-1996, and development expenditure has been confined to what aid funding has allowed.

Inflation has been less than 1 percent per year in the last two years. Because Tuvalu uses the Australian dollar as the domestic currency, inflation is largely a function of movements of Australian prices and of the rate of exchange of the Australian dollar against the currencies of other major exporters to Tuvalu, namely, Fiji, Japan, and New Zealand. Inflation is expected to stay low in the medium term.

The medium-term outlook is that the present economic situation will change little. Living standards will continue to rely on flows of investment income from the Tuvalu Trust Fund, which consists almost exclusively of Australian bonds, remittance income from Tuvaluans working abroad, and licensing fees from deep water fishing nations exploiting Tuvalu's tuna resources. Aid will continue to fund capital development. Projections suggest that the per capita real value of the Trust Fund will be maintained.

In the immediate future, the potential for private sector investment in export-oriented activities is limited, and the development of a substantive merchandise export base is unlikely. While the government has signaled its commitment to limiting the size of the public sector and making it more efficient and to facilitating private sector investment, it needs to pursue such commitments more vigorously if the current development strategy is to succeed and the economy is to become more diversified.

Government plans to reform the public sector through commercializing or corporatizing various activities have stalled and need revitalization. Public sector commercial enterprises have accounted for just over half of the marketed component of GDP in recent years, thus public enterprise reform could have a substantial impact on economic efficiency. The main constraint on the public sector reform program is the continuing control of public sector commercial enterprises by the government's political and civil service arms.

Accelerating moves toward creating a policy environment that encourages private investment and restructuring the economy toward export-oriented business investment are critical for Tuvalu's future economic and social position. The trade deficit has grown since 1991 as exports have declined and imports have risen, and the continued reliance on aid and remittances is undesirable.

The government has passed the Foreign Direct Investment Act to help develop export-oriented businesses. Its salient features include establishment of the Foreign Investment Facilitation Board as a "one-stop shop" for potential investors and removal of the exemption from payment of import duties for public enterprises. However, while economic development through exports is an appropriate aim, the opportunities for such development are limited. Apart from labor exports, such as those Tuvaluans employed overseas in merchant marine fleets, fisheries resources provide the best opportunity for increased exports. Tuvalu must, however, learn from the experience of other Pacific nations and not commit scarce public funds to developing fisheries. Rather, it should pursue possibilities for establishing joint ventures with foreign investors to exploit the fisheries resources. Such an approach should recognize the inherent price and production risks associated with exploiting ocean fish resources.

Access to the scarce land available is a significant constraint to development, and land disputes prevent its easy use as collateral for commercial bor-

rowing and its use as an input into investment projects. Land is central to Tuvaluan culture, so freeing up the land market will be a gradual process. Nevertheless, the need for the government to facilitate access to land by domestic and foreign investors and to ensure security of property rights for those investors is pressing.

Characteristics of the labor force and wage structures present another set of constraints to development. The subsistence sector provides the largest source of employment in Tuvalu (62 percent of the working-age population was engaged in this sector in 1991), and the public sector, where most jobs are in administration, dominates formal employment. Growth in total formal sector employment in the 1990s has been negligible and all indications point to a growing problem of disguised unemployment, particularly in Funafuti. The safety valve of overseas employment, for example, contract work in New Zealand and in the merchant marine with European companies, is critical to reduce the growing pressures of an excess supply of unskilled labor in the domestic labor market. However, the most important source of overseas employment, Nauru, will become progressively less important as Nauru's phosphate mine nears exhaustion.

As well as coping with an excess supply of unskilled labor, Tuvalu faces a continuing shortage of domestically supplied skilled labor, which has affected both the public and private sectors. The supply of accountants, engineers, medical personnel, economists and development planners, teachers, managers, marine officers, and small business advisers is inadequate. A coordinated response to labor market imbalances, with attention to skill deficits and surpluses and education and training needs, is required.

The public sector is more attractive as an employer than the private sector because public sector salaries and casual labor rates tend to be higher, and the public sector also provides job security and extra benefits, such as subsidized housing. The government will need to address such issues if private sector and export industry development is to occur.

VANUATU

In recent years Vanuatu's economy has been typified by modest economic growth and stagnating living standards. GDP is expected to have grown by around 3 percent in 1997, roughly the same as average annual growth rates during 1983-1996, helped by strong contributions from tourism and copra exports. However, during the last 15 years annual growth rates have fluctuated widely from year to year, reflecting the impact of the climate on agriculture, of reduced confidence in the investment climate in the mid-1990s, and of a prolonged public service industrial dispute in 1994. It has barely matched the population growth rate of around 2.8 percent per year. Consequently, living standards have stagnated.

Inflation has declined somewhat in recent years and was around 2.5 percent in 1997. The underlying trend of declining inflation reflects lower imported inflation, subdued economic activity, and the recent absence of hurricanes. The nominal exchange rate has been relatively stable, but could come under pressure in 1998 following the devaluation of Fiji's currency by 20 percent in early 1998.

Vanuatu's trade account is persistently in deficit, but this is generally more than offset by surpluses on the service and transfer accounts. Tourist numbers increased by 7.5 percent in 1997, and while copra exports increased only slightly, the increase

was in addition to already high levels in 1996. Copra exports are expected to increase further in 1998, but tourist arrivals are expected to decline in 1998, possibly because of concerns about the civil unrest that followed an internal report about suspect practices associated with the National Provident Fund.

External grant aid forms a significant component of foreign exchange receipts, representing more than 30 percent of current account receipts. This aid should continue given the successful implementation of the Comprehensive Reform Program (CRP) developed in 1997. The overall balance of payments has reflected a surplus in most years. The surplus largely results from remittances from foreign currency deposits, which reflect residents' preference for saving overseas.

Vanuatu has a low debt-service ratio, indicating its favorable external debt position. Forecasts indicate that in 1997 debt service will have been equivalent to 0.7 percent of exports, and by 2004 will rise to 2 percent of 1997 export levels. While this is still a favorable situation, the recent rapid growth in external debt, which amounted to 18 percent of GDP in 1995, is cause for concern. Most debt has been issued to the government, with some on-lent to public corporations. As funds have been sourced from international agencies, mostly on concessional terms, Vanuatu's debt profile remains modest.

Fiscal policy has aimed to balance the recurrent budget, and this has normally been achieved. However, the recurrent budget has deteriorated somewhat in the past two years, and the recurrent deficit for 1997 is estimated to amount to 3 percent of GDP, compared with less than 1 percent of GDP in 1996, and a surplus that averaged 1.5 percent of GDP during 1992-1995. In addition to the recurrent budget, Vanuatu also has a development budget, and the authorities have not applied the same level of fiscal discipline to the development budget as they have to the recurrent budget. Development expenditures are responsible for the substantial overall budget deficits that have occurred since the late 1980s.

The recent deficits in the recurrent budget have occurred as revenue collections, which rely too heavily on import duties, contracted because of low import growth. At the same time, reductions in public sector expenditures and in import duty exemptions did not occur as expected in 1997. Deficits

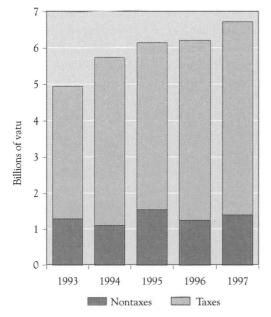

Figure 2.23 Composition of Current Revenue: Vanuatu, 1993-1997

Source: Asian Development Bank data.

have now soaked up the government's entire working capital, and as a result, development expenditures fell from Vt2 billion ($17.8 million) in 1995 to less than Vt1 billion ($9 million) in 1996 and a similar level in 1997.

Greater efforts to collect accounts receivable and delays in making payments are funding the overall deficit in the short term. In the longer term, the introduction of a value-added tax in July 1998 is expected to improve the cash position by increasing revenues to around 27 percent of GDP.

The medium-term outlook for economic growth is modest, and rates are likely to remain at around the same levels as in recent years. Vanuatu's economic position is relatively sound, its fiscal management generally prudent, and its debt levels sustainable. In the longer term, on the assumption that the government implements the recently developed CRP successfully, improves labor skill levels in both the public and private sectors, and achieves greater political stability, Vanuatu can look forward to attaining better living standards for most of its population.

In February 1997 Vanuatu committed itself to major public sector and economic reforms. Subsequently, the government developed the CRP, which emphasizes increased and sustainable economic growth, improved public sector management, and good governance. While private sector development is seen as the key to increasing economic growth, the authorities recognize that such development requires a politically stable environment. Indeed, the increasing politicization of day-to-day operations and administration of government and public enterprises in the early 1990s not only led to inefficiencies, but also destabilized the political system. In 1996 there were three different governments and one major realignment.

A recent policy issue is how aid resources might be invested in the private sector as well as in the public sector, thereby generating a more immediate economic growth response. Aid is normally invested through the public sector, but much of it has been ineffective in facilitating economic growth, and ways should be found to provide aid more directly to the private sector, but in a nondistortionary manner.

The government is involved in a range of commercial functions: it operates eight statutory corporations and has interests in a range of other companies. In nearly all cases business performance and profitability are poor. This indicates that the government is not well equipped to perform business functions efficiently, and efforts to divest the government of its commercial interests and to accelerate the privatization and/or corporatization of public sector enterprises should be accelerated.

The CRP will also receive technical assistance from donors in a number of areas of government. Such assistance needs to be supported by training for local staff, given the generally low level of skills available in the public sector. Skilled labor is also lacking in other sectors, notwithstanding high levels of underemployment. This shortage is constraining increased production in sectors such as agriculture and tourism.

Eighty percent of Vanuatu's population is engaged in subsistence agriculture, and economic development efforts must take this into account. The central medium- and long-term development issue is the transformation of subsistence communities into a more commercially active sector. This calls for developing rural infrastructure, education and other social subsectors, and transport and marketing services. These are currently poorly developed and hinder economic and social development. In addition, the land tenure system prevents the use of land as collateral for credit and, in any case, access to appropriate credit for smallholders and other small business operators is extremely limited. These constraints also hinder economic development and the equitable distribution of the benefits of growth, and policies to address these constraints are needed.

PART III

Population and Human Resources

POPULATION AND HUMAN RESOURCES:

BUILDING BLOCKS OR BINDING CONSTRAINTS TO FUTURE ASIAN DEVELOPMENT?

What is the future of the Asian miracle? While the full answer lies beyond the scope of the Outlook, it does address one of the most important issues the question raises, namely, the dependence of developing Asia's growing prosperity on the effective utilization of its most fundamental of resources—its people. This part of the Outlook highlights the crucial role of human resource development in fast and increasing per capita economic growth. Developing Asia enters the new millennium with the potential advantage conferred by a rapidly growing population and labor force. However, this growth is by itself not enough. To take full advantage of the opportunities requires a major investment in human resources and technological capabilities.

Given the wide disparities in the levels of economic development in developing Asia, no single strategy is applicable across the region. But with the rapid pace of globalization and increasing international competition, all the Asian developing economies will need to face their specific problems of human resource development sooner rather than later. While the challenges are pressing, the rewards are high.

Developing Asia has experienced massive economic transformation in the last 30 years. During this period Asia has emerged as the fastest growing region in the world and closed its economic gap with the industrial countries. Between 1965 and 1990, gross domestic product (GDP) in Asia grew by an average annual rate of 3.8 percent per person, compared with the industrial countries' average annual growth rate of 2.7 percent per person. The newly industrialized economies (NIEs) grew even faster, at a rate of 6.7 percent per person. In 1965 Asia's average income per person was only 13 percent of the US level, but by 1990 it had doubled to 26 percent. The transformation was even more dramatic for the NIEs, where it more than tripled, increasing from 17 percent in 1965 to 57 percent in 1990 (Asian Development Bank 1997a).

A combination of factors accounts for this dramatic transformation of much of the Asian economy, now widely referred to as the Asian miracle. These factors, on which there is wide consensus, include stable macroeconomic policies, openness to trade, high saving rates, generally sound institutional frameworks, high literacy rates, and favorable demographic characteristics. However, not all of developing Asia shares these characteristics, nor has all of developing Asia been part of the Asian miracle in the same manner as East Asia has been. Indeed, the miracle largely bypassed some parts of Asia, such as South Asia and the Philippines. However, things have started to change for these economies. Since 1990 South Asian countries have undertaken significant reforms of their policy frameworks and laid strong economic foundations for growth. The

Philippines has also made significant improvements in its policy and institutional framework, which has been accompanied by greatly improved economic performance. The great convergence toward market-based, outward-oriented economic policies throughout developing Asia in the last few years, a shift that should translate into higher growth in the coming years, has been remarkable.

Nevertheless, despite improvements in policies and institutions, the Asian economies seem to be facing a serious challenge to their economic growth, which declined in both 1996 and 1997. The 1996 slowdown was largely due to a fall in export growth, which has been the principal engine of growth for the miracle economies. The 1997 slowdown largely reflected the financial crisis that has besieged many of Asia's high-performing economies. While much of the 1996 deceleration in export growth was cyclical (caused by the cyclical downturn in demand for electronic products), a good deal is attributable to structural constraints that emerged from gaps in human skills and in technological capabilities. The economic meltdown in the high-performing economies in 1997 has largely been attributed to the lack of an adequate prudential and regulatory framework for the financial sector and a dearth of the sophisticated economic management expected in a globalized economy. These occurrences have raised concerns in many quarters. Is this the end of the Asian miracle?

The full answer to this question is beyond the scope of the Outlook; however, it is considered here in terms of human resource development. This perspective is important, because in the ultimate analysis, the structure of populations and the quality of human beings constitute the basic foundation on which economic miracles are built. This is not to downplay the policies that played a critical role in the economic transformation of developing Asia. Given the convergence of policies in much of Asia, the size, growth, and structure of populations and the quality of the workforce will largely determine the differences in performance across Asia in the future. The population structure has important implications for savings, investment, and growth rates, as well as for unemployment, underemployment, poverty, and dependency. The quality of human resources is consequential because it is a critical determinant of the structure of production, of competitiveness, of exports, and of technological and managerial innovations. It is also a determinant of whether a country can move up the economic ladder from one stage of economic development to another. Observers have suggested that many of the economic woes of some of the Southeast Asian economies are due to a mismatch between the quality of human resources that can support a given production and export structure, and their income levels.

Finally, two other external developments that are shaping the world economy at this time will have critical implications for the development of human resources in developing countries. The first relates to globalization, which implies integration through trade and exchange in goods, capital, and financial and other factor markets. The globally integrated world economy will be more competitive and efficient than ever before. Firms that are inefficient and unable to adapt quickly to changing global conditions will face declining profits and risk eventual demise. Economies that will be quick to adapt and to respond to changing challenges will be those with a highly educated, efficient, flexible labor force. The second development relates to the ongoing revolution in information and communications technology. This technological revolution, which is still unfolding, is likely to change human societies in ways that are beyond anyone's comprehension now. To benefit from this global technological advance, much of which is taking place in the industrial economies, will require significant investment in human resource development in developing Asia.

This part of the Outlook provides a comprehensive assessment of the population and human resource situation in the Asian developing economies (ADEs) and of how adequately prepared they are for the challenges that lie ahead. It begins by describing the trends in various demographic variables that will help determine the structure and composition of the population and workforce—the quantitative dimensions of human resources—in the various ADEs. Many ADEs are experiencing—and many others will soon experience—a large increase in their working-age population. The transition from a regime of high death and birth rates to a regime of low birth and death rates creates a bulge in the age distribution. As the bulge generation ages, rates of saving are also influenced as the proportion in the prime saving ages rises, then eventually declines. Some claim that much of East Asia's spectacular success derives from this age structure, that is, a high proportion of working-age people. Much of South Asia is currently in the process of receiving this demographic bonus.

However, whether prosperity actually ensues or not will depend on whether countries can mobilize sufficient physical capital, along with human capital, to use this bonus. Failing that, the bonus could turn into an onus, creating an additional challenge of providing employment for a larger labor force and risking social and political unrest. In addition to the age structure, demographic factors affect economic growth in numerous other ways. For example, life expectancy (measured at birth) is strongly associated with rapid growth, partly because higher life expectancy enhances growth by increasing the size of the working-age population; partly by raising labor productivity, because a healthier population is more productive; partly by raising the rate of accumulation of human capital, because people invest more in skills and education if they live longer; and partly by promoting more saving for retirement. The discussion examines the various demographic trends ADEs face and explores the implications for their future growth potential.

The discussion then moves on to the qualitative aspects of human resources in terms of the educational, health, and nutritional status of the populations of the ADEs. Some argue that much of the success of the Asian miracle economies is derived from their better human capital endowments (in conjunction with their market-oriented policies). This better human capital endowment ensured them success not only in producing and exporting manufactured goods, but also in transforming their agriculture sectors (exceptions include Hong Kong, China and Singapore). With the recent economic debacle in the miracle economies, some observers claim that much of the problem in some of these economies is due to the vanishing competitiveness in their exports and their inability to move up the value ladder because of human resource constraints. For others, they assert that they have approached the end of growth attainable through input mobilization. Further acceleration of growth would require technological progress attainable through new innovations that stem from a sophisticated endowment of human capital that is absent in these economies. Poorer Asian countries that aspire to the trappings of the miracle economies will require major efforts to improve their human re-

source endowment—in terms of the health, nutritional, and educational status of their workforce— which is necessary to transform their agriculture and expand their manufacturing base. This part of the *Outlook* discusses some of these issues at length.

The ADEs are at different stages of economic development, and by necessity, their strategies for human resource development will differ. The concluding section is devoted to a discussion of strategies, policies, and priorities as developing Asia enters the new millennium.

THE CHANGING DEMOGRAPHIC STRUCTURE IN DEVELOPING ASIA

For a full understanding of the benefits and limitations that changes in the population and labor force can bring to economic development in the ADEs, the significant transformations that are occurring to their populations must be discussed first. Only then will an appreciation of the challenges and opportunities that population growth poses for the ADEs, both now and in the future, be possible.

The ADEs are being transformed by an unprecedented demographic transition (see Box 3.1 for explanations of demographic terms), namely,

---

Box 3.1 Demographic Terms

Infant mortality rate: the annual number of deaths of infants under one year of age per 1,000 live births.

Fertility: the propensity to have children in a population.

Age-specific fertility rate: the average number of children born each year to women in a particular age group.

Total fertility rate: the number of children the average woman will have in her lifetime if age-specific fertility rates remain constant.

Replacement fertility: the fertility level consistent with zero population growth. Note that replacement fertility is slightly greater than two births per woman to replace children that die during childhood. In a low-mortality population, replacement fertility is between 2 and 2.1 births per woman.

Life expectancy at birth: the average number of years a newborn infant could expect to live given current mortality rates.

Child dependency ratio: the ratio of the population under the age of 15 to the population aged 15-64.

Elderly dependency ratio: the ratio of the population over the age of 64 to the population aged 15-64.

a transition from a regime of high fertility and high mortality to a regime of low fertility and low mortality (see Figure 3.1). In most countries the transition began early in the 20th century. At that time birth rates and death rates were high and roughly in balance. As a consequence, population growth rates were relatively low. Innovations in the health sector, improved standards of living, higher educational achievements, and other social and economic developments greatly reduced the incidence of infectious diseases, pushing down death rates and raising life expectancy. In many countries in the region life expectancy has more than doubled during the 20th century. In some countries infant mortality rates have declined to one tenth of the level that prevailed in the early 1950s.

The declines in death rates initially were unaccompanied by declines in birth rates. Consequently, population growth accelerated through the 1960s, and in some instances the 1970s, to levels far greater than previously experienced in Asia. Since 1950 the populations of many Asian countries have approximately tripled. However, population growth rates are slowing throughout the region in response to declining birth rates. A variety of factors are responsible for the changes in childbearing behavior. As child mortality declined, family size increased to levels previously not experienced, and, possibly, greater than desired. Urbanization, industrialization, higher levels of educational attainment (especially among women), and other features of development served to reduce the demand for children. Many Asian governments actively abetted this process by committing themselves to stabilizing population growth, promoting smaller families, and providing the means to regulate childbearing through national family planning programs.

Population growth rates decline gradually, even once birth rates begin to decline. In many countries the decline in death rates is, to some extent, offsetting the decline in birth rates. In the more advanced countries of Asia death rates are so low that further decline is unlikely. Life expectancies will continue to increase, but the proportion of the population dying each year will increase as the percentages of the population in the older age bands increase. Age structure also influences the

decline in birth rates. Rapidly growing populations have a large concentration of women of childbearing age and an even larger group of girls who will bear children in the future. Consequently, even when women are bearing only two children each, the overall birth rate remains high. This phenomenon, called population momentum, is a feature of all countries going through the demographic transition. Even when fertility decline is rapid, population growth continues for decades.

A decline in fertility to the replacement level will eventually produce population stability. At the replacement level, women are bearing just enough children to replace themselves, their husbands, and any children who die before reaching adulthood. In the late 1950s Japan was the first economy in Asia to achieve replacement fertility. Nevertheless, Japan's population continues to grow, and increased by one third between 1960 and 1995. Current projections anticipate that Japan's population will peak in about ten years and will then begin to decline slowly. Only Hong Kong, China and Taipei,China will experience zero population growth before 2050 if current projections prove to be accurate. In particular, the most recent projection for Hong Kong, China, which predates reunification, was for negative growth beginning in 2015. Taipei,China's official projections anticipate zero population growth around 2035.

Although replacement fertility and zero population growth mark the end of the demographic transition, there is little reason to believe that fertility rates will converge to the replacement level. In many European populations and a number of Asian ones,

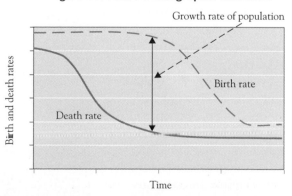

Figure 3.1 Asia's Demographic Transition

the total fertility rate is well below the replacement level. Should low levels of fertility persist, Asia's populations will begin to decline during the 21st century.

The following sections present additional details about the demographic transition and its features. The data required to document the demographic transition fully do not exist. In some countries a rich set of censuses and surveys provide a relatively complete record of the demographic experience, but this is the exception rather than the rule. In other countries the available data are much more incomplete and available estimates of demographic variables are based on methods and models whose reliability varies. Despite the difficulties, the United Nations (UN) has constructed estimates for all member countries. The following discussion relies on the UN data (and national sources for Taipei,China) because they provide a broad and comprehensive picture that is not otherwise available. The discussion will concentrate on the experience of countries with reliable data. This discussion does not, however, limit itself to the past, but relies extensively on population and other projections to anticipate the likely future course of population change in Asia.

The Decline in Mortality and Fertility Rates

Mortality conditions vary enormously among the countries of Asia. Given current mortality conditions the average Japanese can expect to live more than 25 years longer than the average Nepalese. Similarly, only 4 infants die for every 1,000 born in Japan, whereas in Bangladesh more than 100 die. However, all Asian countries have enjoyed enormous improvements in mortality conditions during the 20th century (Table 3.1). The gains have been particularly impressive since the middle of the century. In only three countries is life expectancy at birth

currently under 60 years, namely, Bangladesh, Myanmar, and Nepal; and even in these countries life expectancy increased by nearly 20 years between the early 1950s and the early 1990s. For the region as a whole, life expectancy at birth has increased by 20 years and the infant mortality rate has declined by two thirds since the 1950s.

The gap in life expectancy between low-mortality and high-mortality countries has declined since 1950. Note, however, that the gap between South Asia and East Asia declined only slightly, although Southeast Asia did close the gap with East

Table 3.1 Life Expectancy and Infant Mortality, Selected Asian Economies, 1950-1955 and 1990-1995

Subregion and economy	Life expectancy at birth (years)		Infant mortality rate (per 1,000 births)	
	1950-1955	1990-1995	1950-1955	1990-1995
East Asia	**57.0**	**74.7**	**74.0**	**8.0**
PRC	40.8	68.5	195.0	44.0
Hong Kong, China	61.0	78.6	79.0	7.0
Korea, Rep. of	47.5	71.1	115.0	11.0
Singapore	60.4	74.8	66.0	6.0
Taipei,China	58.9[a]	74.3[b]	36.0[c]	8.0[d]
Southeast Asia	**43.0**	**65.3**	**146.2**	**46.3**
Indonesia	37.5	62.7	160.0	58.0
Malaysia	48.5	70.8	99.0	13.0
Myanmar	36.9	57.6	206.0	84.0
Philippines	47.5	66.3	100.0	44.0
Thailand	47.0	69.0	132.0	37.0
Viet Nam	40.4	65.2	180.0	42.0
South Asia	**41.4**	**60.6**	**169.6**	**77.4**
Bangladesh	36.6	55.6	180.0	108.0
India	38.7	60.4	190.0	82.0
Nepal	36.3	53.5	197.0	88.0
Pakistan	38.9	61.5	190.0	91.0
Sri Lanka	56.6	71.9	91.0	18.0

[a] 1952.
[b] 1992.
[c] 1956.
[d] 1992.

Sources: For all economies, except Taipei,China, United Nations (1994). For Taipei,China: Department of Statistics (1994) and Directorate-General of Budget, Accounting, and Statistics (1986) for life expectancy; Department of Statistics (1994) for infant mortality rates.

Asia. Much of the convergence in life expectancy occurred within the Asian subregions rather than between the Asian subregions.

The total fertility rate began to decline in the 1950s or later. The transition to low fertility began first in East Asia, later in Southeast Asia, and later still in South Asia, with some exceptions. Fertility declined relatively early in Sri Lanka, for example, and recent declines in fertility in Bangladesh have pushed its total fertility rate below Malaysia's. Also significant was the substantial variation in peak fertility. In some countries the total fertility rate never exceeded 5.5 births per woman, while in others the total fertility rate reached 7 births per woman. Differences of this magnitude have major implications for population growth, age structure, and other demographic characteristics.

Current childbearing rates vary enormously (Figure 3.2). Six ADEs have completed their fertility transition and achieved replacement, or below replacement, fertility, namely: People's Republic of China (PRC); Hong Kong, China; Republic of Korea (henceforth referred to as Korea); Taipei,China; Singapore; and Thailand. In contrast, women in Pakistan and Nepal are still averaging close to six and five births, respectively. Other countries are somewhere in between. In Indonesia, fertility decline has been fairly rapid and women are currently averaging about three births. In Malaysia and the Philippines the decline in fertility has been more gradual. Recent surveys indicate that in both Bangladesh and India fertility has declined faster than previously believed: women in these two countries appear to be averaging fewer than 3.5 births over their reproductive spans.

The speed with which fertility declined in many ADEs has been matched in only a few isolated instances outside the region. The shift to low fertility required only 18 years in Hong Kong, China; 22 years in Singapore; and 28 years in

Taipei,China. Current projections for Indonesia anticipate that the shift will take 33 years. A notable exception to this pattern is the Philippines, where projections indicate that completing the fertility transition will take 60 years. By contrast, fertility declines have been drawn out over a much longer period in many African and Latin American countries (Figure 3.3). In the West the fertility transition was even more gradual, extending over a century or two.

Without question, rapid fertility decline in East Asia was partly a consequence of rapid social and economic development, but government policies also played a role. The policy responses of these governments to accelerating population growth were

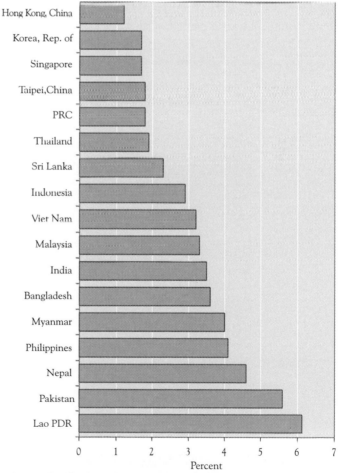

Figure 3.2 Total Fertility Rates, Selected Asian Economies, 1995-1997

Sources: For all economies except Viet Nam, Population Reference Bureau (1996, 1997); for Viet Nam, General Statistics Office (1997).

timely and vigorous, especially compared with African and Latin American governments. Singapore, for example, as part of its draft 1966-1970 Five-Year Plan, explicitly included a commitment to reducing the birth rate by one third, and Singapore's prime minister, along with the heads of state of Indonesia; Korea; Malaysia; Taipei,China; and Thailand were signatories to the 1967 Statement on Population issued by UN Secretary-General U Thant. In many East Asian countries, political leaders were committed to slowing population growth and were willing to devote public resources to that end.

Many Asian countries had adopted population policies and implemented programs by the mid-1960s. Operating through the public sector, nongovernment channels, or both, these countries used public resources to deliver contraceptive information and services to couples of childbearing age. The strength of the commitment to family planning and the programs' effectiveness varied considerably from country to country. Reliable information on the resources devoted is not available for earlier years, but data for the 1980s provide some idea of the size of family planning efforts in Asia. In 1985 Singapore and Sri Lanka had the lowest public expenditure on family planning programs as a percentage of both public health expenditures and gross national product (GNP), while Bangladesh had the highest (Table 3.2).

Judging the success of family planning programs is not a straightforward task. Contraceptive use has increased substantially in many of the countries with a substantial commitment to family planning programs. Thus judged by service delivery criteria, for example, the proportion of ever-married women of childbearing age using contraceptives, many programs can claim success. However, the extent to which private sources would have satisfied contraceptive demand in the absence of public sector involvement is unclear. Most knowledgeable observers believe that family planning programs had a major impact on receptiveness, access, and knowledge about contraception in many countries. The Asian experience also provides several clear examples in which national trends in childbearing appear to be unambiguously related to the government's stance on family planning. In Malaysia, for example, fertility decline virtually ceased when Prime Minister Mahathir adopted pro-population growth views in the early 1980s and the government de-emphasized family planning programs, while Bangladesh's recent experience supports the view that social and economic development do not have to precede fertility decline and slower population growth. Thus these two countries demonstrate that development is neither necessary nor sufficient to guarantee low rates of childbearing.

Differences in Population Growth Rates

Although fertility rates have fallen substantially in many ADEs, every developing country in Asia has experienced a substantial increase in its population during the last four decades:

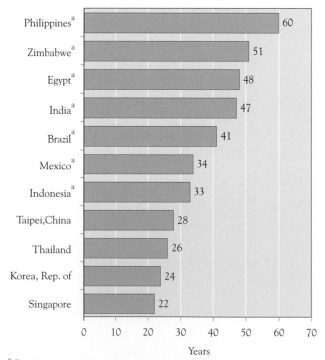

Figure 3.3 Years to Complete Fertility Transition, Selected Economies

Economy	Years
Philippines[a]	60
Zimbabwe[a]	51
Egypt[a]	48
India[a]	47
Brazil[a]	41
Mexico[a]	34
Indonesia[a]	33
Taipei,China	28
Thailand	26
Korea, Rep. of	24
Singapore	22

[a] Projection.
Source: Williamson and Higgins (1997).

Table 3.2 Aggregate Public Expenditures on Family Planning, Selected Asian Economies, 1985 and 1989

Subregion and economy	As a percentage of total public health expenditure		As a percentage of GNP	
	1985	1989	1985	1989
East Asia				
PRC	8.0	8.0	0.09	0.07
Hong Kong, China	0.3	0.2	na	na
Korea, Rep. of	7.0	2.0	0.04	0.02
Singapore	1.0	0.4	0.01	na
Taipei,China	2.0	1.0	0.01	0.01
Southeast Asia				
Indonesia	16.0	20.0	0.12	0.13
Malaysia	2.0	2.0	0.03	0.02
Philippines	12.0	14.0	0.05	0.03
Thailand	4.0	4.0	0.04	0.03
Viet Nam	10.0	5.0	0.06	0.05
South Asia				
Bangladesh	36.0	38.0	0.31	0.37
India	12.0	13.0	0.16	0.17
Nepal	14.0	11.0	0.16	0.16
Sri Lanka	1.0	na	0.01	na

na Not available.

Sources: Ross, Mauldin, and Miller (1993, Table 21, pp. 119-21); Sanderson and Tan (1993, Table 4).

between 1950 and 1995 the population of every country in the region more than doubled. The populations of Bangladesh, Malaysia, Philippines, and Thailand essentially tripled, while the population of Pakistan nearly quadrupled. The five largest ADEs—Bangladesh, PRC, India, Indonesia, and Pakistan—had a combined population of 2.6 billion in 1995, compared with a little less than 1.1 billion in 1950.

Rates of population growth have peaked in many ADEs. In East Asia slower population growth had begun by 1970, in Southeast Asia by 1975, and in South Asia by 1985. For 1995-2000 projected population growth rates are about 1 percent per year for PRC; Hong Kong, China; Korea; Singapore; Sri Lanka; Taipei,China; and Thailand. Indonesia's growth rate is estimated to be 1.5 percent per year and India's to be 1.7 percent per year. By contrast, populations in the other Asian countries are

expected to grow at 2 percent per year or more. By 2025 the populations of Bangladesh, India, Malaysia, Myanmar, Nepal, Philippines, and Viet Nam will be 1.5 times what they are today and Pakistan's population will have doubled (Table 3.3).

Growth of the working-age population is generally more rapid than growth of the total population, which has important implications for the labor force. The East Asian economies will experience an increase of 10 percent or more between 1995 and 2005; in Southeast Asia increases of 25 percent or more are projected in every country except Thailand; and in South Asia increases are likely to average 30 percent (Table 3.4).

The Changing Age Structure

The demographic transition is accompanied by systematic and important changes in age structure (see Box 3.2 for an example). Early in the demographic transition, as rates of infant and child mortality improve, children often become a larger percentage of the population. As couples begin to regulate their childbearing and reduce their fertility, the percentage of children declines and the percentage of the working-age population increases. Toward the end of the transition, the proportion of elderly increases.

The rise in the proportion of working-age people has been a particularly prominent feature of changes in East Asia's age structure. Between 1970 and 1995 the percentage of working-age people increased from 46 to 62 percent of the population (Table 3.5). The countries of Southeast Asia experienced a significant, though smaller, increase from 42 to 50 percent. The average for countries in South Asia was much more modest, rising from 44 to 47 percent.

Although the proportion of the population that is of working age is high in East Asian countries, it has not yet peaked. These countries will experience modest increases until 2005. Thereafter, the proportion of working-age people is projected to decline, in some cases fairly rapidly, except in the PRC. In the other Asian countries the percentage of the population that is of working age will continue to increase for the foreseeable future, but the speed of the projected transition to a high concentration of working-age people will vary considerably from country to country. Over the next ten years, the average

Table 3.3 Population Growth, Selected Asian Economies, 1950-2025

Subregion and economy	Population in 1995 (thousands)	As a percentage of 1995 population				
		1950	1970	1985	2005	2025
East Asia	**75,061**	**39**	**70**	**90**	**107**	**117**
PRC	1,221,462	45	68	88	109	125
Hong Kong, China	5,865	34	67	93	103	101
Korea, Rep. of	44,995	45	71	91	109	121
Singapore	2,848	36	73	90	107	118
Taipei,China	21,353	35	69	90	109	120
Southeast Asia	**465,172**	**36**	**58**	**82**	**118**	**149**
Indonesia	197,588	40	61	85	115	139
Malaysia	20,140	30	54	78	121	157
Myanmar	46,527	38	58	81	122	162
Philippines	67,581	31	56	81	121	155
Thailand	58,791	34	61	87	110	125
Viet Nam	74,545	40	57	80	122	158
South Asia	**1,236,946**	**36**	**56**	**80**	**123**	**167**
Bangladesh	120,433	35	55	82	124	163
India	935,744	38	59	82	118	149
Nepal	21,918	36	52	77	128	186
Pakistan	140,497	28	47	73	132	203
Sri Lanka	18,354	42	68	88	112	136

Sources: For all economies except Taipei,China: United Nations (1994); for Taipei,China: Council for Economic Planning and Development (1993).

changes for Southeast Asia and South Asia are similar. Three countries—Indonesia, Sri Lanka, and Viet Nam—will experience an increase exceeding four percentage points.

The proportion of the population that consists of young dependents (age 0-19) will decrease steadily through 2025, maintaining a trend that has been apparent since 1970 (Table 3.6).

For the most part, significant increases in the proportion of the population aged 65 and older have been confined to the countries of East Asia (Table 3.7). On average, the proportion more or less doubled between 1970 and 1995, rising from 4 percent of the total population to 7 percent. Japan, where 14 percent of the population are elderly, is furthest along in this process, and by 2025 one in four Japanese will be elderly.

Elderly populations are increasing in countries outside East Asia, but rapidly increasing elderly populations are an issue of longer term significance. Between 1995 and 2025 the proportion of the population aged 65 and older will double in Southeast Asia and increase from 4 to 7 percent in South Asia (Table 3.7). Even though rapidly increasing elderly populations are not an immediate feature of demographic change in these countries, many pertinent issues, for instance, policies toward pensions, have long planning horizons. Thus an appreciation of how the population age structure will evolve is essential for establishing sound policies.

DEMOGRAPHIC CHANGE AND SAVINGS

Demographic changes present numerous challenges and opportunities for developing Asia. These challenges and opportunities relate on the one hand to key economic issues, such as education, housing, and

Table 3.4 Growth of Working-Age Population, Selected Asian Economies, 1970-2025

Subregion and economy	Working-age population in 1995 (thousands)	As a percentage of 1995 value			
		1970	1985	2005	2025
East Asia	772,331	52	83	111	113
PRC	726,224	51	77	113	129
Hong Kong, China	3,722	51	89	108	94
Korea, Rep. of	27,906	51	81	112	118
Singapore	1,811	53	86	109	106
Taipei,China	12,668	53	84	115	119
Southeast Asia	235,932	49	76	126	181
Indonesia	102,859	52	76	125	165
Malaysia	9,884	45	74	130	192
Myanmar	22,553	54	77	126	196
Philippines	32,308	47	77	130	192
Thailand	33,157	43	75	117	134
Viet Nam	35,171	52	74	132	204
South Asia	607,784	52	76	131	206
Bangladesh	55,640	50	73	137	216
India	472,444	54	78	125	178
Nepal	9,551	55	77	134	233
Pakistan	60,304	43	72	138	253
Sri Lanka	9,845	57	83	123	151

Note: The working-age population is defined as those aged 20-64.

Sources: For all economies except Taipei,China: United Nations (1994); for Taipei,China: Council for Economic Planning and Development (1993).

employment opportunities, and on the other hand to labor force growth, saving, and social security systems. How economies meet these challenges and use the opportunities will determine the future course of economic development in Asia.

For growth in developing Asia to maintain its rapid pace will require large investments in both physical and human capital. While in theory, domestic saving levels need not constrain investments, in practice, mobilizing domestic savings will be critical.

The idea that demographic forces influence saving rates has a long history in economic research and has been the subject of considerable debate. The so-called dependency model has, in many respects, framed that debate. The idea of the dependency model is simple and focuses on the impact of changes in age structure brought about by the demographic transition. Does the proportion of dependents, whether they be children or the elderly, have any impact on growth, and if so, how and to what extent? These are the issues that will be addressed next.

Low-income countries have populations with a high proportion of young dependents, a characteristic summarized using the child dependency ratio, that is, the ratio of the population under the age of 15 to the population aged 15 to 64. When the child dependency ratio is high, the population consists of a relatively large number of consumers and relatively few workers. Hence consumption will be high relative to earnings, and saving activity will be low. During the demographic transition, the number of workers rises relative to the number of consumers, income rises relative to consumption, and savings increase.

Box 3.2 Republic of Korea's Age Structure

All countries experience broadly similar changes in age structure. The figure below shows the experience of Korea. The figure presents the proportion of the population in three broad age groups: those roughly of working age (20-64), young dependents (under 20), and old dependents (65 or older), starting in 1950 and projected to the year 2050.

Two important changes are apparent. The first is a change in the percentage of the working-age population. Until recently, less than half of all members of the population were working-age adults. In 1970 the percentage began to increase, reaching a high plateau in 1995. For the subsequent 25 years more than 60 percent of the population is expected to consist of working-age adults. In 2020 the percentage will begin to decline, gradually but steadily, until by the latter part of the 21st century the percentage of working age adults may once again be about 50 percent of the population. The change from peak to trough

is substantial, amounting to an increase in the proportion of the population of working age of almost 40 percent.

The second change is a transition in dependency from a society dominated by youth to one in which the elderly figure much more prominently. In 1950 only 1 in every 18 dependents was elderly, in 1995 1 in every 7 dependents was elderly, and by 2050 nearly half of all dependents will be elderly. The bulge in the working-age population has favorable implications for economic growth that should persist for another two to three decades. Beginning around 2025, however, Korea's population will begin to mature. Slower growth in the labor force, lower rates of saving and investment, and lower rates of economic growth are to be expected, but at standards of living comparable to those in other industrial economies. Staying on course will depend, of course, on a variety of factors in addition to the demographic forces portrayed here.

Transition Age Structure, Republic of Korea, 1950-2050

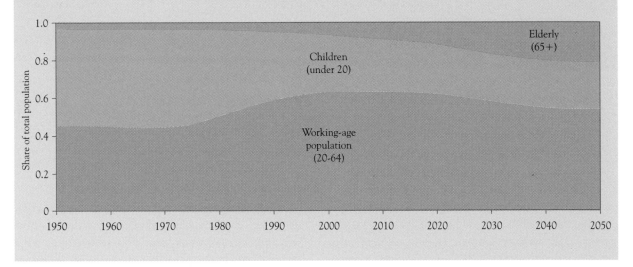

However, savings are also influenced by changes in the relative number of elderly dependents. Populations with relatively large numbers of elderly dependents would have relatively large numbers of consumers and relatively few workers. Hence the rise in the number of elderly at the later stages of the demographic transition would lead to increased consumption relative to earnings, and, therefore to reduced savings.

When these two demographic effects are both at work, saving rates rise in the early part of the demographic transition because of a decline in youth dependency. High levels are sustained for several

decades while overall dependency is low. During the later stages of the transition, saving rates decline because of increases in the proportion of elderly in the population. High saving rates during the demographic transition support the shift to a more capital-intensive economy that is a widely noted feature of the East Asian experience. As saving (and investment) rates decline toward the end of the transition, growth in wealth and capital will moderate. As this occurs, future economic growth will be driven less by capital accumulation and more by changes in productivity.

Table 3.5 Working-Age Population as a Proportion of Total Population, Selected Asian Economies, 1970-2025 (percent)

Subregion and economy	1970	1995	2005	2025
East Asia	45.9	61.6	63.7	59.3
PRC	45.0	59.5	61.2	61.3
Hong Kong, China	48.1	63.5	66.6	58.7
Korea, Rep. of	44.8	62.0	63.6	60.6
Singapore	45.9	63.6	64.4	57.1
Taipei,China	45.5	59.3	62.8	59.0
Southeast Asia	42.3	50.2	53.6	60.1
Indonesia	44.8	52.1	56.5	61.5
Malaysia	41.2	49.1	52.6	60.2
Myanmar	45.0	48.5	50.1	58.5
Philippines	40.5	47.8	51.4	59.2
Thailand	40.2	56.4	60.0	60.6
Viet Nam	42.4	47.2	51.2	60.9
South Asia	43.6	47.4	50.8	57.9
Bangladesh	41.9	46.2	51.2	61.2
India	46.1	50.5	53.4	60.5
Nepal	45.3	43.6	45.8	54.7
Pakistan	39.7	42.9	44.9	53.6
Sri Lanka	44.8	53.6	58.7	59.3

Note: The working-age population is defined as those aged 20-64.

Sources: For all economies except Taipei,China: United Nations (1994); for Taipei,China: Council for Economic Planning and Development (1993).

The evidence on the dependency hypothesis is mixed. The strongest support is found in the Asian experience, where changes in age structure appear to have a substantial impact on saving. The African and Latin American experiences provide less support. While one could therefore simply conclude that Asia is different from other parts of the world and proceed on that assumption, to do so would be incautious, at best. If changes in dependency influence savings only under certain circumstances, understanding what those circumstances are is critical; otherwise, one can neither judge whether changing dependency will influence saving rates in some Asian countries and not in others, nor judge whether dependency will continue to affect saving rates in the future.

Two features of ADEs provide possible explanations for the substantial impact of population change on savings, namely, high rates of economic growth and economic support systems for the elderly.

How Economic Growth and the Life Cycle Affect Saving

One explanation for Asia's high saving rates is that they are the result of changes in age structure. This possibility is an implication of the so-called life cycle saving model (Box 3.3). A further implication of the model is that factors that influence life cycle saving, such as demographic changes, will have a greater impact in a high-growth economy. Thus a combination of high economic growth and rapid demographic change may explain Asia's saving patterns.

Life cycle saving refers to saving that shifts consumption from one period of life to another. The most obvious example is saving for retirement. The motive for saving, however, is essentially irrelevant. What is relevant is that the decision-making unit is using saving as a way to redistribute resources from one age to another, rather than to accumulate wealth that will be passed on to heirs. Therefore, changes in age structure are likely to affect the saving rate.

In an economy with no economic growth, life cycle saving has no impact on aggregate savings. Positive life cycle saving at some ages (by workers, for example) will be offset by negative life cycle saving at other ages (by retirees, for example), leaving the total wealth in society untouched. In a growing economy, however, the positive and negative savings will not balance. Each generation is saving a given percentage of its earnings. If incomes are rising over time, the saving by those who are currently working will exceed the dis-saving by those who are currently retired. The result is aggregate saving and the accumulation of wealth.

The impact of growth on aggregate life cycle saving depends on the direction in time in which resources are being shifted and the magnitude of the shift. If life cycle saving is being used to shift resources from young ages to old ages (retirement saving), economic growth leads to positive aggregate life cycle saving. If resources are being shifted from old ages to young ages, economic growth leads to negative life cycle saving. The more resources that are shifted and the greater the difference between the ages at which the resources are saved and consumed, the greater the impact on aggregate saving.

How large an impact do changes in age structure have on saving rates? The results of different studies cover a wide range of impacts and are not strictly comparable because of differences in the definitions used, the periods and countries analyzed, and the changes in dependency considered. For example, while some studies have found that saving rates increase by three to four percentage points in response to changes in dependency rates of conventional magnitudes, others have put the gains in saving rates to be in excess of ten percentage points. Nevertheless, taken together these different studies provide strong support for the view that changes in age structure have led to substantially higher saving rates, particularly in East Asia.

Saving and Financial Provision for Old Age

Dependency models of saving focus on children in their role as consumers, but children have other important roles that bear on saving behavior. In Asia and other parts of the developing world children are an investment for their parents. Parents who reach old age rely on their children for economic support. This relationship between children and parents has profound implications for saving activity. Children are a substitute for savings. Parents who raise successful children who respect their obligations to their parents have no need for financial wealth when they reach old age and can no longer support themselves with their labor.

The strength of the family support system may have been responsible, in part, for the low saving rates that prevailed in many Asian countries in the 1950s and early 1960s. Living arrangements, at least, were consistent with the view that the elderly "financed" their old age by depending on their children. In 1973 more than 80 percent of elderly parents in Taipei,China lived with their adult, married children. For widowed mothers

or fathers, the figure was even higher. In the 1980s the percentage of those aged 60 and older living with their children was 76 percent in Indonesia, 82 percent in Malaysia, and 92 percent in Thailand.

However, two demographic changes in Asia are influencing the traditional system of family support. The first is the decline in childbearing. Parents who once had four or five surviving children on whom they could rely now have only two. This may create uncertainty among parents, particularly in patrilineal societies in which responsibility for the elderly falls primarily on male heirs and their wives. The decline in childbearing also increases the burden on children, who have fewer siblings with whom they may share responsibility for their elderly parents.

The second demographic change is the increase in life expectancy. Until recently, many

Table 3.6 Young Dependents as a Percentage of Total Population, Selected Asian Economies, 1970-2025 (percent)

Subregion and economy	1970	1985	1995	2005	2025
East Asia	**50.3**	**37.2**	**31.2**	**27.1**	**22.2**
PRC	50.7	42.4	34.4	31.5	26.9
Hong Kong, China	47.9	32.1	26.4	20.6	16.7
Korea, Rep. of	51.9	40.6	32.4	28.6	25.3
Singapore	50.7	33.6	29.7	26.9	22.9
Taipei,China	51.6	39.5	33.1	27.8	23.9
Southeast Asia	**54.5**	**49.6**	**45.6**	**41.4**	**31.9**
Indonesia	52.1	49.6	43.6	38.3	30.2
Malaysia	55.4	49.4	47.0	42.7	31.5
Myanmar	51.3	50.1	47.5	45.4	35.3
Philippines	56.8	51.7	48.8	44.6	33.5
Thailand	56.8	47.4	38.6	33.6	28.4
Viet Nam	53.3	52.2	47.9	43.8	32.1
South Asia	**53.1**	**51.4**	**48.7**	**44.7**	**35.1**
Bangladesh	54.6	55.8	50.7	45.4	33.0
India	50.3	47.9	44.9	41.3	31.2
Nepal	51.7	54.1	53.1	50.6	40.7
Pakistan	57.1	54.8	54.1	51.9	41.4
Sri Lanka	51.6	44.6	40.5	34.4	29.0

Note: Young dependents are defined as those aged 0-19 years.

Sources: For all economies except Taipei,China: United Nations (1994); for Taipei,China, Council for Economic Planning and Development (1993).

Table 3.7 The Elderly as a Proportion of Total Population, Selected Asian Economies, 1970-2025
(percent)

Subregion and economy	1970	1985	1995	2005	2025
East Asia	**3.7**	**5.5**	**7.2**	**9.1**	**17.6**
PRC	4.3	5.2	6.1	7.2	11.9
Hong Kong, China	4.0	7.5	10.2	12.8	24.5
Korea, Rep. of	3.3	4.3	5.6	7.8	14.2
Singapore	3.4	5.2	6.7	8.7	20.0
Taipei,China	2.9	5.1	7.6	9.4	17.2
Southeast Asia	**3.2**	**3.6**	**4.1**	**5.0**	**8.2**
Indonesia	3.1	3.6	4.3	5.3	8.3
Malaysia	3.4	3.7	3.9	4.7	8.3
Myanmar	3.7	3.8	4.1	4.5	6.1
Philippines	2.7	2.9	3.4	4.0	7.2
Thailand	3.0	3.9	5.0	6.4	11.0
Viet Nam	4.3	4.5	4.9	5.0	7.0
South Asia	**3.4**	**3.5**	**4.0**	**4.5**	**7.1**
Bangladesh	3.5	3.2	3.1	3.4	5.8
India	3.7	4.2	4.6	5.3	8.3
Nepal	2.9	2.7	3.4	3.6	4.5
Pakistan	3.2	2.9	3.0	3.2	5.0
Sri Lanka	3.6	4.7	5.8	6.9	11.6

Note: The elderly are defined as those aged 65 and older.

Sources: For all economies except Taipei,China: United Nations (1994); for Taipei,China: Council for Economic Planning and Development (1993).

adults did not survive to old age, and those who did were unlikely to retire. Life expectancy has increased rapidly during the last three decades and further increases appear virtually certain in the future. Throughout the region those who are working today and making decisions about saving can look forward to living well into their 70s and to an extended period of retirement.

Increased survivorship places additional strains on the traditional system of family support. Furthermore, fewer children must support more surviving elderly. Under these circumstances the family support system is an increasingly fragile institution, the erosion of which greatly increases incentives for accumulating material wealth.

Changes in living arrangements in East Asia suggest that the elderly are depending less on their children. In Taipei,China the proportion of older par-

ents living with a married son declined from 82 to 70 percent between 1973 and 1986, and recent data indicate that the shift toward independent living has accelerated greatly since the 1980s. Changes in living arrangements do not, however, definitively establish that elderly parents are now relying on their own financial resources rather than their children's resources. In the case of Taipei,China, for example, the per capita household income of the elderly is raised substantially through co-residence, but we do not know how income is allocated within the household. Further complicating the picture is the possibility that children may exchange personal care (transferring time) for financial support. Alternatively, behavior may be governed by a family compact in which parents accumulate wealth (a farm, a residence) that they will pass on to the younger generation while the younger generation provides support, both financial and personal, during retirement. The kind of detailed survey data needed to assess more fully how intergenerational transfers have evolved over time are not available, and this section must rely on less complete information.

The greater the erosion in the family support system, the greater the impact of changes in life expectancy on aggregate savings. If financial security in old age were provided entirely through the family support system, changes in retirement needs would have no influence on savings. Were the family support system to disappear in its entirety, changes in life expectancy could have an enormous impact on savings. A recent analysis of Taipei,China indicates that taken together, changes in childbearing and increases in life expectancy would have been sufficient to increase national saving rates by 12 percentage points between 1970 and 1995 in the absence of a family support system.

An alternative to family support systems and the accumulation of private wealth is government-sponsored old age security programs. If government programs provide old age security, the implications for savings of increased life expectancy depend on the type of public pension program. Transfer programs, for example, the US Social Security System and the Philippine system, tax those who are currently working to support those who are currently retired. They do not, for the most part, accumulate pension funds nor do they add to national wealth or capital. Funded programs, such as Singapore's Central Provident Fund, where individuals are forced to save and contribute for their own retirement, accumulate wealth. An increase in life expectancy affects savings as it leads to an increase in the contribution rate to support an extended

retirement. If workers rely on their own financial resources for retirement, then an increase in life expectancy or, more generally, the expected duration of retirement, will lead to higher saving rates among those who are currently working and a higher private saving rate.

Future Trends in Saving

The high saving rates that currently characterize many Asian countries should begin to erode as the demographic transition continues. As population

Box 3.3 The Life Cycle Saving Model

The figure below shows key elements of the life cycle saving model in their simplest form. Saving arises because individuals experience enormous swings in their productivity, and thus their earnings, as they age. At young and old ages, individuals produce less than they would prefer to consume. During their working years they produce more. This creates a demand for some way to redistribute resources over the life cycle. Saving is one such means. As the figure shows, children are accumulating debt (dissaving) to finance consumption in excess of their earnings, workers are saving or accumulating wealth, and the elderly are disaccumulating wealth acquired during their working years to support consumption in excess of current earnings.

Given any particular set of consumption and income profiles, aggregate saving is determined by the population's age structure. The greater the concentration at the high-saving, working ages, the greater the saving rate. In the

earlier stages of the demographic transition, changes in age structure favor a higher saving rate as the proportion of the young declines and the proportion of those of working age rises. As the transition proceeds and the proportion of those of working age declines in favor of the proportion of elderly, aggregate saving rates decline.

Whether age structure has a large impact on saving or not depends on the particular features of the age profiles of income and consumption. An alternative consumption profile than that shown in the figure is possible, in which age structure would have considerably less impact on saving. What determines the shape of the consumption profile? Interest rates, costs of rearing children, expectations about economic growth, life expectancy, and the existence of alternative institutions for saving for old age (for example, state-sponsored social security programs) may all play a role.

Stylized Life Cycle

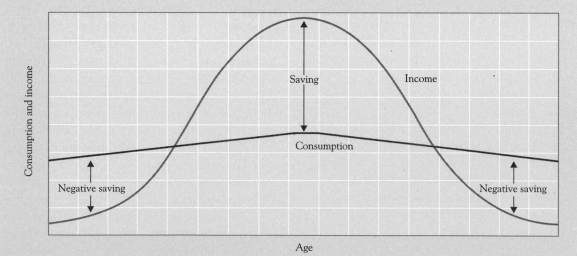

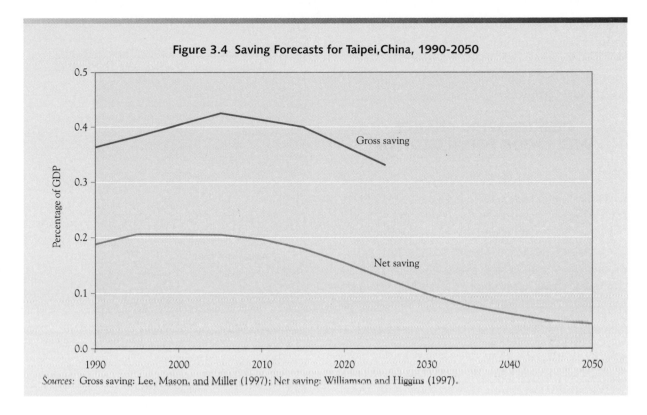

Figure 3.4 Saving Forecasts for Taipei,China, 1990-2050

Sources: Gross saving: Lee, Mason, and Miller (1997); Net saving: Williamson and Higgins (1997).

aging sets in, the number of retirees will rise, thereby depressing national saving rates. With the exception of Japan, Asian countries have not yet begun to experience a substantial increase in their elderly populations because they are in a somewhat different situation. They are not as far along in the demographic transition, and their old age dependency ratios are considerably below those of Japan. Saving rates will likely decline in the future as population aging continues. Two recent forecasts for Taipei,China are relevant in this context (Figure 3.4). Both show that demographic forces will not lead to lower saving rates in Taipei,China for another decade or two. Population aging may begin to play an important role at about the same time in a few other ADEs, namely, PRC, Korea, and possibly Singapore, but in others changes in age structure should not lead to lower saving rates for three or four decades. South Asia will have a rising share of working-age population in the next 30 years. While this does not automatically guarantee higher savings, it points to a possibility that if these economies can manage their demographic transition properly, South Asia can receive its "demographic bonus" of high savings as other countries did in the past.

As the advanced Asian economies mature demographically, saving will decline. However, even a fairly significant decline in saving rates is not necessarily cause for alarm. First, as labor force growth declines, so does the need for capital widening. In an economy with rapid labor force growth, a large share of capital goes to equipping new workers. Increasing capital intensity requires a high rate of investment. This will not be the situation as Asian populations begin to age. Second, the need for savings for old age security will decrease. The more advanced ADEs are now in the process of transition where individuals are relying on individual wealth rather than the family support system for old age security. However, this transition requires rapid accumulation and high savings. Once sufficiently high levels of wealth have been reached (indeed much of the savings of those economies are attributed to the provisioning for old age), no further accumulation is required for old age security needs.

Lower saving rates in more advanced Asian economies may have adverse effects on poorer economies that have relied heavily on foreign capital. A decline in saving rates in Japan, in particular, could slow economic growth elsewhere in the region. Both domestic saving and investment rates will be affected by changing demographic conditions in Japan and, later, in Asia's more demographically advanced economies. Thus whether the saving-investment gaps or current account surpluses will shrink in these economies during the final stages of the demographic transition is uncertain. Consequently, ADEs dependent on foreign capital may find their source drying up.

DEMOGRAPHIC CHANGE AND LABOR FORCE GROWTH

The economies of Asia have experienced an era of particularly rapid labor force growth caused primarily by the rapid growth in the population of working age, but also aided by increased female participation rates. Growth in manufacturing and service sector employment was particularly rapid in the fast-growing economies of East Asia, as large numbers of workers were drawn out of an enormous pool of agricultural workers.

The future will be characterized by considerably more diversity than has existed in the past. Asia's more demographically advanced economies are experiencing much slower growth in their workforces. The number of working-age adults is growing less rapidly, female employment is expanding more slowly, and the lion's share of agricultural workers has been absorbed into the manufacturing and service sectors. These more advanced economies are inevitably entering a new period in their development that will be characterized by relative scarcity in labor.

Most ADEs face quite different prospects with respect to their labor supply than the advanced economies of East Asia: adult populations will experience continued and substantial growth for several decades; substantial growth in the female labor force is likely; and in many instances, the agricultural labor force is well over half of the total; therefore the nonagricultural sectors can draw on this pool of labor.

The countries likely to experience the most rapid growth in their labor forces are also the region's largest countries, which will dominate regional change. Rapid growth in the Asian labor force will be a significant determinant of the future evolution of these economies.

Since World War II Asia has experienced an enormous increase in the size of its workforce (Table 3.8). From 1970 to 1995 the ADEs had labor force growth of between 2 and 4.5 percent per year. The labor forces of Bangladesh and Pakistan have in-

Table 3.8 Labor Force Growth Rates, Selected Asian Economies, 1970-1995 (percent)

Subregion and economy	1970- 1995	1990- 1995	Labor force 1995/ labor force 1970
East Asia	**2.5**	**1.5**	**1.86**
PRC	2.0	1.1	1.66
Hong Kong, China	2.5	1.3	1.89
Korea, Rep. of	2.5	1.9	1.89
Singapore	2.8	1.7	1.99
Southeast Asia	**2.6**	**2.1**	**1.93**
Indonesia	2.7	2.5	1.94
Malaysia	3.1	2.7	2.15
Myanmar	2.1	1.8	1.69
Philippines	2.8	2.7	2.02
Thailand	2.7	1.3	1.95
Viet Nam	2.4	1.9	1.82
South Asia	**2.9**	**2.4**	**2.09**
Bangladesh	4.3	2.1	2.92
India	2.3	2.0	1.76
Nepal	2.1	2.4	1.69
Pakistan	3.4	3.3	2.37
Sri Lanka	2.2	2.0	1.73

Source: World Bank (1997b).

creased the most, followed by Malaysia and the Philippines. Labor force growth has slowed rapidly in East Asia in recent years, falling to only 1.5 percent per year for 1990-1995, while in South and Southeast Asia labor force growth remained either above or close to 2 percent per year, with the lone exception of Thailand.

Rapid growth in the labor force largely reflects growth in the underlying population. Between 1970 and 1995 East Asian labor forces grew at just about the same rate as the population aged 20-64. The Southeast Asian labor forces grew somewhat slower than their working-age populations and the South Asian labor forces somewhat faster. Behavioral decisions, such as decisions about work versus school or participation by women, had a much smaller impact on overall labor force changes than the simple demographic realities.

Growth in the population of working age will continue to influence labor force growth in most

Table 3.9 Labor Force Projections, Selected Asian Economies, 1985-2025

Subregion and economy	Labor force 1995 (millions)	Labor growth index (1995 = 100)		
		1985	2005	2025
East Asia	735.4	83	112	118
PRC	709.3	83	112	120
Hong Kong, China	3.1	na	na	na
Korea, Rep. of	21.6	81	113	124
Singapore	1.4	na	na	na
Taipei,China	na	85	111	112
Southeast Asia	218.7	77	125	173
Indonesia	88.7	78	123	161
Malaysia	8.0	76	31	188
Myanmar	23.0	78	126	192
Philippines	28.3	77	129	190
Thailand	33.8	79	114	129
Viet Nam	36.9	76	128	180
South Asia	522.2	78	129	194
Bangladesh	59.9	75	131	199
India	398.4	79	124	171
Nepal	10.1	76	132	215
Pakistan	46.3	73	138	240
Sri Lanka	7.5	84	120	146

na Not available.

Sources: 1995 figures: World Bank (1997b); projections: staff estimates.

Asian countries for the foreseeable future. Over the next ten years, the labor force increase for Southeast Asian countries will average 25 percent because of growth in the adult population. For the countries of South Asia the average increase will be closer to 30 percent. In East Asia increases of approximately 12 percent are anticipated (Table 3.9).

The most important behavioral change that has influenced labor supply has been the rise in the proportion of women in the labor force (Table 3.10). The increases have been dramatic in many Asian countries. In 1970 and earlier, women were much less likely than men to be in the labor force. In Singapore and Taipei,China, for example, in 1970 only about one quarter of all workers were women. The increases have been the greatest in many of the countries that began with extremely low rates

of female labor force participation; for instance, Bangladesh, Indonesia, Korea, Nepal, Pakistan, and Singapore experienced particularly substantial increases in their female labor forces.

Note that the inclusion of certain activities traditionally performed by women played a role in the measurement of female participation in the labor force; thus in some instances, changes in perceptions played as important a role as changes in activity. In Bangladesh, for example, the definitions of labor force participation were revised to include previously excluded tasks (such as processing and preserving food, caring for poultry, and raising livestock) that were performed primarily by women.

The proportion of women in the labor force converged significantly across subregions: the gaps were considerably smaller in 1995 than they had been in 1970. Despite this convergence, enormous differences between countries persist. In a number of countries little more than one third of the

Table 3.10 Women as a Percentage of the Total Labor Force, Selected Asian Economies, 1970-1995

Subregion and economy	1970	1980	1990	1995
East Asia	33.6	38.4	39.9	39.9
PRC	41.7	44.0	45.7	46.0
Hong Kong, China	34.7	34.2	36.7	36.4
Korea, Rep. of	32.1	38.7	39.3	40.5
Singapore	25.9	36.6	37.9	36.8
Southeast Asia	39.1	40.6	42.0	42.7
Indonesia	30.2	35.8	39.5	40.6
Malaysia	31.0	33.7	35.7	36.8
Myanmar	44.4	43.7	44.1	44.7
Philippines	32.9	35.0	36.2	36.6
Thailand	48.2	47.4	46.7	47.0
Viet Nam	47.7	48.1	50.1	50.2
South Asia	21.6	33.3	34.6	35.8
Bangladesh	5.4	43.0	40.7	42.2
India	29.4	33.8	31.2	32.1
Nepal	39.3	39.4	40.3	40.5
Pakistan	9.0	23.4	26.1	28.5
Sri Lanka	25.0	27.0	34.6	35.7

Source: World Bank (1997b).

Table 3.11 Agricultural Labor as a Percentage of the Total Labor Force, Selected Asian Economies, 1970-1990

Subregion and economy	1970	1980	1990
East Asia	**33.8**	**28.9**	**23.2**
PRC	78.3	75.6	73.5
Hong Kong, China	4.3	1.3	0.9
Korea, Rep. of	49.1	37.1	18.1
Singapore	3.4	1.6	0.4
Southeast Asia	**68.8**	**62.0**	**56.3**
Indonesia	66.3	58.9	56.6
Malaysia	53.7	40.8	27.3
Myanmar	78.4	75.8	73.3
Philippines	57.9	52.3	45.2
Thailand	79.8	70.9	63.8
Viet Nam	76.6	73.2	71.8
South Asia	**72.1**	**70.6**	**65.7**
Bangladesh	81.4	73.9	63.9
India	70.6	69.7	64.1
Nepal	94.4	95.3	95.2
Pakistan	58.8	61.8	56.2
Sri Lanka	55.3	52.1	49.2

Source: World Bank (1997b).

workforce consists of women, while in others close to half of the total labor force consists of women.

Another important source of labor for Asian economies is workers employed in the agriculture sector. In the PRC and many countries in Southeast and South Asia, more than seven out of ten workers were employed in the agriculture sector during 1970-1990 (Table 3.11). Changes in the sectoral composition of output and productivity gains in agriculture led to a substantial decline in the relative size of agricultural employment. In Korea, the agricultural labor force declined from half of the total in 1970 to less than 20 percent in 1990. In other countries, well over half of all workers are still in the agriculture sector. In the region's two largest countries, almost three quarters of Chinese workers and two thirds of Indian workers are still in agriculture. These workers represent an enormous pool of labor that can fuel labor-intensive industrialization over the coming decades.

The overall labor force outlook for the subregions and countries of developing Asia varies enormously because of differences in the growth of the adult population, in female labor force participation, and in the sectoral composition of the labor force. Most important to the regional economy is the situation of the PRC and India. In India the large labor force in agriculture, the rapid growth in the working-age population, and the low rates of female employment all favor continued growth in the labor supply. Other countries in the region, namely, Bangladesh, Indonesia, Pakistan, and Philippines, are in similar situations. In the PRC the growth of the adult population has slowed rapidly and female participation rates are relatively high already. However, the large numbers of workers in agriculture provide an enormous pool that in coming decades will be absorbed into the industry and service sectors.

At the other end of the spectrum are the countries of East Asia and several Southeast Asian countries. In Korea, for example, the working-age population will grow by about 10 percent over the next few years. Female labor force participation rates have increased substantially; male participation rates and the hours men work are extremely high. The demographic trends alone may indicate that labor shortages and higher wages will be among the key features of Korea's future. Of the countries in Southeast Asia, Thailand is most likely to encounter an increasingly tight labor market if economic growth resumes. The adult population is growing at a rate well below that of other Southeast Asian countries and women have particularly high participation rates; however, the percentage of the labor force in agriculture remains relatively high. While these observations need to be verified in the light of the recent turmoil and recessions in Southeast Asian economies, the long-run trends will assert themselves once the current crises are over.

Rapid labor force growth will create many challenges for the countries of Southeast and South Asia, but will also create opportunities. In East Asia, labor force growth during the last 35 years has exceeded population growth by roughly 0.5 percent per year. As a consequence, the number of workers per capita increased by nearly 20 percent.

In many of the Asian economies, changes in age structure are currently leading to an increased concentration of the population in the working ages. The working-age population is growing faster than that of the total population. The largest gap is in six countries—Bangladesh, India, Indonesia, Myanmar, Philippines, and Viet Nam—where projections indicate a difference of 0.7 to 1 percentage points per year for 1995-2005. In Korea, Malaysia, Nepal, Pakistan, Sri Lanka, and Thailand, the working-age population will grow more rapidly than the total population by 0.4 to 0.6 percentage points annually.

The last three to four decades have been an era of rapid labor force growth throughout Asia. The working-age population has grown quickly and women have increased their presence in the labor force. Indeed, in the high-performing economies labor force growth has outstripped population growth. While ADEs have largely accommodated increases in the labor force, the economic implications of such increases have varied from country to country. In some countries, high rates of saving and investment and rapid expansion of the manufacturing and service sectors have led to rapid growth in nonagricultural employment at ever higher wages. In other countries, rapid labor force growth has outstripped growth in employment. For many Asian countries and for the region as a whole, rapid labor force growth will continue in the medium term. However, whether such labor force growth will be a bane or a boon for economic growth will depend on the success with which the countries can turn human beings into human resources and effectively utilize them for economic progress.

IMPROVING PRODUCTIVITY BY INVESTING IN HUMAN RESOURCES

The challenge much of Asia faces is not only to ensure the generation of adequate employment opportunities for its growing labor force, but also to ensure that the standard of living of its people continues to rise. To achieve these goals, Asia's policymakers will have to focus on improving the productivity of their workers. Improving the productivity of workers involves producing a greater amount of goods and services from a given amount of human effort. This may be achieved by equipping workers with more tools, that is, investing in physical capital, but may also be achieved by improving the efficiency of workers through investments in their health, knowledge, and skills. Such investments, termed investments in human resources (or human capital), enable in-

dividuals to produce more with given tools, natural resources, and technology. But improvements in the productivity of workers can also come about because of the adoption and generation of new and innovative technologies. However, this process of adopting and generating new technologies is not independent of investments in human resources: an economy must possess the capability to create and manage new technologies, that is, technological capability. This requires continuous improvements in human resources, particularly knowledge and skills.

In the absence of adequate investment in human resources, Asia's developing economies would be seriously hindered in their efforts to sustain economic growth in an increasingly competitive and integrated world. Indeed, the current economic crisis in those ADEs that have seen rapid economic growth in the last decade or two seems to indicate that the challenge of augmenting human capabilities is not limited to those ADEs that have lagged behind in economic growth. This is because the economic crisis afflicting Indonesia, Malaysia, Philippines, and Thailand is only partly macroeconomic. On a more fundamental level it is structural. Some of these structural problems relate to the frailties of the financial sectors, but others relate to the weaknesses that have tended to erode the growth and dynamism of the "real" sectors. In particular, a lack of high-quality secondary- and tertiary-educated workers seems to have undermined the economies' dynamism by constraining their ability to shift their exports to higher value-added goods and services in the face of fierce competition from countries such as PRC, India, and Viet Nam that have a cost advantage in unskilled labor.

While investment in human resources is critical for the ADEs' growth prospects, the nature and composition of this investment will vary from one economy to the next. This is because of the considerable diversity in the state of human resources across the ADEs, which parallels their diversity in demographic features. Outlining strategies for human resource development thus entails understanding not only the state of human resources in the ADEs, but also the links between the various types of investments in human resources and the improvements in productivity and technological capability they may bring about.

HEALTH AND PRODUCTIVITY IN THE ADEs

This part of the *Outlook* will now turn to an examination of health and productivity in the ADEs and then consider the empirical evidence on the relationships between investment in human resources and productivity and technological capability.

Healthier Workers Are More Productive

Experts generally agree that improved nutrition, especially at low levels of energy intake and income, can increase labor productivity, but what is the magnitude of this effect? A study by Deolalikar (1988) in rural south India provides some estimates. The study used data from an integrated household survey undertaken during 1975-1977 in six semiarid villages in the states of Andhra Pradesh and Maharashtra, among the poorest and most nutritionally deficient areas of India.

The study was able to take into account other factors that affected productivity besides nutrition (such as individual characteristics and other inputs, apart from labor, into farming). Thus, by allowing for these, it was possible to determine the effect on productivity solely of nutrition. The study found that this was a long-run rather than a short-run phenomenon. The daily calorie intake (a short-run factor) had little effect on productivity. In contrast, the long-run nutritional status of the family workers, measured by their weight-for-height, had a large impact on productivity. This suggests that while the human body can adapt to a lack of nutrition in the short run (in the sense of maintaining its productivity), it cannot cope with persistent malnutrition.

The study also examined the effect of nutrition on labor productivity by estimating the relationship between an individual's nutritional intake and the wage rates that the same individual earned in casual agricultural labor. The results confirmed the farm productivity results: weight-for-height (but not calorie intake) had a large and positive effect on agricultural wage rates. As daily wage rates for specific agricultural tasks, such as plowing, weeding, and harvesting, are generally fixed, the empirical results suggest that better nourished individuals choose more physically demanding tasks, like plowing, which pay higher wages.

Other recent research has confirmed these findings in such varied settings as Bangladesh, India, Philippines, Sierra Leone, and Sri Lanka, and suggests that improved health and nutrition could result in substantial productivity gains, especially in agriculture. The evidence from Bangladesh, for example, suggests that workers' nutritional status, in this case measured by body mass index, increases the likelihood of their engaging in strenuous, and usually relatively high-paying, work in rural Bangladesh.

The important message that emerges from these empirical studies is that the adverse effects on productivity of poor nutrition—as reflected in inadequate calorie intake, low weight-for-height, or low body mass—are considerable. In addition, available evidence indicates that inadequate nutrition has long-term and lasting adverse effects on children's cognitive development and school performance, both of which contribute to lower labor productivity in adulthood.

The productivity effects of nutrition and health are strongest at low levels of nutrition and income, and level off at higher income and nutrition levels. Consequently, these effects are unlikely to be significant for workers in ADEs' manufacturing sectors, because in most developing countries, workers in urban-based manufacturing tend to be better off than agricultural workers. Consequently, improved health and nutrition are more likely to enhance productivity in the agriculture sector than in the manufacturing sector.

Given the importance of health, both in its own right and as a factor that enhances productivity, this section turns next to a consideration of the question: What is the state of health in the ADEs?

The State of Health in the ADEs

Despite the progress made in improving the health and nutritional status of people in ADEs during the last five decades, there is room for considerable improvement, particularly in the poorest ADEs. As the following discussion will reveal, deficiencies in health and nutrition are more of a problem for rural populations and for females (particularly in South Asia). Health-related policies must address these imbalances. In addition, policymakers may also have to reconsider the focus of health expenditures, which in most ADEs remains excessively oriented toward providing curative care rather than preventive care, which emphasizes control of communicable diseases and immunization programs.

Life Expectancy and Infant Mortality. Health and nutrition conditions in Asia have improved dramatically during the past three to four decades, although the magnitude of the changes has varied considerably across countries. As described earlier in the section on demographic change, infant mortality rates and average life expectancy at birth have undergone dramatic changes during the last 40 to 50 years for a number of ADEs. Economies such as Hong Kong, China; Korea; Malaysia; Singapore; Sri Lanka; and Thailand were able to reduce infant mortality rates more than countries such as Bangladesh, PRC, India, Indonesia, Philippines, and Viet Nam. Nevertheless, even the changes in the latter economies have been remarkable. Some economies, however, such as Cambodia and the Lao People's Democratic Republic (Lao PDR) have had much smaller reductions in infant mortality.

Life expectancy, another indicator of health outcomes, underwent a transition similar to that of the infant mortality rate in much of Asia. Life expectancy increased dramatically, but with large variations between countries. Bangladesh, Cambodia, Lao PDR, Pakistan, and Philippines experienced relatively little change in life expectancy between 1960 and 1990. By contrast, PRC, Korea, Myanmar, Sri Lanka, and Thailand recorded extraordinary improvements in life expectancy during the same period.

Despite the remarkable progress made in the last 40 to 50 years, with the exception of Sri Lanka, infant mortality rates in South Asia, Cambodia, Lao PDR, and Myanmar are still unacceptably high (and approaching levels found in sub-Saharan Africa).

Illnesses. Data on morbidity are notoriously difficult to obtain. They can only be reliably obtained from household health surveys, as facility-based data are biased and do not include individuals who are ill, but who do not seek treatment. These reporting biases are evident in Table 3.12, which shows the incidence of AIDS, tuberculosis, and malaria in selected ADEs. For example, the table shows Sri Lanka as having the highest incidence of malaria, but the high reported rate may simply reflect

Sri Lanka's superior reporting system. The table similarly shows that Cambodia, India, and Philippines have the highest incidence of tuberculosis in the region.

The HIV/AIDS epidemic is likely to pose serious problems for the ADEs. Although it started in the region later than elsewhere in the world, its spread has been especially fast in Asia. Estimates indicate that by 2000, half of those with HIV will be living in the ADEs. Table 3.12 shows the extent of the AIDS problem in the ADEs, especially in Cambodia, Myanmar, Singapore, and Thailand. Surveys of pregnant women attending prenatal clinics also suggest that the HIV/AIDS epidemic is most severe in Cambodia and Thailand.

Asian policymakers generally seem to be unprepared for the rapidity with which the AIDS epidemic has spread in the region. Only Thailand

Table 3.12 Reported Cases of AIDS, Tuberculosis, and Malaria, Selected Asian Economies and Years (number of cases per 100,000 people)

Subregion and economy	AIDS (1995)	Tuberculosis (1994)	Malaria (1992)
East Asia			
PRC	na	30.1	5.7
Hong Kong, China	0.8	na	na
Korea, Rep. of	na	85.7	na
Singapore	2.0	51.3	10.8
Southeast Asia			
Cambodia	0.9	155.3	1,015.6
Indonesia	na	25.5	72.3
Lao PDR	0.1	24.0	882.3
Malaysia	0.7	59.4	202.5
Myanmar	1.3	35.2	254.9
Philippines	0.1	271.2	97.9
Thailand	30.5	82.7	199.4
Viet Nam	0.2	71.5	215.6
South Asia			
Bangladesh	na	41.4	107.6
India	0.1	122.0	241.6
Pakistan	na	na	69.8
Sri Lanka	0.1	35.9	2,045.4

na Not available.

Source: United Nations Development Programme (1997).

has taken substantial measures to confront the problem and has achieved some success in limiting the spread of the disease. However, projections indicate that by 2000, nearly 1 million children in Thailand will have one or both parents infected by HIV. Asian governments must give immediate priority to this problem.

Malnutrition among Children. An indicator of malnutrition among children that is used extensively in the literature is the proportion of children who are underweight for their age and sex. As with infant mortality, most ADEs (with the exception of Myanmar) reduced the prevalence of childhood malnutrition during 1975-1996. However, the prevalence of childhood malnutrition is still exceptionally high in much of the region, with a quarter to a third of all children under five years old being underweight even in such countries as Indonesia, Philippines, and Thailand. In India half of all children under five are underweight, while in Bangladesh the figure stands at two thirds.

How to Improve Health Care

Experts believe that an inadequate supply of preventive health services, such as immunizations and prenatal care, and an inability to provide prompt curative attention for early symptoms, contribute significantly to the poor health status and high mortality rates prevalent in the poorest ADEs. Indeed, some observers have argued that places such as PRC, Sri Lanka, and the Indian state of Kerala have primarily achieved low morbidity and mortality rates relative to their per capita incomes through their success in sensitizing individuals to even minor illnesses and in getting them to seek early treatment.

Many ADEs have committed sizable resources to establishing large public health care systems, most of which provide services at little or no cost to patients to promote access to health for all socioeconomic groups. However, health care providers and programs are often concentrated in urban areas; are frequently characterized by an indifferent quality of services; and provide little access to health services for populations in rural areas, where most of the poor typically live. In this context, examining the experience of the state of Kerala in India is instructive. Kerala has one of the lowest per capita incomes and

average calorie and protein intakes of any Indian state. Surprisingly, it also has the lowest mortality rates of any Indian state. This paradox is partly the result of Kerala's success in controlling infections, achieved largely by means of successful immunization programs and prompt curative intervention, made possible by the rural population's easy access to primary health services. This suggests that high incomes, and even high nutrient intakes, may not be strictly necessary for achieving low mortality levels.

The provision of primary health services varies greatly from country to country. At one extreme are Viet Nam and the countries of East Asia, which have the highest per capita availability of physicians (Table 3.13). At the other extreme are Bangladesh, Myanmar, and Philippines, which have the lowest per capita supply of physicians. The evidence suggests, however, that there is little correlation

Table 3.13 Population Per Physician and Per Nurse, Selected Asian Countries, 1988-1991

Subregion and economy	Per physician	Per nurse
East Asia		
Korea, Rep. of	1,205	1,538
Singapore	725	na
Southeast Asia		
Indonesia	7,143	2,857
Lao PDR	4,545	na
Malaysia	2,564	na
Myanmar	12,500	na
Philippines	8,333	na
Thailand	4,762	1,064
Viet Nam	247	1,149
South Asia		
Bangladesh	12,500	20,000
Bhutan	11,111	6,667
India	2,439	3,333
Nepal	16,667	33,333
Pakistan	2,000	3,448
Sri Lanka	7,143	1,754

na Not available.

Source: United Nations Development Programme (1997).

between the per capita availability of physicians and a country's actual health status. Indeed, an inverse relationship between the per capita availability of physicians and average health status seems to be apparent.

While the availability of appropriate health services is important for improving a population's health status, it is not sufficient by itself. For the health care system to have an impact on health, individuals and households need to use health services effectively. A rough measure of overall utilization that is often used in the literature is the annual number of per capita contacts with the health services. Obviously, an appropriate average level of annual health contacts per capita depends on the population's age and sex distribution, as well as on prevalent morbidity levels. However, an average of three to four per capita annual contacts with the health services is thought to be adequate to achieve basic preventive health care goals. For instance, this level of contact with mothers and children would assure a high level of immunization among children and proper monitoring of pregnancies and deliveries. A few developing countries, such as the PRC and Sri Lanka, average four to five contacts per year, but most others average less than one health service contact per year. Even in a middle-income country such as Indonesia, the annual per capita contact rate is estimated to be as low as 0.3 to 0.5. Inpatient hospital admission rates are much lower. Note that an average annual contact rate of less than one signifies that up to half of the total population, and a much larger proportion of the rural population, is effectively outside the health system, because of the extremely skewed nature of the distribution of service contacts in many developing countries.

Are Women Disadvantaged in Health Care? In South Asia in particular, women do not have adequate access to primary health services, partly because of discrimination within the household. Many studies that have analyzed health outcomes, especially in South Asia, have documented evidence of poorer nutritional and health status for females than for males. A number of studies have also documented higher postneonatal mortality rates for female children than male children.

The greater incidence of poor health and mortality among female children does not appear to be the result of lower food or calorie intakes, but reflects general parental neglect in providing medical care for their female children. For example, in rural Punjab, while calorie intakes were roughly equal for male and female infants under one year old, parents spent well over double the amount on medicines for their male infants than their female infants. Pakistan's experience indicates that the demand for health care is more responsive to price for girls than for boys, so that girls are more vulnerable than boys to increases in health charges. Evidence also suggests that as household income improves, utilization of health services is greater for boys than for girls. As the evidence suggests the presence of sex discrimination in the way households decide how much health care each family member gets, clearly the mere provision of primary health services by public authorities will not have much impact on women's health. Aggressive attempts will be needed to increase their uptake by women.

Other Reasons for the Low Uptake of Health Provision. Factors responsible for the generally low utilization of health services, especially in the rural areas of developing countries, may include price, distance, and quality. Some countries, often under pressure to reduce fiscal deficits as part of their structural adjustment and stabilization programs, have had to cut back health expenditures in real terms. As a result, these countries have attempted greater cost recovery in primary health care by charging user fees for health services. For instance, as part of its adjustment package Indonesia doubled user fees for health centers in 1987.

Another reason for the low utilization of existing health services may be the abjectly low quality of health services in many developing countries. As the total cost of using health services includes the time spent traveling to health centers and waiting for treatment, lack of nearby health facilities may also deter people from using health services. At any rate, the low utilization of health services is extremely unlikely to reflect a low need for medical attention. If anything, the high mortality and morbidity rates in many developing countries suggest that the true requirement for appropriate health services is substantial and largely unmet. Health service utilization rates of individuals covered under health insurance schemes, who in most developing countries tend to be public sector employees, are often three to four times as large as those for the uninsured population. This suggests that the actual demand for health services by the uninsured population might well be much greater if they had better access to these services.

Another factor that contributes to the low uptake is the fact that many ADEs are under increasing pressure to recover even more of the costs of primary health care than they are currently recovering by charging user fees. Recent research indicates that the demand for health services may be quite elastic with respect to price, so that a small increase in price results in a substantial fall in demand. Some evidence also indicates that the price responsiveness of medical care varies inversely with income, so that demand for health care among low-income patients is very price elastic, while that among high-income patients is quite inelastic. If this is the case, not only would utilization of health services fall because of cost recovery, increasing user fees for health services could also price the rural poor completely out of the organized health care system.

Problems in the Provision of the Correct Type of Health Care. The functional distribution of government health expenditures in many ADEs also leaves much to be desired. A much larger proportion of resources than is justifiable goes to curative care, while preventive care in the form of communicable disease control and immunization programs typically receives token funding. Within the curative sector, hospitals, which typically cater to high-income, urban patients, generally have much larger allocations than public health centers and village health posts, which cater to low-income, rural patients. Even worse, when public health expenditures are cut back sharply, say because of a macroeconomic shock or an adjustment program, communicable disease control programs are among the first casualties, while expenditures on hospitals are relatively protected. For example, when Indonesia slashed public expenditures on health by nearly 50 percent in real terms between 1983 and 1987 (the period of Indonesia's adjustment program), the brunt of the cut was felt most by real expenditures on communicable disease control programs, which fell by 75 percent, while real expenditures on hospitals fell by only 23 percent. The authorities virtually suspended the tuberculosis control program and cut back extensively on malaria

control activities. This is contrary to standard economic principles, which suggest that the government should give greater priority to funding for public goods, such as communicable disease control programs and immunization against communicable diseases, for which private willingness to pay is typically low. By contrast, as hospital care yields mostly private benefits, especially for higher income individuals, the hospital sector is the least in need of large government subsidies.

The burden of health expenditure cuts often also falls heavily on new investment and nonpersonnel recurrent expenditures, with relative protection for salaries and personnel expenses. Taking the case of Indonesia again, the burden of budgetary cuts fell largely on investment expenditures, which fell by nearly 80 percent in real terms between 1984/85 and 1987/88, and to a smaller extent on recurrent nonpersonnel expenditures, which fell by about 18 percent in real terms during the same period. Recurrent expenditures on staff salaries, however, increased by 32 percent in real terms during the same time. Lower nonsalary recurrent expenditure means fewer outreach activities and an inadequate supply of drugs and medical supplies at health facilities. If existing investments, primarily those in health personnel, are to be better utilized, recurring expenditures on operations and management, including the purchase of drugs and supplies, need to be increased, not decreased, during periods of adjustment.

EDUCATION AND PRODUCTIVITY IN THE ADEs

As noted earlier, education, as well as health, improves productivity. By promoting the acquisition of knowledge and skills, education not only enables individuals to make more effective use of existing technologies, it is also a critical ingredient for generating and managing new technologies. Thus this section will examine the effects of education on productivity.

Educated Workers Earn More

To what extent is workers' productivity associated with human resources? A large literature is available on the many economic benefits of formal education, and it is beyond the scope of this discussion to survey this literature extensively. However, reviewing some of the salient findings is important.

Economists now generally accept that schooling yields important pecuniary returns to individuals in the form of higher earnings. These returns can be relatively large in developing countries. Estimates indicate that private rates of return to schooling in Asia are as high as 40 percent. This view of education is known as the human capital view. According to this view, education is an investment in individuals that makes them more productive. An alternative view of education is that it serves as a screening device that allows employers to distinguish between high-ability and low-ability individuals, because high-ability individuals will go through school more easily than low-ability individuals.

There is also more direct evidence linking education to productivity. A survey in eight ADEs revealed that on average, farmers with four years of schooling are 9 percent more productive than farmers with no schooling. Recent evidence from Korea, Malaysia, and Thailand suggests that a year of schooling is associated with a net increase in farm production of roughly 2, 5, and 3 percent, respectively. Thus the high pecuniary returns to schooling reflect, at least in part, the productivity augmenting effect of schooling, which the labor market recognizes and rewards.

Recent evidence also suggests that women face higher returns to schooling, especially postprimary schooling, than men. For example, the private rate of return to secondary and tertiary education is 25 percent greater for women than for men in Indonesia and more than 10 percent greater in Cambodia.

What accounts for the large gender difference in the returns to secondary and tertiary schooling? If most salaried men were in occupations where physical strength is important, such as manufacturing or construction, the wage premium for men in unskilled factory positions and with low schooling would be considerable. The estimated returns to postprimary schooling would then be higher for women than for men. Both the Cambodia and Indonesia studies provide some evidence for this conjecture. For example, they find that earnings growth, although larger in magnitude for men early in the life cycle, falls off more rapidly beyond age 50 for men than for women, which suggests that

physical strength matters more for men. Schooling is often the only vehicle by which women can move out of low-paid, physically demanding jobs. This is what happened in the United States from about 1880 to 1920, when women acquired secondary schooling and moved into clerical occupations in large numbers. This trend already appears to be under way in Asia. Although secondary school enrollment rates are lower for girls than for boys in many ADEs, secondary school enrollments have been rising faster for girls.

The productivity impact of education on the nonmarket time women spend in home production activities is also large. Numerous studies for a large number of ADEs have documented the significantly lower prevalence of malnutrition and morbidity and higher rates of survival among children of literate mothers than among children of uneducated mothers. In addition, research during the last two decades on the determinants of fertility has shown that increased female education is the single most important variable in explaining fertility decline in virtually all developing countries.

A large empirical literature, spawned by the revival of interest in growth theory, is available on the relationship between educational attainment and economic growth. A recent empirical study by Barro and Sala-I-Martin (1995) showed that for males, the average years of secondary and tertiary schooling are significantly related to subsequent economic growth across a cross-section of countries. However, attainment at the primary level is not a significant determinant of growth rates, while initial levels of female secondary and tertiary education are inversely related to growth rates. While the literature is beset with many conceptual and data problems, the results are suggestive of a link between education and technological change. Evidence that provides further support for this proposition is discussed in Boxes 3.4 and 3.5. Box 3.4 documents a study where education facilitates the adoption of technology in agriculture and Box 3.5 illustrates this in the case of industry.

The central message of this research is compelling: education enables individuals to take advantage of technical progress and, at a minimum, education and skills produce a flexible labor force able to adapt rapidly to changing production conditions.

Box 3.4 Does Education Facilitate the Adoption of New Agricultural Technologies?

While it may be obvious that the skills and knowledge acquired through education are important for generating useful technologies, the relationship between education and the successful adoption of technology is less clear. For the users of technology—as low-income developing countries tend to be—the latter relationship is perhaps the more relevant one.

Recent research by Foster and Rosenzweig (1996) uses India's experience with the green revolution to shed light on this issue. Using data on rural households, crop yields, and schools, Foster and Rosenzweig found that farmers with a primary education were better able to exploit the technical advances embodied in the new high-yielding variety seeds than those without an education. In districts particularly conducive to the cultivation of high-yielding varieties, educated farmers' profits were as much as 46 percent more than those of uneducated farmers. The reason for the difference in profitability is that the potential productivity benefits of high-yielding variety seeds over the traditional varieties require a precise understanding of allocations of complementary inputs, such as water and fertilizer.

On the basis of this and other studies, education does appear to be important for facilitating the adoption of new agricultural technologies.

Box 3.5 Does Education Facilitate the Adoption of New Industrial Technologies?

Further corroboration of the superior ability of educated and skilled individuals to gain from technological advances comes from two recent papers by Tan and Batra (1995, 1997). Using industrial data from firms in three developing economies, including Taipei,China, the results indicate that while firms' investments in activities to enhance workers' knowledge, such as training programs, lead to higher wages and productivity for both skilled (typically well-educated) and unskilled labor, the gains made by skilled workers are much larger. For example, the results for the firms in Taipei,China indicated that skilled workers in firms that invest in training see, on average, a 54 percent wage premium over similar workers in firms that do not invest in training, while unskilled workers in the investing firms see, on average, only a 15 percent wage premium over their counterparts in noninvesting firms. Moreover, the results also revealed that training skilled workers leads to large gains in productivity, while training unskilled workers does not.

Education Promotes Technological Capability and Economic Growth

While the evidence indicates that education is important to enable workers to make more effective use of technology, education is a key building block for developing technological capability, that is, the capability to create and manage technological change. Box 3.6 discusses the need to develop human resources alongside the adoption of new technology—the two are complementary. Without sufficient education to develop the required skills, a country will not be able to benefit fully from the introduction of advanced technology.

The links between education, technological capability, and economic growth are perhaps the clearest in the case of research and development (R&D) activities. While it may be obvious that education—particularly tertiary education in science, engineering, and management—provides the knowledge and skill base required to carry out R&D activities, how important are such activities for the ADEs?

In general, investigators have looked most closely at the economic benefits to developing countries from R&D activities in the field of agriculture. In this context, the evidence from public sector agricultural research programs in Asia suggests that the internal rates of return to R&D activity have been in the range of 25 to 100 percent. Few estimates of the rate of return for industrial R&D in the developing world exist. Those that do are based on studies that have used data from private Indian manufacturing firms and report returns in the range of 25 to 80 percent.

The paucity of studies of industrial R&D in the ADEs should not be taken as an indication of its general lack of relevance to these economies. R&D can be of many types, and it is important to distinguish between basic R&D, which is geared toward extending the frontiers of scientific and technical knowledge, and more applied forms of R&D such as adaptive R&D, which is conducted with a view to adapting and assimilating technologies developed elsewhere, typically in the industrial world. For the ADEs, adaptive R&D clearly makes sense. Such R&D has not only enabled firms in some ADEs to use imported equipment and technology more effectively, it has also facilitated the acquisition of technology from foreign firms on more economic

Box 3.6 Complementarity between Human Resources and Technology

Raising productivity often requires the use of better technologies, but being able to use such technologies efficiently depends on the availability of a sufficiently skilled labor force. In other words, technology and human resources have to work together in a complementary fashion. Any attempt to introduce the use of more advanced technology may be of only limited success if the human resources (in terms of the numbers of engineers, scientists, and other skilled workers) to take full advantage of it are insufficient. Consider a simple analogy: importing high technology from abroad when complementary skills are lacking is like buying an extremely expensive shoe for one foot only. To be able to walk properly, the other shoe—in this case human resources—must be in place.

Some recent studies have looked empirically at the degree of complementarity that exists between technology and human resources at the industry level and have found that without sufficient human resources, the introduction of new technology may not lead to greater output, and indeed, it may even lead to a fall in output. To return to the analogy, it is like trying to walk faster wearing only one shoe. Walking barefoot might have been a better alternative.

Clearly, determining whether complementarity between technology and human resources is essential for the Asian economies as a whole is critically important. If it is, then a failure to develop the human resource base could seriously hinder the rate of economic development, despite the importation of costly advanced technology.

Khan (forthcoming) developed a model to address this issue by linking complementarities at the sectoral level with the economy as a whole. What emerges, perhaps not surprisingly, is that the advanced countries, with their greater skills base, benefit more from the introduction of new technology than the ADEs. For example, in both Japan and the United States, a 1 percent increase in investment in high technology increases output by 3 percent. By contrast, because of their relative lack of skills, the increase in output is considerably lower for the ADEs. The Asian economies in the best position to benefit from advanced technology are Korea and Taipei,China. However, even there, the gain in output from a 1 percent increase in investment in high technology is only slightly greater than 1 percent. This implies that the skill levels in ADEs are still not sufficiently developed to yield social returns comparable to those in the industrial countries. Thus appropriate research and development, technology acquisitions, and human resource development are paramount if the ADEs are to become competitive in the production of more sophisticated products.

A virtuous circle is at work here: greater skills lead to progressively greater benefits from the introduction of new technology, which in turn will lead to the further development of human resources. Without an initial skills base, no amount of new high-technology imports will lead to sustained development. The term positive feedback loop innovation system (POLIS) has been coined to describe this process.

terms. The international market for technology is different from that for goods, in that prices for licensing or purchasing technologies are not set, and the scope for negotiation between the buyer and seller in setting the terms of technology purchases is much greater. Case studies from a number of developing countries have shown that enterprises with greater local technological capability are able to purchase foreign technology on better terms than less technologically capable firms.

Adaptive R&D in some ADE firms has enabled them to modify technologies that they had previously imported and to export it successfully on the basis of their modifications. The technological capability to do this is fundamentally important in creating new bases of comparative advantage. While emphasizing industrial R&D and technology development may not be critical for building a solid base in the production and export of low value-added,

low-technology goods, it is critical as the industrial structure becomes more complex and a shift to the production of higher value-added goods occurs.

Efforts to develop technological capability pay dividends not only to the people or firms that are engaged in such efforts, but also to the rest of the economy. The "externality" produced by R&D occurs because the knowledge it generates is difficult to keep secret and spills over to others. These spillovers take place as highly skilled and trained workers switch jobs and as knowledge leaks to other firms through demonstration effects and reverse engineering. (Reverse engineering is the attempt to learn about competitors' technology through careful study of their products.)

While evidence from industrial countries indicates that R&D conducted by firms and industries has led to productivity gains in other firms and industries, is there any evidence of such spillover effects in developing countries? The limited evidence available indicates positive and significant spillover effects from privately conducted industrial R&D. These spillover effects are not limited to domestic R&D, but transcend national borders. A recent study by Evenson and Singh (1997) used data from 11 Asian countries collected during 1970-1993 to examine the determinants of gross domestic product (GDP) growth. The study found that both the stock of domestic R&D (domestic R&D expenditures accumulated over time) and the stock of spillover R&D undertaken internationally have a strong positive effect on GDP growth. The magnitude of the international R&D effect on output is about half of the effect of domestic R&D, indicating that knowledge and technologies are transmitted across countries, and that the productivity effects of these international transmissions of technology and R&D are not trivial. The study also showed that the productivity effect of international spillover R&D increases with the level of education and training in a country. This indicates that a country's efforts to improve the scientific ability of its manpower—that is, its domestic technological ca-

pabilities—induce spillover effects (see Box 3.7 for more details).

The State of Education

Given that education is a crucial factor in determining the productivity of the workforce, a clear picture of current educational standards in the ADEs is important, so that the challenge they face in developing their human resources can be understood more readily. Consequently, this section describes the present state of education in the ADEs.

The state of education in the ADEs has a number of salient features. First, in most countries in South Asia around half or more of the adult population continues to be illiterate. To the extent that, as already noted, an educated workforce is an important determinant of productivity, adult illiteracy will continue to constrain these economies' growth prospects, albeit to a diminishing extent as the illiterate ultimately leave the workforce. Second, while the ADEs have made important strides in increasing enrollments in primary and secondary education, gender biases, income biases, or both are

---

Box 3.7 Economic Growth and International Technological Spillovers

What is the effect of domestic and international technology activity on economic growth? Using data from 11 Asian countries from 1970-1993, a study by Evenson and Singh (1997) estimated an aggregate production function (the relationship between an economy's output and its inputs, such as capital and labor, together with an allowance for the rate of technical change). The study differs from most previous work in this area in that it considers both the stock of domestic R&D in a country as well as the stock of international R&D to be important inputs in addition to labor and capital in explaining a country's GDP. The idea is that the R&D undertaken in the industrial nations results in a spillover of knowledge and innovation to developing countries. However, developing countries need to have trained and educated manpower to make use of knowledge in the public domain. Thus a hypothesis the study tested is that international R&D spillovers will not contribute to productivity gains in a country until that country has invested sufficiently in higher education. The study also tested the hypothesis that the productivity impact of international R&D will be larger for those developing countries that are more globally integrated through international trade flows.

The results suggest that after controlling for other inputs and unobserved country-specific factors, both domestic and international R&D have strong positive effects on economic growth: a 10 percent increase in domestic R&D results in a 3.5 percent increase in GDP growth, while an equivalent increase in international R&D results in a 1.5 percent increase in GDP growth. However, as hypothesized, the effect of international spillover R&D on a country's growth increases with the country's secondary school enrollment rate and with its import share.

The implications of this study are clear. There is a major externality to developing countries from the technological activity and R&D done in the industrial nations. However, to benefit from the vast pool of technical knowledge that is being created in those nations, a developing country needs to have some technological capability (which comes about from both having a stock of trained, scientific manpower and undertaking some domestic R&D) and an outward trade orientation. Closed economies that underinvest in education and R&D are especially unlikely to reap the rewards of international technological spillovers.

important stumbling blocks to further improvement, particularly in Cambodia, Lao PDR, Viet Nam and some of the economies of South Asia, and especially in rural areas. Third, the quality of education in many ADEs, particularly the lower income ones, is less than adequate. While in principle the quality of education may be improved by devoting more resources to providing more and better instructional materials and paying teachers better salaries to improve their motivation and morale, resources are not unlimited. Thus policymakers are likely to be confronted with a tradeoff between the quantity and quality of education provided.

The situation as concerns education varies widely among the ADEs. The provision of education is generally best in the NIEs and worst in the South Asian economies, but even within these categories large disparities are sometimes apparent.

Adult Literacy. Education at all levels has expanded enormously in the ADEs, resulting in a general increase in literacy rates throughout Asia. While countries such as Korea, Philippines, Sri Lanka, and Thailand already had generally high literacy rates by 1970, in most other countries in the region, fewer than two thirds of the adult population were literate (Figure 3.5). By 1994, however, these other countries had increased their literacy rates by 40 to more than 100 percent. Nevertheless, despite these large increases, literacy rates in South Asia remain pitifully low, with rates in Bangladesh, Nepal, and Pakistan currently being less than 40 percent. Even in India, nearly half of all adults remained illiterate as of 1994.

As newly schooled cohorts of children become adults, the adult literacy rates in most ADEs will continue to rise. However, this rise will necessarily be slow, because of the continued presence of large numbers of older, illiterate adults. Literacy programs targeted to this group are vital, as these adults will continue to be economically active for several decades and their illiteracy will be a drag on economic productivity and competitiveness.

Primary Education. As in other areas, the ADEs' performance in the provision of primary education has been mixed. East and Southeast Asian economies have for some time had a record of which they can be justifiably proud. As long ago as 1965, the primary school enrollment rate was 90 percent in these countries and today it is, to all intents and purposes, universal. In South Asia the situation has improved rapidly in the last 30 years, with 90 percent of children now going to primary school, compared with only 70 percent in 1965. Consequently, despite large increases in the school-age population of most ADEs during the last three decades, school enrollment rates have improved impressively in every ADE, indicating that school enrollments have expanded more rapidly than the population of school-age children.

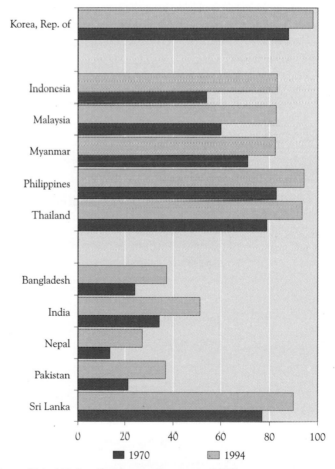

Figure 3.5 Adult Literacy Rates, Selected Asian Economies, 1970 and 1994 (percent)

Source: United Nations Development Programme (1997).

As noted, however, these averages conceal a wide variety of different experiences. For example, the most spectacular increase in the gross enrollment rate occurred in Nepal, where it grew from a mere 10 percent in 1960 to 109 percent in 1992 (Figure 3.6). (The gross enrollment rate can exceed 100 percent because some children enrolled in primary education are above or below the ages defined to be appropriate for those receiving primary education.) At the other extreme is Pakistan, which only increased its gross enrollment rate from 30 to 44 percent between 1960 and 1992.

In general, countries that had the lowest primary enrollment rates in 1960 experienced the largest increases in enrollment rates. As a result, the gap in expected years of primary schooling between the low- and high-income ADEs has narrowed substantially during the last three decades. Indeed, enrollment of children aged 6-12 in school is virtually universal except in Afghanistan, Bangladesh, and Pakistan. However, in virtually all the countries for which data are available, except Korea, the net enrollment rates at the primary level are significantly lower than the gross enrollment rates, which suggests that overage enrollment in primary schools is common in most ADEs. This occurs both because of late entry into school and because of high levels of grade repetition. Especially in the rural areas of Cambodia, Lao PDR, Viet Nam, and the South Asian countries, finding children starting school as late as eight or nine years old is not unusual.

While, on average, gross enrollment rates for primary school-age children are not a problem in most ADEs with the sole exception of Pakistan, the average enrollment figures mask large differences between income groups and genders. Boys generally have higher gross rates of primary enrollment than girls, particularly in the South Asian countries. For instance, in India the gross enrollment rate of girls is only 80 percent that of boys, while in Pakistan the figure is only 50 percent. Thus access to primary schooling opportunities is by no means universal among ADEs and substantial expansion of primary schooling opportunities is needed, especially for girls in South Asia.

Large disparities in enrollment by different income groups are also apparent. While data reported by school facilities are unable to indicate the extent of income disparities, evidence from household surveys in some ADEs suggests that the differences in enrollment rates between income groups can be substantial. For instance, in Cambodia and the Lao PDR, the gross primary school enrollment rate for children from the wealthiest 20 percent of families is, respectively, 35 and 43 percent greater than that for the poorest 20 percent. The differences in the net enrollment rates are even larger, because poor children typically enter primary school late and also have higher rates of grade repetition.

Even though the overall quantity of primary schooling opportunities may be

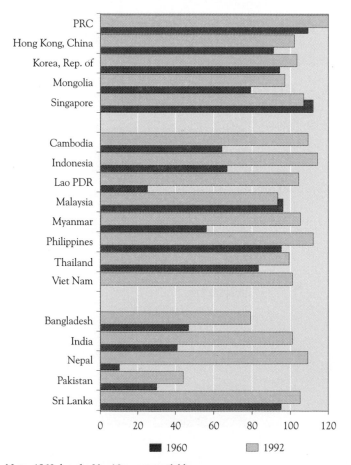

Figure 3.6 Gross Primary Enrollment Rates, Selected Asian Economies, 1960 and 1992 (percent)

Note: 1960 data for Viet Nam not available.
Source: United Nations Development Programme (1997).

adequate in most ADEs, the quality of primary schools is problematic in many low-income ADEs. Several factors are responsible for the low quality of schooling, including poorly paid teachers; low expenditures on nonsalary items, such as teaching and learning materials, including textbooks; inappropriate and overloaded curricula; and a generally unsupportive learning environment. The low quality of schooling is manifested in the form of low test scores, high levels of grade repetition, and high dropout rates. In some low-income ADEs, about a quarter of all children repeat a grade and, as a consequence, some children spend two to four years longer in primary school than normal.

Some ADEs may encourage repetition in primary schools as a matter of school policy, because they lack sufficient secondary school spaces to accommodate all primary school-leavers. This might help explain why repetition rates are much lower at the secondary level: secondary schools need to promote students irrespective of their academic performance to make space for new entrants.

Dropout rates are also high. The combination of high repetition and dropout rates means that enormous wastage occurs in education systems that are strapped for resources in the first place. The evidence suggests that of the cohort of children who enter primary school in low-income ADEs, only about half complete grade 6. The high dropout and repetition rates also mean, of course, that many students leave school unable to read or write.

Average pupil-teacher ratios are often considered a good indicator of school quality, because large class sizes may inhibit learning. Average pupil-teacher ratios in primary school vary considerably across the ADEs, ranging from class sizes of 20 or fewer pupils in Malaysia and Thailand to class sizes of 60 or more students in Bangladesh and India in 1990. Thus based on this criterion, the quality of primary education in Bangladesh and India is considerably worse than that in Malaysia and Thailand. Note, however, that pupil-teacher ratios in the NIEs at comparable levels of development averaged more than 40. Indeed, Korea had a pupil-teacher ratio of about 35 as recently as 1990. Meanwhile, achievement test scores of school children in the NIEs have been quite high—comparable to those in economies of the Organisation for Economic Co-operation and Development—and indicate that imparting a high quality education is possible despite high pupil-teacher ratios.

The NIEs seem to have been able to maintain high pupil-teacher ratios without compromising the quality of education by paying teachers high salaries relative to average incomes, thereby encouraging high standards of teaching. Indeed, a fundamental problem with the quality of primary education in most ADEs may be traced to the lack of motivation on the part of primary school teachers, many of whom, especially in public school systems, are poorly paid. As would be expected, the problem is much more severe in the poorer countries.

As concerns total government current spending on primary education across countries, although variation is wide, generally, the wealthier the country, the more it spends per capita on education.

Secondary Education. The cross-country variation in enrollment rates is much greater at the secondary level than at the primary level. At one end of the spectrum is Bangladesh, which has a gross secondary enrollment of less than 20 percent, while at the other end Korea's rate is greater than 90 percent (Figure 3.7). As these enrollment rates are totals, they mask a bias against the secondary schooling of girls in some of the ADEs. For example, while the male-female differential in enrollment rates was only 1 percentage point in Korea in 1993, it was as high as 14 percentage points in Bangladesh.

As may be expected, countries with higher per capita incomes also tend to have higher enrollment rates. However, as Figure 3.8 makes clear, the relationship is by no means a watertight one. For instance, whereas Indonesia and Sri Lanka have similar per capita incomes when adjustments are made for differences in local purchasing power, Sri Lanka has an enrollment rate that is 30 percentage points greater than that of Indonesia. Thailand, which has extremely high rates of enrollment in primary education, has a surprisingly low enrollment rate in secondary education, not only in relation to its level of per capita income, but also in absolute terms.

Many of the problems that plague primary education in the ADEs are also prevalent in secondary schools, including internal inefficiency (in the form of high repetition and dropout rates), low quality of schooling, poorly paid teachers, and inadequate current expenditures per pupil. Some countries with low enrollment rates may nevertheless spend more per student than countries with higher enrollment rates. This raises the problem of comparing the quality of secondary education and not just enrollment rates when comparing secondary education across countries. Moreover, to the extent that higher pupil-teacher ratios reflect poorer quality of education, an economy, for example, the Philippines, which has a much higher secondary enrollment rate than, say, Indonesia, may be achieving high enrollment rates at the expense of quality: the average pupil-teacher ratio in the Philippines is more than twice that in Indonesia.

Gender and income disparities are even greater at the secondary level than at the primary level. This is because in most ADEs, parents have to contrib-

ute financially to their children's secondary education, even in the public sector. As a result, low-income households are much less likely than high-income households to send their children to secondary school. This points to the need for government action to encourage wider access to secondary education, which is vital if countries are to realize the full potential of all, and not just part of, their populations.

A concept with great intuitive appeal is that the quality and efficiency of education may be improved by "diversifying" secondary school curricula by substituting a portion of the academic program with a vocational component. For instance, some educators believe that much of the problem in some developing country education systems stems from the lack of relevance to rural life of much of what is taught in rural schools. Thus they argue that the teaching of basic literacy should be combined with the teaching of practical skills for rural employment and agricultural production. A diversified curriculum that combines academic instruction with some vocational education may offer students a wider choice of future career opportunities than the typical technical or purely academic curricula offer. It may also make the curriculum more relevant to the needs of the labor market, and thus not only improve school-leavers' employment prospects, but also reduce wastage and repetition within secondary schools.

The evidence on the outcomes of curriculum diversification is not encouraging, however. For example, a World Bank study of curriculum diversification in Colombia and Tanzania—countries where diversification has been in place since the 1970s—found that while students in the diversified secondary schools generally performed better in terms of test scores in both vocational and academic subjects than students in traditional secondary schools, the gains in average test scores were achieved at the expense of significant additional costs per pupil. The

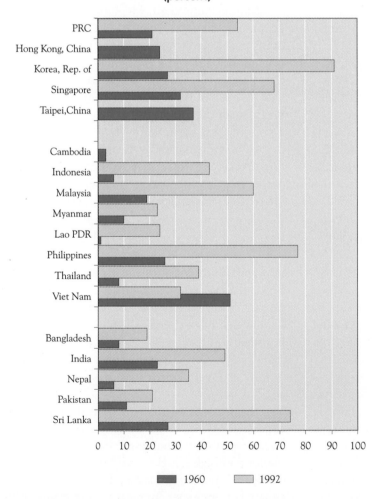

Figure 3.7 Gross Secondary Enrollment Rates, Selected Asian Economies, 1960 and 1992 (percent)

■ 1960   □ 1992

Source: UNESCO database.

Figure 3.8 Gross Secondary Enrollment Rates and Per Capita Income, Selected Asian Economies, 1990

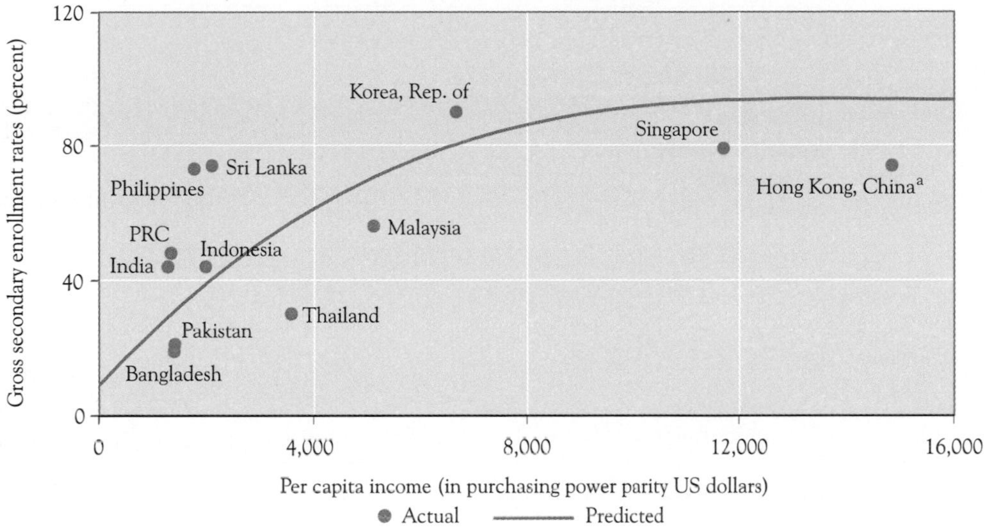

Note: The figure plots actual enrollment rates along with enrollment rates predicted on the basis of per capita incomes. The predicted values were obtained from cross-country regressions based on 92 countries. The dependent variable is gross enrollment rate at the secondary level and the independent variables include an intercept, per capita income, per capita income squared, and per capita income cubed.
[a] For the enrollment rate, figure for 1987 was used.
Sources: Per capita incomes: Penn World Table (Mark 5.6); enrollment data: World Bank (1994, 1997b).

higher costs stem from the need to compensate instructors of vocational courses for their specialized skills and the costs of equipment and special instructional material required in the vocational courses.

In addition, the data on graduates' employment prospects and earnings similarly offered no evidence of significant cost-benefit advantages of diversified secondary curricula over traditional secondary curricula. Similarly, a study in Indonesia that analyzed the performance of secondary school graduates in the labor market found that academic curricula were a better investment in terms of having higher rates of return than vocational programs.

These results do weaken the case for curriculum diversification and suggest that an attempt to reform secondary school curricula must be preceded by a careful analysis of the potential benefits and costs.

The finding that curriculum diversification is not a cost-effective way to deliver vocational education and training suggests that a better approach may be to focus on ways to improve the quality of existing academic secondary education. One such way might be through "technology" education

(World Bank 1991). Rather than attempting to develop occupation-specific skills, the emphasis of technology education is to improve students' understanding of the principles of science and mathematics that underlie modern technologies. As vocational skills are necessary, providing them is still important, but there is no compulsion to provide them in schools, or even within the formal educational system. A more sensible policy may be to encourage the private sector to provide the required training. This would not only increase the likelihood that the skills imparted to trainees would be relevant to employers' needs, but would also reduce the financial burden on the public sector by shifting it toward employers, and even to the students themselves.

Tertiary Education. Tertiary-level enrollment rates are generally relatively small in the ADEs. In 1990 enrollment rates for tertiary education averaged between 3 and 10 percent in South Asia and between 9 and 16 percent in Southeast Asia with the exception of the Philippines (Figure 3.9). The relatively more developed East Asian economies have higher enrollment rates, with the gross enroll-

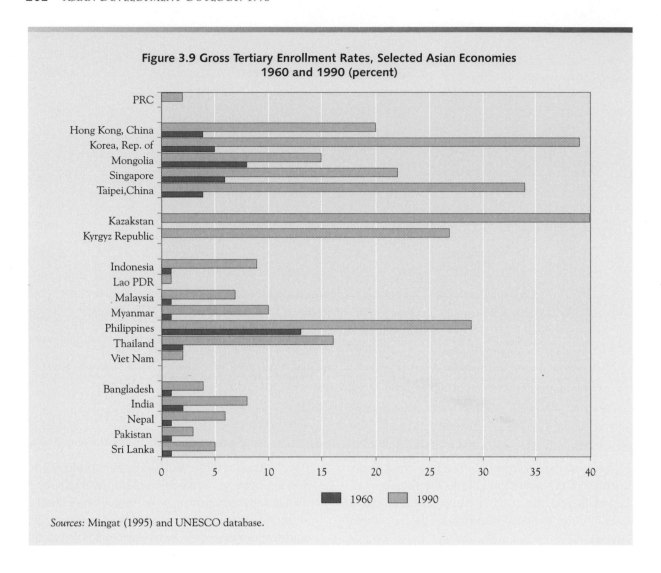

Figure 3.9 Gross Tertiary Enrollment Rates, Selected Asian Economies 1960 and 1990 (percent)

Sources: Mingat (1995) and UNESCO database.

ment rates in Korea and Taipei,China exceeding 33 percent.

The percentage of students in tertiary institutions who are enrolled in science and applied fields shows wide disparities between countries. In the PRC and Korea, for example, 40 to 50 percent of all students are in such fields. By contrast, Nepal and Thailand have among the lowest numbers of students enrolled in science and applied fields.

Scientific Education and R&D Activity. Insofar as scientists and technicians carry out R&D activities and contribute to productivity growth and technological capability, the stock of scientists and technicians in a country will be important. Figure 3.10 suggests that Korea and Singapore have around ten times as many R&D scientists and technicians per capita as the other countries in the region and are compa-

rable to the industrial economies in this regard. The PRC and Viet Nam have the next largest stock of scientists and technicians per capita, although the absolute numbers involved are quite small (fewer than 0.5 scientists and technicians per 1,000 persons). Given their higher per capita incomes, finding that Malaysia and Thailand have approximately the same number of scientists and technicians per capita as the lower income ADEs in South Asia is somewhat surprising.

Figure 3.10 also displays R&D spending as a percentage of GNP for the same cross-section of countries and shows that it follows the same broad pattern implicit in the data on R&D personnel. Among ADEs, Korea spends more than three times its GNP on R&D than India or Pakistan does. Indonesia, Philippines, and Thailand are among the lowest relative spenders on R&D in the region.

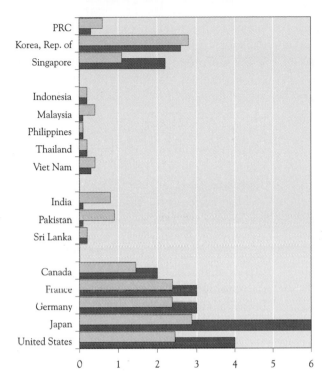

Figure 3.10 The Status of Research and Development Capabilities, Selected Countries and Years

☐ R&D expenditure as a percentage of GNP
■ R&D scientists and technicians per 1,000 persons

Sources: International Institute for Management Development (1996) and United Nations Development Programme (1997).

Other indicators of human resource development are also available, though for a smaller cross-section of countries. While books are not indicators of human resources as such, they are closely related to the development of human resources. An examination of the number of book titles published per 100,000 persons across countries reveals that Korea emerges as a leader among the ADEs (77 book titles published per 100,000 persons). In contrast, India, and surprisingly the Philippines, emerge as laggards in comparison (one and two book titles published per 100,000 persons, respectively).

One could also look at the use of personal computers and the Internet as indicators of the ADEs' use of information technology, both recent innovations that have large potential productivity effects. The data, however, indicate that with the excep-

tion of the NIEs, which have more than 100 personal computers per 1,000 persons, the diffusion of personal computers is still quite limited. Malaysia, however, with about 40 personal computers per 1,000 persons, stands out among the remaining ADEs and has more than twice as many computers per 1,000 persons than either Thailand or the Philippines (15 and 11, respectively). Most other countries in the region have between one and four personal computers per 1,000 persons. The number of Internet hosts per capita (a rough indicator of Internet usage) displays a pattern similar to that for personal computers. The NIEs are once again the clear leaders, with Malaysia the leader among the remaining economies.

HUMAN RESOURCE DEVELOPMENT IN AGRICULTURE

The previous section completed the examination of the state of human resources in the ADEs. The following sections will now draw upon the information presented to highlight some of the problems of human resource development facing the ADEs. For convenience, the discussion will treat agriculture, industry, and services separately, and will start with an examination of the first.

The notion that economic development is synonymous with industrialization is an old one. It may also be a dangerous one, as it has tended to lead to a neglect of agriculture in the belief that it is an inherently less dynamic sector than industry. In large part this neglect explains the bias in the provision of health and education services against rural, and thus agricultural, populations noted earlier. However, agriculture may be just as dynamic as industry, as demonstrated by Chile's recent experience, whereby it has experienced robust export-led growth over the last decade, with agricultural exports leading the way. Moreover, while the share of manufacturing in Chile's GDP has declined over the last two decades, the share of agriculture has risen. The scope for improving agricultural productivity appears to be plentiful, but this will depend on a number of factors, of which a crucial one is appropriate investment in human resources.

Agricultural productivity varies significantly across Asia. The yields of three major crops in particular—wheat, rice, and maize—show enormous variability. For example, with the exception of Indonesia, ADEs, and Viet Nam, every other country in Asia has rice yields that are less than half of Korea's rice yield. Similarly, the PRC's wheat yield per hectare is nearly double that of Pakistan. There is thus a great deal of potential for raising crop yields in most ADEs.

One effective way to improve productivity in agriculture through education and training is extension. The primary objective of agricultural extension is to help farmers produce more by teaching them about improved farming practices, new techniques, and more productive technology packages. An agricultural extension system is a conduit between international and national agricultural research systems on the one hand, and farmers on the other. A comprehensive extension system also performs other functions, such as providing assistance in the marketing and supply of farm inputs, helping farmers form service or community organizations, and communicating farmers' technical problems and needs to agricultural research organizations. The latter is particularly important in ensuring the relevance and usefulness of agricultural research to real-world issues and practical problems.

While many developing countries have had agricultural extension systems since the late 1950s, a renewed interest in agricultural extension has arisen throughout the developing world. A Food and Agriculture Organization (FAO) survey of agricultural extension systems in 113 countries conducted in 1988-1989 (FAO 1989) indicated that more than half of all agricultural extension organizations around the world were established or had been reorganized since 1970. The number of agricultural extension workers also appears to have increased significantly. While a 1980 survey identified a total of 290,592 extension workers in 138 agricultural extension organizations, the FAO survey identified 542,133 extension workers worldwide, of whom more than 70 percent were located in the Asian and Pacific region.

According to the FAO survey, agricultural extension expenditures worldwide constituted approximately 0.9 percent of agricultural GDP in 1988. However, this ratio had declined between 1980 and 1988. Thus the recent expansion of extension activities, as reflected by the increased number of extension organizations and workers, seems to have taken place concomitantly with declining average expenditures per extension worker. If the downward trend in real extension expenditures continues, the impact on extension programs and staffing could be serious.

Several approaches to agricultural extension have been tried out in various countries over the years. These include (i) the general agricultural extension approach, (ii) the commodity specialized approach, (iii) the training and visit approach, (iv) the agricultural extension participatory approach, (v) the project approach, (vi) the farming systems development approach, (vii) the cost-sharing approach, and (viii) the educational institution approach. Each approach differs in terms of its assumptions about farmers' problems and behavior and in terms of organizational set-up, that is, degree of centralization, extent of cost sharing and farmer participation, and focus on a particular commodity or crop. While a detailed analysis of the advantages and disadvantages of each approach is beyond the scope of this section, note that no single approach is universally appropriate. Depending on the nature of local problems and the capabilities of the local agricultural research establishment and extension system, different approaches may work in different settings. Indeed, the eight approaches listed above are not mutually exclusive, and many countries often employ combinations of the various approaches. The FAO's recently introduced Strategic Extension Campaign is an example of a combination of methods that offer considerable promise.

The contributions of agricultural extension have been widely documented around the world. The rapid spread of high-yielding varieties of wheat, corn, and rice in large parts of Latin America, Asia, and to a minor extent Africa, in what came to be known as the green revolution was largely the result of agricultural extension workers effectively disseminating information about the improved seeds and the fertilizer and water requirements of the new technology to farmers. The Masagana 99 Program in the Philippines, the Farm Extension/Credit Program in Indonesia, and the agricultural extension system of Korea established in the late 1950s are additional examples of extension programs that have succeeded in raising farm yields and farm incomes.

One study of agricultural extension in India estimated the marginal rate of return to investment in extension to be 17.5 percent, after controlling for investment in agricultural research. While this rate of return may appear modest, it is probably substantially underestimated, because separating the productivity effects of agricultural extension from those of agricultural research is often difficult, if not impossible, because of the strong complementarity between the two activities.

More recently, the FAO (1989) has calculated simple cost-benefit ratios, defined as the annual cost of the extension operation divided by the increase in annual value of production, for selected extension programs in developing countries. The major finding was that the cost-effectiveness of an agricultural extension program depends largely on the extension approach followed. For instance, approaches that embrace large numbers of farmers, such as general, participatory, and training and visit approaches, have lower per farmer costs, and therefore lower cost-benefit ratios. By contrast, approaches that maintain high agent-to-farmer ratios, such as the project and specialized commodity approaches, have higher per farmer costs, and therefore higher cost-benefit ratios. The cost-benefit ratios the FAO calculated based on case studies of selected approaches within countries (and thus not representative of entire countries) ranged anywhere from a low of 1:1 for Rwanda to a high of 1:32 for the Philippines. An FAO assessment of Ireland's Farm Modernization Scheme found that those participants with advisory contact expanded the size of their businesses by 56 percent, while participants with no advisory contact expanded their businesses by only 19 percent. By contrast, the businesses of nonparticipants actually contracted by 17 percent. The FAO estimated the rate of return to resources used in the extension service to be 25 percent.

Thus there is considerable scope for raising agricultural production in many, if not all, the ADEs by introducing appropriate extension schemes. However, it is one thing to make these programs available, and quite another for farmers to implement them successfully. Successful implementation requires a level of basic education sufficient for agricultural workers to understand the proposed methods fully, which will imply, at the very least, a

basic level of literacy. Thus the development of human resources is a necessary prerequisite for any significant increase in productivity in the agriculture sector.

HUMAN RESOURCE DEVELOPMENT IN INDUSTRY

By and large, industrial workforces in the ADEs are healthier and more educated than agricultural workforces. The importance of investment in human resources, especially higher education, also tends to be more widely accepted in the industry sector. Nevertheless, there are signs of a human resource weakness that may well pose a serious constraint for future industrial growth in the ADEs, especially for the middle-income Southeast Asian economies that have posted remarkably high rates of export-led growth in the last two decades. The danger for these economies lies in not taking the particular human resource weakness as seriously as they should.

The Competitiveness Problem

The term competitiveness has figured extensively in recent policy discussions and the popular press. For example, Thailand's export slowdown in 1996 may be viewed as a problem of competitiveness. The appreciation of the US dollar since 1995, to which the Thai baht was pegged, resulted in Thai products becoming more expensive internationally. Growing competition from producers of similar products in lower wage economies such as PRC, India, and Viet Nam exacerbated the competitiveness problems of Thailand's exports. The notion of competitiveness being used in this illustration focuses on the cost side of production. Accordingly, the lower a firm's unit costs (the costs of producing one unit of output) relative to competing firms' unit costs, the greater the competitiveness of that firm. As competing firms are located domestically as well as internationally, competitiveness has a national dimension as well as an international one.

Two aspects of competitiveness are worth emphasizing. First, measures to improve competitiveness in the sense of lowering production costs must focus on improving efficiency and productivity. Second, competitiveness is concerned not only with lowering production costs, but also with the technological capability required to produce a different set of products in response to a changing economic environment. Thus Thailand's competitiveness problem can be seen not only as one of higher costs of production relative to other nations producing similar products, but also as an inability to alter the structure of production toward more skill-intensive activities. These activities may entail designing, developing, and marketing new and improved products as opposed to the unskilled or semiskilled activities typical of manual assembly line operations. Therefore, the key to improving competitiveness in ADEs lies in raising human resource capabilities by making appropriate investments in people's education.

Competitiveness and Productivity

Three factors affect the relative unit costs of products across countries: the nominal exchange rate, unit nonlabor costs, and unit labor costs. The more overvalued a country's local currency, the greater the cost, as measured in international prices, of goods produced in that country, and the less internationally competitive will that country's firms be. Likewise, higher land, capital, or infrastructure prices will drive up the unit nonlabor cost of goods and lower international competitiveness. Finally, the higher a firm's unit labor costs, other things being equal, the lower that firm's international competitiveness.

To gauge an economy's competitiveness in labor-intensive products, one shorthand method entails focusing on a single component of unit costs, that is, unit labor costs. Labor productivity and wage rates are the two determinants of unit labor costs. If two firms or economies have the same wage rates, then the one with higher labor productivity will have lower unit labor costs. Similarly, if the labor productivity is the same in two firms or economies, then the one with lower wage rates has the lower unit labor costs and is more competitive.

An economy could be more competitive relative to others if it could somehow suppress wages while ensuring that labor productivity did not decline. However, in addition to political economy reasons, this goes against the entire objective of economic development, which is to improve living standards. Thus lowering unit labor costs to improve competitiveness should be driven by improvements in labor productivity. Eventually, wages will catch up with labor productivity, and this is exactly what economic development is about. Indeed, as Figure 3.11 reveals, the two variables that make up unit labor costs—labor productivity (output per worker measured by value added per employee) and annual wages per employee—tend to move together across manufacturing sectors in ADEs. Thus countries with higher labor productivity also tend to pay higher wages.

To get an idea of how investment in human resources can influence labor productivity in the manufacturing sector, labor productivity (as measured by value added per employee) can be plotted against mean schooling attainment for a cross-section of ADEs. This results in a strong positive correlation between value added per employee and mean years of schooling (Figure 3.12). Wages per worker also increase with mean years of schooling, as would be expected on the basis of the foregoing discussion, and this may be considered to be an indicator of higher standards of living of workers.

Competitiveness and the Changing Structure of Production

According to one argument, many of the economic difficulties of Southeast Asian countries can be attributed to their failure to produce and export more skill-intensive goods and services in the face of competition from countries such as the PRC and India that enjoy a cost advantage in unskilled and semiskilled labor. In particular, the PRC, with its huge supply of unskilled and semiskilled labor and its enormous expansion of manufacturing capacity during the last decade, has become a formidable player in low-skill manufacturing. The failure of Indonesia, Malaysia, Philippines, and Thailand, to move into higher skill exports to a large extent reflects a weak human resource base, in particular, a lack of well-qualified secondary- and tertiary-educated workers.

How compelling is this argument? Of course, one must realize that a number of factors precipitated the Asian financial crisis of 1997 and 1998, most of them of a macroeconomic nature, namely: high current account deficits; exchange rates that were pegged to the US dollar, which in turn led to overvaluation of local currencies in relation to European currencies, the Japanese yen, and the Chinese renminbi; and overextended lending to the real estate sector and other imprudent loans, which led

Figure 3.11 Wages and Productivity in Manufacturing, Selected Asian Economies, 1990

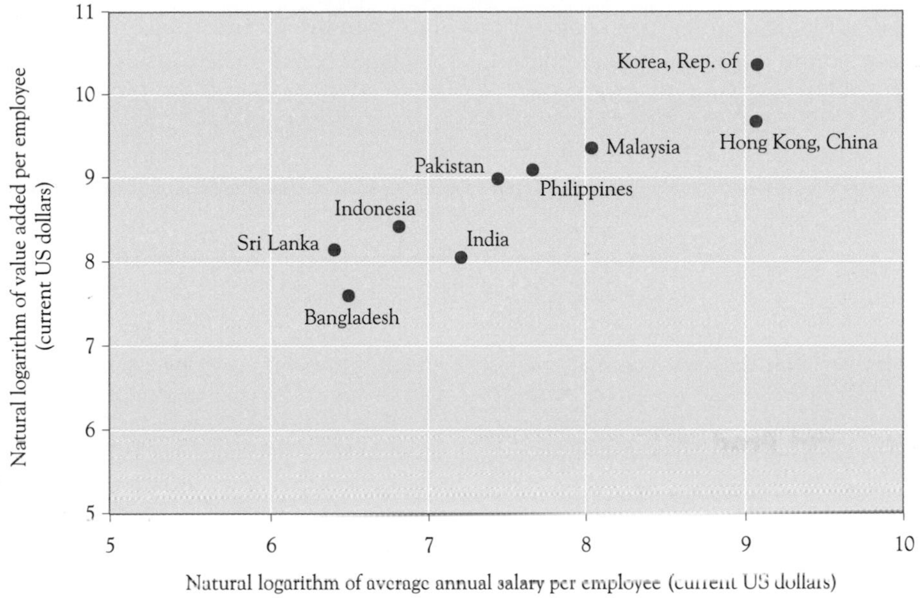

Source: UNIDO Industrial Statistics Database 1994.

to bank and finance company failures. However, the lack of an adequate supply of well-trained technicians, engineers, and scientists has contributed significantly to the longer-term difficulties these nations face in moving from simple assembly-line operations in foreign-built plants toward designing and developing products in the face of competition from lower wage economies (see Box 3.8).

In summary, perhaps the most succinct way to describe the problem of competitiveness for the ADEs is to emphasize the need for continuous increases in productivity and improvements in technological capability.

An examination of the distribution of wage rates across ADEs may permit identification of low-wage economies and give a rough indication of those economies likely to have a cost advantage in producing unskilled and semiskilled labor-intensive products. Table 3.14 shows average wage rates in various sectors for the ADEs. The table clearly shows that ADEs such as Bangladesh, India, Pakistan, and Sri Lanka will have an advantage over such ADEs as Malaysia and the Philippines in the manufacture of unskilled and semiskilled labor-intensive products.

This makes it less likely that the latter group of countries can continue to specialize in traditional manufactured exports in which the primary unit cost advantage stems from low wages and grow as rapidly as they have in the last 10 to 15 years.

Other evidence that points to the need for some ADEs to move away from the manufacture and export of unskilled or semiskilled labor-intensive products comes from comparing relative unit labor costs across the ADEs. Note that comparing unit labor costs across sectors in different countries is not easy because of the paucity of appropriate data. Nevertheless, using data on value added, number of employees, and wage rates by sector, Table 3.15 presents, by sector, selected countries' unit labor costs relative to Thailand's unit labor costs. A number less than one implies lower unit costs than Thailand's, while a number greater than one implies the converse. In general, low-income economies such as Bangladesh, PRC, Pakistan, and Sri Lanka appear to have lower unit labor costs than middle-income Thailand in a number of sectors, whereas high-income economies such as Hong Kong, China; Singapore; and Taipei,China have higher unit labor costs relative to those of Thailand. Low-income India and high-income Korea are the two anomalies in this general pattern.

What these numbers suggest is a simple fact: a middle-income developing country like Thailand will find that maintaining its international competitiveness in the production of unskilled and semi-

skilled labor-intensive goods is difficult in the face of challenges from the low-income countries. This is because these goods are precisely the ones where low unit labor costs driven by low wages are the main determinant of international competitiveness. Nonlabor costs for these goods tend to be either relatively unimportant or are roughly the same across

---

Box 3.8 Are Deficiencies in Human Resources Constraining Thailand's Movement Up the Export Ladder?

A pattern is discernible in the changing industrial structure of the East and Southeast Asian economies. As the most technologically advanced countries, such as Japan, moved away from being exporters of labor-intensive manufactured goods such as textiles to more high-technology products, so the NIEs of East Asia took their place. Similarly, as these countries developed more skill-intensive exports, so other Asian countries stepped in to fill the vacancy, a process sometimes described by the metaphor of the "flying geese."

At first glance, Thailand would seem to be a good example of this process, but a more careful examination suggests that there is cause for concern about its future export performance. Certainly, Thailand follows the pattern in that it has shown a marked increase in the proportion of its total exports that are manufactured, from 32 percent in 1980 to 80 percent in 1995, with a consequent decline in the share of agricultural exports. Moreover, manufactured exports have shifted away from labor-intensive products to products classified as medium to high-technology, so that by 1993 the latter exceeded the former. In 1995-1996 the growth of exports fell well below the average for the preceding four years, but the medium- to high-technology products performed relatively less badly than the other categories.

Why then is there cause for concern? The problem is that the decline in the growth of Thailand's low-technology exports has come from the increasing competition from the low-wage economies of Bangladesh, PRC, India, and Viet Nam. This would not be serious if it were more than compensated for by sustained growth in the medium- to high-technology exports. Indeed, it could be said to be highly desirable if it reflected increasing sophistication of Thailand's industrial base. However, the crux of the problem is that Thailand is merely acting as an assembly point for these medium- to high-technology exports. Thus while these goods, such as electronics and cars, are classified as medium- to high-technology products, they do not require a highly skilled labor force for that part of their production that actually takes place in Thailand. Hence, Thailand's production of these exports

is likely to come under increasing pressure from the low-wage and unskilled labor economies.

If the process of the hollowing out of the industrial and export base continues, it will spell new difficulties for the economy. To avoid such difficulties, Thailand needs to foster and develop industries that are not only high value added, but require considerable skills for their domestic production.

The difficulty is that Thailand does not, at the moment, have the human resource base to produce those exports where skills are important and that provide a measure of protection from competition from the low-wage, unskilled economies. The benefits of Thailand's almost universal enrollment rates in primary education are more than offset by low enrollment rates in secondary education and a tertiary education that appears to be biased against basic and applied science. Estimates suggest that Thailand is producing less than half the number of engineers and scientists with undergraduate and graduate degrees than it requires, and a comparison across the ADEs reveals that Thailand has a lower proportion of tertiary-level students enrolled in scientific and applied fields than Bangladesh and India. Moreover, while Thailand purchases a tremendous amount of technology—as indicated by its payments for foreign patents, copyrights, industrial processes, trademarks, and so on—it receives disproportionately smaller payments from foreigners for the use of its intellectual property than even lower income ADEs such as Pakistan and the Philippines. In 1995 Thailand paid $630 million, but received only $1 million, compared with Pakistan's payment of $12 million and receipt of $2 million and the Philippines' payment of $99 million and receipt of $2 million.

All of this is not to deny the importance of financial sector weaknesses in contributing to Thailand's current economic crisis. However, bolder strategies toward developing a stronger human resource base oriented toward technical and scientific fields are needed for Thailand's growth to be on a firmer footing and for its exports to be able to meet the test of international competition.

Table 3.14 Average Annual Salary per Employee, Selected Asian Economies, 1990
($ thousands)

Subregion and economy	Total manufacturing	Food, beverages	Textiles, apparel, footwear	Wood products, furniture	Paper products, publishing, printing	Chemicals (including petroleum, rubber, plastics)	Pottery, china, glass products	Iron, steel, non-ferrous metals	Fabricated metal products, machinery equipment	Other manufacturing
East Asia										
Hong Kong, China	8.69	12.45	8.08	7.05	9.76	10.69	8.81	11.02	9.49	8.83
Korea, Rep. of	8.76	10.67	6.74	7.69	9.78	11.73	9.21	11.46	9.59	6.89
Southeast Asia										
Indonesia	0.91	0.94	0.71	0.81	1.33	1.51	0.95	2.60	1.24	0.73
Malaysia	3.11	4.52	2.28	2.39	3.90	5.92	3.52	4.30	3.43	2.05
Philippines	2.13	2.44	1.34	1.55	2.40	3.97	3.50	2.45	2.19	1.40
South Asia										
Bangladesh	0.66	0.74	0.84	0.61	0.91	1.28	0.61	1.03	0.72	0.47
India	1.35	0.74	0.84	0.76	1.32	1.99	0.91	1.56	1.69	1.42
Pakistan	1.71	1.60	1.56	1.25	1.70	2.52	1.79	2.06	1.79	1.25
Sri Lanka	0.60	0.69	0.56	0.43	0.74	1.04	0.96	1.02	0.72	0.59

Source: United Nations Industrial Development Organization industrial statistics database.

economies because of the use of easily importable plant and equipment with only standardized assembly-type operations required of labor.

For economies that have lost their competitiveness in the production of such goods because of the entry of lower wage economies into the international economy, regaining competitiveness in the absence of cuts in wage rates will involve either improving productivity in the production of the same goods or moving into the production of new and improved goods, with a greater emphasis on the design, development, and marketing of these goods as opposed to assembly-line operations. While both options require workforces to possess greater technological capabilities, the latter option is typically the more viable one, because of the diminishing returns to investments to improve productivity in any given activity.

NURTURING TECHNOLOGICAL CAPABILITY

Technological capability does not develop automatically with production capability. While the capability to produce, and to do so efficiently, does require

a certain type of knowledge and skills, the capability to create technology requires another type of knowledge and skills. While the two are related, they are not the same. In addition, the existence of important externalities from activities such as R&D, which are directly concerned with developing technological capability, leads to a tendency to underinvest in them. In other words, while the operation of private markets is likely to encourage efficiency and enhancements in production capabilities, it may not encourage building technological capability to the same extent.

For these reasons economies such as Korea; Singapore; and Taipei,China have invested heavily in technology production and R&D, both in public institutions and in the private sector, while at the same time encouraging the importation of new technologies from more developed nations. (See Box 3.9 for a discussion of the complex relationship between local R&D and the imports of foreign technology, drawing on the case of India.) Some of the most sweeping technology development policies were pursued in Korea, which simultaneously encouraged the importation of technology and a comprehensive strategy for developing local R&D capability. While government research institutes (often in collaboration with industry) spearheaded a great deal of technological activity in the initial years, in later years Korea succeeded in shifting the burden of research to the large private conglomerates known as the *chaebol*. Taipei,China opted for public provision of technological support to industry based on a system of extension and contract research undertaken by government research institutes for private industry.

Much as technology development, especially by locals, is necessary for developing international competitiveness in high-end manufacturing, a strong base of tertiary-level education, especially in the natural sciences, is indispensable for technology development. Developing local technological capability in the absence of a higher education system that produces well-trained, high-caliber scientists, engineers, and technicians is impossible.

At the same time, while competitiveness in high value-added manufacturing cannot be sustained without a supply of skilled scientific workers, the reverse is not necessarily true, that is, a supply of highly skilled workers will not automatically enable a country to become competitive in high-end

manufacturing. The Central Asian republics of Kazakstan, Kyrgyz Republic, and Uzbekistan are examples of countries that enjoy high secondary and tertiary enrollment rates and have generally abundant supplies of skilled labor; however, they have not succeeded in establishing international competitiveness in any high-skill industry. It is the combination of a skilled and well-trained labor supply, macroeconomic stability, market orientation and discipline, and outward orientation that enables a country to become internationally competitive in a skill-intensive industry. In addition, it must often identify a niche product or market in which to develop export competitiveness.

India is a classic example of an ADE that developed export competitiveness in a niche industry. In absolute terms, India has always had a large supply of skilled workers, scientists, and technicians (although given India's large population, this supply is small on a per capita basis). However, India had developed export competitiveness in virtually no knowledge-based industries during the first four decades following independence. With the liberalization of the economy in the mid-to late-1980s, the

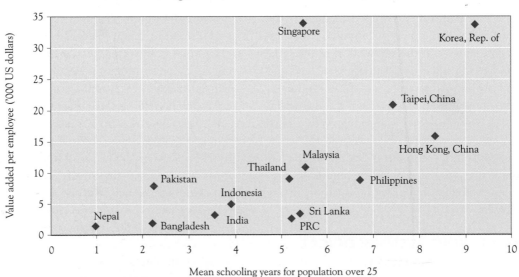

Figure 3.12 Value Added per Employee in Relation to Mean Years of Schooling, Manufacturing Sector, Selected Asian Countries, 1990

Sources: UNIDO Industrial Statistics Database 1994 and Barro and Lee (1993).

presence of a pro-active government with a positive attitude toward technology, and the enormous growth of personal-computer use in business in the United States and Europe, India launched a big push toward establishing custom software as a niche product for export. Indian software exports have increased more than twentyfold in the last few years, with annual software exports currently running at $1 billion. Many large companies in the United States and Europe have outsourced their in-house custom software needs to India.

Obviously, the development of competitiveness in high-skill industries does not mean that low-skill industries need to be abandoned, especially by low-wage, surplus labor economies. For the latter, stagnation in low value-added exports is premature and undesirable, as these exports hold great potential for growth in the manufacturing sector. After all, the rapid growth of Indonesia, Malaysia, and Thailand during the 1980s and of Korea and

Taipei,China before that came about largely from growth in low-technology consumer industries like apparel, toys, footwear, and wood products. The latter are far from sunset industries in low-wage, surplus labor economies.

The Philippines has pursued an approach that appears to move prematurely into higher end exports at the cost of low-wage manufacturing exports. During 1991-1996, electrical and electronic exports increased by 37 percent per year, while exports of textiles and garments increased by merely 8.2 percent, the slowest growth rate among all ADEs with the exception of Korea and Taipei,China. Thus relative export stagnation occurred in an industry that could be a mainstay of Philippine exports, because the Philippines, unlike many of its neighbors, remains a low-wage, labor surplus economy. Export growth in such industries as garments, toys, leather goods, and footwear still has great potential for the Philippine economy. To make matters worse, electrical and

Table 3.15 Unit Labor Costs in Manufacturing, Selected Asian Economies, 1990
(index, Thailand = 1)

Subregion and economy	Total manufac- turing	Food, beverages	Textiles, apparel, footwear	Wood products, furniture	Paper products, publishing, printing	Chemicals (including petroleum, rubber, plastics)	Pottery, china, glass products	Iron, steel, non- ferrous metals	Fabricated metal products, machinery, equipment	Other manufac- turing
East Asia										
PRC[a]	0.57	0.74	0.32	0.37	0.51	0.58	0.51	0.44	0.44	0.41
Hong Kong, China	1.94	1.59	1.85	1.86	1.51	1.64	1.43	1.11	1.46	2.46
Korea, Rep. of	0.99	0.81	1.09	1.20	0.90	0.85	0.95	0.61	0.87	1.55
Singapore	1.12	1.58	1.52	1.57	1.04	0.99	0.94	0.73	1.07	1.80
Taipei,China	1.45	1.23	1.35	2.31	1.37	1.50	1.25	0.70	1.43	1.16
Southeast Asia										
Indonesia	0.71	1.15	0.79	0.84	0.80	1.01	0.83	0.16	0.68	1.15
Malaysia	0.95	1.04	1.35	1.31	1.03	0.69	0.80	0.65	0.79	1.41
Philippines	0.85	0.77	1.44	1.38	0.88	0.75	0.84	0.28	1.06	1.96
Thailand	1.00	1.00	1.00	1.00	1.00	1.00	1.00	1.00	1.00	1.00
South Asia										
Bangladesh	1.16	0.88	0.92	1.20	1.23	0.67	0.73	0.89	1.06	0.68
India	1.52	1.99	1.50	1.88	1.66	0.97	1.36	0.81	1.30	1.71
Pakistan	0.76	0.65	0.93	1.04	1.28	0.68	0.74	1.22	0.97	1.14
Sri Lanka	0.62	0.42	0.86	1.46	0.81	0.62	1.06	0.59	0.91	0.85

[a] Data are for 1986.

Source: United Nations Industrial Development Organization industrial statistics database.

Box 3.9 Do Technology Imports Inhibit or Promote Local Efforts in R&D?
Evidence from India

Many economists believe that an important benefit of international trade for developing countries is the access that trade provides to the world's knowledge base. Although developing countries have access to several mechanisms by which they may tap into this knowledge base, two important ones are transfers of technical knowledge through either foreign direct investment or arm's-length licensing of technology and imports of physical inputs, such as equipment, that embody new technology.

Studies based on data from Indian firms report high private returns to technology imports. In particular, they estimate that the returns from a dollar of imported technology are at least three times higher than a dollar of expenditure on in-house R&D, holding all else constant. This finding is not surprising, because R&D is a costly and risky undertaking, in which capabilities develop cumulatively and over time. Firms in industrial countries are at an advantage given their larger R&D outlays and greater previous experience.

Thus a reasonable question is why Indian firms bother to conduct in-house R&D in the first place. One reason is that India's government has, until recently, imposed barriers to technology imports, including equipment. While the authorities have traditionally cited the need to conserve foreign exchange as the primary reason for restricting the importation of technology, they have also put forward an infant industry argument for the domestic production of knowledge. The implicit assumptions behind the infant industry argument have been that in-house R&D and imported technologies are substitutes for each other, and that domestic R&D efforts generate externalities.

By contrast, some economists argue that Indian firms conduct R&D to adapt foreign technology to local conditions. If this is the case, then dismantling India's import restrictions would serve to promote in-house R&D rather than inhibit it. A careful analysis of available data reveals that technology transfers are substitutes for in-house R&D. This is corroborated by surveys of firm managers' decisions. This is not to say, however, that R&D efforts are not needed for assimilation and adaptation. Indeed, the evidence also indicates that firms with larger R&D efforts can use their new imports of equipment more effectively.

Thus the relationship between local efforts and imports of foreign technologies is more complex than the simple either/or position described above and points to a tricky tradeoff. A liberal policy of technology imports may dampen overall incentives for conducting in-house R&D, but it can lead to substantial improvements in firms' productivity and competitiveness. However, if investment in domestic R&D has an important externality component, then firms may underinvest in R&D, with possibly adverse consequences for future competitiveness.

---

electronics exports of the Philippines have extremely low value added as they mostly involve final assembly of imported components. Average local content is only 15 to 25 percent in electrical and electronic manufacturing, compared to 45 percent in Malaysia and 75 percent in Taipei,China. Even worse, local content has not increased appreciably in the Philippines during the past two decades, indicating low development of technology.

Finally, much of Asia's past economic success can be attributed to its success in transforming agriculture. A key determinant of future agricultural growth will be agricultural research. Without continued private and public support for agricultural research and development, future productivity growth will slacken. In view of the past successes and with the specter of famine largely banished from most countries, interest and investment in agricultural research has diminished greatly in recent years.

INTERNATIONAL INTEGRATION AND THE RETURNS TO SKILLS

In the last 15 years scores of developing countries, including many in Asia, have moved to liberalize their trade policies and integrate themselves more closely with the world economy. Because developing countries have relatively larger supplies of unskilled labor than industrial countries, conventional wisdom argues that integration will lead to greater demand for unskilled labor relative to skilled labor in developing countries. This is because, so the argument goes, the developing countries should specialize in those industries that make use of their abundant factor, namely unskilled workers. The result should be an increase in the relative wages of unskilled workers as the demand for them rises.

However, recent studies of the movements in relative wages following large increases in trade flows show declines in the relative wages of unskilled workers. One set of explanations for this that is gaining currency relies on the widely accepted notion that trade liberalization leads to increased technology flows from industrial to developing countries. These flows take place through imports of inputs that embody new technology, such as modern equipment, and through technology transfers via foreign direct investment or licensing agreements between industrial and developing country firms. If the incoming technology requires skills to operate, then the demand for skilled workers will rise. Even if the technology itself does not require skilled workers to operate it, initial adoption of the technology may require a high degree of skills before a standardized set of operating procedures can be developed. Either way, the introduction of new technology will lead to a premium for skilled workers. The premium may well be large enough to offset the increase in relative wages of unskilled workers attributable to conventional wisdom, which relies on differences in factor endowments rather than on technology as the driving force of international trade.

Thus trade liberalization, and more generally openness, provide one more reason why policymakers in developing countries should concentrate on improving access to education and training.

HUMAN RESOURCE DEVELOPMENT IN SERVICES

The discussion has thus far examined the role of human capital from the perspective of agriculture and industry. However, the development of human resources is just as important for the service sector. This sector typically increases in importance as an economy undergoes economic development. For the low-income economies, the share of services in GDP is about one third, whereas it is typically double this for the high-income economies. The importance of the service sector also varies widely among the ADEs. Whereas the share of the service sector is less than 30 percent in some ADEs such as PRC, Lao PDR, and Uzbekistan, it rises to 50 percent or more in the NIEs. However, a wide disparity is apparent even among the NIEs: the share ranges from 50 percent in Korea to 85 percent in Hong Kong, China. In fact, Hong Kong, China is the most service-oriented economy in the world.

The output of the service sector—essentially intangibles—is a diverse one. It includes not only such traditionally important services as transport, tourism, retailing, wholesaling, finance, and insurance, but also others that are now rapidly growing in importance. These include telecommunications, information, and computer services. With the exception of transport and tourism, the service sector was formerly viewed essentially as catering for the domestic economy. However, a number of forces have combined to change this. Advances in telecommunications and information technology, together with financial deregulation and trade liberalization, have led to new trends in international trade, and the trade in services has been the most rapidly growing component of international trade. During the last 15 years, it has grown at an average rate of 8 percent per year, compared with 6 percent for merchandise trade. The most rapidly expanding services are financial, brokerage, and leasing services.

For the highly service-oriented NIEs such as Hong Kong, China; Singapore; and Taipei,China services, which represent opportunities for further rapid growth, also present challenges for the continued development of their skills base. All three of these economies are aiming to consolidate and expand their positions as international financial centers. A highly skilled workforce is a necessary prerequisite for this. In particular, financial centers require not just a skilled workforce trained in banking and finance, but also such professionals as accountants, lawyers, actuaries, economists, management consultants, systems analysts, and computer programmers.

However, the future of the NIEs' service sectors does not lie in financial services alone, important though these are. Other services, such as medical services in Singapore and education in Hong Kong, China, are also likely to be factors in the future growth of the NIEs. The NIEs are now in a position where they can reap benefits from concentrating their efforts on developing indigenously both basic and applied research, which are at the frontiers of knowledge. This will not only benefit other sectors of their economies, but will lead to increased royalty payments from abroad. All these developments require a substantial investment in producing a highly skilled and educated workforce.

In addition, with globalization, innovations are rapidly being introduced in telecommunications and information technology (which are essential for finance and related business services). This has meant that adeptness in the use of the computers and the Internet, along with proficiency in English, are emerging as requirements for entry into virtually all high-end service sectors. The Internet deserves special mention, because it is rapidly emerging as a vital tool for business. Advertising, sourcing of inputs, and so on can all be conducted over the Internet, and the main language of the Internet remains English.

The available evidence on the per capita number of Internet hosts, which are required for access to the Internet, suggests that even the NIEs are far behind the United States. Singapore, which is the leader among the NIEs in this regard, has less than half the number of Internet hosts per head of population than the United States. Part of this difference may simply be the result of a time lag in catching up, because the use of the Internet for business is a relatively new phenomenon, but a generally low proficiency in English among the NIEs (and the other ADEs) may also be part of the explanation. This is suggested by the fact that the other vital equipment for Internet access—personal computers, software, and telephone lines—are more readily available, at least in the NIEs.

Deficiencies in the provision of many business services—particularly banking and finance—will affect the growth in industry and agriculture. Earlier this part of the *Outlook* noted the view that the current economic crisis affecting the NIEs and Southeast Asia stems partly from a weakness in human resources. While the arguments were couched in terms of deteriorating international competitiveness in manufacturing, human resource weaknesses in the financial sector have played perhaps an even greater role in leading to the crisis. Both public sector agencies (including regulatory bodies) and private financial sector companies lack the necessary skills and expertise. The public sector's inability to design effective prudential regulations to govern the activities of the private financial sector has been widely noted. The regulatory authorities' lack of understanding of the development of new financial instruments, such as derivatives, has been a particular problem in many developing countries.

FINANCING HUMAN RESOURCE AND TECHNOLOGY DEVELOPMENT

Given that the development of human resources and of technology are important for improving productivity and for raising standards of living, the crucial question is how to finance such development, in particular, the extent to which the government should fund their provision. Clearly, however, even if they wanted to, governments simply could not take on exclusive responsibility for providing education and health and conducting R&D, because many ADE governments are seriously short of funds for financing social expenditures.

However, there is a strong case for public financing of primary, and to a lesser extent secondary, education, which rests primarily on two grounds (but note that some of the NIEs have successful secondary education systems that are largely private). The first is that education brings substantial benefits to society as a whole, and not just to those individuals who receive it, that is, education has a significant positive externality. The second justification is on grounds of equity and income distribution. If education is left entirely to private financing, the poor and disadvantaged are likely to be denied access to it. Even though poor people may wish to partake of education in the knowledge that this would greatly enhance their future earnings, they may have no way to pay for it. In addition, future earnings cannot be used as collateral for a loan, so they cannot borrow against the stream of future incomes to pay for the education.

The case for public funding of higher education is less readily justifiable. Social returns to tertiary education are not as high as for primary and secondary education, at least for the lower income ADEs. It does not have the impact on the nonpecuniary aspects of the quality of life that primary and secondary education does. Moreover, those who go on to higher education are largely the children of higher income, urban families, who can afford to pay for it. If this situation is likely to remain unchanged in the near future, that is, no increase is likely in participation in higher education by children of the poor and of rural families, then the public provision of higher education is merely subsidizing those who are already relatively better off. However, if higher education is completely privately funded, this is likely to exclude the poorer members of society. Consequently, the system would have to provide scholarships and loans for the less well off.

By contrast, agricultural extension and training, an activity that is generally associated with large positive externalities, almost always has to be publicly provided. Indeed, the past success of the NIEs was at least partly due to their education policies, which focused on public financing of primary education and agricultural extension and on private financing of secondary and higher education.

Many kinds of health and nutrition interventions are associated with strong positive externalities, including the supply of safe drinking water and sanitation, as well as programs to control communicable diseases. Implementing these kinds of interventions is much more cost-effective than many other health and nutrition programs, such as policies on curative health and nutrition supplementation. In addition, many believe that everyone in society should have access to a certain minimum level of health care. Thus the activities associated with strong positive externalities are strong candidates for public support.

The case of technology development is more complex, because it has elements of both a public and a private good. As noted earlier, enterprises will be able to import technology on better terms and to absorb and assimilate this technology better, thereby lowering their production costs, if they engage in some technology development and adaptive R&D activities. As they can appropriate the benefits of their technology development activities, they will be willing to pay for these activities. However, as technology development and R&D have large interindustry and interfirm spillover effects, firms will tend to underinvest in these activities. In this sense, technology development and innovative activities are public goods, and to the extent that firms in ADEs substitute their own efforts at technology development with technology imports, the underinvestment in R&D activities will be exacerbated.

Clearly, in all the countries that have recently shifted into higher value-added manufacturing and exports, such as Korea, Singapore, and Taipei,China, government support of technology development and innovation was strong, and included the establishment of special R&D institutions. Many of these countries now aspire to move beyond manufacturing and to become part of the sophisticated, international information economy, which will entail moving beyond imitation to innovation and technical advances. Given the public good nature of technological research, public support in favor of such activity will have to be stronger than it has been in the past.

STRATEGIES AND POLICIES FOR IMPROVING HUMAN RESOURCES

The policies and strategies for improving productivity and competitiveness will obviously differ for each group of ADEs depending on its socioeconomic situation. For the low-income ADEs, such as Cambodia, Lao PDR, Viet Nam, and those in South Asia, where wage costs are still relatively low, the focus should be on raising labor productivity in labor-intensive industries, such as agriculture, forestry, fisheries, and low-technology manufacturing (agroprocessing, food and beverages, footwear and apparel, textiles, and so on). Productivity in these industries, including crop yields in agriculture, is still low, and the potential for increasing productivity, and thereby international competitiveness, is large. This group of countries is characterized by high levels of adult illiteracy, less than universal primary schooling, and varying levels of malnutrition and morbidity. The high levels of adult illiteracy, which often amount to as many as half to two thirds of all adults, and of malnutrition present obstacles to productivity growth.

This group of ADEs can realize large improvements in productivity by introducing targeted basic literacy programs, expanding access to primary education, and improving the quality of primary education. In addition, farmers need to be targeted through agricultural extension programs that can teach them improved farming practices and new cropping techniques and introduce them to more productive technology packages. Finally, targeted policies to combat malnutrition and morbidity would have high payoffs in the form of increased agricultural productivity.

Middle-income ADEs such as the countries in Southeast Asia need a different set of human resource strategies. These countries need to move toward more skill-intensive activities and production, because their competitiveness in goods and services manufactured or provided by unskilled and low-skill labor has eroded. With rapid growth during the last two or more decades, the wages paid to unskilled workers in these countries have increased to the point where they do not have a cost advantage over the low-income ADEs. To develop international competitiveness in more skill-intensive manufactures, this group of countries has to address deficits and shortcomings in secondary- and tertiary-level education, and in R&D.

These ADEs need to focus on three distinct areas. First, while they enjoy universal primary enrollment rates, with the exception of the Philippines, their secondary- and tertiary-level enrollment rates are relatively low. Thailand, in particular, has an unusually low secondary school enrollment rate, while Indonesia and Malaysia have unusually low tertiary-level enrollment rates. Unless these rates increase substantially, they could act as a binding constraint on the countries' ability to move into higher value-added manufacturing.

Second, these ADEs will need to place greater emphasis on basic and applied science and technology in their tertiary-level curricula. This is virtually a prerequisite for developing export competitiveness in higher value-added manufactured goods and services. Unfortunately, the proportion of tertiary-level students in Indonesia and Thailand studying science and applied fields is even smaller than in Bangladesh and India.

Third, besides having a weak science and technology base, this group of ADEs grossly underspends on national R&D programs. Indeed, national R&D expenditures in Indonesia, Philippines, and Thailand expressed as a proportion of GNP are only a quarter or less of those in India and 7 percent of those in Korea. The experiences of Korea and Taipei,China underscore the importance of having a strong R&D program to develop competitiveness in higher value-added industries. Indeed, the high-growth industries of the next three decades are likely to be even more knowledge-, technology-, and information-based than those of the past three decades, so these countries will need to invest even more in R&D and technology than Korea and Taipei,China did during the corresponding stage of their development. Some evidence indicates that a few of the middle-income ADEs—Malaysia in particular—have realized the importance of technology, and have begun making large, targeted investments in this area. However, having a strong national R&D and technology program without having a higher education system that can produce well-trained, qualified scientists and technicians is virtually impossible. This further underscores the importance of expanding both the quantity as well as the quality of secondary and tertiary education and emphasizing scientific and applied fields of study.

Given the success of Asian NIEs in transforming their economies, they now rightly aspire to a position of leadership in scientific innovations and technological advances, rather than remaining as imitators. Hong Kong, China and Singapore, which provide high-technology services in finance, trade, and transport, will require more sophisticated information infrastructure and basic scientific and technological development. To achieve all this calls for further upgrading of tertiary education in general, and of science and technology in particular. This would entail not only making greater investments in research infrastructure in universities, but also establishing an environment to foster creativity through greater administrative flexibility and unfaltering commitment to academic and research excellence.

The final group of ADEs is the transitional economies, especially the Central Asian republics. Because of their socialist backgrounds and their past association with the former Soviet Union, these countries are generally well endowed with skilled manpower. They enjoy high rates of secondary and tertiary enrollment, and their education systems have a strong technological and scientific orientation. However, because these countries were isolated for so long, they were unable to use their trained manpower to develop international competitiveness in knowledge-based industries. They will need to identify niche products and areas in which they have a distinct cost advantage, and will need to make their R&D and higher education programs more market-relevant. These countries need to draw lessons from India's successful experience in using its vast supply of low-cost scientists, technicians, and programmers to become a major international exporter of computer software.

How should ADEs implement these broad strategies and options? In discussing the various options available, listing some important issues that policymakers need to keep in mind while designing specific human resource development interventions is important.

Introducing Targeted Programs to Raise Enrollments

The least developed ADEs need to expand access to primary education, especially for groups with low enrollment rates, such as girls and children from low-income households. However, improved access does not always imply that the public sector must establish new school facilities. Often what is needed are new approaches to encourage groups with low enrollment rates to attend school and to stay in school, for instance, establishing teacher training schools for training women teachers, educating girls during the evenings (as in India), and providing scholarships to girls (as in Bangladesh) and to low-income students. Targeted assistance in the form of scholarships, bursaries, or loans can go a long way toward improving access to primary education, especially among those groups that have the lowest enrollment rates.

Establishing Partnerships with Communities and the Nongovernment Sector

If an expansion of school facilities is required, generally an efficient way to proceed is for governments to locate these facilities in regions where the nongovernment sector is unwilling to invest in school facilities and to build and run schools in close partnership with communities. Experience worldwide has shown that schools are likely to be more sustainable and impart education of higher quality when local communities have an ownership and management stake in these schools. As the demand for private and nongovernment organization schools is strong among middle- and high-income households, governments do not need to be the exclusive providers of education.

Improving School Quality Versus Quantity

Another issue that is important in both the low- and middle-income economies is school quality, which remains abysmally low in most of these countries. The low quality of schooling is the result of many factors, including the inferior quality of teachers, which reflects poor teacher training and lax teacher training requirements; low teacher morale caused largely by extremely low salaries; low expenditures on nonsalary items, such as learning aids, textbooks, and other teaching materials; and large class sizes. The results are high rates of grade repetition and dropouts and poor examination performance by students.

Thus while improving the quality of schools should be high on the priority list for education policymakers in developing countries, conflict can sometimes arise between expanding quantity and improving quality. A recent study in Kenya (Deolalikar, forthcoming) indicates that policies to expand the number of school facilities increase the net primary enrollment rate of the poor much more than the enrollment rate of the better off. This implies that primary school spaces are rationed as far as the poor are concerned, or that an increase in the number of schools is likely to lower schooling costs, that is, the equilibrium "price" of schooling, for poor households and thereby improve their enrollment rates.

By contrast, an improvement in the quality of primary schools through an increase in the teacher-pupil ratio has exactly the opposite effects on enrollment: it reduces primary school enrollments among poor children, especially in rural areas, but increases enrollments of better-off children, particularly in urban areas. One reason for this might be that improvements in the teacher-pupil ratio might take place at the expense of other schooling inputs, such as bursaries and scholarships, that primarily help poor students to gain access to primary school. Another reason might be that improvements in the teacher-pupil ratio at the community level are often financed out of higher user fees and supplements, which can have an adverse effect on the enrollment rate of poor children.

These results suggest that in countries with less than universal primary school enrollment, expanding access to primary school might be a more pressing concern than improving quality. However, in middle-income ADEs that already have universal primary enrollment, the overriding concern should be improving the quality of primary education.

Achieving Better Resource Allocation across Education Levels

Economic research indicates that the returns to schooling are much higher at the primary and lower secondary levels than at the upper secondary and tertiary levels, especially in the lowest income ADEs. In these economies, therefore, allocating a larger share of public resources to primary and lower secondary education would enhance internal efficiency. Such an allocation would also be more equitable, because in most ADEs the children who attend primary and lower secondary schools are typically less affluent than those that go on to upper secondary and higher education.

However, those middle-income ADEs, which already have universal primary enrollment, need to increase spending on higher levels of education because, as noted earlier, some evidence indicates that these economies have underfunded secondary and tertiary education. Again, the strategy in these economies should be to rely as much as possible on the private and nongovernment sectors in the provision of such education, but to use public funds for targeted scholarships and incentives that will raise enrollments in secondary and higher education institutions.

Eliminating Constraints to Private Sector Provision

Many countries have explicit and implicit restrictions—such as regulatory constraints, more stringent financial requirements, and stricter standards—on private and nongovernment provision of education and health services. These constraints often mean that government and nongovernment providers of social services are not operating on a level playing field. The opportunity cost of these restrictions is high, because the presence of nongovernment providers in the health and education sectors not only improves household access to schooling and health opportunities at little or no cost to the government, but also introduces competition, thereby raising the quality of the services provided.

Investing in Environmental Hygiene and Communicable Disease Control

A predominance of communicable diseases and water- and food-borne infections characterizes the disease pattern in most South and Southeast Asian economies. Relatively inexpensive public health interventions can be used to manage these diseases, such as vector control, health education, environ-

mental health, immunizations, and screening. One of the key messages in health economics is that such interventions should have the first claim on public resources, both because of the substantial externalities they create for the society, and because of underspending on them by private agents. However, with half to three quarters of the government health budget in most ADEs going to curative services to treat these diseases and to other, much lower priority health problems, the scope for improved expenditure allocations on a more economically-sound mix of services is considerable.

HIV/AIDS deserves special attention, because several ADEs, namely, Cambodia, India, Lao PDR, Myanmar, and Thailand, have among the most serious HIV epidemics in the world, and the economic and human implications of HIV/AIDS for these countries in the near future could be staggering. In addition to the enormous human costs of HIV/AIDS in terms of suffering, loss of livelihoods, and disruption of families, the disease has economic costs. The direct costs of HIV/AIDS include the public and private costs of (i) prevention, including testing the blood supply; (ii) treatment and care; (iii) funerals; and (iv) care of those orphaned by the disease. The indirect costs of HIV/AIDS include the value of output lost by society because of the premature mortality of AIDS victims. The indirect cost is large because AIDS mostly affects young adults of prime working (and earning) age.

Estimates of the indirect economic costs of HIV/AIDS in Cambodia, based on projections of the spread of the disease, range from a low estimate of $1.97 billion to a high estimate of $2.82 billion during 1997-2006. If the direct costs are added in, these figures increase even more. The colossal amounts indicate how seriously the AIDS epidemic could affect the poorest ADEs in the absence of intervention.

Setting Up R&D Institutions

One way to promote technology development is to use special R&D institutions. This is the approach Korea followed. In 1966 the government established the Korean Institute of Science and Technology to undertake applied research for industry. In its early years, the institute concentrated on solving the relatively simple problems associated with technology transfer and absorption. In the 1970s the government set up other specialized research institutes, many of them spun off from the institute, in a number of fields, including machinery, metals, electronics, nuclear energy, resources, chemicals, telecommunications, standards, shipbuilding, and marine sciences. By the end of the 1970s Korea had 16 R&D institutions, some of which were consolidated under the Ministry of Science and Technology in 1981. An important reason for the success of Korea's R&D institutions was that they worked in close partnership with industry. Similar technology and R&D institutions in India have not worked as well, because they did not foster close partnerships with industry. As a result, these institutions have produced research and technologies that have not found many applications in industry.

Increasing Reliance on the Private Sector for R&D and Technology Development

While initially governments may have to take the initiative for technology promotion and development, eventually firms and enterprises need to undertake technology development. Again, Korea's experience is relevant to many ADEs. In the early 1970s the government accounted for nearly three quarters of the national R&D expenditures, but by the early 1990s, 80 percent of R&D expenditures were borne by the private sector. Note, however, that because R&D is lumpy and often risky, R&D expenditures are highly concentrated. Estimates indicate that in 1995, 20 *chaebols* accounted for 80 percent of total private R&D in Korea.

Providing Vocational and Technical Education and Training

Recent studies on vocational and technical education and training show that when government policies on vocational and technical training are designed to encourage rather than to supplant the private sector, the private sector response is usually strong. For example, when public funding mechanisms require public providers to compete on the same terms with private trainers, private training institutions end up with a large share of the market for vocational education programs. The studies indicated that clear and balanced legislation on training was more important for an expansion of vocational training than government subsidies to that sector. Another important finding was that government preoccupation with providing, regulating, or financing vocational training often results in governments neglecting their role as providers and facilitators of information about the availability and effectiveness of vocational programs. An expansion of this role is often the most effective way for governments to further the development of an appropriate and cost-effective vocational education and training system.

Providing vocational education may not be as crucial as promoting basic academic and learning skills, such as building analytical capacities and numeracy at the secondary level. Such an orientation will enable the education system to produce highly trainable and versatile graduates who can adjust to various employment situations and add to their skills through on-the-job vocational training.

CONCLUSIONS

The past few decades have seen the spectacular growth of a number of Asian economies. These miracle economies have compressed into the length of one generation the process of economic development that took many advanced countries more than a century to achieve. Although a number of commentators have quibbled as to whether the term economic miracle should be applied to these economies, it is difficult not to be impressed by the massive strides these countries have made in improving their living standards in a comparatively short time. Indeed, in this respect, economic miracle is not an inappropriate term.

The recent financial crisis that has affected some of these economies should not obscure their long-term success story. Ironically, the concern with which the industrial countries view the financial crisis demonstrates just how important these Asian countries have now become to the world economy. If this were not the case, the rest of the world would view their current financial crisis with equanimity, rather than with alarm.

However, not all the ADEs have a long way to go to emulate the NIEs. Bangladesh, Myanmar, Nepal, and Viet Nam, for example, are among the world's poorest nations.

The question this section of the *Outlook* posed is whether the current state of human resources is going to act as a building block for or a binding constraint to the future economic growth of the Asian economies. The answer lies in identifying the extent to which investment in human resources can affect growth, and determining the degree to which the less developed ADEs can emulate the NIEs in developing their human resources. A related issue is how much the NIEs should invest in human resources to maintain their spectacular growth rates in the future, and whether or not it is a feasible objective.

The rapid demographic transition, with falling birth and death rates and with the latter preceding the former, especially in the NIEs, has led to a bulge in the proportion of young people in the population that is working its way through the age structure. The NIEs' economic success is attributable in part to an increase in the proportion of workers in the population and to the increased level of savings that resulted from the fast economic growth rates. These factors mutually reinforce each other: high growth leads to high savings, and hence to investment, which in turn further stimulates growth. More recently, Southeast Asia has begun to experience a bulge in its working-age population, and might also benefit from this demographic bonus. Eventually, the same may hold true for South Asia.

However, an increase in the labor force is not by itself a prerequisite for economic growth. It could merely result in higher unemployment and greater poverty. What is crucial in this context is how this resource is enhanced. One of the key elements behind the economic miracle, and one that the relatively less developed Asian countries ignore at their peril, has been the effective use and development of that most fundamental of all resources, the people. Economists have coined the term human capital for this investment in human resources, which conveys the idea that investing in people is like investing in tangible capital goods, such as machinery and equipment. Both will nearly always improve productivity, earn a rate of return, and help raise living standards. In addition, human capital formation and investment in new technology complement each other. The effective utilization of investment in new technology imported from abroad often requires the development of new skills, and hence investment in people. Skilled human resources are also required to develop, not simply adapt, new technology through, for example, R&D.

For the poorest countries, however, an increase in nutrition and health is of paramount importance for economic development, because malnutrition and poor health lead to an inability to undertake strenuous work, to lethargy, to apathy, and to a sense of fatalism. As development occurs, so the emphasis must shift to increasing skills.

Notwithstanding this, some of the ADEs tend to neglect the need to invest in people, to improve their health, and expand their knowledge and skills. However, in the low-income countries in particular, many people do not have the financial wherewithal to provide adequate levels of nutrition, health, and education for themselves. In addition, important externalities are involved in such provision, and this provides another reason why, if left to the private sector, provision would be less than optimal.

Consequently, governments have a crucial role to play in this area. In many countries governments directly fund a large proportion of spending on health and education, but despite the importance of such expenditure, it is still often inadequate. This is partly because the benefits from increased expenditure on health, education, and training, although crucial for sustained economic development, take a long time to materialize. Furthermore, they are not as immediately discernible as expenditures on more tangible investments, such as building a new factory or dam or improving the infrastructure. Many of these latter projects also carry an element of prestige for policymakers that is not associated with investment in education or health. Even where the private sector plays a major role in health and education provision, governments are still responsible for ensuring that the provision is of sufficient quality and quantity for their countries' long-term development. Many ADE governments face severe budgetary problems, and are thus tempted to skimp on their investment in human resources, but as this part of the *Outlook* demonstrates, any such economy would indeed be a false economy if it were not offset by a compensatory increase in private provision.

In addition, scope exists for improving the allocation of resources currently expended on health and education in many ADEs. For example, as far as government expenditure on health is concerned, some ADEs should give more emphasis to preventive rather than curative health care. Some governments also need to address the current gender bias in health provision, whereby women have less access to health care than men.

Governments in the lowest income ADEs should allocate more public resources to primary and lower secondary education. This would enhance internal efficiency, as the social returns to primary and lower secondary education tend to be much higher than those to higher education in these economies. It would also be more equitable, because children who proceed to higher education tend to come from more affluent backgrounds. However, the economically better-off ADEs that have achieved universal primary enrollments need to increase expenditures on higher levels of education, especially given the evidence that such levels of education have been underfunded in the past. While the case for public funding of education is strong, governments do not need to be the exclusive providers of education, nor do they need to provide subsidized education to all. Removing constraints to the provision of education by the private and non-government sector will help not only to expand education facilities without impinging on government resources, it is also likely to introduce some measure of competition in the provision of education, and thereby help to raise quality. However, for those children whose access to education is limited by their socioeconomic backgrounds, governments must make special efforts to ensure that these children are not left behind. Targeted assistance in the form of scholarships or loans and innovative approaches to encourage groups with low enrollment rates are required.

Moreover, it is not just the quantity of formal education that matters, but also the quality. This can vary greatly between countries that devote the same per capita expenditure to education. A curriculum that is appropriate to a relatively advanced country may be irrelevant to one that is relatively less developed. The concentration in some ADEs on university syllabuses borrowed from industrial countries that emphasize the humanities and social sciences at the expense of science, engineering, and medicine is a case in point.

Economic success is related to the notion of industrial competitiveness. Competitiveness has three facets, namely, the wage rate and other costs of production; the level of productivity; and the structure of production, that is, the type and extent of technical sophistication of the goods being produced. Successful growth is related to a high degree of competitiveness, but as development takes place, a particular ADE will find itself progressively challenged by less developed, lower wage economies. Nations can maintain their competitiveness either by reducing real wages (or perhaps their growth), increasing productivity in industries that produce traditional low value-added goods, or diversifying into higher technology products. The first is not a long-run option, because it is the antithesis of the concept of successful economic development, which implies sustained growth in living standards. The second option, increasing the level of productivity in traditional labor-intensive industries, is likely to become progressively more difficult, and there is no guarantee that such improvements will not be matched in the low-wage, unskilled economies. The key to success is the third option, moving into high-technology production, but this is easier said than done.

The rapid growth rates some Southeast Asian economies achieved in the past were no doubt partly influenced by demographic factors and by an outward-oriented policy environment. By using abundant cheap labor, these economies were able to specialize in exports of labor-intensive products. However, the era of rapid growth through the pursuit of traditional, labor-intensive, low value-added production and exports may be over, because of the adoption by other ADEs, such as Bangladesh, PRC, India, and Viet Nam, which have an abundance of low-wage workers, of macroeconomic policies and an outward orientation similar to those of the Southeast Asian economies.

Many of the economies suffer from a shortage of the scientists and engineers necessary to modify the advanced technology that would enable the country to develop an indigenous medium- to high-technology industry. What was indeed for them the foundation for high export volumes and rapid economic growth in the past may now prevent these countries from effecting a timely transition to a more diversified and higher value-added export structure in the future. Moving toward higher value-added activities will require expanding the technological capabilities of the workforce. Without developing the human resources needed to undertake such activities, the path to future prosperity may well be arduous for these economies. What they now need is a highly flexible, highly skilled labor force. Such a labor force must be flexible, because with increasing globalization and international competition, skill requirements will continuously be changing. The typical worker will have to be prepared to acquire new skills throughout his or her working life, and this cannot be done without high enrollment rates in primary, secondary, and increasingly tertiary, education. Even economies such as the NIEs, which have already attained high enrollment rates, cannot afford to neglect further investment in their human resources, because the high-growth industries of the future, such as information technology and biotechnology, are precisely those areas for which an increasingly skilled labor force will be vital.

The hope is that the lessons derived from the current economic crisis are not limited to the need for prudential regulations to govern private financial institutions and for more general reforms of the financial sector. All the ADEs can learn important human resources lessons from current events, including those ADEs that are not facing the full brunt of the crisis. With appropriate policy responses, all the ADEs can move ahead in developing human resources further.

This part of the *Outlook* has offered a detailed analysis of the specific problems particular groups of ADEs face. Within this context it has also offered some broad strategies for formulating appropriate policies. These range from the need for targeting programs to increase school enrollments to encour-

aging a private-public partnership in vocational training. Obviously a single set of policies will not be appropriate for every economy, because different ADEs are in different stages of their development. For those ADEs with low per capita incomes, better health, improved nutrition, and basic education are the prime prerequisites. For the more advanced Asian economies, the focus must be on education and training, broadly defined, as the way to enhance productivity growth.

Because improved human resources and expanded technological capability are ultimately the key to a successful transition to a more sophisticated and prosperous economic structure, the ADEs would do well to formulate the necessary policies and implement them as soon as possible. In any case, the forces of globalization are inexorably pushing these economies into increasing expenditures in these areas. Preparing for the change by launching the appropriate policies sooner, rather than being overwhelmed by the changing world economy later, would be wise. In the future, advantages in world trade, like important discoveries, may also come only to countries that are prepared to create them.

The road the ADEs will travel depends largely on their policymakers' foresight and initiative and on the quality of leadership. The cost of doing nothing could be enormous in terms of lost opportunities, as could be the cost of wrong policies. Only timely and appropriate policies, implemented pragmatically, can keep the door to continuing prosperity open for the Asian economies.

SELECTED BIBLIOGRAPHY

SELECTED BIBLIOGRAPHY

Asian Development Bank (ADB), 1996a. "Consultative Group Report." Manila.

_____, 1996b. "Economic Report 1996 for Marshall Islands." Manila.

_____, 1997a. *Emerging Asia: Changes and Challenges.* Manila.

_____, 1997b. *Key Indicators of Developing Asian and Pacific Countries 1997.* Vol. XXVlll. Hong Kong: Oxford University Press for the Asian Development Bank.

_____, 1997c. "Country Economic Review for Bangladesh." Manila.

_____, 1997d. "Country Economic Review for Kazakstan." Manila.

_____, 1997e. "Country Economic Review for Kyrgyz Republic." Manila.

_____, 1997f. "Country Economic Review for Thailand." Manila.

_____, 1997g. "Country Economic Review for Uzbekistan." Manila.

_____, 1997h. "Country Economic Review for the Socialist Republic of Viet Nam." Manila.

_____, 1998. "Country Economic Review for Nepal." Manila.

Azis, I., 1997. "Short-Term Outlook of the Indonesian Economy." Background paper prepared for the *Asian Development Outlook 1998.* Cornell University, Ithaca, New York. Mimeo.

Banerjee, A. V., 1992. "A Simple Model of Herd Behavior." *Quarterly Journal of Economics* 107(3):797-817.

Bangko Sentral ng Pilipinas, 1998a. *The Philippines: Staying on Course.* Manila.

_____, 1998b. *Selected Economic Indicators.* Manila.

Bank of Indonesia, 1997. *Weekly Report.* Jakarta. December 15.

Bank of Thailand, 1997. *Monthly Bulletin.* Bangkok.

Barro, R. J., and J. W. Lee, 1993. "International Comparisons of Educational Attainment." *Journal of Monetary Economics* 32(5):363-94.

Barro, R. J., and X. Sala-I-Martin, 1995. *Economic Growth.* New York: McGraw-Hill.

Basant, R., and B. Fikkert, 1996. "The Effects of R&D, Foreign Technology Purchase, and International and Domestic Spillovers on Productivity in Indian Firms." *The Review of Economics and Statistics* 78(2):187-99.

Behrman, J. R., 1988. "Nutrition, Health, Birth Order, and Seasonality: Intrahousehold Allocation among Children in Rural India." *Journal of Development Economics* 28(1-3): 43-62.

Behrman, J. R., and A. B. Deolalikar, 1991. "School Repetition, Dropouts, and the Returns to School: The Case of Indonesia." *Oxford Bulletin of Economics and Statistics* 53(4):467-80.

Bhattarcharya, A., S. Claessens, and L. Hernandez, 1997. "Recent Financial Turbulence in Southeast Asia." Paper presented at the Tenth Asian Economic Outlook Workshop, 21-22 October, Asian Development Bank, Manila. Mimeo.

Bikhchandani, S., D. Hershleifer, and I. Welch, 1992. "A Theory of Fads, Fashion, Cultural Change as Informational Cascades." *Journal of Political Economy* 100(5):992-1026.

Birdsall, N., 1988. "Economic Approaches to Population Growth." In H. C. Chenery and T. N. Srinivasan, eds., *Handbook of Development Economics.* Vol. I. North Holland: Elsevier Science Publishers.

Caramazza, F., 1997. "World Economic Outlook." Paper presented at the Tenth Asian Economic Outlook Workshop, 21-22 October, Asian Development Bank, Manila. Mimeo.

Central Bank of Samoa, 1997. *Central Bank of Samoa Bulletin* 12(3) (September). Apia, Western Samoa.

Central Bank of Sri Lanka, 1997. *Sri Lanka Socioeconomic Data 1997.* Colombo.

Central Bureau of Statistics, 1997a. *FY1997-98 GDP Forecast.* Kathmandu, Nepal.

_____, 1997b. *National Accounts of Nepal 1997.* Kathmandu, Nepal.

Central Statistical Organisation, 1998. *Press Note on Quick Estimates of National Income, Consumption Expenditure, Saving, and Capital Formation, 1996-97.* Delhi, India: Department of Statistics.

Cheung, S., 1997. "Hong Kong Country Report." Background paper prepared for the *Asian Development Outlook 1998.* City University of Hong Kong, Hong Kong, China. Mimeo.

Cheung, S. Y. L., and V. Kakkar, 1997. "Recent Currency Crisis, Short- and Medium-Term Economic Prospects and Issues of Macroeconomic Management in Asia." Paper presented at the Tenth Asian Economic Outlook Workshop, 21-22 October, Asian Development Bank, Manila. Mimeo.

Coale, A., and E. Hoover, 1958. *Population Growth and Economic Development in Low-Income Countries: A Case Study of India.* Princeton, New Jersey: Princeton University Press.

Collins, I., 1997. "Country Report for Cambodia." Background paper prepared for the *Asian Development Outlook 1998.* Policy Development and Planning, Sydney, Australia. Mimeo.

Council for Economic Planning and Development, 1993. *Taiwan Statistical Data Book 1993.* Taipei,China.

Das, D. K., 1997. "Recent Macroeconomic Developments and Short-Term Growth Prospects for the Developing Asian Economies." Paper presented at the Tenth Asian Economic Outlook Workshop, 21-22 October, Asian Development Bank, Manila. Mimeo.

Deolalikar, A. B., 1988. "Nutrition and Labor Productivity in Agriculture: Wage Equation and Farm Production Function Estimates for Rural India." *The Review of Economics and Statistics* 70(3):406-13.

_____, 1997. "Education, Training, and International Competitiveness in Asia." Paper presented at the Tenth Asian Economic Outlook Workshop, 21-22 October, Asian Development Bank, Manila. Mimeo.

_____, forthcoming. "Increasing School Quantity Versus Quality: Impact on Children from Low-Income Versus High-Income Households." *Journal of Policy Reform.*

Department of Statistics, 1994. *Statistical Abstract.* Taipei,China: Ministry of Interior.

Diel, M., and R. Schweickert, 1998. Currency Crisis: Is Asia Difficult? Kiel Discussion Papers. Kiel, Germany.

Directorate-General of Budget, Accounting, and Statistics, 1986. *Statistical Yearbook.* Taipei,China.

Economic Adviser's Wing, 1997. *Economic Survey 1996-97.* Islamabad: Finance Division, Government of Pakistan.

Evenson, R. E., and Y. Kislev, 1975. *Agricultural Research and Productivity.* New Haven, Connecticut: Yale University Press.

Evenson, R. E., and L. Singh, 1997. Economic Growth, International Technological Spillovers, and Public Policy: Theory and Empirical Evidence from Asia. Center Discussion Paper No. 777. Yale University, Economic Growth Center, New Haven, Connecticut.

Fallon, J., 1998. "Recent Economic Performance and Medium-term Prospects for Pacific Islands Economies." Background paper prepared for the *Asian Development Outlook 1998.* Economic Insights, Brisbane, Australia. Mimeo.

Flood, R., and P. Garber, 1984. "Collapsing Exchange Rate Regimes: Some Linear Examples." *Journal of International Economics* 16-17(1-4): 1-13.

Food and Agriculture Organization (FAO), 1989. "Agricultural Extension Approaches: What FAO's Case Studies Reveal." Paper presented at the Global Consultation on Agricultural Extension organized by the FAO, 4-8 December, Rome, Italy.

Foster, A., and M. Rosenzweig, 1996. "Technical Change and Human-Capital Returns and Investments: Evidence from the Green Revolution." *American Economic Review* 80(4):931-53.

General Statistical Office for the Socialist Republic of Viet Nam, 1996. *Statistical Yearbook 1996.* Hanoi: Statistical Publishing House.

_____, 1997. *Viet Nam Demographic and Health Survey.* Hanoi: Statistical Publishing House.

Giap, T. K., and C. Kang, 1997. "Economic Outlook for Singapore." Background paper prepared for the *Asian Development Outlook 1998*. Nanyang Business School and Nanyang Technological University, Singapore. Mimeo.

Government of Singapore, 1997. *1997 Annual Economic Survey*. Singapore.

Hasan, R., 1997. "Productivity Growth and Technological Progress in a Reforming Economy: Evidence from India." Unpublished Ph.D. dissertation, University of Maryland.

Institute of International Finance, 1998. *Capital Flows to Emerging Market Economies*. Washington, D.C.

International Institute for Management Development, 1996. *The World Competitiveness Report Yearbook 1996*. Lausanne, Switzerland.

International Monetary Fund (IMF), 1997a. *Balance of Payments Statistics Yearbook 1997*. Washington, D.C.

_____, 1997b. *World Economic Outlook, Initial Assessment*. Washington, D.C.

_____, 1998. *International Financial Statistics*. Washington, D.C.

Jaleel, M., 1998. "Country Report for Maldives." Background paper prepared by the Maldives Monetary Authority for the *Asian Development Outlook 1998*. Mimeo.

Jun, K. W., 1997. "Presentation on World Economic Prospects." Paper presented at the Tenth Asian Economic Outlook Workshop, 21-22 October, Asian Development Bank, Manila. Mimeo.

Khan, H. A., 1997. "The Future of Miracles; Interpreting East Asian Growth." Graduate School of International Studies, University of Denver, Colorado. Unpublished manuscript.

_____, forthcoming. *Technology, Development, and Democracy: Limits of National Innovation Systems in the Age of Postmodernism*. Cheltenham, UK: Edward Elgar.

Kim, J. I., 1997. "The Korean Economy 1997-1999: Recent Trends and Future Prospects." Background paper prepared by the Korea Development Institute, Seoul, for the *Asian Development Outlook 1998*. Mimeo.

Krugman, P., 1979. "A Model of Balance of Payments Crisis." *Journal of Money, Credit and Banking* 11(1-4):311-25.

_____, 1997. "Currency Crisis." Unpublished manuscript.

_____, 1998. "What Happened to Asia?" Unpublished manuscript.

Lee, R., A. Mason, and T. Miller, 1997. Savings, Wealth, and the Demographic Transition. East-West Center Working Papers, Population Series 88-7. East-West Center, Honolulu, Hawaii.

Leff, N. H., 1969. "Dependency Rates and Savings Rates." *American Economic Review.* 59(December):886-95.

_____, 1984. "Dependency Rates and Savings Rates: Another Look." *American Economic Review* 74(March):231-33.

Mason, A., 1987. "National Saving Rates and Population Growth: A New Model and New Evidence." In D. Gale Johnson and R. D. Lee, eds., *Population Growth and Economic Development: Issues and Evidence*. Madison, Wisconsin: University of Wisconsin Press.

_____, 1988. "Saving, Economic Growth, and Demographic Change." *Population and Development Review* 14(March):113-44.

_____, 1996. "Population and Housing." *Population Research and Policy Review* 15(December):419-35.

_____, 1997. "Population Change and Asia's Economies." Paper presented at the Tenth Asian Economic Outlook Workshop, 21-22 October, Asian Development Bank, Manila. Mimeo.

Mingat, A., 1995. "Towards Improving Our Understanding of the Strategy of High Performing Asian Economies in the Education Sector." Paper presented at the Conference on Financing Human Resource Development in Advanced Asian Countries, 17-18 November, Asian Development Bank, Manila.

Minister for Finance, 1996. "The 1997 Budget Finance Statement." Presented to the National Parliament, Papua New Guinea. September.

Ministry of Finance, Government of Malaysia, 1997. *Economic Report 1997/98*. Kuala Lumpur.

Ministry of Finance, Government of the Solomon Islands, 1996. "Summary of Economic Performance and Prospects for 1996." Honiaria. Mimeo.

Ministry of Trade and Industry, Department of Statistics, 1996. *Yearbook of Statistics Singapore 1996*. Singapore.

Mishkin, F. S., 1997. "Understanding Financial Crisis: A Developing Country Perspective." In M. Bruno and B. Pleskovi, eds., *Annual World Bank Conference on Development Economics 1996*. Washington, D.C.: World Bank.

Monetary Authority of Singapore, 1997. *Monthly Statistical Bulletin.* Singapore.

Mujahid-Mukhtar, E., 1997. "Pakistan: Economic Performance in 1996/97 and Prospects for 1997/98 and 1998/99." Background paper prepared for the *Asian Development Outlook 1998.* Islamabad, Pakistan. Mimeo.

National Reserve Bank of Tonga, 1997. *Quarterly Bulletin* 8(2).

National Statistical Coordination Board, various years. *Philippine Statistical Yearbook.* Manila.

_____, 1998. "National Accounts of the Philippines, CY 1995 to CY 1997." Manila. Mimeo.

National Statistics Office, 1997. *Korea Statistical Yearbook 1997.* Seoul: National Statistical Organization.

Nguyen, V. Q., 1997. "Viet Nam: Economic Situation in 1997 and Outlook." Background paper prepared for the *Asian Development Outlook 1998.* Central Institute of Economic Management, Hanoi, Viet Nam. Mimeo.

Pissarides, C., 1997. "Learning by Trading and the Returns to Human Capital in Developing Countries." *The World Bank Economic Review* 11(1):17-32.

Pitt, M., M. R. Rosenzweig, and Md. N. Hassan, 1990. "Productivity, Health, and Inequality in the Intrahousehold Distribution of Food in Low-Income Countries." *American Economic Review* 80(5):1139-56.

Population Reference Bureau, various years. *World Population Data Sheet.* Washington, D. C.

Pray, C. E., and V. W. Ruttan, 1990. "Science and Technology Policy: Lessons from the Agricultural Sector in South and Southeast Asia." In R. E. Evenson and G. Ranis, eds., *Science and Technology: Lessons for Development Policy.* Boulder, Colorado: Westview Press.

Psacharopoulos, G., and W. Loxley, 1985. *Diversified Secondary Education and Development: Evidence from Colombia and Tanzania.* Baltimore, Maryland: The Johns Hopkins University Press.

Psacharopoulos, G., and M. Woodhall, 1985. *Education for Development: An Analysis of Investment Choices.* New York: Oxford University Press.

Quibria, M. G., 1997. "Labor, Migration, and Labor Market Integration in Asia." *World Economy* 20(1):21-42.

Rana, P. B., 1997. "Trends in Private Capital Flows to Asian Developing Countries." Paper presented at the Tenth Asian Economic Outlook Workshop, 21-22 October, Asian Development Bank, Manila. Mimeo.

Reserve Bank of India, various years. *Annual Report.* Mumbai.

Ross, J. W., P. Mauldin, and V. C. Miller, 1993. *Family Planning and Population: A Compendium of International Statistics.* New York: Population Council.

Salleh, I. Md., 1998. "Country Economic Outlook: Malaysia." Background paper prepared for the *Asian Development Outlook 1998.* Kuala Lumpur, Malaysia. Mimeo.

Sanderson, W., and J. P. Tan. 1993. *Population Issues in Asia.* Washington, D. C.: World Bank.

Sen, P., 1998. "Recent Economic Performance and Prospects of India." Background paper prepared for the *Asian Development Outlook 1998.* Planning Commission, Delhi, India. Mimeo.

Sharma, S., 1997. "Nepal: Trends and Prospects." Background paper prepared for the *Asian Development Outlook 1998.* Ministry of Finance, Kathmandu, Nepal. Mimeo.

Siripala, N., 1997. "Country Report: Sri Lanka, Brief Discussion of the Economic Outlook and Assumptions Underlying the Forecast." Background paper prepared for the *Asian Development Outlook 1998.* Department of National Planning, Colombo, Sri Lanka. Mimeo.

State Bank of Pakistan, various years. *Annual Report.* Karachi.

State Statistical Bureau, People's Republic of China. 1997. *China Statistical Yearbook 1997.* Beijing.

Stiglitz, J., 1997. "Building Robust Financial Systems." Lecture at the Asian Development Bank, 19 November, Manila.

Strauss, J., 1986. "Does Better Nutrition Raise Farm Productivity?" *Journal of Political Economy* 94(2):297-320.

Strauss, J., and D. Thomas. 1995. "Human Resources: Empirical Modeling of Household and Family Decisions." In J. R. Behrman and T. N. Srinivasan, eds., *Handbook of Development Economics.* Vol. 3. North Holland: Elsevier Science Publishers.

Summers, R., and A. Heston, 1994. *World Penn Tables, Mark 5.6* (online). Philadelphia: University of Pennsylvania.

Tan, H., and G. Batra, 1995. "Enterprise Training in Developing Countries: Incidence, Productivity Effects, and Policy Implications." World Bank, Washington, D.C. Mimeo.

_____ , 1997. "Technology and Firm Size-Wage Differentials in Colombia, Mexico, and Taiwan (China)." *The World Bank Economic Review* 11(1):59-83.

United Nations (UN), 1994. *World Population Prospects, 1950-2050.* New York.

United Nations Development Programme (UNDP), 1997. *Human Development Report 1997.* New York: Oxford University Press.

United Nations Educational, Scientific, and Cultural Organization (UNESCO), 1995. *World Education Report 1995.* Paris: Oxford University Press.

Williamson, J., and M. Higgins, 1997. The Accumulation and Demography Connection in East Asia. East-West Center Working Papers, Population Series 88-6. East-West Center, Honolulu, Hawaii.

World Bank, 1988. Indonesia: Poverty Assessment and Strategy Report. Report No. 8034-IND. Asia Region, Country Department V, Washington, D.C. Mimeo.

_____ , 1991. "Vocational and Technical Education and Training." Policy Paper. Population and Human Resources Department, Education and Employment Division, Washington, D. C.

_____ , 1994. *Socioeconomic Time-Series Access and Retrieval System* (online), version 3.0. (STARS database.) Washington, D. C.

_____ , 1997a. Philippines: Managing Global Integration. Report No. 17024-PH. East Asia and Pacific Regional Office, Poverty Reduction and Economic Management Sector Unit, Washington, D. C. Mimeo.

_____ , 1997b. *World Development Indicators.* CD-ROM version. Washington, D. C.

_____ , 1997c. *Private Capital Flows to Developing Countries.* Washington, D. C.

_____ , 1997d. *Global Development Finance.* Washington, D. C.

Wu, C. S., 1997. "Recent Developments and Near Future Outlook for Taipei,China Economy." Background paper prepared for the *Asian Development Outlook 1998.* The Institute of Economics, Taipei,China. Mimeo.

Yushi, M., 1997. "Country Report for People's Republic of China." Background paper prepared for the *Asian Development Outlook 1998.* Unirule Institute of Economics, Beijing, People's Republic of China. Mimeo.

STATISTICAL APPENDIX

STATISTICAL NOTES

This Statistical Appendix comprises 23 tables containing selected economic indicators for the developing member countries (DMCs) of the Asian Development Bank (ADB). The selected indicators are presented by account, namely, sector components of the national income accounts, consumer price index, money supply, components of the balance of payments, external debt outstanding and debt-service ratio, exchange rate, and the budget accounts of the central government. These tables present a historical series for 1992-1996 and preliminary data for 1997. Except for the exchange rate and budget account, which are treated as policy variables, and foreign direct investment, where data are not available for the current year, the tables contain projections for 1998 and 1999. What follows are notes that describe the source, scope, and conceptual definition of the data in each table.

Most of the historical data are obtained from updated statistical publications available from official local sources; publications; and internal documents from the ADB, World Bank, International Monetary Fund (IMF), and United Nations. Some of the preliminary data for 1997 are ADB staff projections derived from quarterly or monthly data available for the year. Projections for 1998 and 1999 are purely staff estimates.

Efforts were made to standardize the data to allow comparability over time and across the DMCs, and to ensure consistency across accounts. However, limitations exist because of differences in statistical methodology, definitions, coverage, and practice. The informed judgment of the staff was relied upon in cases where there were peculiarities in selected accounts. In particular, breaks in time-series data were unavoidable, and data-splicing and

data-rebasing techniques were used to make the series consistent. However, there remain data breaks due to changes in definitions and methodologies.

For most countries, we have adopted the calendar/fiscal year reference cited in various economic accounts from official country sources. For India, Maldives, and Myanmar, all data are on a fiscal year basis. For Bangladesh, Nepal, and Pakistan, the national accounts, consumer price index, and balance of payments are fiscal year data. For all countries, data on government finance are reported on a fiscal year basis.

Nine tables display regional averages or totals for the DMCs as a whole and for each of the subregions, namely, the newly industrialized economies (NIEs), People's Republic of China (PRC) and Mongolia, Central Asian republics (CARs), Southeast Asia, South Asia, and the Pacific islands. These are the tables on growth rate of gross domestic product (GDP), growth rate of per capita GDP, changes in consumer prices, growth rate of merchandise exports and imports, balance of trade, current account balance in absolute level and as a percentage of GDP, and level of outstanding external debt. The averages are simple weighted arithmetic means computed using contemporaneous GDP values in current US dollars, for 1992 to 1996, as weights. From 1997 onward the weights used are the values of GDP in 1996. For the CARs, the weight used is the average GDP value in current US dollars from 1994 to 1996. The computation of the averages or totals for the DMCs exclude data for Myanmar and the CARs. Owing to sizable devaluation/depreciation of the currencies in Indonesia, Republic of Korea, Malaysia, Philippines, and Thailand, adjustments of the weights were implemented for 1998 and 1999 to reflect the declining shares of these countries in total regional output. The method used was to substitute the three-year moving average for the annual nominal GDP values for 1996. The effect of this adjustment was to minimize the sharp downturn in regional output arising from the effects of the currency crisis.

Tables A1, A2, A3, A4, A5, and A6. Growth and Structure of Production. In most countries, the definitions relating to national income accounts are based on the United Nations System of National Accounts. Table A1 shows the annual growth rate of GDP valued either at constant market prices or at constant factor costs. For this issue, we tried to use market prices uniformly for all the DMCs, but owing to data quality and informed preferences of ADB staff regarding developments in the factor markets, GDP valued at constant factor cost were used in some cases. The GDP data for Bhutan, Fiji, India, Mongolia, Nepal, Pakistan, Sri Lanka, and Tonga are reported in constant factor cost. For Papua New Guinea, the growth rate is based on GDP at constant purchaser's value. Tables A3, A4, and A5 present annual growth rates for real gross value added in agriculture, industry, and services, respectively. Agriculture includes agricultural crops, livestock, poultry, fisheries, and forestry. The industry sector comprises mining and quarrying, manufacturing, construction, and utilities. The services sector consists of trade, transportation and communications, finance, public administration, and other services. The sector growth rates are consistently defined with the reported GDP values in Table A1, and adding up restrictions are imposed where numerical discrepancies were noted or where reclassifications of the sectors were implemented.

The growth rate figures for per capita real GDP are presented in Table A2. Per capita real GDP is obtained by dividing GDP at constant market prices by population. In countries where GDP growth rate is based on constant factor costs, except for India, the per capita real GDP growth in constant market prices is used for uniformity. This creates a residual item between GDP growth, per capita GDP growth, and population growth. For most DMCs, the 1996 data for per capita gross national product (GNP) in US dollars were obtained from the World Bank.

Table A6 shows the sector shares of GDP based on constant market prices. For Bangladesh, Cook Islands, Fiji, India, Lao People's Democratic Republic, Mongolia, Nepal, Pakistan, Sri Lanka, and Tonga, the sector shares of GDP are based on constant factor costs. In the case of Hong Kong, China the sector value added and GDP figures used in computing the sector shares are in current factor costs because constant price estimates are not available. The sector shares for Bhutan are based on value added at current factor cost.

Tables A7 and A8. Saving and Investment. Gross national saving (GNS) or gross domestic saving (GDS) is computed as the difference between GNP or GDP and total consumption expenditure in the national accounts statistics. For some countries, gross saving data were obtained from official country sources. Gross savings differ from GNS/GDS in that it is derived from the consolidated income and outlay account, and includes the amount of private transfers from the balance-of-payments account. Gross domestic investment (GDI) is the sum of gross fixed capital formation and increases in stocks. For the Pacific islands, except Fiji, where reliable estimates of consumption expenditures are not available, GDS is taken as the sum of GDI and current account balance minus the sum of net factor income from abroad and net transfers. For Nepal, Pakistan, and Philippines, GNS/GDI as a ratio to GNP was used and was also obtained from official country sources. For Bhutan, Cambodia, and Viet Nam, gross saving/

GDI as a ratio to GDP was used and was obtained from official country sources. For India, GNS/GDI as a ratio to GDP was used and was obtained from official country sources. For the rest of the DMCs, GDS/GDI as a ratio to GDP was used and was obtained from official country sources. All figures used in computing the GNS/GDS/GDI ratios to GNP/GDP are in current prices.

Table A9. Consumer Prices. The table presents the annual inflation rate (period average) based on the consumer price index obtained from official local sources and from the IMF *International Financial Statistics* (January 1998) for DMCs for which data are not available locally. For Cambodia, the inflation rate for 1997 was based on the fourth quarter basis. For Lao PDR, end-of-period inflation rate for Vientiane is reported. The rate reported for Viet Nam is an end-of-period inflation rate. For India, the inflation rate refers to the general index for the country, while for Bangladesh and the Philippines, the inflation rates refer to Dhaka middle class and Metro Manila, respectively.

Table A10. Growth of Money Supply. The annual growth rates of M2 are given in Table A10. M2 is defined as M1—the sum of currency in circulation and demand deposits with deposit money banks— plus quasi money. Data for M2 are obtained from country sources, except for Fiji, Indonesia, Papua New Guinea, Samoa, and Vanuatu, which are taken from the ADB *Key Indicators of Developing Asian and Pacific Countries* and IMF *International Financial Statistics*. For India, M3 is used for liquidity.

Tables A11 and A13. Growth Rate of Merchandise Exports and Imports. Historical data on merchandise exports and imports are taken from the balance-of-payments accounts from country sources. These are generally on a free on board basis. Data for Cambodia, PRC, Republic of Korea, Lao PDR, Malaysia, Mongolia, and Thailand were obtained from IMF documents. Of these countries, data for Bangladesh, Bhutan, India, Maldives, Myanmar, Nepal, and Pakistan refer to fiscal years.

Table A12. Direction of Exports. The table presents the annual growth rate of exports to the DMCs and other major trading partners (Japan, United States, European Union, and Australia/New Zealand) from the individual DMCs for the years 1985 and 1996. The data were extracted from the tape of IMF's *Direction of Trade Statistics Yearbook 1997*. Data for Taipei,China are from a local source.

Tables A14, A15, and A16. Balance of Payments. The balance of trade is the difference between merchandise exports and merchandise imports. The current account balance is the sum of the balance of trade, net trade in services and income, and net unrequited transfers. In the case of Cambodia, India, Lao PDR, and Viet Nam, official transfers are excluded. Data reported for Cambodia, PRC, Indonesia, Republic of Korea, Malaysia, and Thailand are from *International Financial Statistics* (January 1998). The balance-of-payments data for other countries are from local sources.

Table A17. Foreign Direct Investment (FDI). The data on gross FDI flows were obtained from the United Nations Conference on Trade and Development, *World Investment Report 1997*. Direct investment capital includes equity capital, reinvested earnings, and other capital that is associated with the transactions of enterprises.

Tables A18 and A19. External Debt. For most countries, external debt outstanding includes long-term debt, short-term debt, and use of IMF credit. Debt-service payments consist of principal repayments and interest payments on long-term debt and IMF credit, and interest payments on short-term debt. For Cambodia and Viet Nam, external debt includes medium- and long-term debt in convertible currency only. For Mongolia, medium- and long-term debt includes payment on Council for Mutual Economic Assistance (CMEA) debts but excludes unresolved claims of former CMEA members. For all countries, the debt-service ratio is defined as debt-service payments as a percentage of exports of goods and services. The data were obtained from local sources for most countries. Data provided by the World Bank were used for Cambodia, PRC, Indonesia, Lao PDR, Malaysia, Maldives, Myanmar, and Thailand.

Tables A20. Foreign Exchange Rates. The foreign exchange rate quoted is the annual average of the exchange rate of the currency of each of the countries to the US dollar. Basic data were obtained from local sources except for Bangladesh; Cambodia; Indonesia; Lao PDR; Mongolia; Taipei,China; and

Thailand where the data were sourced from IMF documents.

Tables A21, A22, and A23. Government Finance. These tables relate only to central government finance. Government expenditure includes both current and capital expenditure. Total revenue includes current revenue and capital receipts. In most countries, the overall budget surplus/deficit is the balance between government revenue and expenditure, excluding grants. In the case of Bhutan, Republic of Korea, Marshall Islands, Federated States of Micronesia, Nepal, Pakistan, and Vanuatu, the overall balance includes grants. For India, the overall balance includes recovery of loans and asset sales. For Pakistan, the account reported refers to consolidated federal and provincial accounts, and includes surpluses of autonomous bodies. All ratios are reported as a percentage of GDP in current prices. Data are taken from official country sources and are on a fiscal year basis.

Table A1 Growth Rate of GDP
(percent per annum)

	1992	1993	1994	1995	1996	1997	1998	1999
Newly Industrialized Economies	5.9	6.4	7.6	7.4	6.4	6.0	2.2	4.3
Hong Kong, China	6.3	6.1	5.4	3.9	5.0	5.2	3.0	3.5
Korea, Rep. of	5.1	5.8	8.6	8.9	7.1	5.5	-1.0	3.1
Singapore	6.2	10.4	10.5	8.7	6.9	7.8	3.0	4.5
Taipei,China	6.8	6.3	6.5	6.0	5.7	6.8	5.8	6.2
People's Rep. of China and Mongolia	14.2	13.5	12.6	10.5	9.6	8.8	7.2	6.8
China, People's Rep. of	14.2	13.5	12.6	10.5	9.6	8.8	7.2	6.8
Mongolia	...	-3.0	2.3	6.3	2.4	3.3	...	...
Central Asian Republics	-13.5	-13.3	-16.5	-5.5	3.9	7.8	...	...
Kazakstan	-14.0	-12.9	-12.6	-8.2	0.5	2.0	...	...
Kyrgyz Republic	-13.8	-15.5	-20.1	-5.3	5.6	10.4	...	...
Uzbekistan	-11.1	-2.3	-5.2	-0.9	1.6	5.2	...	...
Southeast Asia	6.6	7.2	7.7	8.2	7.1	3.9	-0.4	2.4
Cambodia	7.0	4.1	4.0	7.6	6.5	2.0	...	...
Indonesia	7.2	7.3	7.5	8.2	8.0	4.6	-3.0	1.0
Lao People's Democratic Rep.	7.0	5.9	8.1	7.0	6.9	7.2	...	...
Malaysia	7.8	8.3	9.2	9.5	8.6	7.5	3.5	4.5
Myanmar	9.7	6.0	7.5	6.9	5.8	5.0	...	...
Philippines	0.3	2.1	4.4	4.8	5.7	5.1	2.4	4.0
Thailand	8.1	8.7	8.6	8.8	5.5	-0.4	-3.0	1.0
Viet Nam	8.6	8.1	8.8	9.5	9.3	9.2	5.0	6.5
South Asia	5.5	5.4	7.0	6.6	6.8	4.8	6.4	6.7
Bangladesh	4.2	4.5	4.2	4.4	5.4	5.7	6.0	6.2
Bhutan	4.5	6.1	6.4	7.4	6.1	6.6	...	...
India	5.3	6.0	7.8	7.2	7.5	5.0	6.7	7.0
Maldives	6.3	6.2	6.6	7.2	6.5	6.0	...	...
Nepal	4.6	3.3	7.9	2.8	6.1	4.3	3.7	4.0
Pakistan	7.7	2.3	4.5	5.2	4.6	3.1	5.1	5.5
Sri Lanka	4.3	6.9	5.6	5.5	3.8	6.3	5.6	6.0
Pacific Islands	9.2	12.1	3.0	-1.7	3.3	-4.1	...	...
Cook Islands	11.0	1.5	1.5	-5.7	-5.3	0.5	...	...
Fiji	4.9	2.2	3.9	2.0	3.1	-1.0	...	...
Kiribati	2.5	3.1	6.8	12.8	1.7	2.0	...	...
Marshall Islands	1.1	2.5	4.7	4.7	-5.0	-5.0	...	...
Micronesia, Federated States of	1.3	1.4	-1.9	0.8	0.8	-5.0	...	...
Papua New Guinea	11.8	16.6	3.1	-4.7	3.9	-6.5	...	...
Samoa	-0.9	6.3	-7.8	9.5	5.9	3.0	...	...
Solomon Islands	12.5	2.3	5.6	7.6	3.5	-1.0	...	...
Tonga	...	2.8	4.7	2.6	1.6	3.0	...	...
Tuvalu	2.7	5.2	6.2	2.0	2.5	2.5	...	...
Vanuatu	1.0	4.5	2.5	3.2	3.0	3.0	...	...
Average for DMCs	8.1	8.4	8.7	8.2	7.5	6.1	4.0	5.1

Table A2 Growth Rate of Per Capita GDP
(percent per annum)

	1992	1993	1994	1995	1996	1997	1998	1999	Per Capita GNP (US$) 1996
Newly Industrialized Economies	4.7	5.1	6.3	5.3	5.1	4.6	0.9	3.1	
Hong Kong, China	5.4	4.3	3.1	1.9	2.4	2.1	0.5	1.5	24,290
Korea, Rep. of	4.0	4.7	7.5	7.8	6.1	4.5	-1.9	2.1	10,610
Singapore	4.1	8.3	8.4	6.5	5.1	5.7	0.4	3.2	30,550
Taipei,China	5.7	5.2	5.7	5.1	4.9	6.0	5.0	5.4	13,310
People's Rep. of China and Mongolia	12.9	12.2	11.3	9.3	8.5	7.7	6.1	5.7	
China, People's Rep. of	12.9	12.2	11.3	9.3	8.5	7.7	6.1	5.7	750
Mongolia	...	-4.4	0.9	4.5	0.8	1.2	...	...	360
Central Asian Republics	-14.4	-13.8	-15.7	-6.8	3.7	7.1	...	...	
Kazakstan	-13.3	-12.8	-12.2	-6.5	1.5	3.1	...	...	1,350
Kyrgyz Republic	-15.0	-15.8	-18.9	-7.7	5.3	10.0	...	...	550
Uzbekistan	-13.2	-4.5	-6.0	-2.9	-0.1	...	...	...	1,010
Southeast Asia	4.4	5.2	5.8	5.3	5.2	1.7	-2.3	0.6	
Cambodia	1.6	0.3	1.8	4.0	1.5	-0.7	...	...	300
Indonesia	5.4	5.5	5.8	6.5	6.2	2.9	-4.4	-0.5	1,080
Lao People's Democratic Rep.	4.3	3.2	5.4	4.3	4.3	4.6	...	...	400
Malaysia	3.3	5.0	6.5	6.4	6.1	5.1	1.2	2.1	4,370
Myanmar	7.6	4.1	5.5	4.9	3.9	4.5	...	...	...
Philippines	-2.1	-0.5	2.0	2.3	3.3	2.8	-0.4	1.7	1,160
Thailand	6.8	7.4	7.3	7.6	4.3	-2.8	-4.7	-0.5	2,960
Viet Nam	6.1	5.6	6.6	7.4	7.3	7.0	3.0	4.4	290
South Asia	3.4	3.3	4.4	4.3	4.8	3.1	4.5	4.9	
Bangladesh	2.5	2.8	2.0	2.6	3.5	3.8	4.1	4.3	260
Bhutan	1.3	2.9	3.5	3.8	2.9	2.9	...	...	390
India	3.3	4.1	5.3	5.5	5.6	3.4	5.0	5.4	380
Maldives	2.8	2.8	3.3	5.7	...	...	...	...	1,080
Nepal	2.5	1.2	5.7	0.8	3.9	2.2	1.6	1.9	210
Pakistan	4.7	-1.0	0.9	2.4	1.3	0.6	2.3	2.5	480
Sri Lanka	3.3	5.6	4.2	4.0	2.6	5.2	4.5	4.9	740
Pacific Islands	7.1	10.6	1.0	-0.6	-0.4	0.3	...	...	
Cook Islands	10.5	0.4	0.4	-3.2	-6.3	3.5	...	...	...
Fiji	4.5	-0.1	2.3	1.3	1.4	0.9	...	...	2,470
Kiribati	-21.4	-1.4	-0.7	5.3	-0.2	1.0	...	...	920
Marshall Islands	-4.0	0.3	-1.2	0.9	...	...	...	...	1,890
Micronesia, Federated States of	-0.7	-0.3	-3.2	-0.5	-0.5	...	...	...	2,070
Papua New Guinea	9.5	14.5	1.0	-2.0	-2.4	...	...	...	1,150
Samoa	-0.3	2.9	-7.0	7.6	5.3	2.4	...	...	1,170
Solomon Islands	2.0	7.4	-0.8	6.9	13.9	...	...	...	900
Tonga	-14.9	0.2	2.8	1.2	-3.7	0.1	...	...	1,790
Tuvalu	1.4	3.9	1.8	0.7	0.7	1.2	...	...	...
Vanuatu	-1.7	7.5	-0.1	0.7	0.6	...	...	...	1,290
Average for DMCs	6.5	6.9	7.1	6.2	6.0	4.6	2.5	3.7	

Table A3 Growth Rate of Value Added in Agriculture
(percent per annum)

	1992	1993	1994	1995	1996	1997	1998	1999
Newly Industrialized Economies								
Hong Kong, China	...	...	...	...	...	...	...	...
Korea, Rep. of	6.0	-2.9	1.6	3.7	3.5	0.6	1.0	1.0
Singapore	0.6	-2.4	5.4	11.0	6.0	-5.8	...	...
Taipei,China	1.4	8.1	3.9	5.4	-4.1	-3.4	0.5	1.4
People's Rep. of China and Mongolia								
China, People's Rep. of	4.7	4.7	4.0	5.0	5.1	3.5	3.5	3.5
Mongolia	-2.1	-2.7	2.7	4.2	10.0	2.6	...	...
Central Asian Republics								
Kazakstan	0.5	-12.1	-20.8	-23.7	-6.9	3.5	...	...
Kyrgyz Republic	-3.2	-9.1	-9.0	-2.0	13.0	...	...	...
Uzbekistan	-9.7	1.5	-3.4	2.0	-7.3	5.8	...	...
Southeast Asia								
Cambodia	1.9	-1.0	-0.0	6.5	1.8	4.9	...	...
Indonesia	6.3	1.7	0.6	4.4	3.0	0.6	1.5	2.5
Lao People's Democratic Rep.	8.3	2.7	8.3	3.1	2.8	5.8	...	...
Malaysia	4.7	4.3	-1.0	1.1	2.2	3.5	2.0	2.0
Myanmar	10.5	4.6	5.9	4.8	4.6	6.4	...	...
Philippines	0.4	2.1	2.6	0.8	3.1	2.8	-1.0	2.0
Thailand	6.0	0.5	2.8	2.5	3.8	1.2	3.0	...
Viet Nam	7.1	3.8	3.9	5.1	4.4	4.9	3.0	3.5
South Asia								
Bangladesh	2.2	1.8	0.3	-1.0	3.7	6.0	3.2	3.4
Bhutan	-2.0	3.6	3.9	4.0	6.4	4.1	...	...
India	6.1	3.6	4.6	-3.0	7.9	-2.0	4.5	3.0
Maldives	-1.1	0.0	2.6	1.5	...	...	...	...
Nepal	-1.1	-0.6	7.6	-0.3	4.4	4.1	2.0	3.5
Pakistan	9.5	-5.3	5.2	6.6	5.3	0.7	5.0	3.0
Sri Lanka	-1.6	4.9	3.3	3.3	-4.6	5.4	3.0	3.0
Pacific Islands								
Cook Islands	-8.3	0.2	1.9	...	5.0	...	...	...
Fiji	3.5	0.6	9.4	-2.8	4.2	-2.3	...	...
Kiribati	...	-5.6	11.4	-8.3	-9.4	...	...	...
Marshall Islands	-3.0	2.3	24.4	-3.1	...	...	...	...
Micronesia, Federated States of	...	...	...	...	...	...	...	...
Papua New Guinea	6.1	9.5	6.0	0.7	3.0	...	...	...
Samoa	-10.1	10.8	-22.6	11.5	4.2	...	...	...
Solomon Islands	-0.5	18.9	-1.4	18.7	3.5	-2.2	...	...
Tonga	-7.6	-0.1	4.7	4.4	-7.3	-3.8	...	...
Tuvalu	-1.6	0.9	0.6	0.5	0.5	1.0	...	...
Vanuatu	1.9	18.4	2.2	6.4	1.6	...	...	...

Table A4 Growth Rate of Value Added in Industry
(percent per annum)

	1992	1993	1994	1995	1996	1997	1998	1999
Newly Industrialized Economies								
Hong Kong, China	...	...	...	...	...	...	...	...
Korea, Rep. of	3.4	6.2	9.0	10.3	6.2	5.4	-2.5	4.0
Singapore	5.8	9.3	13.2	9.5	6.5	6.6	...	...
Taipei,China	3.6	4.0	1.8	3.1	4.0	5.7	3.1	4.1
People's Rep. of China and Mongolia								
China, People's Rep. of	21.2	19.9	18.4	13.9	12.1	10.8	8.0	7.0
Mongolia	-12.9	-6.9	2.1	14.6	0.5	2.3	...	...
Central Asian Republics								
Kazakstan	-23.2	-19.7	-25.9	-21.9	5.1	-3.5	...	...
Kyrgyz Republic	-25.9	-22.0	-38.5	-11.5	-1.2	...	...	...
Uzbekistan	-15.5	-4.2	-6.6	-5.6	1.7	6.5	...	...
Southeast Asia								
Cambodia	15.5	13.0	7.7	9.8	13.3	0.6	...	...
Indonesia	8.2	9.8	11.2	10.4	10.6	5.4	-3.0	1.5
Lao People's Democratic Rep.	7.5	10.3	10.7	12.9	17.5	9.8	...	...
Malaysia	8.9	10.1	12.4	13.8	11.2	10.5	5.0	6.0
Myanmar	12.7	11.0	10.3	12.5	10.7	9.8	...	...
Philippines	-0.6	1.6	5.8	7.0	6.3	5.7	3.0	3.5
Thailand	9.9	10.4	10.2	10.5	7.0	-0.1	0.3	...
Viet Nam	14.0	13.1	14.0	13.9	14.4	13.6	7.3	10.0
South Asia								
Bangladesh	7.1	8.0	7.8	8.4	5.3	3.6	8.1	8.0
Bhutan	15.1	7.3	13.9	17.0	8.4	1.6	...	...
India	4.2	6.8	9.4	14.1	7.2	6.0	7.0	9.0
Maldives	9.1	8.9	6.6	8.2	...	...	...	...
Nepal	16.8	4.8	9.0	3.9	5.9	3.2	4.6	4.0
Pakistan	7.7	5.5	4.5	4.8	3.6	3.3	4.5	6.5
Sri Lanka	7.1	9.8	8.1	7.8	5.6	7.9	7.5	8.5
Pacific Islands								
Cook Islands	24.0	-17.1	10.6	...	2.0	...	...	...
Fiji	7.1	6.0	5.6	1.9	3.9	-0.1	...	...
Kiribati	...	1.8	1.4	2.9	2.6	...	...	...
Marshall Islands	1.3	-7.5	13.3	20.7	...	...	...	...
Micronesia, Federated States of	...	...	...	...	...	...	...	...
Papua New Guinea	28.5	35.8	-0.8	-8.0	7.6	...	...	...
Samoa	19.7	2.2	-3.2	26.6	14.0	...	...	...
Solomon Islands	8.4	6.7	11.5	39.7	...	1.7	...	...
Tonga	12.3	1.6	-2.2	-2.7	6.3	-1.7	...	...
Tuvalu	38.8	-8.1	-10.1	-6.5	2.7	2.7	...	...
Vanuatu	-8.4	1.2	7.3	6.4	-9.2	...	...	...

Table A5 Growth Rate of Value Added in Services
(percent per annum)

	1992	1993	1994	1995	1996	1997	1998	1999
Newly Industrialized Economies								
Hong Kong, China	...	...	...	...	...	...	...	...
Korea, Rep. of	7.6	7.4	8.6	7.6	8.1	7.1	0.1	2.6
Singapore	6.0	10.7	9.5	8.2	7.3	8.8	...	...
Taipei,China	9.5	7.8	9.9	7.9	7.3	7.9	7.6	7.5
People's Rep. of China and Mongolia								
China, People's Rep. of	12.4	10.7	9.6	8.4	7.8	8.2	7.5	8.4
Mongolia	-13.2	1.0	2.0	0.2	-4.1	5.3	...	...
Central Asian Republics								
Kazakstan	-9.0	-7.0	0.7	3.8	0.1	5.0	...	...
Kyrgyz Republic	-11.6	-16.4	-19.3	-7.8	0.8	...	...	...
Uzbekistan	-49.5	-3.0	-5.4	-0.5	5.1	4.6	...	...
Southeast Asia								
Cambodia	11.2	7.2	7.4	7.9	8.8	-0.4	...	...
Indonesia	6.8	7.4	7.1	7.6	7.3	5.3	-4.6	-0.1
Lao People's Democratic Rep.	3.9	7.7	5.5	10.2	8.5	10.0	...	...
Malaysia	8.5	9.7	9.5	9.2	9.5	8.5	6.0	7.0
Myanmar	7.6	6.1	8.3	7.2	5.3	5.1	...	...
Philippines	1.0	2.5	4.2	5.0	6.5	5.6	3.5	5.0
Thailand	7.2	9.6	8.8	9.0	4.6	-1.1	-0.3	...
Viet Nam	7.0	9.2	10.2	10.6	10.0	9.5	5.0	6.0
South Asia								
Bangladesh	4.8	5.3	5.8	6.9	6.5	6.2	7.1	7.2
Bhutan	6.6	10.1	6.2	5.9	5.2	13.9	...	...
India	5.5	7.3	7.5	9.8	7.3	9.1	7.9	8.1
Maldives	8.7	7.9	8.1	8.7	...	...	...	...
Nepal	6.5	7.3	7.7	6.0	7.9	5.0	5.0	4.5
Pakistan	6.8	4.6	4.2	4.8	4.7	4.1	5.5	6.2
Sri Lanka	5.3	6.2	5.1	4.9	6.0	5.6	5.3	5.4
Pacific Islands								
Cook Islands	13.7	3.1	5.9	...	-8.9	...	...	...
Fiji	5.5	0.2	1.7	4.3	2.3	2.7	...	...
Kiribati	-4.5	0.7	0.7	3.7	3.4	...	...	...
Marshall Islands	2.0	4.5	-0.8	3.4	...	...	...	...
Micronesia, Federated States of	...	...	...	...	...	...	...	...
Papua New Guinea	2.9	3.0	5.6	-9.1	0.5	...	...	...
Samoa	2.0	-1.8	11.0	-0.5	2.4	...	...	...
Solomon Islands	8.3	4.7	2.9	-0.2	1.7	2.4	...	...
Tonga	-19.8	-0.7	2.1	0.8	-1.8	8.6	...	...
Tuvalu	59.5	-16.6	-8.5	-9.2	3.0	2.9	...	...
Vanuatu	3.0	9.8	1.7	1.4	6.2	...	...	...

Table A6 Sectoral Share of GDP
(percent)

	Agriculture			Industry			Services		
	1970	1980	1997	1970	1980	1997	1970	1980	1997
Newly Industrialized Economies									
Hong Kong, China	...	0.9	0.2	...	32.0	15.5	...	67.2	84.4
Korea, Rep. of	29.8	14.2	6.1	23.8	37.8	43.7	46.4	48.1	50.2
Singapore	2.2	1.1	0.1	36.4	38.8	34.3	61.4	60.0	65.5
Taipei,China	...	7.9	2.9	...	46.0	35.3	...	46.1	61.8
People's Rep. of China and Mongolia									
China, People's Rep. of	42.2	25.6	17.2	44.6	51.7	54.9	13.2	22.7	27.9
Mongolia	33.1	17.4	36.9	26.3	33.3	34.0	40.6	49.3	29.1
Central Asian Republics									
Kazakstan	...	...	13.4	...	...	30.5	...	...	51.6
Kyrgyz Republic	...	...	49.8	...	...	25.0	...	...	25.2
Uzbekistan	...	...	21.3	...	...	18.0	...	...	60.7
Southeast Asia									
Cambodia	...	...	43.9	...	...	19.6	...	...	36.5
Indonesia	35.0	24.4	14.8	28.0	41.3	43.2	37.0	34.3	42.0
Lao People's Democratic Rep.	...	...	52.5	...	...	21.5	...	...	26.0
Malaysia	...	22.9	11.7	...	35.8	47.6	...	41.3	40.8
Myanmar	49.5	47.9	44.5	12.0	12.3	16.8	38.5	39.8	38.7
Philippines	28.2	23.5	20.5	33.7	40.5	35.9	38.1	36.0	43.6
Thailand	30.2	20.2	10.8	25.7	30.1	42.2	44.1	49.7	47.0
Viet Nam	...	42.7	31.2	...	26.3	30.1	...	31.0	38.7
South Asia									
Bangladesh	...	49.4	32.4	...	14.8	19.2	...	35.8	48.4
Bhutan	...	56.7	36.2	...	12.2	28.0	...	31.1	35.9
India	44.5	38.1	24.3	23.9	25.9	31.9	31.6	36.0	43.8
Maldives	...	...	...	...	...	...	...	...	...
Nepal	...	61.8	41.0	...	11.9	19.1	...	26.3	39.8
Pakistan	40.1	30.6	24.2	19.6	25.6	26.4	40.3	43.8	49.4
Sri Lanka	30.7	26.6	18.3	27.1	27.2	32.3	42.2	46.2	49.4
Pacific Islands									
Cook Islands	...	...	...	...	...	...	...	...	...
Fiji	30.2	22.5	22.1	23.1	21.7	23.4	46.7	55.8	54.5
Kiribati	...	...	...	...	...	...	...	...	...
Marshall Islands	...	...	...	...	...	...	...	...	...
Micronesia, Federated States	...	...	...	...	...	...	...	...	...
Papua New Guinea	...	...	...	...	...	...	...	...	...
Samoa	...	...	...	...	...	...	...	...	...
Solomon Islands	...	52.5	35.7	...	10.0	23.7	...	37.4	40.6
Tonga	...	47.6	35.3	...	11.0	15.4	...	41.4	49.3
Tuvalu	...	...	...	...	...	...	...	...	...
Vanuatu	...	...	...	...	...	...	...	...	...

Table A7 Gross Domestic Savings
(percentage of GDP)

	1992	1993	1994	1995	1996	1997	1998	1999
Newly Industrialized Economies								
Hong Kong, China	33.8	34.6	33.1	30.5	30.7	30.6	30.0	32.0
Korea, Rep. of	35.2	35.4	36.5	36.8	35.2	34.5	34.9	33.9
Singapore	45.6	46.3	48.8	51.0	51.2	51.8	50.0	50.0
Taipei,China	27.0	27.0	25.8	25.6	25.1	24.7	24.9	25.2
People's Rep. of China and Mongolia								
China, People's Rep. of	38.3	41.5	42.2	41.9	41.4	42.6	39.0	39.0
Mongolia	23.9	12.4	11.3	21.8	19.9	19.3	...	...
Central Asian Republics								
Kazakstan	...	...	13.4	15.8	10.3	...	...	...
Kyrgyz Republic	7.9	4.0	2.7	5.5	2.2	3.0	...	...
Uzbekistan	6.7	-5.4	7.8	20.4	8.2	9.0	...	...
Southeast Asia								
Cambodia	6.2	5.3	4.8	5.4	5.4	4.4	...	...
Indonesia	35.3	32.5	32.2	30.6	30.2	31.0	24.0	25.0
Lao People's Democratic Rep.	...	...	...	...	...	...	...	...
Malaysia	36.5	37.7	38.8	39.5	42.6	43.8	42.0	42.5
Myanmar	12.8	11.4	11.7	13.4	14.0	14.6	...	...
Philippines	17.0	15.2	17.0	16.8	18.8	19.2	17.0	19.0
Thailand	35.2	35.6	36.0	33.6	33.7	31.0	31.4	32.0
Viet Nam	16.9	17.4	16.9	17.0	16.7	17.7	16.0	18.0
South Asia								
Bangladesh	5.8	7.0	13.4	12.8	7.5	9.0	8.6	8.8
Bhutan	16.1	26.8	28.4	27.0	29.0	30.0	...	...
India	22.5	21.1	23.0	24.4	25.6	25.5	25.6	27.1
Maldives	...	...	...	...	...	...	...	...
Nepal	12.7	15.5	16.5	15.2	10.3	12.5	13.1	13.0
Pakistan	16.9	13.5	15.6	14.2	11.6	11.4	12.5	13.5
Sri Lanka	15.0	16.0	15.2	15.3	15.5	16.5	17.5	18.0
Pacific Islands								
Cook Islands	...	...	...	...	...	...	...	...
Fiji	9.3	10.3	11.2	11.0	12.7	...	...	...
Kiribati	-50.4	...	...	...	...	...	...	...
Marshall Islands	...	...	...	...	...	...	...	...
Micronesia, Federated States of	...	...	...	...	...	...	...	...
Papua New Guinea	19.7	...	...	...	...	...	...	...
Samoa	...	...	...	...	...	...	...	...
Solomon Islands	...	...	...	...	...	...	...	...
Tonga	-24.8	...	...	...	...	...	...	...
Tuvalu	...	...	...	...	...	...	...	...
Vanuatu	20.3	19.3	18.9	23.0	...	...	...	...

Table A8 Gross Domestic Investment
(percentage of GDP)

	1992	1993	1994	1995	1996	1997	1998	1999
Newly Industrialized Economies								
Hong Kong, China	28.5	27.6	31.9	34.8	32.3	34.5	31.0	32.0
Korea, Rep. of	36.6	35.1	36.1	37.0	38.2	34.6	26.4	29.4
Singapore	36.0	37.7	32.7	33.7	35.3	37.4	32.0	33.0
Taipei,China	24.9	25.2	23.9	23.7	21.2	21.8	22.6	23.4
People's Rep. of China and Mongolia								
China, People's Rep. of	37.3	43.5	40.9	40.2	39.2	39.8	39.0	39.0
Mongolia	29.3	27.7	24.8	26.4	25.2	23.3	...	...
Central Asian Republics								
Kazakstan	...	...	21.4	20.1	14.0	...	...	...
Kyrgyz Republic	19.9	11.7	9.0	18.3	23.5	19.0	...	...
Uzbekistan	13.1	3.0	5.7	20.9	16.1	15.0	...	...
Southeast Asia								
Cambodia	9.8	17.8	18.5	21.6	20.9	17.6	...	...
Indonesia	32.4	29.5	32.5	31.9	30.8	31.6	25.0	27.0
Lao People's Democratic Rep.	...	...	...	...	...	...	...	...
Malaysia	35.1	37.8	40.4	43.5	41.5	42.0	40.5	41.5
Myanmar	13.5	12.4	12.4	14.3	14.8	16.8	...	...
Philippines	20.8	23.6	23.5	21.6	23.3	23.9	20.0	22.0
Thailand	40.0	39.9	40.3	41.6	41.7	35.0	26.0	29.0
Viet Nam	17.6	24.9	25.5	27.1	27.9	25.4	23.0	25.0
South Asia								
Bangladesh	12.1	14.3	18.1	19.1	17.0	17.4	17.2	18.0
Bhutan	47.7	47.1	50.3	47.6	48.0	47.0	...	...
India	24.0	21.7	24.0	26.2	27.1	26.6	27.1	29.0
Maldives	...	...	...	...	...	...	...	...
Nepal	21.2	23.1	22.4	23.4	23.2	23.4	24.9	25.0
Pakistan	19.9	20.5	19.4	18.3	18.7	18.4	20.0	22.0
Sri Lanka	24.3	25.6	27.0	25.7	24.2	25.8	26.7	27.6
Pacific Islands								
Cook Islands	...	...	...	...	...	...	...	...
Fiji	13.4	14.6	12.2	13.0	12.1	...	...	...
Kiribati	69.0	...	...	...	...	...	...	...
Marshall Islands	...	...	...	...	...	...	...	...
Micronesia, Federated States of	...	...	...	...	...	...	...	...
Papua New Guinea	23.8	...	...	...	...	...	...	...
Samoa	...	...	...	...	...	...	...	...
Solomon Islands	25.4	19.6	...	...	...	...	...	...
Tonga	33.8	...	...	...	...	...	...	...
Tuvalu	58.4	41.1	46.1	71.6	...	...	...	...
Vanuatu	26.2	25.5	26.5	30.5	...	...	...	...

Table A9 Changes in Consumer Prices
(percent per annum)

	1992	1993	1994	1995	1996	1997	1998	1999
Newly Industrialized Economies	5.8	4.6	5.6	4.6	4.3	3.5	6.1	4.9
Hong Kong, China	9.3	8.5	8.1	8.6	6.0	5.7	4.5	5.0
Korea, Rep. of	6.2	4.8	6.2	4.5	4.9	4.5	9.8	7.2
Singapore	2.3	2.2	3.1	1.7	1.4	2.0	3.2	3.3
Taipei,China	4.5	2.9	4.1	3.7	3.1	0.9	3.2	2.2
People's Rep. of China and Mongolia	6.7	14.9	24.2	17.1	8.3	2.8	4.0	6.0
China, People's Rep. of	6.4	14.7	24.1	17.1	8.3	2.8	4.0	6.0
Mongolia	153.8	268.4	87.6	56.8	49.6	20.0	...	...
Central Asian Republics	987.1	1,277.3	782.5	83.6	36.5	24.8	...	...
Kazakstan	1,381.0	1,658.7	1,878.3	175.8	39.1	20.4	...	...
Kyrgyz Republic	854.6	1,208.7	278.1	42.8	30.3	25.5	...	...
Uzbekistan	906.1	880.4	1,281.4	116.9	64.4	30.0	...	...
Southeast Asia	7.1	6.5	7.1	7.3	6.6	5.6	12.9	8.7
Cambodia	112.5	41.0	17.9	3.5	9.0	9.1	...	...
Indonesia	7.6	9.6	8.5	9.5	7.9	6.6	20.0	15.0
Lao People's Democratic Rep.	9.8	6.3	6.8	19.6	13.0	19.5	...	...
Malaysia	4.7	3.6	3.7	3.4	3.5	4.0	5.0	4.5
Myanmar	21.9	31.8	24.1	25.2	16.3	...	...	...
Philippines	8.9	7.6	9.0	8.1	8.4	5.1	10.0	8.0
Thailand	4.1	3.3	5.2	5.8	5.9	5.6	15.0	9.0
Viet Nam	17.6	5.2	14.4	12.7	4.5	3.2	4.0	4.0
South Asia	...	4.8	10.7	9.9	9.3	7.1	7.4	7.5
Bangladesh	5.1	1.3	1.8	5.2	4.0	3.9	5.5	5.0
Bhutan	15.9	11.2	7.0	9.5	8.8	7.0	...	...
India	...	3.8	11.8	10.0	9.2	6.5	7.0	7.2
Maldives	16.8	20.2	16.5	5.4	6.2	8.0	...	...
Nepal	21.0	8.9	8.9	7.6	8.1	7.8	7.5	8.0
Pakistan	9.6	9.8	11.2	13.0	10.8	11.6	10.0	10.2
Sri Lanka	11.4	11.7	8.4	7.7	15.9	9.6	10.0	9.0
Pacific Islands	4.8	4.3	2.9	11.7	8.6	3.9	...	...
Cook Islands	3.5	7.3	2.6	0.9	-0.5	-2.0	...	...
Fiji	4.9	0.5	0.8	2.2	3.0	2.9	...	...
Kiribati	4.0	6.1	5.3	3.6	-0.6	2.0	...	...
Marshall Islands	10.3	5.0	5.6	7.3	6.0	4.0	...	...
Micronesia, Federated States of	5.0	6.0	4.0	4.0	3.0	3.0	...	...
Papua New Guinea	4.3	4.9	2.9	17.3	11.6	3.9	...	...
Samoa	9.0	1.7	18.4	1.0	7.1	8.0	...	...
Solomon Islands	10.7	14.3	7.3	9.8	15.8	12.0	...	...
Tonga	8.0	0.9	2.4	0.3	2.8	1.8	...	...
Tuvalu	2.2	2.3	1.4	5.0	0.0	0.6	...	...
Vanuatu	4.1	3.6	2.5	2.3	2.5	2.5	...	...
Average for DMCs	5.6	8.0	11.3	9.4	6.7	4.3	6.9	6.5

Table A10   Growth Rate of Money Supply (M2)
(percent per annum)

	1992	1993	1994	1995	1996	1997	1998	1999
Newly Industrialized Economies								
Hong Kong, China	10.8	16.2	12.9	14.6	10.9	8.4	9.4	9.6
Korea, Rep. of	14.9	16.6	18.7	15.6	15.8	14.7	13.1	13.2
Singapore	8.9	8.5	14.4	8.5	9.8	10.3	8.6	7.5
Taipei,China	19.1	15.4	15.1	9.4	9.1	7.2	7.4	7.4
People's Rep. of China and Mongolia								
China, People's Rep. of	31.3	36.8	35.1	29.5	25.8	17.3	20.0	22.0
Mongolia	31.6	227.6	79.5	32.9	25.8	36.0	...	...
Central Asian Republics								
Kazakstan	389.0	691.9	576.1	110.4	17.4	29.6	...	...
Kyrgyz Republic	428.2	179.9	117.8	77.8	22.2	17.0	...	...
Uzbekistan	468.2	782.2	680.0	158.1	113.7	24.0	...	...
Southeast Asia								
Cambodia	214.0	34.4	34.9	44.3	40.4	16.6	...	...
Indonesia	20.2	22.0	20.2	27.6	29.6	27.7	25.0	26.1
Lao People's Democratic Rep.	49.0	64.6	31.9	16.4	26.7	68.8	...	...
Malaysia	19.1	22.1	14.7	24.0	20.9	18.5	18.0	20.0
Myanmar	35.6	26.8	33.9	40.5	39.5	...	...	...
Philippines	11.0	24.6	26.8	25.2	15.8	20.5	17.0	17.0
Thailand	15.6	18.4	12.9	17.0	12.6	16.4	6.8	7.5
Viet Nam	33.7	19.0	33.2	22.6	22.7	24.0	15.0	15.0
South Asia								
Bangladesh	14.1	10.6	15.4	16.0	8.2	10.8	12.0	12.5
Bhutan	-2.3	16.2	21.5	29.9	30.4	20.0	...	...
India	15.7	18.4	22.3	13.7	15.9	16.5	16.7	15.0
Maldives	12.9	36.4	24.2	15.6	24.0	20.0	...	...
Nepal	21.1	27.7	19.6	16.1	14.4	10.7	12.0	12.0
Pakistan	30.3	18.0	16.9	16.6	14.9	13.1	14.2	15.0
Sri Lanka	17.4	23.4	19.7	19.2	10.8	14.7	14.0	13.0
Pacific Islands								
Cook Islands	26.9	6.5	...	...	...	...	...	...
Fiji	15.0	17.9	0.2	7.5	15.4	...	...	...
Kiribati	...	...	...	...	...	...	...	...
Marshall Islands	...	...	...	...	...	...	...	...
Micronesia, Federated States of	...	...	...	...	...	...	...	...
Papua New Guinea	24.9	7.0	2.6	-12.5	8.1	...	...	...
Samoa	0.8	2.3	12.9	21.8	1.6	6.2	...	...
Solomon Islands	26.2	14.7	24.1	9.6	...	...	...	...
Tonga	22.5	4.1	8.8	17.1	2.6	9.3	...	...
Tuvalu	...	...	...	...	...	...	...	...
Vanuatu	-2.6	4.9	2.9	12.2	...	...	...	...

Table A11 Growth Rate of Merchandise Exports
(percent per annum)

	1992	1993	1994	1995	1996	1997	1998	1999
Newly Industrialized Economies	12.1	10.7	15.0	20.9	4.5	3.4	4.0	4.9
Hong Kong, China	21.2	13.2	11.9	14.8	4.0	4.0	2.2	3.5
Korea, Rep. of	8.0	7.7	15.7	31.5	4.1	7.2	5.8	5.6
Singapore	8.5	17.0	25.8	21.0	6.4	-3.1	2.0	4.0
Taipei,China	6.9	4.5	9.4	20.0	3.8	5.2	6.8	7.0
People's Rep. of China and Mongolia	18.0	8.7	35.4	24.9	17.8	20.0	3.0	3.0
China, People's Rep. of	18.1	8.8	35.6	24.9	17.9	20.0	3.0	3.0
Mongolia	2.7	2.8	0.3	32.3	-12.8	8.9	...	...
Central Asian Republics	-66.3	29.7	0.5	37.2	13.1	7.1	...	...
Kazakstan	-65.1	0.7	-0.9	45.3	21.8	7.7	...	...
Kyrgyz Republic	-93.1	31.7	0.1	20.3	29.9	13.7	...	...
Uzbekistan	-88.0	102.0	2.2	29.4	-0.6	5.3	...	...
Southeast Asia	14.7	13.3	19.3	24.3	6.0	8.7	8.2	10.4
Cambodia	24.5	7.2	62.8	75.2	-18.5	-4.9	...	...
Indonesia	14.0	8.3	9.9	18.0	5.8	11.2	5.0	7.0
Lao People's Democratic Rep.	37.3	81.4	24.9	3.5	3.8	-1.0	...	...
Malaysia	18.1	16.1	23.1	26.6	7.3	6.0	8.0	10.0
Myanmar	37.2	17.8	31.8	-2.8	4.6	7.5	...	...
Philippines	11.1	15.8	18.5	29.4	17.7	22.8	21.0	21.0
Thailand	13.7	13.4	22.7	24.8	-1.9	3.2	5.0	8.0
Viet Nam	21.2	20.6	35.8	28.2	41.0	22.2	15.0	16.0
South Asia	8.0	15.4	13.0	20.5	5.5	5.1	8.0	8.9
Bangladesh	16.1	19.5	6.0	37.2	12.2	13.7	15.0	16.0
Bhutan	-9.6	4.9	-4.2	11.7	9.3	8.5	...	...
India	3.3	20.2	18.4	20.8	4.1	5.0	7.5	7.8
Maldives	10.0	-19.0	43.1	12.7	8.0	5.8	...	...
Nepal	56.1	25.4	-2.7	-9.6	1.7	10.3	4.0	6.0
Pakistan	14.6	0.3	-1.4	16.1	7.1	-2.7	6.0	9.0
Sri Lanka	20.6	16.3	12.0	18.7	7.9	13.0	9.0	10.0
Pacific Islands	25.2	28.2	7.9	2.3	-1.3	-12.0	...	...
Cook Islands	-41.4	21.9	7.7	9.5	...	...	...	...
Fiji	-3.5	6.1	32.2	6.0	23.3	-11.4	...	...
Kiribati	64.8	-27.4	51.9	40.7	-31.1	...	...	...
Marshall Islands	9.1	-17.7	87.3	14.9	...	...	...	...
Micronesia, Federated States of	94.4	33.8	135.9	5.0	-1.6	2.0	...	...
Papua New Guinea	31.4	33.7	2.5	0.4	-5.6	-13.3	...	...
Samoa	-10.1	10.5	-45.3	149.1	15.1	...	...	...
Solomon Islands	22.1	25.5	10.1	18.4	4.3	4.0	...	...
Tonga	78.2	-42.4	82.8	-11.8	-25.1	0.8	...	...
Tuvalu	-40.5	4.5	4.3	-54.2	9.1	25.0	...	...
Vanuatu	30.2	-4.2	10.1	13.2	6.7	0.3	...	...
Average for DMCs	13.2	11.3	18.3	22.1	6.8	7.2	5.0	6.0

Table A12 Direction of Exports
(percent share)

From \ To	DMCs 1985	DMCs 1996	JAPAN 1985	JAPAN 1996	USA 1985	USA 1996	EU 1985	EU 1996	AUSTRALIA/ NEW ZEALAND 1985	AUSTRALIA/ NEW ZEALAND 1996	OTHERS 1985	OTHERS 1996
Newly Industrialized Economies												
Hong Kong, China	35.6	46.0	4.2	6.5	30.8	21.2	11.8	15.8	2.3	1.8	15.3	8.7
Korea, Rep. of	12.9	38.4	15.0	12.3	35.6	16.8	10.4	13.3	1.3	1.4	24.7	17.8
Singapore	36.7	48.4	9.4	8.2	21.2	18.4	10.1	13.4	4.4	2.4	18.1	9.2
Taipei,China	15.6	...	11.3	...	15.5	...	5.5	...	2.4	...	49.7	...
PRC and Mongolia												
China, People's Rep. of	38.2	36.6	22.3	20.4	8.5	17.7	7.8	15.0	0.8	1.3	22.5	9.0
Mongolia	3.1	38.5	11.2	21.5	5.5	8.0	20.5	...	0.0	...	59.6	32.0
Central Asian Republics												
Kazakstan	...	15.1	...	1.4	...	...	...	...	...	...	...	...
Kyrgyz Republic	...	53.8	...	0.2	...	...	...	...	...	...	...	...
Uzbekistan	...	15.8	...	2.1	...	...	...	...	...	...	...	...
Southeast Asia												
Cambodia	67.9	52.1	7.0	1.8	...	1.2	13.2	14.0	...	...	11.9	30.9
Indonesia	17.2	31.5	46.2	28.8	21.7	16.5	6.0	18.3	1.2	2.8	7.6	2.1
Lao People's Democratic Rep.	71.9	64.9	6.6	6.6	2.7	4.8	0.5	27.0	5.5	...	12.7	-3.3
Malaysia	38.1	45.9	24.6	13.4	12.8	18.2	13.6	14.8	1.9	1.7	9.1	6.0
Myanmar	47.1	54.1	8.4	7.4	0.8	8.3	8.4	6.3	...	...	35.4	23.9
Philippines	19.5	25.1	19.0	17.1	35.9	32.6	13.8	18.6	2.1	1.1	9.7	5.5
Thailand	27.1	34.0	13.4	16.8	19.7	18.0	17.8	15.7	1.9	1.4	20.1	14.1
Viet Nam	50.4	24.6	17.4	26.4	...	4.5	6.2	25.0	2.2	4.0	23.8	15.5
South Asia												
Bangladesh	14.5	7.6	7.2	3.1	18.1	31.0	13.0	45.0	1.8	0.6	45.5	12.7
Bhutan	...	...	...	...	...	...	...	...	...	...	...	...
India	8.9	24.1	11.1	7.4	18.9	17.3	16.7	29.4	1.4	1.3	43.0	20.5
Maldives	50.8	41.9	10.1	7.0	24.3	8.5	4.0	38.0	...	...	10.9	4.6
Nepal	41.4	12.4	0.7	0.6	35.3	34.4	20.3	52.0	0.1	0.3	2.3	0.3
Pakistan	16.0	21.4	11.3	6.5	10.0	16.7	20.9	30.1	1.1	1.3	40.6	24.0
Sri Lanka	11.2	8.1	5.1	6.2	22.3	34.1	17.9	34.4	1.7	1.2	41.9	16.0
Pacific Islands												
Cook Islands	...	...	...	...	...	...	...	...	...	...	...	...
Fiji	22.5	4.9	3.0	8.4	4.9	10.6	31.0	21.3	18.2	28.2	20.4	26.6
Kiribati	7.2	...	4.3	...	...	...	44.5	...	0.5	...	43.5	100.0
Marshall Islands	...	...	...	...	...	...	...	...	...	...	...	...
Micronesia, Federated States of	...	...	...	...	...	...	...	...	...	...	...	...
Papua New Guinea	9.9	19.0	22.1	21.5	4.0	0.4	46.5	21.0	12.0	...	5.6	38.1
Samoa	0.3	2.7	0.9	0.3	59.4	1.7	5.8	1.6	29.7	...	3.9	93.7
Solomon Islands	11.1	...	52.1	...	2.4	...	26.3	13.5	3.2	3.1	5.0	83.4
Tonga	5.9	...	0.2	...	3.2	...	0.5	5.5	83.1	5.0	7.1	89.5
Tuvalu	...	...	...	...	...	...	...	...	...	...	...	...
Vanuatu	1.4	...	6.7	...	...	...	25.4	42.9	1.6	15.1	65.0	42.0
Total for DMCs	25.6	39.2	16.5	12.9	26.3	16.4	10.7	15.8	2.1	2.0	18.8	13.1

Table A13 Growth Rate of Merchandise Imports
(percent per annum)

	1992	1993	1994	1995	1996	1997	1998	1999
Newly Industrialized Economies	13.1	10.1	17.4	22.9	5.2	3.0	-0.4	8.1
Hong Kong, China	23.0	12.3	16.7	19.1	3.0	5.1	1.0	6.0
Korea, Rep. of	1.0	2.3	22.4	32.1	12.2	-2.3	-12.3	14.0
Singapore	11.3	17.8	19.8	21.6	5.4	0.1	2.0	4.0
Taipei,China	13.6	7.1	10.4	21.2	-0.1	10.1	9.5	10.0
People's Rep. of China and Mongolia	27.9	33.8	10.3	15.6	19.5	2.5	12.0	12.0
China, People's Rep. of	28.3	34.1	10.4	15.5	19.5	2.5	12.0	12.0
Mongolia	-14.0	-10.5	-3.3	32.0	5.4	-1.5	...	...
Central Asian Republics	-55.5	32.6	-7.8	16.6	27.3	6.2	...	...
Kazakstan	-65.0	9.9	-2.7	7.6	22.9	9.4	...	...
Kyrgyz Republic	-91.4	34.7	-4.6	24.6	47.5	-9.4	...	...
Uzbekistan	-85.1	96.3	-16.2	31.9	31.0	4.2	...	...
Southeast Asia	8.9	14.4	21.8	29.7	6.3	2.4	-1.1	5.6
Cambodia	43.1	34.3	56.5	64.6	-8.5	-8.5	...	...
Indonesia	7.8	6.0	13.9	26.6	8.1	4.8	-5.0	2.0
Lao People's Democratic Rep.	58.8	60.1	30.6	4.4	17.2	-14.7	...	...
Malaysia	10.1	17.8	28.1	30.4	1.7	7.0	6.0	7.0
Myanmar	19.9	28.9	14.3	2.3	8.2	7.0	...	...
Philippines	20.5	21.2	21.2	23.7	20.8	14.0	9.0	10.0
Thailand	6.0	12.2	18.1	31.9	0.6	-9.3	-15.0	3.0
Viet Nam	20.4	39.3	48.5	43.8	39.0	-1.6	5.0	5.0
South Asia	9.2	14.5	18.1	25.7	7.7	5.6	8.3	10.7
Bangladesh	0.5	15.5	-7.5	39.4	17.8	3.0	8.0	10.0
Bhutan	14.0	50.4	-25.7	22.1	-8.2	25.0	...	...
India	10.3	15.1	34.3	28.0	5.1	8.2	9.9	11.2
Maldives	18.4	5.9	9.7	20.9	12.6	12.0	...	...
Nepal	15.8	22.2	14.6	21.9	9.0	10.3	5.0	6.0
Pakistan	7.3	11.7	-13.6	18.5	16.7	-5.0	0.5	10.0
Sri Lanka	15.3	14.6	18.6	11.6	2.5	7.0	10.0	9.0
Pacific Islands	80.1	-1.8	11.6	1.3	7.2	-0.3	...	...
Cook Islands	34.5	4.4	-15.4	1.5	...	...	...	...
Fiji	-1.9	21.2	10.3	5.8	8.0	-0.5	...	...
Kiribati	43.4	-25.1	-5.0	33.3	-6.4	...	...	...
Marshall Islands	7.5	1.3	11.1	8.5	...	...	...	...
Micronesia, Federated States of	0.8	11.2	16.6	2.8	-0.8	1.0	...	...
Papua New Guinea	-5.8	-14.2	17.2	-4.5	19.3	8.0	...	...
Samoa	17.1	-6.7	-22.0	15.2	7.3	...	...	...
Solomon Islands	-0.9	22.7	1.9	10.4	-4.4	8.7	...	...
Tonga	6.6	2.3	31.6	2.7	-9.1	-13.1	...	...
Tuvalu	-2.5	33.3	4.0	32.1	4.1	2.7	...	...
Vanuatu	1.2	8.0	2.6	7.2	8.0	2.7	...	...
Average for DMCs	13.6	14.0	17.4	23.6	7.3	3.0	1.7	8.3

Table A14 Balance of Trade
($ million)

	1992	1993	1994	1995	1996	1997	1998	1999
Newly Industrialized Economies	4,421	6,836	-868	-10,040	-13,809	-11,767	13,520	-4,288
Hong Kong, China	-4,329	-3,808	-10,923	-19,594	-18,352	-21,121	-19,076	-25,025
Korea, Rep. of	-2,146	1,860	-3,146	-4,746	-15,306	-2,802	22,438	13,356
Singapore	-1,823	-2,724	1,354	1,065	2,281	-1,770	-1,806	-1,878
Taipei,China	12,718	11,508	11,847	13,235	17,568	13,926	11,963	9,259
People's Rep. of China and Mongolia	5,154	-10,633	7,324	18,017	19,448	46,354	35,647	23,119
China, People's Rep. of	5,183	-10,654	7,290	18,050	19,535	46,396	35,647	23,119
Mongolia	-29	21	34	-33	-87	-42	...	...
Central Asian Republics	-1,430	-2,047	-1,326	-136	-1,509	-1,499	...	...
Kazakstan	-1,121	-1,561	-1,453	-222	-326	-465	...	...
Kyrgyz Republic	-74	-107	-86	-122	-252	-106	...	...
Uzbekistan	-235	-379	213	208	-931	-929	...	...
Southeast Asia	1,033	-177	-3,493	-13,167	-14,587	-1,723	20,248	33,263
Cambodia	-86	-187	-275	-404	-450	-388	...	...
Indonesia	7,022	8,231	7,901	6,533	5,948	9,456	14,565	17,787
Lao People's Democratic Rep.	-137	-191	-264	-278	-368	-269	...	...
Malaysia	3,150	3,037	1,577	-100	3,933	3,435	5,281	8,306
Myanmar	-419	-606	-571	-631	-715	-760	...	...
Philippines	-4,695	-6,222	-7,850	-8,944	-11,342	-11,127	-9,100	-6,700
Thailand	-4,161	-4,297	-3,392	-7,629	-9,157	-1,472	10,032	13,295
Viet Nam	-60	-547	-1,190	-2,345	-3,151	-1,358	-530	576
South Asia	-9,729	-10,859	-14,653	-20,464	-23,110	-24,657	-26,570	-30,424
Bangladesh	-1,532	-1,688	-1,240	-1,782	-2,296	-1,947	-1,794	-1,668
Bhutan	-20	-59	-30	-43	-27	-46	...	...
India	-4,368	-4,056	-9,049	-13,516	-14,530	-16,802	-19,317	-22,776
Maldives	-103	-125	-120	-151	-174	-200	...	...
Nepal	-427	-512	-655	-922	-1,031	-1,137	-1,198	-1,270
Pakistan	-2,236	-3,267	-2,000	-2,537	-3,704	-3,328	-2,900	-3,275
Sri Lanka	-1,043	-1,153	-1,559	-1,513	-1,348	-1,197	-1,363	-1,435
Pacific Islands	21	766	738	802	559	116	...	...
Cook Islands	-51	-53	-44	-44	...	-34	...	...
Fiji	-189	-282	-229	-242	-197	-266	...	...
Kiribati	-32	-24	-21	-28	-28	...	...	...
Marshall Islands	-51	-53	-53	-57	...	...	...	...
Micronesia, Federated States of	-102	-109	-94	-95	-95	-95	...	...
Papua New Guinea	625	1,470	1,339	1,410	1,015	557	...	...
Samoa	-104	-96	-77	-83	-89	...	...	...
Solomon Islands	10	15	26	40	53	49	...	...
Tonga	-35	-44	-53	-57	-55	-46	...	...
Tuvalu	-5	-7	-7	9	10	9	...	...
Vanuatu	-44	-50	-50	-52	-56	-58	...	...
Total for DMCs	900	-14,067	-10,952	-24,852	-31,499	8,324	42,845	21,671

Table A15 Balance of Payments on Current Account
($ million)

	1992	1993	1994	1995	1996	1997	1998	1999
Newly Industrialized Economies	10,261	12,475	14,869	11,723	2,249	13,511	38,394	25,001
Hong Kong, China	...	...	...	...	...	...	...	...
Korea, Rep. of	-3,939	1,016	-3,855	-8,250	-23,061	-8,840	21,138	11,356
Singapore	5,653	4,417	12,226	14,499	14,283	14,630	13,160	11,430
Taipei,China	8,547	7,042	6,498	5,474	11,027	7,721	4,096	2,215
People's Rep. of China and Mongolia	6,345	-11,578	6,954	1,566	7,143	19,947	10,000	5,000
China, People's Rep. of	6,401	-11,609	6,908	1,618	7,243	20,000	10,000	5,000
Mongolia	-56	31	46	-52	-101	-53	...	...
Central Asian Republics	-1,384	-1,608	-1,308	-753	-2,214	-2,116	...	...
Kazakstan	-1,073	-1,072	-1,367	-518	-752	-1,016	...	...
Kyrgyz Republic	-74	-107	-59	-185	-388	-195	...	...
Uzbekistan	-237	-429	118	-50	-1,075	-906	...	...
Southeast Asia	-12,339	-15,670	-19,943	-33,046	-34,309	-24,123	-6,138	-900
Cambodia	-50	-251	-329	-476	-487	-409	...	...
Indonesia	-2,780	-1,944	-2,790	-6,431	-7,660	-5,713	-1,598	2,702
Lao People's Democratic Rep.	-108	-143	-223	-235	-302	-207	...	...
Malaysia	-2,167	-2,991	-4,520	-7,362	-4,964	-5,384	-4,860	-4,090
Myanmar	-275	-292	-195	-303	-386	-421	...	...
Philippines	-858	-3,016	-2,950	-3,287	-3,914	-4,328	-2,619	-955
Thailand	-6,304	-6,364	-7,802	-13,207	-14,351	-6,272	4,590	3,211
Viet Nam	-72	-961	-1,329	-2,048	-2,631	-1,810	-1,651	-1,767
South Asia	-6,746	-6,824	-7,374	-10,661	-11,277	-9,840	-11,436	-14,415
Bangladesh	-578	-618	-430	-1,040	-1,627	-875	-1,100	-1,000
Bhutan	-25	-69	-39	-57	-48	-79	...	...
India	-3,889	-1,526	-3,785	-5,903	-3,700	-4,000	-5,700	-8,500
Maldives	-20	-54	-12	-16	-27	-28	...	...
Nepal	-275	-314	-224	-343	-569	-354	-455	-501
Pakistan	-1,346	-3,688	-1,965	-2,484	-4,575	-4,187	-3,500	-3,700
Sri Lanka	-613	-556	-920	-818	-731	-317	-681	-714
Pacific Islands	46	485	473	694	234	-290	...	...
Cook Islands	...	...	...	...	...	...	...	...
Fiji	11	-81	-69	-36	65	-24	...	...
Kiribati	4	3	14	2	-6	...	...	...
Marshall Islands	-0	-1	0	-6	...	...	...	...
Micronesia, Federated States of	2	-2	13	16	9	8	...	...
Papua New Guinea	95	646	573	767	188	-305	...	...
Samoa	-44	-52	-18	-16	-10	...		
Solomon Islands	-8	-7	-1	10	16	49	...	...
Tonga	-3	-3	-21	-24	-8	-0	...	...
Tuvalu	6	1	2	...	...	...	...	...
Vanuatu	-18	-18	-20	-19	-20	-19	...	...
Total for DMCs	-2,433	-21,111	-5,021	-29,724	-35,961	-796	30,819	14,687

Table A16 Balance of Payments on Current Account
(percentage of GDP)

	1992	1993	1994	1995	1996	1997	1998	1999
Newly Industrialized Economies	1.5	1.7	1.8	1.2	0.2	1.4	4.5	2.7
Hong Kong, China	...	...	...	...	...	...	...	...
Korea, Rep. of	-1.3	0.3	-1.0	-1.8	-4.8	-2.0	6.9	3.4
Singapore	11.4	7.6	17.2	17.0	15.4	15.2	12.9	10.3
Taipei,China	4.0	3.2	2.7	2.1	4.0	2.7	1.5	0.8
People's Rep. of China and Mongolia	1.3	-1.9	1.3	0.2	0.9	2.2	0.9	0.4
China, People's Rep. of	1.3	-1.9	1.3	0.2	0.9	2.2	0.9	0.4
Mongolia	-5.0	5.3	6.7	-5.5	-10.0	-5.6	...	...
Central Asian Republics	-8.4	-9.4	-7.3	-10.8	-17.2	-8.5	...	...
Kazakstan	-7.4	-9.5	-11.6	-3.1	-3.6	-4.6	...	...
Kyrgyz Republic	-9.2	-9.5	-7.5	-15.6	-24.1	-10.5	...	...
Uzbekistan	-6.4	-8.4	2.1	-0.5	-7.9	-6.0	...	...
Southeast Asia	-3.3	-3.7	-4.2	-5.9	-5.5	-4.1	-1.4	-0.2
Cambodia	-2.5	-12.5	-13.7	-16.2	-15.5	-13.2		
Indonesia	-2.0	-1.2	-1.6	-3.2	-3.4	-2.7	-1.6	2.5
Lao People's Democratic Rep.	-9.2	-10.7	-14.4	-13.3	-16.1	-11.8	...	...
Malaysia	-3.7	-4.7	-6.2	-8.4	-5.0	-5.3	-4.9	-3.8
Myanmar	-0.7	-0.5	-0.2	-0.3	-0.3	-0.3	...	...
Philippines	-1.6	-5.5	-4.6	-4.4	-4.7	-5.2	-3.8	-1.3
Thailand	-5.7	-5.1	-5.4	-7.9	7.9	4.0	3.4	2.0
Viet Nam	-0.7	-7.5	-8.6	-10.1	-11.2	-7.7	-7.0	-7.0
South Asia	-1.9	-2.0	-1.8	-2.4	-2.4	-2.0	-2.1	-2.4
Bangladesh	-2.5	-2.6	-1.2	-2.7	-5.2	-2.6	-3.1	-2.7
Bhutan	-10.5	-29.9	-14.9	-19.2	-15.0	-22.0	...	...
India	-1.4	-0.6	-1.2	-1.8	-1.0	-1.2	-1.5	-2.0
Maldives	-10.2	-23.8	-4.3	-6.1	-9.2	-8.2	...	...
Nepal	-7.9	-7.9	-5.5	-7.8	-12.8	-7.2	-8.7	-8.8
Pakistan	-2.8	-7.1	-3.8	-4.1	-7.1	-6.5	-5.1	-5.2
Sri Lanka	-6.3	-5.4	-7.9	-6.3	-5.3	-2.1	-4.2	-4.0
Pacific Islands	0.7	6.5	5.7	8.3	2.8	-3.9	...	...
Cook Islands	...	...	...	...	...	...	...	...
Fiji	0.7	-5.8	-4.0	-2.4	0.8	0.8	...	...
Kiribati	14.3	11.4	43.6	6.3	-21.0	...	...	...
Marshall Islands	-0.1	-1.3	...	-5.5	...	...	...	...
Micronesia, Federated States of	-65.2	-64.2	-56.4	-54.6	-53.1	-56.4	...	...
Papua New Guinea	2.2	12.7	10.6	15.6	3.8	-6.2	...	...
Samoa	-37.1	-42.6	-13.2	-10.3	-11.2	...	...	...
Solomon Islands	-3.8	-2.8	-0.3	3.0	4.6	...	...	...
Tonga	-4.2	-4.4	-28.0	-6.8	-6.3	-6.3	...	...
Tuvalu	57.6	8.6	16.4	...	...	...	...	...
Vanuatu	-9.4	-9.0	-9.2	-8.5	-8.3	-7.6	...	...
Average for DMCs	-0.1	-1.0	-0.2	-1.1	-1.2	-0.0	1.1	0.5

Table A17 Foreign Direct Investment
(\$ million)

	1991	1992	1993	1994	1995	1996
Newly Industrialized Economies	7,876	5,861	7,858	9,664	12,347	15,650
Hong Kong, China	538	2,051	1,667	2,000	2,100	2,500
Korea, Rep. of	1,180	727	588	809	1,776	2,308
Singapore	4,887	2,204	4,686	5,480	6,912	9,440
Taipei, China	1,271	879	917	1,375	1,559	1,402
People's Rep. of China and Mongolia	4,366	11,158	27,523	33,794	35,859	42,305
China, People's Republic of	4,366	11,156	27,515	33,787	35,849	42,300
Mongolia	...	2	8	7	10	5
Central Asian Republics	...	140	195	245	430	381
Kazakstan	...	100	150	185	280	310
Kyrgyz Republic	...	...	...	10	30	16
Uzbekistan	...	40	45	50	120	55
Southeast Asia	8,512	9,899	10,734	10,325	14,315	19,804
Cambodia	...	33	54	69	151	350
Indonesia	1,482	1,777	2,004	2,109	4,348	7,960
Lao People's Democratic Rep.	7	8	30	59	88	104
Malaysia	3,998	5,183	5,006	4,342	4,132	5,300
Myanmar	238	171	149	91	115	100
Philippines	544	228	1,238	1,591	1,478	1,408
Thailand	2,014	2,114	1,730	1,322	2,003	2,426
Viet Nam	229	385	523	742	2,000	2,156
South Asia	470	703	1,141	1,922	2,643	3,468
Bangladesh	1	4	14	11	2	9
Bhutan	...	...	...	...	...	...
India	155	233	574	1,314	1,929	2,587
Maldives	7	7	7	6	5	7
Nepal	2	1	4	6	5	5
Pakistan	257	335	347	419	639	690
Sri Lanka	48	123	195	166	63	170
Pacific Islands	260	390	69	106	573	362
Cook Islands	...	...	...	...	...	...
Fiji	15	51	29	65	67	47
Kiribati	...	...	-1	...	...	1
Marshall Islands	...	...	...	...	...	...
Micronesia, Federated States of	...	...	...	...	...	...
Papua New Guinea	203	294	-2	-5	453	230
Samoa	3	4	2	3	2	4
Solomon Islands	15	14	13	11	18	21
Tonga	...	1	2	2	1	23
Tuvalu	...	...	...	...	...	...
Vanuatu	25	26	26	30	31	36
Total for DMCs	21,485	28,151	47,520	56,056	66,166	81,970

Table A18 External Debt Outstanding
($ million)

	1992	1993	1994	1995	1996	1997	1998	1999
Newly Industrialized Economies	...	...	...	...	...	...	...	...
Hong Kong, China	...	...	...	...	...	...	...	...
Korea, Rep. of	...	...	...	...	...	...	...	...
Singapore	...	...	...	...	...	...	...	...
Taipei,China	...	...	...	...	...	...	...	...
People's Rep. of China and Mongolia	72,726	86,294	100,931	118,594	128,571	134,008	140,000	145,000
China, People's Rep. of	72,428	85,928	100,457	118,090	128,015	133,415	140,000	145,000
Mongolia	298	366	474	504	556	593	...	...
Central Asian Republics	101	2,966	4,237	6,122	7,315	2,800	...	...
Kazakstan	35	1,724	2,669	3,712	4,397	...	...	...
Kyrgyz Republic	1	294	450	610	618	...	...	...
Uzbekistan	65	948	1,119	1,800	2,300	2,800	...	...
Southeast Asia	194,116	211,735	235,559	270,785	265,903	291,792	293,897	217,818
Cambodia	1,873	1,862	1,944	2,030	2,108	2,239	...	...
Indonesia	88,004	89,148	96,543	107,831	120,246	135,000	142,657	150,748
Lao People's Democratic Rep.	412	492	579	687	803	...	...	...
Malaysia	19,960	23,300	22,518	27,379	...	...	...	...
Myanmar	5,355	5,756	6,555	5,771	5,553	...	...	...
Philippines	30,934	34,282	37,079	37,778	38,300	49,500	50,000	53,000
Thailand	43,621	52,107	64,869	82,568	90,536	94,900	89,240	...
Viet Nam	3,957	4,788	5,473	6,741	8,357	10,153	12,000	14,070
South Asia	132,068	138,909	150,612	148,384	149,254	145,740	151,299	159,529
Bangladesh	13,200	14,100	15,700	16,500	17,600	18,700	19,800	20,800
Bhutan	128	125	130	129	113	164	...	...
India	90,023	92,695	99,008	92,199	90,900	95,300	98,700	104,600
Maldives	116	131	142	167	195	...	...	...
Nepal	1,802	2,004	2,320	2,399	2,413	2,576	2,799	3,129
Pakistan	19,629	22,046	24,482	27,072	28,603	29,000	30,000	31,000
Sri Lanka	7,171	7,809	8,830	9,919	9,429	...	...	...
Pacific Islands	4,507	4,136	3,586	2,862	2,759	...	...	...
Cook Islands	108	126	...	...	...	...	...	...
Fiji	339	330	299	...	...	...	...	...
Kiribati	19	18	...	...	...	...	...	...
Marshall Islands	...	...	...	...	...	...	...	...
Micronesia, Federated States of	...	...	...	...	...	...	...	...
Papua New Guinea	3,740	3,224	2,879	2,431	2,329	...	...	...
Samoa	118	194	154	162	164	...	...	...
Solomon Islands	94	151	155	157	152	...	...	...
Tonga	50	51	52	64	64	...	...	...
Tuvalu	...	...	...	...	...	...	...	...
Vanuatu	40	42	47	48	50	...	...	...
Total for DMCs	403,517	444,041	494,924	546,748	553,801	574,340	585,196	522,347

Table A19 Debt-Service Ratio
(percentage of exports of goods and services)

	1992	1993	1994	1995	1996	1997	1998	1999
Newly Industrialized Economies								
Hong Kong, China	...	...	...	...	...	...	...	...
Korea, Rep. of	...	...	...	...	...	...	...	...
Singapore	...	...	...	...	...	...	...	...
Taipei,China	...	...	...	...	...	...	...	...
People's Rep. of China and Mongolia								
China, People's Rep. of	10.2	11.1	8.9	9.9	10.1	9.8	11.0	11.0
Mongolia	10.5	10.6	16.3	12.0	11.5	9.0	...	...
Central Asian Republics								
Kazakstan	...	0.2	1.7	4.0	5.6	...	...	...
Kyrgyz Republic	...	0.4	3.9	20.7	12.2	10.0	...	...
Uzbekistan	0.4	0.7	4.0	5.0	8.9	10.0	...	...
Southeast Asia								
Cambodia	4.1	20.5	0.7	3.0	5.3	3.2	...	...
Indonesia	33.0	33.6	30.7	30.9	29.5	30.0	28.0	30.0
Lao People's Democratic Rep.	6.9	4.0	3.3	5.2	6.0	...	...	...
Malaysia	6.6	7.8	4.9	6.2	...	...	...	...
Myanmar	6.2	11.8	14.5	16.7	18.1	...	...	...
Philippines	17.0	17.1	17.4	15.8	12.0	10.4	11.4	11.0
Thailand	13.7	18.5	11.3	11.4	12.2	25.0	15.0	15.0
Viet Nam	11.3	10.7	5.7	6.3	8.7	11.0	12.0	12.0
South Asia								
Bangladesh	9.0	10.2	11.6	10.3	12.1	11.4	10.7	10.5
Bhutan	6.7	18.0	20.5	14.8	24.0	12.0	...	
India	28.6	26.9	27.5	37.3	41.9	31.8	29.9	28.9
Maldives	3.9	4.8	3.7	3.6	3.6	...	...	
Nepal	7.4	8.1	6.8	7.9	8.4	8.2	8.4	8.2
Pakistan	24.9	27.4	33.4	34.9	33.9	37.0	35.0	34.0
Sri Lanka	14.6	11.8	11.2	11.6	12.9	11.4	11.2	11.0
Pacific Islands								
Cook Islands	...	...	...	...	...	...	...	...
Fiji	9.3	8.2	7.0	4.6	...	...	...	...
Kiribati	21.7	27.0	...	...	...	...	...	...
Marshall Islands	...	...	...	...	...	...	...	...
Micronesia, Federated States of	...	...	...	...	...	...	...	...
Papua New Guinea	28.2	28.7	30.4	20.8	17.5	...	...	...
Samoa	5.5	6.9	7.3	4.2	4.2	4.2	...	...
Solomon Islands	5.5	4.4	6.2	2.8	6.2	...	...	...
Tonga	3.0	3.0	4.5	5.5	9.5	...	...	...
Tuvalu	...	...	...	...	...	...	...	...
Vanuatu	1.3	1.4	1.6	1.5	0.7	...	...	...

Table A20   Exchange Rates to the Dollar
(Annual Average)

	Currency	1992	1993	1994	1995	1996	1997
Newly Industrialized Economies							
Hong Kong, China	HK$	7.7	7.7	7.7	7.7	7.7	7.7
Korea, Rep. of	Won	780.7	802.7	803.5	771.3	804.5	951.4
Singapore	S$	1.6	1.6	1.5	1.4	1.4	1.5
Taipei,China	NT$	25.2	26.4	26.5	26.5	27.5	28.6
People's Rep. of China and Mongolia							
China, People's Rep. of	Yuan	5.5	5.8	8.6	8.4	8.3	8.3
Mongolia	Tugrik	42.6	283.0	412.7	448.7	548.4	793.7
Central Asian Republics							
Kazakstan	Tenge	...	2.6	35.6	61.0	67.3	75.4
Kyrgyz Republic	Som	...	5.8	10.9	10.8	12.8	...
Uzbekistan	Sum	...	...	9.8	29.8	40.2	...
Southeast Asia							
Cambodia	Riel	1,266.6	2,689.0	2,545.0	2,450.8	2,624.0	2989.0
Indonesia	Rupiah	2,029.9	2,087.1	2,160.8	2,248.6	2,342.3	2946.0
Lao People's Democratic Rep.	Kip	716.1	716.3	717.7	804.7	921.1	1256.7
Malaysia	Ringgit	2.5	2.6	2.6	2.5	2.5	2.7
Myanmar	Kyat	6.1	6.2	6.0	5.7	5.9	6.2
Philippines	Peso	25.5	27.1	26.4	25.7	26.2	29.5
Thailand	Baht	25.4	25.3	25.2	24.9	25.3	30.8
Viet Nam	Dong	11,179.0	10,640.0	10,978.0	11,037.0	11,032.0	12,500.0
South Asia							
Bangladesh	Taka	39.0	39.6	40.2	40.3	41.8	42.6
Bhutan	Ngultrum	25.9	30.5	31.4	32.4	35.4	36.1
India	Rupee	25.9	31.4	31.4	33.5	35.5	37.8
Maldives	Rufiyaa	10.6	11.0	11.6	11.8	11.8	11.8
Nepal	Rupee	42.8	43.0	49.3	49.9	55.2	57.0
Pakistan	Rupee	24.8	26.0	30.2	30.9	33.6	39.0
Sri Lanka	Rupee	43.8	48.3	49.4	51.3	55.3	59.0
Pacific Islands							
Cook Islands	NZ$	1.9	1.8	1.7	1.5	1.6	1.7
Fiji	F$	1.5	1.5	1.5	1.4	1.4	1.4
Kiribati	A$	1.4	1.5	1.4	1.3	1.3	1.4
Marshall Islands	US$	...	...	...	...	...	...
Micronesia, Federated States of	US$	...	...	...	...	...	...
Papua New Guinea	Kina	1.0	1.0	1.0	1.3	1.3	1.3
Samoa	Taka	2.5	2.6	2.5	2.5	2.5	2.5
Solomon Islands	SI$	2.9	3.2	3.3	3.4	3.6	3.7
Tonga	T$	1.3	1.4	1.3	1.3	1.2	1.2
Tuvalu	A$	1.4	1.5	1.4	1.3	1.3	...
Vanuatu	Vatu	113.4	121.6	116.4	112.1	111.7	114.5

Table A21 Central Government Expenditure
(percentage of GDP)

	1992	1993	1994	1995	1996	1997
Newly Industrialized Economies						
Hong Kong, China	14.5	16.4	16.2	17.0	15.3	14.9
Korea, Rep. of	19.5	19.8	17.2	21.4	22.7	20.1
Singapore	19.6	17.4	12.9	12.9	14.7	18.1
Taipei,China	30.7	30.5	30.2	29.9	29.1	28.0
People's Rep. of China and Mongolia						
China, People's Rep. of	14.0	13.4	12.4	11.7	11.6	12.5
Mongolia	38.9	30.0	30.1	29.8	36.0	38.8
Central Asian Republics						
Kazakstan	31.4	24.7	24.4	20.5	19.0	18.0
Kyrgyz Republic	25.0	23.4	24.4	28.6	23.2	19.5
Uzbekistan	43.7	38.7	33.3	37.6	36.2	35.5
Southeast Asia						
Cambodia	9.8	11.2	16.5	16.7	16.4	13.9
Indonesia	17.2	16.3	16.4	15.4	15.1	14.3
Lao People's Democratic Rep.	20.7	18.1	42.7	41.2	22.3	20.7
Malaysia	27.4	24.9	23.7	22.4	22.4	21.0
Myanmar	10.5	9.0	9.3	9.5	6.6	...
Philippines	19.7	18.5	18.5	18.2	18.3	19.1
Thailand	15.0	15.9	16.0	15.3	17.8	18.2
Viet Nam	22.7	28.5	26.7	25.1	24.7	17.1
South Asia						
Bangladesh	16.9	17.8	13.5	14.2	17.8	17.6
Bhutan ·	36.3	36.7	38.9	37.9	37.3	44.2
India	17.4	17.5	16.9	16.4	15.8	16.0
Maldives	59.5	58.3	48.8	52.2	47.8	45.2
Nepal	17.7	18.0	16.9	17.6	18.9	18.3
Pakistan	26.5	26.0	23.2	23.0	23.9	23.6
Sri Lanka	27.5	28.1	29.0	30.0	27.9	24.0
Pacific Islands						
Cook Islands	48.3	52.8	60.8	45.6	...	...
Fiji	39.3	51.2	43.3	0.6	20.6	6.2
Kiribati	144.1	119.3	120.6	168.3	155.9	168.0
Marshall Islands	102.8	97.4	88.1	95.3	70.0	63.9
Micronesia, Federated States of	91.7	84.8	79.1	77.5	73.8	71.8
Papua New Guinea	32.9	32.3	29.7	27.2	28.4	32.5
Samoa	70.7	79.9	62.7	65.7	57.5	31.6
Solomon Islands	52.6	42.9	41.9	40.3	38.1	33.7
Tonga	56.1	55.1	45.3	46.8	29.0	29.0
Tuvalu	110.6	104.8	54.8	50.5	55.7	58.7
Vanuatu	22.4	21.4	20.7	22.0	22.0	22.6

Table A22 Central Government Revenue
(percentage of GDP)

	1992	1993	1994	1995	1996	1997
Newly Industrialized Economies						
Hong Kong, China	17.4	18.6	17.3	16.7	17.5	20.7
Korea, Rep. of	19.2	19.9	17.8	21.9	22.8	21.0
Singapore	32.9	35.7	21.9	20.5	21.4	21.4
Taipei,China	25.3	25.3	24.5	22.5	21.7	22.3
People's Rep. of China and Mongolia						
China, People's Rep. of	13.1	12.6	11.2	10.7	10.8	11.7
Mongolia	23.9	31.2	29.3	30.6	27.8	30.2
Central Asian Republics						
Kazakstan	24.6	23.3	17.2	18.5	16.5	13.8
Kyrgyz Republic	15.9	16.1	16.7	17.0	17.6	15.0
Uzbekistan	31.5	35.9	29.2	34.6	34.2	32.3
Southeast Asia						
Cambodia	6.2	5.4	9.6	8.9	9.1	9.2
Indonesia	16.8	15.9	17.4	15.7	15.9	14.1
Lao People's Democratic Rep.	10.7	11.9	15.4	16.4	13.1	11.4
Malaysia	26.4	25.2	26.0	23.3	23.3	23.1
Myanmar	8.4	7.6	6.8	6.1	5.1	...
Philippines	18.0	17.7	19.9	18.9	18.7	19.2
Thailand	17.7	17.9	18.7	18.6	18.6	17.3
Viet Nam	18.3	21.7	24.0	23.2	22.9	21.8
South Asia						
Bangladesh	10.5	11.7	8.9	9.1	11.9	12.1
Bhutan	19.5	23.6	20.4	19.5	18.7	18.3
India	15.6	16.2	16.8	15.7	15.5	16.7
Maldives	36.3	35.1	35.9	37.3	37.9	37.0
Nepal	9.0	8.8	9.8	11.2	11.3	11.2
Pakistan	19.1	18.0	17.3	17.4	17.5	17.3
Sri Lanka	20.2	19.7	19.0	20.4	19.0	19.2
Pacific Islands						
Cook Islands	37.2	36.7	36.2	39.7	...	...
Fiji	67.7	43.0	39.2	30.6	29.1	28.1
Kiribati	185.6	171.0	151.6	159.3	141.9	172.0
Marshall Islands	84.4	83.6	74.9	73.9	72.1	61.8
Micronesia, Federated States of	31.1	31.5	29.0	29.4	23.6	27.0
Papua New Guinea	22.4	22.7	23.8	23.0	24.8	26.8
Samoa	54.5	58.7	51.5	56.8	59.4	34.8
Solomon Islands	33.0	26.7	28.7	27.7	27.4	30.3
Tonga	47.8	52.8	58.2	60.0	63.3	63.4
Tuvalu	126.6	101.3	47.5	41.8	47.0	47.0
Vanuatu	22.8	20.8	23.0	23.1	22.8	24.0

Table A23 Overall Budget Surplus/Deficit of Central Government
(percentage of GDP)

	1992	1993	1994	1995	1996	1997
Newly Industrialized Economies						
Hong Kong, China	2.8	2.1	1.1	-0.3	2.2	5.8
Korea, Rep. of	-0.3	0.1	0.6	0.5	0.0	-0.5
Singapore	12.6	15.5	8.9	7.6	6.8	3.3
Taipei,China	-5.4	-5.2	-5.7	-7.4	-7.4	-5.7
People's Rep. of China and Mongolia						
China, People's Rep. of	-1.0	-0.8	-1.2	-1.0	-0.8	-0.8
Mongolia	-15.0	1.2	-6.5	-3.8	-8.2	-8.6
Central Asian Republics						
Kazakstan	-6.8	-1.4	-7.2	-2.0	-2.5	-4.2
Kyrgyz Republic	-17.4	-7.4	-7.7	-11.5	-5.6	-4.5
Uzbekistan	-18.5	-10.4	-6.1	-4.1	-3.3	-3.0
Southeast Asia						
Cambodia	-3.6	-5.9	-6.8	-7.7	-7.2	-4.8
Indonesia	-0.4	-0.4	1.0	0.4	0.8	-0.2
Lao People's Democratic Rep.	-10.0	-6.2	-27.3	-24.8	-9.1	-9.2
Malaysia	-0.8	0.2	2.3	0.9	0.7	1.8
Myanmar	-2.1	-1.4	-2.5	-3.4	-1.5	...
Philippines	-1.2	-1.5	1.0	0.6	0.3	0.1
Thailand	2.8	2.1	2.7	3.0	0.9	-0.9
Viet Nam	-2.5	-5.3	-1.8	-1.3	-1.2	-3.2
South Asia						
Bangladesh	-6.4	-6.1	-4.6	-5.1	-5.9	-5.5
Bhutan	-8.5	-0.7	-2.3	-2.0	-0.6	-4.9
India	-5.7	-7.4	-6.1	-7.1	-7.0	-6.7
Maldives	-24.2	-23.2	-12.9	-14.9	-9.9	-8.2
Nepal	-7.5	-7.0	-5.8	-4.6	-5.6	-5.3
Pakistan	-7.4	-8.0	-5.9	-5.5	-6.3	-6.3
Sri Lanka	-7.3	-8.4	-10.0	-9.6	-8.9	-4.9
Pacific Islands						
Cook Islands	-11.1	-16.1	-24.7	-5.9	...	...
Fiji	28.4	-8.1	-4.1	0.7	5.7	9.2
Kiribati	-29.4	1.8	-10.3	-66.8	-49.9	-52.8
Marshall Islands	-79.5	-65.0	-58.6	-61.7	-41.7	-40.2
Micronesia, Federated States of	-3.3	-1.2	1.7	3.4	-2.2	-1.3
Papua New Guinea	-10.4	-9.6	-5.9	-4.2	-3.6	-5.7
Samoa	-16.2	-21.2	-11.2	-8.9	1.9	3.2
Solomon Islands	-5.9	-10.9	-9.2	-8.5	-6.1	-6.1
Tonga	-9.8	-3.9	5.6	5.8	1.5	2.6
Tuvalu	46.2	16.1	...	...	...	...
Vanuatu	0.4	-1.0	2.3	1.6	0.7	1.5